T3-BPX-815

A GARLAND SERIES

THE ENGLISH
WORKING CLASS

A Collection of
Thirty Important Titles
That Document and Analyze
Working-Class Life before
the First World War

Edited by

STANDISH MEACHAM
University of Texas

Unemployment
A Social Study

B. Seebohm Rowntree
Bruno Lasker

Garland Publishing, Inc.
New York & London
1980

For a complete list of the titles in this series,
see the final pages of this volume.

The volumes in this series are printed on acid-free,
250-year-life paper.

This facsimile has been made from a copy in
the Library of Congress.

Library of Congress Cataloging in Publication Data

Rowntree, Benjamin Seebohm, 1871–1954.
Unemployment, a social study.

(The English working class)
Reprint of the 1911 ed. published by Macmillan, London.
Includes index.
1. Unemployed—England—York. 2. Working-men's
gardens. I. Lasker, Bruno, 1880–1965, joint author.
II. Title. III. Series: English working class.
HD5766.Y67R68   1980   305.5'6   79-56970
ISBN 0-8240-0121-4

Printed in the United States of America

UNEMPLOYMENT

MACMILLAN AND CO., LIMITED
LONDON · BOMBAY · CALCUTTA
MELBOURNE

THE MACMILLAN COMPANY
NEW YORK · BOSTON · CHICAGO
ATLANTA · SAN FRANCISCO

THE MACMILLAN CO. OF CANADA, LTD.
TORONTO

UNEMPLOYMENT

A SOCIAL STUDY

BY

B. SEEBOHM ROWNTREE

AUTHOR OF 'POVERTY: A STUDY OF TOWN LIFE'
'LAND AND LABOUR: LESSONS FROM BELGIUM,' ETC.

AND

BRUNO LASKER

MACMILLAN AND CO., LIMITED
ST. MARTIN'S STREET, LONDON
1911

INTRODUCTION

THIS book gives an account of a detailed investigation of unemployment in York, together with suggestions for remedying the evils which it disclosed. Perhaps its chief value lies in the fact that it covered the whole city, and so far as we are aware, no detailed inquiry over a similar area has previously been made. There have, of course, been a great number of inquiries into the unemployment of particular sections of the people, as, for instance, those applying to distress committees, or registering at the Labour Exchange, or the members of trade unions, etc. But the partial character of such investigations has always laid them open to the criticism that they have given no complete picture of the problem, since the unemployed persons considered were not typical of the whole class. It was to remedy this defect in a small measure that the present inquiry was undertaken, and so far as the city of York is concerned, we are now able to state not only how many people were unemployed on the day of the inquiry, but in nearly all cases to give their industrial record since they left school, and other information concerning them. Thus we can trace the immediate cause of their unemployment, and the apparent obstacles to their finding fresh work. We can also say approximately in how far they consist of capable men who are eager for work, but unable to obtain it, and in how far of men who are inefficient or disinclined for regular work, even if they could get it. We can in large measure trace the influences leading up to this inefficiency and unwillingness to work steadily. It is clearly important to possess such knowledge, since wise measures for the remedy of any disease cannot be suggested until its precise nature is known.

Obviously, the proportions of the various sections of the unemployed will vary according to the time of year and the general condition of trade in the country. For instance, certain men are likely to be unemployed in winter and others in summer, and when trade is depressed the proportion of good workmen unemployed will be greater than when it is active. Moreover, every town has its special industrial characteristics. Nevertheless, our inquiry has more than local interest, for in the absence of any industrial conditions which are entirely exceptional, and allowing for variations in trade activity and time of year, it may reasonably be assumed that similar investigations in other towns would, as a rule, furnish results not differing fundamentally from our own.

The inquiry here described was made in York on the 7th of June 1910. The weather was fine, and had been so for a week. It will be remembered that at that time the trade of the country had just recovered from a period of unusual depression. The proportion of unemployed members in those trade unions which report to the Board of Trade was 3·7 per cent, the lowest recorded during the preceding ten years being 3·3 per cent in April 1907, and the highest 9·5 per cent in October 1908. Thus, so far as we can judge by these figures, trade generally was exceptionally good.[1]

But this was not the case in York. We have gone to considerable pains to ascertain the state of trade in the city in June 1910, and have discussed the question with bank managers, retail tradesmen and manufacturers, and with the secretary of the co-operative distributing society, which, having more than 6000 working-class members in York, is exceptionally sensitive to any fluctuation. The Railway Company has also kindly furnished us with statistics covering several years, showing the number of passengers leaving York station, and the tonnage of

[1] For reasons which need not here be discussed, the statistics of unemployment published by the Board of Trade only indicate very roughly the relative amount of unemployment at different times ; they do not show the absolute amount of unemployment in the country.

goods arising in and forwarded from York. Basing our opinion on all the evidence collected, we are able to say with confidence that trade in York in the summer of 1910 had not entirely recovered from the depression which had affected the whole country during the preceding two years. Perhaps we can best describe the condition by saying that it was about half-way between normal trade and acute depression. Some of those whom we have consulted have informed us that the movements of trade in York, both upwards and downwards, are always somewhat behind those of the country generally.

So far as the time of year of the inquiry is concerned, those who have made a special study of unemployment are divided in opinion as to whether it is generally worse in winter or in summer, some industries being busier at one period and some at the other. We believe that so far as York is concerned, it is most severe during the winter, the proportion of trades then busy being smaller than in the summer.

The mention of local conditions leads up to a brief statement of those facts connected with York which have a bearing on this investigation. When it took place the population of the city was about 82,000. The chief industries are those of the North Eastern Railway Company, employing altogether between five and six thousand men, with scarcely any women, and

the various cocoa and confectionery works, employing
between them about 2000 men and boys, and 3000
women and girls. In addition to these, about 1600
men were engaged in the building trades, and 600 in
flour-milling, and the remainder of the workers in
the city in many minor industries, no individual one
of which employs any large number. Employment
on the railway and in the confectionery industries
is very stable, though in connection with the former
there has, during the last two or three years, been a
large amount of short time.

Before returning to the results of our inquiry, a
few words must be said as to the methods adopted.
First, it must be clearly understood that all the
figures given refer only to individuals unemployed
on June 7, 1910, and must never be looked upon as
indicating the total number of those who, during the
year 1910, suffered from unemployment. It may be
urged that such an inquiry would have been more
valuable had it taken into account all those who were
unemployed in the course of the year, but any who
have had experience of social investigations of this
kind will appreciate the difficulties they involve,
and will recognise that it would have been almost
impossible for private individuals to make an investigation on so extensive a scale. But the restric-
tion of the inquiry to a particular date does not

appreciably lessen its value in so far as it accurately indicates the character of the various sections of the unemployed.

The method of inquiry was as follows :—On June 7 and the two succeeding days, sixty investigators, selected by the writers as being men who would do the work conscientiously, called on every working-class house in York, and ascertained whether any person residing there was out of work, and desirous of finding it. They further ascertained whether the unemployed person was male or female, and the occupation which he or she was seeking. As it was desired to cover the whole of the city within three days, further investigations were left over to be made at subsequent visits.

Once the city had been covered, and a statement obtained of the names and addresses of all persons un-employed on the 7th of June, the next step was care-fully to investigate every case. For this purpose a much smaller number of investigators was employed, and the information which they supplied was strictly checked. As always occurs in similar cases, some of the investigators proved to be inefficient, and their work had to be done over again, while inquiry showed that the work of others was intelligent and reliable. The information to be obtained in the case of this subsequent inquiry was as follows :—

INQUIRY SCHEDULE

Number. Name. Address. Age. Relation to head of household.

Last regular occupation :
  Its nature. Earnings per week. Duration. Name and Address of
  Employer. Date and cause of leaving.

Previous Employments :

Nature.	Lasted From	To	Name and Address of Employers.	Cause of Leaving.	Followed by unemployment lasting for

Earnings at best time :

Earnings when out of regular Employment: Occupation. | Amount per week.

Member of :
  Trade Union ? Friendly Society ? Church or other organisation ?
    Which ?
    Entitled to benefit ?
    Drawing benefit ?

Birthplace : How long in York ? At what age left school ?
  Which Standard ?

First employments : What training ?
  Continuation education ? Army or { When ?
    Navy ? } How long ?
  What occupation looked for ? How ?

Other members of family.	Relation to head.	Sex.	Age.	Occupation (or if at school, which standard ?)	Earnings per week.

Condition of street and house. Number and size of rooms. Rent.

Total earnings of household. Other sources of income (gifts, charities, poor relief) ? Credit ?

Disposal of furniture, clothing, etc. ? Are children fed at school ?

Physical condition of unemployed. | How does unemployed spend
  Of family. | his time ?
Character of unemployed. Of family. | Special circumstances.
Moral effect of unemployment on | Information supplied by
  unemployed. On family. |

Date. Signature of investigator.

Obviously much of the above information could only be supplied by the unemployed person himself, or by members of his family, but the cause of his leaving his last employment and the investigator's impression regarding his character were, whenever it was possible, checked from other sources, especially from the last employer. In the great majority of cases, where a man had been employed within the last three or four years, we were able, by reference to the employer, to ascertain why he had lost his post, and what were his qualifications as a workman. The work involved in these inquiries was very considerable. In the first place, it frequently took much time to obtain the information from the unemployed person, while to check it adequately in a single case often involved a number of visits to different persons. The work was, however, practically complete by October 1910, and while it is impossible in an investigation of this kind to vouch for the perfect accuracy of all the information, we believe the proportion of error is small.

To those who have not given much thought to the subject, it would appear easy to define unemployment, but, in point of fact, this is far from being the case. For instance, many people who would not call themselves "unemployed" are certainly "underemployed," that is, they would be glad to undertake more work if they could get it. At what point does under-employment lapse into unemployment? Again, is a man to be considered unemployed who is practically unemployable? If so, is a man who has worked steadily all his life, but grown too old for further work, to be counted among the unemployed? If not, why count among them a young man who, through some physical defect, is no more employable than the veteran of labour? Again, is a man to be counted unemployed who is ill, but whose employment is waiting for him when he recovers? Or is a trade unionist to be counted unemployed who cannot find work at the trade union rate of wages, but who could do so if he would accept a farthing an hour less, or who could not find work in York, but could in Leeds if he would go there? These illustrations, which might readily be multiplied, will serve to show how difficult it is to define unemployment precisely, and how easy it would be to compile statistics of it which might be very misleading. The working definition which we have adopted throughout this book is as follows :—

A person is unemployed who is seeking work for wages, but unable to find any suited to his capacities and under conditions which are reasonable, judged by local standards.

This definition rules out a number of persons who returned themselves as unemployed when our census was originally made. The reasons why, on further investigation, we ruled them out, were as follows :—

	M.	F.
Still at school on date of Census . . .	17	2
Temporarily ill ,, ,, . . .	11	4
Mentally deficient	7	3
Chronically ill or infirm—		
Under 65 years of age . . .	55	16
Over ,, ,, ...	31	5
	121	30

Although these people were not, according to our definition, unemployed, many of them were destitute, and some in a truly pitiable condition.[1]

Before passing to a discussion of the results of our investigation, a few words may here be said as to the exact ground covered, and the way in which we have arranged our subject matter. We begin with a chapter dealing with the unemployment of youths under 19, of whom a surprisingly large number were found not only to be without work, but to have been without it for a considerable time. The serious consequences of such an experience when the character is especially impressionable, will at once be recognised.

[1] We have also excluded (a) 41 men and 5 women enumerated in our census, who either refused all information or who had left the neighbourhood in the interval between June 7 and the date of subsequent inquiry. We cannot say what proportion of these would have come within the limits of our definition of unemployment. (b) All persons working on their own account, who, although anxious for additional work, were not looking for employment as wage-earners proper (i.e. such persons as cobblers, signwriters, dressmakers, etc.).

The educational attainments of the youths are
studied, as well as their industrial records.

Chapter II. is concerned with the unemployment
of men who have been in regular work within the
last two years—" regular work " here implying un-
interrupted employment for one master lasting for
at least twelve months. The reasons for its loss, and
any apparent obstacles in the way of finding fresh
work are examined. In the latter connection, the
parts played by age, physical condition, personal
character and degree of efficiency, are all discussed.

Chapter III. deals with casual workers, whose
number is much greater than we had imagined, since
there are in York no important industries which are
known to rely largely on casual workers for their
labour supply. The characters and other personal
qualities of the casuals are studied, and also the
reasons why they are relying on casual, rather than
regular work. Interesting questions are opened up
by an examination of their industrial history.

The building trades are studied in Chapter IV.,
and Chapter V. deals with the " work-shy "—men
who only work when forced to do so by sheer
necessity. After a general description of the class
we give some details regarding its individual
members, and analyse the causes of their present
condition.

The unemployment of women and girls is dealt with in Chapter VI. It is in comparatively small compass, for the demand for girl labour in York is greater than the supply, and unemployment becomes a serious problem only in the case of widows and women too old to be taken on in the factories.

Chapter VII. is devoted to a detailed description of the way in which a few typical families, whose chief wage-carner is unemployed, manage to exist. Particulars are given of their weekly income and expenditure, and the food they have consumed, the nutritive value of which is shown, with the extent to which the families are underfed.

By thus separating the unemployed workers into classes, we see clearly how diverse are the causes of their unemployment, and a part of each chapter is devoted to considering the remedies which the special facts suggest. Chapter VIII. describes in considerable detail a method of reducing the volume of unemployment and of mitigating its evil consequences, the importance of which has been strongly impressed on us in the course of social investigations in Belgium.

In Chapter IX. we summarise the various facts set forth in the preceding chapters, and the proposals for reform suggested.

In conclusion, we wish very cordially to thank all those who have in any way helped us in connection with our investigation, especially Mr. Joseph Rowntree, who has read through each chapter— never without making suggestions of the utmost value. We also wish to thank various friends who have been so good as to read individual chapters, and Mr. J. St. G. Heath, lecturer on Economics at Woodbrooke, Birmingham, who has read through the greater part of the manuscript. It is impossible personally to thank all our investigators, but we must make an exception in the case of Mr. H. S. Barnes, who has with great thoroughness done some of the most difficult work. And especially we would thank those unemployed persons, employers, and others, whose public spirit often prompted them to devote much time and trouble to supplying the information we sought. Lastly we would thank Miss May Kendall, who has written the descriptions of unemployed families given in Chapter VII., and supervised the keeping of the budgets. She has also read through the manuscript of all the chapters.

B. S. R.

B. L.

YORK, *September* 1911.

CONTENTS

xix

CHAPTER VIII

CHAPTER IX

CHAPTER I

IN view of the special problems affecting juvenile workers, and their close connection with those of education, the cases of youths found unemployed on the date of the inquiry have been grouped separately. We shall in this chapter, after stating the size of the group, seek first to show why the lads are unemployed, and especially in how far their unemployment is due to personal defects. In this connection the home influences under which they have been brought up, and the character of their education, are factors of prime importance. We recognise, of course, that even if all boys were thoroughly efficient there might still be unemployment among them, for if there is a surplus of boy labour, some must go without work. But none the less the character and efficiency of the unemployed are important, if only because schemes for absorbing surplus labour largely depend for their success on its adaptability and general efficiency. We shall next show in how far the organisation of the

B

industries which boys enter is responsible for the unemployment of this group, and conclude with such suggestions for reform as the facts appear to warrant.

Altogether 129 lads are included in this group, their ages being as follows :—

14 years	.	.	23 [1]	17 years	.	.	29
15 „	.	.	25	18 „	.	.	25
16 „	.	.	26	doubtful	.	.	1

Thus about two-thirds are between 16 and 18 years of age. We have not included 40 boys who were returned as unemployed in our original census, but who, on subsequent inquiry, were found to be still at school, though on the look-out for work; nor 13 others under 19 years of age suffering from physical or mental defects so grave as to render them practically unemployable.

All but 9 of the lads live with their parents; of the exceptions 8 live with other relatives, and 1 in lodgings.

Before going farther we may state that 15 of the youngest lads in the list given above only left school a few weeks before the inquiry was instituted, and although they were not yet working, it would be stretching a point to include them among the genuine "unemployed." Some of them probably wanted a holiday before beginning the serious work of life, and,

---

[1] The age of leaving school in York is 14 years, except in the case of boys obtaining a labour certificate. These may leave after they are 12 years old, if they pass the necessary examination and have been in the sixth standard for at least six months. As a matter of fact, however, only 27 boys left the York schools with labour certificates during 1910, and only 14 passed the qualifying annual examination in 1911.

in any case, the fact that they did not immediately step into a situation does not necessarily reflect upon their ability or industrial fitness, or suggest any disorganisation of the labour market. Although, therefore, we have included them for the sake of completeness, we shall not refer to them further, but shall confine our attention to the remaining 114 lads.

EDUCATIONAL RECORD OF UNEMPLOYED YOUTHS

The first questions naturally asked in considering why these lads cannot secure work are : What sort of education have they had? Is their unemployment due to exceptional incapacity or lack of school training?

On comparing the percentage of the 114 lads who left from various standards with that of all the boys who left the York elementary schools during the year 1910,[1] it is at once evident how inferior, on the

| | School standard reached by boys who | |
	left school during the year ended September 30, 1910 (710).	were unemployed on June 7, 1910 (known for 107).
	Per cent	Per cent
II.	0·1	0·9
III.	1·1	3·8
IV.	3·8	10·3
V.	10·1	27·1
VI.	19·3	27·1
VII.	37·8	25·2
Ex-VII.	27·8	5·6
	100·0	100·0

The age at which they left school is unknown for 5 of the unemployed lads. Of the remainder, 8 left school under 14 years of age.

average, are the scholastic attainments of the unemployed. Whereas, taking the city as a whole, 66
per cent of the lads reached the seventh standard, it
was only reached by 31 per cent of those now under
consideration. The latter, therefore, have evidently
had a bad educational start.

In order to ascertain in how far this was due to
innate physical or mental defects and in how far to
bad home influences, or lack of control, resulting
often in irregular school attendance, a supplementary
inquiry was undertaken. In all cases where it was
possible to ascertain the school attended by the lads,
the head teachers were visited and questioned concerning their record and its possible connection with
their unemployment at a later date. Such information was obtained for 69 boys, and in the case of 55
of these we were told that there had been reason to
forebode an unsuccessful industrial career. Two of
the remaining 14 lads were rather dull, but not
sufficiently so to render them unsuited to ordinary
unskilled labour ; and in the case of another lad the
school record was excellent, but it was known to the
teacher that, soon after leaving, he became associated
with a very inferior set of lads who induced him to
quit work and loaf with them, until eventually the
gang was broken up by the police. In the following table a résumé is given of the various reasons
which led the teachers to expect that the future
of 55 of the 69 boys would reflect little credit on
the school.

Mentally deficient	1
Abnormally dull	10
Delicate and frequently ill	4
Seriously undersized	1
One-eyed.	1
Very short-sighted	1
One arm paralysed	1
Underfed and generally neglected . . .	7
Without energy	1
Bad attendance (irregular and often late) . .	7
Bad influences at home	12
Insufficient control at home	2
Frequent change of neighbourhood and school .	3
Bad character of boy	4
	55

It will be noted that in approximately half the 55
cases, the bad start which the lads have made in their
industrial careers was attributable to home influences,
and in the other half to mental dullness or physical
weakness. It must, however, be borne in mind that
in framing the table we have only taken into account
what appeared to us the prime cause, and that often
more than one cause was in operation. For instance,
physical or mental unfitness was often the outcome
of neglect at home, due either to poverty or to the
character of the parents. Indeed, speaking generally,
it would not be an exaggeration to say that the great
majority of these 55 boys came from homes where
the influence was definitely bad, or the children were
carelessly brought up. In some cases there was no
appreciation of the advantages of education, and even
a moderately regular attendance was only secured
through the constant supervision of the school attend-

ance officer; in others, the physical or mental unfitness of the boys was the direct result of parental
ignorance or indifference, as in a case where a lad
had such bad eyesight that he could not see the
blackboard, and yet the mother refused to let him
wear spectacles.

Perhaps a few examples, taken at random, of the
notes furnished us by teachers regarding some of
the boys, will illustrate more clearly the handicap
with which they are starting their industrial careers.

"Thriftless family. Father dead. Mother drinks. Bad school
attendance. Often in rags and underfed. Normal intelligence."

"Apparently dodged Education Committee by many removals.
School attendance can only have been very irregular. Poor home."

"Nervous and rather delicate. Not energetic. Spoilt and
pampered at home. Always had his own way. Constantly moved
from one school to another."

"Suffers from asthma. Bad school attendance partly owing to ill-
health : but was allowed to play about more than was necessary."

"Very clever, but bad home. Mother blind and father casual
labourer of unsatisfactory character."

"Undersized, ulcerated eyes, not strong. Wretched home.
Backward, underfed, bad stock."

"Very dull. Fairly decent home. Parents both illiterate."

"Unhealthy and ill-nourished. Father chronically out of work.
Children neglected in every respect. Dull, and was not put to
regular work when leaving school, but to selling firewood."

"Very deaf. Abnormally dull, thin, and weak. Indifferent and
stupid parents. A hopeless case from the beginning."

"Father drinks and is often in gaol. Hawker of notorious
character. Home full of children. None of the boys seek employment, but all hawk cinders or sell newspapers, at which they are
doing well for the time being. No member of the family would take
regular work if it were offered. They are not really idling, but
prefer this mode of living."

"Very sharp. Good scholar : especially clever at arithmetic.

Mother dead, consequent lack of home control. Too much in the
street, and has learned to cadge for coppers."

"Dull, heavy, and no initiative. Only half alive. Lack of sleep and
food. Mother dead. Father drinks and is shiftless and very stupid."

To sum up our knowledge of the lads in this
class prior to their entry upon industrial careers,
assuming, as we may fairly do, that the 69 about
whom information was obtained from the teachers
were typical of the rest, we note that about 80 per
cent of the lads found unemployed have begun badly.
This was primarily due to their home conditions, an
important fact when we come to consider remedial
measures.

In examining these figures it must, however, be
borne in mind that a teacher when asked whether
there was anything in a lad's school record to
account for his unemployment in later life, would
naturally search for such causes, and thus his
criticism may, to a certain extent, have been biased.
Statistics depending on personal judgment must not
be too rigidly interpreted.

INDUSTRIAL RECORD OF BOYS FOUND UNEMPLOYED

Now let us trace the history of the lads after they
left school. First we note that there has frequently
been a considerable interval between leaving school
and beginning work—an interval spent in "larking
about" in the streets. Teacher after teacher has
complained to us that boys left school on the
day they attained their 14th year without having

a situation in view. Frequently they play about in the streets so long that when they actually begin work they resent discipline, and will throw up a job on the slightest provocation. Many of them learn to prefer an easy life as casual "hands," with considerable intervals of loafing at street corners, to regular work. These periods of idleness are sometimes due to apathy on the part of the boys or parents in looking for work, but in many cases to the fact that the supply of boy labour in York is permanently in excess of the demand. But whatever may be their cause, they have a harmful influence on the industrial efficiency of the lads. Yet teachers often find that all their efforts to secure promising situations for boys who leave school are frustrated by indifference on the part of the parents. Cases have come to our notice where all necessary arrangements have been made for apprenticing clever lads to trades which they were anxious to follow, but the parents, although comparatively well off, have refused their consent. They would rather have their boys bringing home comparatively high wages in blind-alley occupations, than entering trades with a reasonable certainty of remunerative employment in the future, but smaller present earnings.

That this has been the case with many of the lads here considered, may be seen from the following table which shows the first occupations entered by each of them.

FIRST EMPLOYMENTS OF JUVENILE UNEMPLOYED

Errand boys	. . .	48
At glass works [1]	. .	11
Page boys .	. .	5
Catch jobs or nil	. .	5
Telegraph boys .	. .	3
Casual field work	. .	1
Labouring in brick-yard	.	1
Printer's feeder .	. .	1
Hawker .	. . .	1
Van boy .	. . .	1
Bottle packer	. . .	1
Selling papers .	. .	2
Musician .	. . .	1
Factory hands [2] .	. .	14
Junior clerks and office boys		4
Ropeworker	. . .	1
Joiners .	. . .	2
Farm hands	. . .	2
Gardeners .	. . .	2
Printer's labourer	. .	1
French polisher .	. .	1
At motor works .	. .	1
Apprenticed to moulder	.	1
Apprenticed to bootmaker	.	1
Barber's lather boy	. .	1
Milk delivering .	. .	2

It is almost certain that the great majority of those boys had entered blind-alley occupations, while those who had begun to learn a skilled trade were few.

We do not, of course, forget that circumstances not infrequently compel boys to take situations in which, regardless of the future, they can earn the highest possible present wage, and thus eke out the all too meagre family income, and that sometimes their parents can find no better work for them, although they would much prefer to place them in more promising posts.

But whatever may be the cause, the fact remains that the great majority, probably three-fourths, of the lads found unemployed, had entered blind-alley occupations, while, as we have already seen, four-fifths of them were also handicapped by bad physique

[1] They were "takers-in" or "wetters-off." The prospect of continued work as glass workers is small.

[2] Chiefly in confectionery works.

or home circumstances. These facts indicate pretty clearly what kind of industrial material is being produced by the processes under observation. The future of most of these boys can be safely foretold. Thrown upon the labour market in early manhood, with neither the knowledge of a skilled trade nor adaptable hands and minds, and untrained in methodical habits, they will almost certainly become casual workers of a poor type. Some of them will undoubtedly drift into workhouses, and some into prisons. Indeed the steps by which they become " casuals " can be traced, if we follow their industrial careers a little farther. Hitherto we have only considered the *first* occupations they have entered ; but examination shows how frequently many of them change their work, moving, often for the most trivial reasons, from one situation to another. The intervening periods of unemployment, shorter or longer, are usually spent in the streets, where they pick up odd jobs, a mode of living which certainly does not increase industrial efficiency. Thus they lose even that training in sticking to one occupation which, however unskilled the work may be, has considerable value.

Perhaps a few concrete examples will illustrate these facts better than further comment. We are obliged to delete some details from the descriptions to avoid identification.

A. P., age 18, left school at the age of 14 from Standard VI., and was engaged as an errand boy. He threw up the job after four or five weeks, owing to " differences with the employer," and went to an oil-

refining works. Here he stayed a year on piece-work and left for
unknown reasons, only to find himself unable to secure another place
for several months. Finally he became a bottle washer at a chemical
works, and again stayed for about a year, when he left because the
steam and dampness of the place did not agree with him. After another
period of several months' unemployment, he secured a temporary
job as attendant at a skating rink, where he received no wages, but good
tips. This work only lasted for three and a half months, and at the
beginning of June he was again without employment. This lad is
living with his parents and does not suffer want, since the earnings of
the household are good. But there can be no doubt that his career is
on a downward plane, and that he may ultimately find himself unable
to retain any permanent occupation worthy of the social position of
his father and brother, who are skilled tradesmen.

F. S., age 16, left school at the age of 14 from Standard VII., and
was engaged by a printer as errand boy. He left after a few months,
because his father wished him to learn the bottle trade, at which the
earnings of young lads were larger. He therefore became " taker-in "
at a glass works, earning six shillings a week for eight months, and
then went on strike for higher wages with a number of other lads.
In any case this employment would hardly have led to work at the
same factory at a higher wage, since the large majority of boys
employed as " takers-in " have to leave when they outgrow boyhood.
Since May this boy has been attending furniture sales with his father
to seek porterage work, his earnings only averaging about three shillings
per week. It is a most demoralising occupation for a mere lad, and
his industrial career, in all probability, has already come to an end.
In this case bad influences in the home would have put almost over-
whelming difficulties in the way of even an exceptionally steady and
industrious lad.

T. L., age 16, left school at the age of 14 from Standard VI., and
became an errand boy at a retail shop. In a few months he left, and
after being out of work for nine weeks, was engaged as a page boy.
In this situation again, he only stayed for a year or so, and left of his
own accord to learn French polishing. At this occupation he earned
seven shillings a week, but had to be dismissed after ten months
because he did not give satisfaction. " He is on the whole a good
worker," said his last employer, " but like others, he got into bad
company, and we had to part with him. Under fair supervision he
ought to do well." Since then he has obtained temporary work as an

errand boy, earning 5s. 6d. a week, and since the inquiry was made has been at an engine works at a wage of ten shillings a week. It is obvious that such frequent changes make for general instability. Taking into account periods of unemployment, probably a permanent occupation at a lower wage would have yielded a better financial result than this constant change with occasional short periods of relatively high wages ; as well as being morally more desirable.

D. F., age 17, comes from a good home in a large industrial town. After leaving school he worked in a factory for eight or nine months, earning six shillings a week and only leaving because his parents had died and he wished to go into another neighbourhood. He worked for about a year at a colliery where he earned ten shillings a week, until he went on strike with other workers. After this he seems to have had a period of excessive bad luck, for when found in York a few months later, staying with relatives, he was without respectable clothes, and had to be fitted up entirely by a shopkeeper who employed him for charity, although a younger boy would have done as well. In this shop, where he cleaned the windows and acted as errand boy, he earned four shillings a week and all meals ; but after a few months a dispute arose about working overtime, which led to his dismissal, and at the time of inquiry he had been entirely dependent on his relatives for over a month. He is strong, and nothing is known against his character, so that with better luck he may still retrieve his position as a regular wage-earner.

J. R., age 17, has had three different situations as errand boy, the first lasting for six months, the second for three months, and the third for six months. He is a strong and intelligent lad of good character, but is handicapped by having only one eye. At the time of inquiry he was temporarily engaged in timber carrying, an occupation at which he could earn about 7s. 6d. a week. This lad's home is a very unsatisfactory one, and it is thought by those who know it intimately, that he has, from the beginning, been exploited by his elders, who put him to immediately remunerative jobs without a thought of his future. It is almost impossible that he should now enter upon a regular industrial career.

M. N., age 17 years and 9 months, was brought up in a poor part of York and left school at the age of 14. He entered the services of a tradesman as errand boy after having, apparently, been unemployed for about six months, but only stayed for a year or less, because, as he says, " he quarrelled with one of the masters." Another situation as errand boy lasted only three months, and was followed by two months' employment as cellar boy in a wine and spirit business. Then he drifted into the services of a private family as boots and " gardener " (sic), where he stayed for fourteen months. He left, it appears, in the spirit of comradeship, with another boy who wanted to better himself. At the age of 17 we find him engaged as a bottle washer for his previous employers in the wine and spirit business, but being dissatisfied with his earnings of six shillings per week, he left again two weeks before the date of our inquiry. During this last fortnight he had earned 9d. for organ blowing, and enough money to buy cigarettes from occasional " floor washing " and similar occupations. There is little likelihood of his ever resting content in a permanent situation.

P. B., age 17, served as errand boy for a very short time after leaving school at the age of 14. His father is a carter, and seems to have used his influence to find him a place as groom at the cavalry barracks. The boy did not, however, stay for more than a few months, when he " bettered himself " by taking a paper round in the city. He worked for one newspaper agent for eighteen months, and for another for nine months. His next move was to take employment as machine attendant at a soap works outside York. This seemed more promising, but he only stuck to it for two months, after which he went off again in search of higher earnings. This lad has a good character given him by several of his employers.

F. R. S., age 18, though a good scholar, was obliged to enter a blind-alley occupation at a glass works to help his father and mother to maintain the family, he being the oldest of six children. He left at the end of a year to better himself and got employment as bottle washer for a firm of chemical manufacturers. This engagement, however, only lasted for about half a year, and he had to go back to his former employers, who willingly reinstalled him, since he was an intelligent and decent lad. He earned ten shillings a week, but after nineteen months he was suspended for staying off without permission, in search of work elsewhere. As he wanted to be a clerk he took this opportunity of leaving his unskilled labour, without, however, having secured another situation. It had not occurred to him or his parents that it might be wise to add to his attainments by attending evening classes before taking the plunge, and on the date of inquiry he had been entirely without work or prospect of it for nearly two months.

B. M., age 18, was for less than a year in a confectionery works, and was dismissed for a reason not known. He immediately found casual work with various employers, the jobs being of brief duration and alternating with short periods of idleness. He had last worked for any length of time as watchman on a work of public improvement for seven months. This was followed by three months' unemployment in the heart of winter. In the spring of 1910 he was employed for fourteen weeks as labourer by a printer, his wages being fifteen shillings, but was dismissed as unsatisfactory. After an interval of unemployment, came six weeks' navvying and one month's work at a Bone Mill. At the time of inquiry there was no longer any endeavour to secure a permanent situation, and he had lost, through his own fault, several prospects of regular employment at rising wages.

Many more examples could be given, but these will suffice to show the frequency with which many of the lads change their work, and the tendency of these changes to induce a casual mode of life. For it must be remembered that the occupations which they follow in succession are of the most varied description, and are entered without any idea whatever of progressive training of any kind. Here, for instance, is a list, selected at random, of the jobs successively undertaken by a number of lads :—

  1. Bottle washer—errand boy—waiter.
  2. Errand boy—groom—selling papers—machinist at oil mill.
  3. Printer's machine attendant—errand boy—pottery labourer.
  4. Bottle washer—errand boy—labourer at glass works.
  5. Stable boy (at two places)—machine feeder—errand boy—stableman.
  6. Bottle washer—button maker—errand boy—rink attendant.
  7. Errand boy (two places)—cellar boy—boots and gardener.
  8. Junior clerk—telegraph messenger—printer's feeder.
  9. Errand boy—page—errand boy.
  10. Beer bottler—butcher's errand boy—van boy.

This list would be much fuller if it had included the great number of catch jobs undertaken by the lads when out of what they euphemistically call "regular work."

The intervals between the periods of comparatively regular employment are frequently of considerable length. For instance, of the 114 lads unemployed on the date of our census, 7 had been out of regular work for over a year, 16 others for over six months, and 4 for over three months. In the case of a number of others the exact period was doubtful; but from such information as we obtained, in not a few cases it was at least three months. The power of steady application of such lads must have been gravely impaired.

In the foregoing pages we have given especial attention to lads who began their industrial career with a bad prospect, because the problems they suggest are so large and so important as to call for grave consideration. But we must not forget that a certain number of lads, perhaps between 20 and 30 per cent of the whole, were unemployed although they had not entered blind-alley occupations, and there was nothing especially unsatisfactory in their home circumstances or previous history. Their unemployment was due to a number of causes, such as reduction of staff, ill-health, the committal of some minor offence, and so forth. Now it must be borne in mind that such enforced idleness, though the problem it presents is less difficult and complex than that with which we have just dealt, is not without its dangers. The choice of occupations for youths aged from 16 to 18 is more limited than for those of 14, as many employers needing apprentices or other lads prefer to take them direct from school, and we have noticed that sometimes, to avoid protracted unemployment, a lad who has left a situation with apparently good prospects, accepts one which is distinctly inferior. On the other hand, if he remains too long without work, there is a grave risk of his contracting habits which will unfit him to do justice to a good post, should he finally obtain one.

Proposals for Reforms

We now come to consider what reforms the facts which we have been discussing suggest. And first let us remember that the lads out of work on the day of our census only represent those members of a long procession who happened to be passing a given point at a given moment, and that their ranks are constantly being reinforced by others who will come under the same influences. We shall then realise that juvenile unemployment has a vital connection with adult unemployment, and that the latter problem can never be solved if the former is neglected. We urge this point with some insistence, since its importance has often been overlooked.

Reform must begin with the children, while they are yet attending the elementary schools.[1] As a

---

[1] We do not, of course, forget the part played by heredity in determining the quality of each generation. The consideration of this interesting subject would, however, lead us too far from the specific question before us.

rule, the teachers have a considerable knowledge of their home circumstances, which, combined with observation of their conduct and progress at school, will enable them to distinguish all those who are making a bad start in life Such a bad start will probably be due to one or another of the following causes :—

(a) Physical or mental defect.
(b) Bad moral influence at home.
(c) Great poverty or neglect at home.
(d) Lack of adequate home control.

With regard to (a), physical and mental defects, it is now generally recognised by educationists that provision should be made in connection with our educational system for giving specialised treatment to all very slow or otherwise defective children ; and the experience already gained in this connection, both in this country and abroad, has been encouraging. Medical inspection in the elementary schools will facilitate the selection of children suitable for special treatment, and also reduce the number of cases in which the neglect of minor ailments leads to serious consequences in later life. The effect of this special treatment will be to reduce the number of defectives who would otherwise, at a later age, have to be maintained, wholly or in part, out of public funds.

(b) With regard to children suffering from bad

Nor can we discuss the effects of our system of elementary education on industrial efficiency or the formation of character. We must content ourselves with expressing the opinion that there is much room for improvement in this respect.

C

moral influences at home, we suggest that there should be much greater readiness to send them to day or residential industrial schools, or otherwise to remove them from their demoralising environment; and a more generous interpretation of existing powers would enable this to be done. It would be necessary strictly to enforce payment for their maintenance at the schools, to avoid undermining the parental responsibility.

Cases (c) and (d), *i.e.* cases of children coming from very poor or neglected homes, or homes where the control over them is inadequate, could probably be best dealt with by a well organised system of School Care Committees, working in close connection with the local Education Authorities. These committees would be composed of voluntary workers attached to the different schools, each member of which would be made responsible for a few children, and give such help as might be needed in connection with them. In one case, the help given might take the form of seeing that they were fed at school and provided with proper clothing; in another, children who had outgrown home control might be brought under the influence of such agencies as Sunday schools, boys' clubs, the Boy Scout movement, and the like. It is clear that if Care Committees are to be effective bodies, the number of children placed under the control of each worker must be very small, and it is not unlikely that this work may develop so extensively that, in larger centres at any rate, experienced secretaries must be engaged at the public expense to organise it, and to undertake the necessary correspondence. One result of the work of these Care Committees would, no doubt, be that existing laws for securing the proper care of children would be more strictly enforced.

Turning now to the entry of the lads into the industrial world, the first desideratum is that head teachers should be periodically informed by the local Labour Exchanges of the relative demand for workers in different industries, so that the advice which they give their pupils as to suitable occupations may be based on the best available knowledge. In addition, however, there should be a closer intercourse and a more frequent interchange of views between the representatives of the educational and of the industrial worlds. Advisory Committees on Juvenile Employment, consisting of teachers and other persons specially interested in boys, along with employers of labour, trade unionists, and a representative of the local Labour Exchange, have already been started by several local Education Authorities, for the purpose of helping boys to find suitable situations. The experience of these Committees will, no doubt, indicate with increasing clearness the lines on which they can most usefully advance. It might be well if the local Education Authorities appointed special officers to act as a link between the Labour Exchanges and the head teachers.[1]

[1] The same officers might also help in organising Continuation Classes and encouraging their use.

The foregoing proposals, after all, only amount to carrying out more systematically and thoroughly methods which are already in vogue, to a greater or less extent, here and there; and yet their universal adoption would go far to remove the handicap with which so many children start their industrial careers. But there will still remain difficult problems to solve, and one of these will be that in many towns, as in York, the supply of boy labour usually exceeds the demand, and no matter how efficient it may be, a surplus is left after all demands have been met, while even those lads who find work immediately on leaving school may, from one cause or another, have to pass through periods of unemployment during the next few years. The solution does not necessarily lie in the direction of increasing the demand for boy labour, but rather in that of decreasing the available supply of it, by extending the period of compulsory education. But though the latter course would lessen unemployment among youths it would not end it, and then, as now, periods of enforced idleness would too frequently be spent in the streets, either in " larking" or in seeking to " pick up a catch job." It is difficult to say which of these two methods of passing the time is the more detrimental to industrial efficiency. It is of supreme importance that during boyhood and youth, say up to the age of 19, lads should never be subject to the temptations inseparably connected with periods of idleness. How can they be avoided? Only, it seems to us, by compelling youths who are not regularly engaged for weekly wages, to spend their time in training schools designed to fit them for their future work.

The system would work out in this way : before a lad left an elementary school, he would be obliged either to produce a certificate signed by a prospective employer, stating that he would forthwith be engaged in regular work at a weekly wage, or else immediately to enter a training school where he would remain until he found work. In this school, which might be in connection with an existing technical school, he would receive such instruction as would develop his general intelligence and render him adaptable to any employment that might be forthcoming. He would, for instance, add to his knowledge of applied mathematics and drawing—both freehand and mechanical. He would be taught to express himself clearly in writing, and would receive carefully regulated instruction in physical drill. An important place in the curriculum would be given to industrial training, the character of which would depend upon the local industries, and it is to be hoped that some teaching of horticulture or agriculture would be included wherever practicable.[1] The lad would remain in this school until he could produce an employer's certificate to the effect that he had

---

[1] In making this last suggestion we have in mind a proposal amplified in Chap. VII. for the decentralisation of a large proportion of our town populations. It is important that those who might, under such a system, move into the country, although continuing to work in the towns, should have some knowledge of rural occupations.

obtained regular work. The exact definition of what should be held to constitute regular work would require consideration, but we suggest that, at any rate, no promise of work for less than a week should be so considered.

It will not, however, be sufficient for a lad to go to the training school only during the interval between his leaving the elementary school and entering his first occupation. Up to a given age— say 19—he should return there during any period of unemployment, and develop the knowledge and faculties gained in his previous work. As soon as he becomes unemployed it should, therefore, be the duty of the employer, under penalty, to advise the head of the training school of the fact, possibly through the medium of the local Labour Exchange. It would forthwith become compulsory for the boy to re-enter the training school until he was again able to bring a certificate that he had secured employment.[1] On his re-entry his case would be considered by the Advisory Committee, and if any industrial misfit had occurred, an attempt would be made to rectify the error.[2]

If this system were carried out, periods of un-

---

[1] It might be advisable to require local Education Authorities to extend their existing registers of scholars so as to include all ages up to 19. This would bring all young people under the supervision of the school attendance officers, and make it easier to ensure the attendance of unemployed youths.

[2] We suggest that in starting such a system, a beginning should be made with the boys leaving school, so as to avoid mixing them in training schools with older lads, who possibly have already become demoralised by frequent periods of idleness.

employment, so far from being demoralising, would be educational; and whatever had been the character of the employment that the lad had been engaged in, the time spent at the training school would either render him more efficient in the industry which he had left, or more adaptable to a new one. In this connection it must be remembered, that among the unemployed there is always likely to be an undue proportion of lads whose educational attainments are considerably below the average, and who, therefore, stand especially in need of the instruction which the training school would give.

From the physical standpoint the time spent there would be valuable, and if the exercises involved not only muscular development, but discipline and concerted action, there would be a double gain.

We believe it would be advisable to give at any rate one substantial meal per day free to those who attend these schools, not only because it is of the utmost importance that their physical efficiency should be maintained, but also because it is only a reasonable compensation for the catch jobs they miss. The granting of this meal would also extend the area which each school could serve, by making it unnecessary for the lads to return home for dinner.

This extension would be an important matter, for since lads possessing widely differing educational attainments would be dropping into the school at all times of the year, the classes should be numerous enough to allow them to be suitably graded.

This grading would not, of course, be the only difficulty to surmount. We should have to face the uncertainty of the period for which each lad would stay. We need not, however, magnify this difficulty by comparing the conditions with those of an ordinary school, in which some of the boys intended to leave at their 14th and others at their 16th year of age. It would be practically impossible to frame a curriculum suited to both those classes, because the character of the teaching would, from the beginning, have to be entirely different, according to the age at which school education was to cease. In the proposed training schools, however, the teaching would not vary according to its probable duration, but only according to the previous attainments of the lads, since the aim would not be to acquire a definite minimum of knowledge, but the best possible development of knowledge already possessed.

This brings us to another piece of necessary machinery, namely the keeping of a continuous record for each lad. This should be commenced by his teacher when he leaves the elementary school, and should contain such information as would enable the head of the training school to place him in a suitable class. The entries would be continued whenever he left the training school, so that should he enter it or a similar school again, information would be easily available which would secure for him, with the least possible delay, the kind of help which he most needed.   It is important that the head teachers of training schools, like those of elementary schools, should be in close touch with the local Labour Exchanges and Advisory Committees, and so well acquainted with the relative demand for labour in the different industries as to give their pupils the best advice.

The schools would vary largely with the industrial characteristics of the locality, and there is no doubt that in their management head teachers should have much more liberty than is now given them in elementary schools.

One difficulty to be met is that the number of lads in attendance would vary greatly with the state of trade.   We believe that it could only be overcome by making both staff and buildings adequate to the greater rather than the lesser demand.   It may be thought that this course would involve unnecessary extravagance at times of trade activity, when the number of boys in the schools was small, but, on the other hand, it may be urged that the lads unemployed at such times would probably be the least efficient, and therefore those standing most in need of the increased personal attention which could be given by an ample teaching staff.

We recognise that any scheme of training schools such as has been outlined could not be satisfactorily carried out in very small towns or in country districts. In such areas, either some arrangement must be made whereby suitable boys should travel daily to the nearest school, or the few cases which presented themselves must be dealt with through the existing educational institutions. This method would, no doubt, be less satisfactory, but it would be rare, as the problem of unemployment in its acutest form is urban and not rural.

It may be objected that if unemployed lads are kept constantly under training, they will have no adequate opportunity of searching for work. But the establishment of Labour Exchanges has already rendered the unsystematic tramping of the streets in search of work much less inevitable than hitherto; and as they come to be more generally used by employers, the old methods should be entirely superseded. Meanwhile, although all the lads would be registered, the hours spent at the training school should be such as to leave them free to seek employment on their own account if they thought it desirable. Work might be, for instance, from nine to twelve and from two to five, with a holiday on Saturdays; and special leave of absence might also be given to any lad who could show that it was necessary to apply for some particular post during the working hours of the training school.

But while these institutions would overcome some of the worst evils of juvenile unemployment, they would leave other serious evils unremedied, as, for example, the continued existence of blind-alley occupations which often keep lads fully occupied up

to the age of 19, and then leave them stranded
as entirely unskilled labourers, with much of their
education forgotten, and less generally adaptable than
when they left the elementary schools. While we believe that in any serious attempt to grapple with the
problem of juvenile unemployment, the system outlined in the preceding pages will come first, we hope
that its advantages would soon be so far appreciated
as to facilitate legislation demanding that all lads, or
at any rate lads who follow occupations scheduled as
holding out no prospect of continued employment,
should, up to a certain age—say 19—spend a considerable proportion of each week—possibly one-third—
in training schools such as we have described. Such
a scheme is definitely proposed in the Minority Report
of the Royal Commission on the Poor Laws. The
question of compulsory education for all juvenile
workers is a wide and difficult one, upon which a
good deal has already been written. We believe that
in time the nation will recognise the necessity for this
reform, which alone can overcome the chief evils of
blind-alley occupations.

Meanwhile, however, we believe that public opinion
would support proposals such as we have outlined
in this chapter. At present incompetent and casual
workers are being manufactured in appalling numbers
between the years of 12 and 20, and it is absolutely
necessary to remedy this state of things. The problem
of adult unemployment will remain insoluble so long
as a large proportion of the workers lack skill and

intelligence, and have never acquired habits of regular work.[1]

[1] Since this chapter was written, based as it was not on theory, but upon the facts ascertained in York, we have had the satisfaction of learning that another worker in this field, Arthur Greenwood (*Juvenile Labour Exchanges and After-Care*, P. S. King & Son, 1911), has come to conclusions similar in many respects to our own. We do not, however, agree with the author that the training of unemployed lads should be non-compulsory, since we are convinced that the boys who are most in need of it would be the very last to exchange the liberty of the streets for the comparatively rigid discipline of a school.

It will also be known that in the Report of the Consultative Committee on Attendance at Continuation Schools (Cd. 4757, 1909) a paragraph is devoted (p. 65) to outlining a scheme for the compulsory education of all unemployed boys and girls up to their 16th year.

CHAPTER II

REGULAR WORKERS

(291 men)

In this chapter we shall consider 291 men over 18 years of age, who, though many of them, under pressure of circumstances, have been obliged to accept casual employment, have, with a few exceptions, within the last two years been in regular work, *i.e.* for one employer for at least one year without a break, and are, for the most part, definitely seeking it.[1]

We shall inquire into the reasons which appear to prevent the men from obtaining work; in how many cases, for instance, they consist of personal failings, and in how many they are purely economic. After reviewing the effect of periods of unemployment on the efficiency of the workers, we shall conclude with an examination of various schemes for dealing with the problem, and ask to what extent they might benefit the men whose circumstances we have studied.

Our first and most important inquiry is : Why

[1] For purposes of simplifying classification, a few men who, although they had been without regular employment for rather over two years were obviously looking for it, are here included.

MEN WHO HAVE BEEN IN

Last Regular Employment.					Previous Regular Employments.[1]	Present Age.	Present Condition.
Nature.	Dura-tion (years).	Date of Leaving.	Cause of Leaving.	Age at date of Leaving.			Physique.
Groom and coachman .	27	1908	Death of master . .	57	Errand boy, groom .	59	Good . .
Coppersmith . .	2	1909	End of contract . .	34	Coppersmith (17) .	35	,, . .
Shop porter . . .	2	Jan. 1910	Laziness . . .	25	Errand boy, brewer's labourer (3), tram conductor (4)	26	,, . .
Errand boy . . .	5	1909	Displaced by younger boy	19	Errand boy (1) . .	20	Fairly healthy
Flour-mill labourer .	1½	April 1910	Bad time-keeper . .	20	Confectioner's labourer (2 or 3), unemployed (about 2)	20	Good . .
Confectionery labourer	7	Nov. 1909	To better himself .	24	Helping in shop at home (4)	25	Often ill . .
Errand boy and carter.	1¾	1909	Firm wound up . .	19	Helping father, school caretaker (3)	20	Underfed. .
Steam lurry driver .	5 or 6	,,	Left to avoid temptation to drink	34	Farm lad (1), carter (3), cement worker (6), carter (6)	35	Good . .
Box-maker . . .	11	Jan. 1910	To emigrate. . .	25	Rope-maker, engineer's labourer (½)	25	,, . .
Railway labourer . .	Over 15	June 1908	Bad time-keeping .	39	....	41	Underfed
Barman. . . .	18	Dec. 1909	Work only temporary	24	Clerk	25	?
Warehouseman . .	3½	April 1909	Illness	33	Warehouseman (15) .	34	Not strong
Engine-driver . .	17	April 1910	Firm wound up . .	32	Engineer's labourer (1), railway labourer (1)	33	Strong . .
Box-maker . . .	25	July 1909	Accident and temporary disablement	47	Box-maker (7 months), printer's labourer, general labourer, various	48	?
Laundry vanman . .	4	June 1908	To better himself .	18	....	19	Good . .
Bookbinder's apprentice	7	Dec. 1909	End of apprenticeship	21	....	21	,, . .
School caretaker . .	8	March 1910	To open provision shop (chiefly to find work for son)	46	Tailor . . .	46	Not strong enough for own trade
Baker's apprentice .	5½	Feb. 1910	End of apprenticeship	21	....	21	Good . .
Drayman . . .	5	1909	Slackness . . .	38	At colliery, grooming, shunter	39	,, . .
Lithographic printer .	1½	June 1909	,, . . .	53	Confectioner's labourer, lithographic printer	54	,, . .
Flour packer . .	16	July 1909	Quarrel with foreman.	30	Paperhanger (2) .	31	,, . .
Beer bottler . . .	3	Sept. 1909	To better himself .	20	Errand boy (1), confectioner's labourer (3), relief signalman (½)	21	Not strong enough for heavy work

1 Number of years in brackets.   2 Member of Trade Union.

REGULAR WORK (291 IN NUMBER)

Present Condition. Character.	Nature of Temporary Occupations.	Nature of Permanent Occupations sought.	Apparent Personal Handicaps in Search for Regular Work.	Average Weekly Casual Earnings.[3]	Average Weekly Income of Rest of Household.[3]	Adults.	Children (under 16).	Is Family under Poverty Line?[4]
Excellent	Groom, odd jobs	Stableman or coachman	Age . . .	10/-	25/-	3	..	No
Good	Assisting in sister's fruit and confectionery shop	Own trade or any	None . .	8/6	20/-	2	5	,,
Very lazy, betting and drinking	....	Any labouring .	Bad reputation	..	..	1	..	?
Very lazy	Casual painting . .	,,	Laziness and bad home influence	?	39/-	5	1	No
Fair . .	....	,,	None . .	..	?	?	?	?
Slow and inefficient, in danger of degenerating	Shop messenger 6 months	,,	Bad record .	?	..	2	3	?
Steady and willing	....	,,	None . .	..	14/-	3	2	Yes
Good, but inclined to drink	Gas works 6 months .	,,	,, . .	?	..	2	..	,,
Good . .	....	,,	,, . .	..	..	1	..	,,
,, . .	Painting and other catch jobs	,,	Has become casual	13/-	3/-	2	3	,,
Satisfactory worker	Catch jobs . . .	,,	None ,, ,,	12/-	?	7	1	No
Excellent, well educated	Railway summer porter	Clerk or timekeeper	None . .	9/-	?	?	?	,,
Good . .	Haymaking . . .	Any	,, . .	?	?	3	5	?
,, . .	Poor Law relief work .	,, ...	Age . . .	12/6	10/-	3	5	Yes
,, . .	....	Vanman . .	Not worked for 12 months. Likely to deteriorate	..	32/-	5	..	No
Fully trained, satisfactory worker	....	Bookbinding "or any"	None . .	..	?	?	?	?
Excellent . .	Own provision shop which does not pay	Caretaker . .	Ill-health and age	..	..	3	..	Yes
Good . . . / Good reference, but was least efficient of four draymen employed	Helps in above . . / Temporarily for last employer	Baker's improver . / Drayman "or any".	None . . / Not very efficient	5/-	8/-	3 / 2	4	,, / ,,
Efficient. .	One week in 52 at his trade	Own trade[2] .	Age . . .	?	?	6	..	No
Steady . .	....	Any	Not worked for 12 months	..	?	?	?	?
"Good, steady lad"	....	Light work .	Delicate health	..	58/-	3	..	No

[3] Including all regular pensions, poor relief, etc., but not occasional gifts or savings.   [4] See note, p. 61.

MEN WHO HAVE BEEN IN REGULAR

Last Regular Employment.				Age at date of Leaving.	Previous Regular Employments.[1]	Present Age.	Present Condition.
Nature.	Dura-tion (years).	Date of Leaving.	Cause of Leaving.				Physique.
Shop assistant . .	11	Aug. 1909	Charge of criminal offence which, however, was not proved	35	Shop assistant . .	36	Poor . .
Errand boy . . .	2	Nov. 1909	To better himself .	21	Errand boy . .	22	Good . .
Baker	5	Feb. 1910	Slackness . . .	30	Baker (not apprenticed)	30	,, . .
French polisher .	3	May 1910	To resist reduction of wages	40	French polisher .	40	,, . .
Flour-mill labourer .	3	Dec. 1909	Dispute with foreman	29	Frame maker (3), bolt maker (8), bricklayer's labourer (3)	30	Strong . .
Wagoner . . .	5 or 6	1909	Slackness . . .	24	Confectioner's labourer (5)	25	,, . .
Piano action fitter .	6	April 1910	Fighting . . .	21	Page-boy (2) . .	21	,, . .
Factory labourer . .	3	1908	Drink, after many warnings	21	Box-maker (1), brick yard (3)	23	,, . .
Out porter . . .	18	Nov. 1909	Slackness . .	42	Van boy (1), farm labourer (7½), flour packer (4), porter (1)	43	Good . .
Moulder . . .	9	Sept. 1909	,, . . .	55	Moulder . . .	56	Strong . .
Flour-mill labourer .	11 or 12	May 1910	To better himself .	32	?	32	Good . .
Carter	1½	Aug. 1908	Drink	26	Confectioner's labourer (5), carter (5)	28	Strong . .
,, . . .	3	May 1910	To better himself .	22	Stonemason's labourer (½), unemployed (2)	22	Healthy, but mentally defective
Factory labourer . .	4	Aug. 9	Accident and temporary disablement	26	Confectioner's labourer (4), shop porter (4)	27	Healthy, but ruptured
Glass polisher . .	Many	1908	Age	56	Some forty years with same firm	58	?
Flour-mill labourer .	1¼	,,	?	18	Ropemaker (1), errand boy (1), box-maker (2)	20	Strong . .
,, ,, .	2	May 1910	To better himself .	40	Farm labourer (8), engine-driver (14)	40	,, . .
Electrician . . .	2	June 1909	Bad time-keeping .	24	Electrician . .	25	Often ill . .
Druggist's packer .	1¾	?	Bad time-keeping and drink	?	Confectioner's labourer (10)	27	Not very strong
Flour-mill labourer .	1	May 1909	Bad time-keeping due to ill-health	23	Confectioner's labourer (6), factory labourer (3)	24	Delicate . .
Barman	9½	Spring 1910	Ill-health . . .	25	. . . .	25	,, . .
Groom	7	,, 1909	Put on casual staff .	24	Training home (1), carter (3)	25	Very good .
Machinist . . .	2	1905	Illness (more or less permanent)	35	Machinist (5), then irregular	40	Seems consumptive
Railway loader . .	34	March 1910	Series of petty thefts .	50	Farm service (4) .	50	Very good .

[1] Number of years in brackets.　　　　　　[2] Member of Trade Union.

WORK (291 IN NUMBER)—continued

Present Condition / Character	Nature of Temporary Occupations.	Nature of Permanent Occupations sought.	Apparent Personal Handicaps in Search for Regular Work.	Average Weekly Casual Earnings.[3]	Average Weekly Income of Rest of Household.[3]	No. of Persons in Household. Adults	Children (under 16).	Is Family under Poverty Line?[4]
Very doubtful	Parish relief work	Any	Suspicion against his character	10/-	11/-	2	5	Yes
Excellent	Nil since Nov. 1909	,,	Probably got under bad moral influences	..	1/-	3	..	,,
,,	At his trade one night per week	Baker	None	3/-	?	2	3	?
Sometimes intemperate	Casual at his trade	Own trade	,,	6/6	5/-	2	..	Yes
Good	Bricklayer's labourer	Any labouring	,,	8/6	5/-	2	..	No
Dishonest; given to drink and gambling	Casual factory porter and cattle market	Any	Bad reputation. On down grade	12/-	..	2	2	Yes
Good worker, but inclined to be lazy	....	,,	None	..	?	4	..	?
Very good	Brickyard, and casually at flour mill	,,	Has become casual	7/-	28/-	3	4	No
Hot tempered and sometimes intemperate	Distress Committee relief work	Out porter	,, ,,	..	20/3	4	5	Yes
Very good	....	Own trade[2]	Age	..	28/-	4	2	No
,,	....	General labourer	None	..	..	2	..	Yes
Given to drink and loafing	Gas works stoker, twice for half year; factory porter	,,	Bad record	Say 10/-	50/-	5	..	No
Good	....	,,	Mental deficiency	..	20/-	5	1	Yes
"Poor type"	Carter and railway porter	,,	Probably getting confirmed casual	15/3	..	2	1	No
Must have been good	Parish relief work	Any	Age	?	?	4	..	?
Good	Skin-yard labourer about 4 days per week	Only at skin-yard	Probably become casual	17/-	31/-	4	1	No
Very good	Brush-hand and catch jobs	Carter or labourer	None	?	?	2	..	?
Seems inclined to loaf	A few weeks at own trade	Own trade	Laziness	?	over 60/-	5	..	No
Given to drink and loafing	....	Any light work	Delicate health and laziness	..	26/-	4	..	,,
Doubtful	....	Labourer	Delicate health and probably inclined to loaf	..	24/3	3	..	,,
Good	Casual outdoor portering	Casual portering	Delicate health	?	?	?	?	,,
,,	Groom (casual)	Groom or carter	None	?	..	1	..	?
,,	Catch jobs such as snow shovelling	Light work	Physical inefficiency	?	42/-	3	..	No
Dishonest	Timber carrying and other catch jobs	Any	Age	?	29/-	4	..	,,

[3] Including all regular pensions, poor relief, etc., but not occasional gifts or savings. [4] See note, p. 61.

D

MEN WHO HAVE BEEN IN REGULAR

| Last Regular Employment. | | | | | | Present Age. | Present Condition. |
Nature.	Dura-tion (years).	Date of Leaving.	Cause of Leaving.	Age at date of Leaving.	Previous Regular Employments.[2]		Physique.
Coachman	1	Feb. 1910	Horses sold	50	Coachman (9), previous occupation unknown	50	Good
Railway striker	12	1908	Illness due to heavy work	45	?	47	Fair
Caretaker and messenger	8½	Aug. 1908	Ill-health	45	Errand boy, farm labourer, packer, and warehouseman (6)	47	Poor
Blacksmith	12	Oct. 1909	Temporary illness	28	Errand boy	29	Fair
Coachman and gardener	1½	May 14, 1910	Employer left York	46	Groom, coachman (22)	46	,,
Railway mechanic	about 3	1908	Insubordination	17	....	19	Good
Railway labourer	about 2½	July 1908	"Slackness"[1]	28	Errand boy, confectioner's labourer, railway labourer	29	,,
Grocer's manager	3	March 1910	Slackness	46	Commercial college, grocer	46	Strong
Shunter	34	Oct. 1909	Theft	49	Farm labourer (3)	50	Healthy
Groom	¾	May 1910	Horses sold	19	Errand boy (¾), blacksmith (¼), gardener (1½)	19	Strong
Grocer on own account	12	March 1910	Bankruptcy	38	Grocer	38	Good
Blacksmith's apprentice	5	April 1910	End of apprenticeship	21	Blacksmith's labourer (1)	21	Very healthy
Clerk	1	Sept. 1909	Removal of firm	21	Clerk	22	Healthy
Stud-groom	2	April 1910	End of hunting season	45	Errand boy, groom, groom-gardener (13)	abt. 45	Fair
Fitter	1	early 1909	Slackness	22	Fitter	23	Good
Warehouseman	8½	Nov. 1909	Drink	40	Page-boy, warehouseman	41	,,
Insurance agent	4 or 5	1909	To better himself	51	Joiner	52	Healthy
,,	1	March 1910	Inefficiency at this particular work	25	Farmer (6), china and glass trade (4)	25	Strong
Dairyman on own account	3	Oct. 1909	Loss of stock and bad season	45	Joiner and cabinet-maker (to 1906)	46	Good
Farmer's labourer	1	April 1910	Temporary ill-health	35	Farm labourer and dairyman	35	Strong
Naval engineer	1¼	May 1910	Overworked	28	Pupil teacher, packer and checker, naval engineer	28	Fair
Railway labourer	23	July 1908	"Slackness"[1]	44	Whitesmith (10)	46	Fair, but very deaf
Mechanical engineer	1?	April 1910	Temporary slackness	25	Fitter(5), mechanic(5)	25	Strong
Confectioner's labourer	10	Dec. 1908	Inefficiency	24 or 25	Errand boy (¼)	26	Good
Iron-moulder	2	Nov. 1909	Slackness	25	Iron-moulder	26	Underfed
Electrician	2¼	April 1910	Temporary slackness	21	Electrician	21	Strong
Railway labourer	2	1908	Probably bad time-keeping	21 or 22	Farm labourer (4)	23	Good

[1] Reason given not checked. [2] Number of years in brackets. [3] Member of Trade Union.

WORK (291 IN NUMBER)—continued

Present Condition. Character.	Nature of Temporary Occupations.	Nature of Permanent Occupations sought.	Apparent Personal Handicaps in search for Regular Work.	Average Weekly Casual Earnings.[4]	Average Weekly Income of Rest of Household.[4]	No. of Persons in Household. Adults.	Children (under 16).	Is Family under Poverty Line?[5]
Excellent	Groom (casual)	Coachman or any	Age . . .	3/-	?	2	..	No
Good	Cabman, barman, waiter, and catch jobs	Any	Age and illiteracy	7/6	6/-	2	..	,,
Excellent	Casual outdoor employment for former employer	Casual only	Age . .	8/-	18/-	2	2	,,
Good	(Was laid up till March)	Own trade or any	None . .		16/-	4	..	Yes
Excellent	Helps wife to keep shop	Own trade	Age . . .		?	8	2	No
Lazy and troublesome	Some months butcher's assistant	Mechanical engineer	Lack of energy	?	over 90/-	6	1	,,
"Unsatisfactory and very slow," lazy	Factory porter (rare)	Labourer . .	Inefficiency	?	..	1	..	,,
Good	....	Any . . .	Age . . .		23/-	4	5	Yes
Dishonest	Chimney sweep, haymaking	,, . .	,, . .	10/-	..	2	8	,,
Capable	....	Groom or any .	None . .		47/-	5	1	No
Excellent	....	Grocer or clerk	,, . .			2	8	Yes
Very satisfactory	Casual at own trade	Own trade . .	,, . .	4/-	116/-	8	..	No
Excellent character but not clever	Casual clerk . .	Clerk or any .	,, . .	5/-	28/-	4	..	,,
Excellent	Gardener and coachman	In stables . .	Age . . .	?	?	2	..	,,
Very good	Six months and catch jobs at own trade	Fitter or turner	None . .	10/-	58/-	6	8	,,
Given to drink and lazy	....	Warehouseman	Intemperance .	..	?	2	1	?
Good character but shiftless	Night watchman, joiner, commission and insurance agent	Joiner or any .	Age . . .	7/-	6/-	2	..	No
Very good	....	"Any suitable"	None . .	..	..	1	..	?
Excellent character, good joiner	....	Cabinetmaker .	,, . .	..	..	8	8	No (has savings)
Good	....	Horse-breaker or labourer	,, . .	..	..	1	..	,,
Very good	....	Packer, stock-keeper, engine-driver, fireman[3]	,, . .	..	..	2	2	Yes
Good	Furniture remover, relief work	Labourer . .	Age and deafness	10/-	17/-	5	1	No
Very good	....	Fitter . .	None . .			2	2	Yes
Good character, but slow and inefficient	Catch jobs . .	Confectioner's labourer	Inefficiency .	?	?	8	..	No
Good	Signwriter . .	Own trade .	None . .	2/-	44/-	5	..	,,
,,	....	Electrician .	,, .		?	8	1	,,
Lazy	Carter . .	Groom or carter	Deteriorating into loafer	..	50/-	4	..	,,

4 Including all regular pensions, poor relief, etc., but not occasional gifts or savings. 5 See note, p. 61.

MEN WHO HAVE BEEN IN REGULAR

Last Regular Employment.					Previous Regular Employments.[1]	Present Condition.	
Nature.	Dura-tion (years).	Date of Leaving.	Cause of Leaving.	Age at date of Leaving.		Present Age.	Physique.
Confectioner's labourer	5	June 1909	Suspended for larking	19	....	20	Very good
Iron-moulder	2	,, 1908	Slackness . . .	28	Errand boy (3), moulder (10)	29	Often ill .
Blacksmith's striker .	7	May 1909	Theft	34	Sold newspapers, confectioner's labourer, wagon builder (4), footballer	25	Good
Bottle packer	2	April 1910	Too old for boy's work	19	Errand boy (casual 3)	19	Strong
Confectioner's labourer	2 or 3	1910	To resist transfer into other department	19	?	19	Good
Shop porter .	16	Dec. 1908	Firm wound up . .	48	Errand boy, shop porter (9)	50	Fair .
Gardener	4	Sept. 1909	Difference with head gardener	41	Page-boy (?), gardener (10)	42	Not strong
Stableman	2½	1909	To better himself .	24½	Box-maker, stable-boy, stableman	25	Strong
Cabman	2	1908	Difference with employer	51	Groom (12), cab driver (6), groom (2), fitter (3), striker (3), groom (10)	53	Healthy .
Shop assistant	10	Apr. 30, 1910	Business (mother's) given up	24	....	24	Good
Fitter's labourer .	11	Jan. 1910	" Reduction of staff".	46	Match mill (5), taker-in (2), railway labourer (5), builder's labourer (3), platelayer(3), casual work (3)	46	Fair .
Confectioner's labourer	17 or 18	Oct. 1909	Bankruptcy of firm .	36	Comb worker, glass worker (4)	37	Good
Fitter	5	June 1909	Bad time-keeping .	31	Errand boy (3 or 4), Fitter	32	Fair .
Water buffer (Comb Works)	3	April 1910	Insubordination . .	20	Errand boy (3)	20	Strong
Shop porter .	4	Dec. 1909	Superseded by motor van [had really been employed by charity]	61 or 62	Candlemaker (1), beer bottler (7), engineer's labourer (34)	62	Underfed and weak
,, . .	3	1909	Slackness . . .	22	Painter's labourer (6)	23	Good
Chemist's labourer	3	Nov. 1909	Inefficiency due to nervousness	44	Farm labourer (22), engineer's labr. (8)	45	,,
Grocer on own account	2	Apr. 30, 1910	Failure . . .	25	Grocer and traveller (9)	25	Good, but under fed
Grocer's assistant	?	1908	Slackness . . .	33	Grocer . . .	35	Good
Warehouseman .	3	June 1909	Illness (six months) .	20	Errand boy (3), farm labourer (1)	21	,,
Shop assistant	7½	Feb. 1910	Drink (after frequent warnings)	50	Draper (15), clerk (7), draper (2)	50	,,
Turner . . .	1½	June 1909	Slackness . . .	22	Errand boy, fitter (7)	23	,,
Railway wagon builder's apprentice	4 or 5	1908	To better himself .	20	....	22	Strong

[1] Number of years in brackets.   [2] Member of Trade Union.

WORK (291 IN NUMBER)—continued

Present Condition. Character.	Nature of Temporary Occupations.	Nature of Permanent Occupations sought.	Apparent Personal Handicaps in Search for Regular Work.	Average Weekly Casual Earnings.[3]	Average Weekly Income of Rest of Household.[3]	Adults.	Children (under 16).	Is Family under Poverty Line?[4]
Good . . .	In winter: gas-works labourer	Any . . .	None . .	..	?	7	..	No
Very good .	Furniture auctions and other catch jobs	Moulder or any suitable	? Perhaps now bookmaking	10/-	?	3	3	,,
Dishonest . .	Navvy and catch jobs .	Striker ² . . .	Stained record	?	?	2	3	Yes
Slow and bad time-keeper	Catch jobs . . .	Labourer . . .	Inefficiency .	3/-	15/6	3	..	No
Good . . .	....	?	None . .	?	?	?	?	?
,, . . .	Allotment holder, furniture auctions	Any . . .	Age . . .	12/-	10/-	2	..	No
,, . . .	....	Gardener or any .	Perhaps age .	?	?	?	?	?
Bad time-keeper, hasty temper	Vanman (6 months, lost through bad time-keeping)	Stable or factory work	None . .	?	19/6	6	1	?
Good . . .	Cab driver (casual) .	Any . . .	Age . . .	4/6	81/-	7	2	No
,, . . .	....	Factory labourer .	Never worked outside home	..	?	2	1	Yes
Drinker . . .	Railway porter (casual), relief work	General labourer .	Age . . .	2/-	10/-	4	..	,,
Excellent, hard worker	Confectioner's labourer (2 months)	Any . . .	None .	?	..	2	..	,,
Bad time-keeper, disreputable	Fitter's labourer (casual)	Fitter or labourer .	Laziness .	20/-	48/-	5	..	No
Good . . .	Station tout, farm labourer	Any . . .	None .	1/-	15/-	2	2	,,
Excellent . .	....	Factory labourer .	Age . .	..	..	1	..	Yes
Good . . .	Station tout, cattle-drover	Any . . .	Deteriorating .	5/-	..	2	1	,,
Very good .	Gardener, snow shovelling	Gardener . .	Age . . .	13/6	65/-	5	1	No
Excellent . .	....	Any . . .	None .	...	..	2	2	Yes
,, .	Grocer's assistant (temporary)	Grocer or clerk .	,, . .	?	..	2	1	?
Good, but given to drink	Manure mixing, covering boilers, deal carrier	Any . . .	,, . .	?	26/-	8	..	No
Good . . .	Temporary clerk . .	,, ...	Age . .	18/-	10/-	4	2	,,
,, . . .	Own trade (two temporary jobs, 6 months each)	Fitter or labourer .	None .	?	70/-	6	2	,,
Good, but perhaps rather lazy	Boots at hotel (9 months), signal fitter (6 months), barman (3 months)	Labourer . . .	,, . .	7/-	18/-	8	..	,,

3 Including all regular pensions, poor relief, etc., but not occasional gifts or savings.   4 See note, p. 61.

MEN WHO HAVE BEEN IN REGULAR

Last Regular Employment.					Previous Regular Employments.[1]		Present Condition.
Nature.	Dura-tion (years).	Date of Leaving.	Cause of Leaving.	Age at date of Leaving.	Previous Regular Employments.[1]	Present Age.	Physique.
Lithographic draughts-man	1¼	Mar. 31, 1910	Firm in liquidation	29	Office - boy (¼), draughtsman	29	Good
Boilersmith . . .	1½	Oct. 1909	Slackness . . .	24	Errand boy (2), boiler-maker (6), labourer (1)	25	,,
Spokeshaver . . .	15	April 1910	Bronchitis and age .	55	Spinner (5), ship car-penter (7), engine cleaner (¼), police-man (9), engine-driver (5)	55	Suffering from bronchitis
Sawyer	30	Jan. 1910	Machine scrapped .	52	Milkman (3), under-gardener (3), plate-layer (2)	52	Good
Assistant school care-taker	8	April 1910	To better himself .	22	Errand boy (3 weeks)	22	,,
Signal fitter . . .	1	1909	Contract finished .	22	Confectioner's labourer (1), fitter (7)	23	,,
Groom and gardener .	1½	April 1910	To better himself .	35	Farm servant (12), market gardener (8), milkman (1)	35	,,
Railway fireman . .	9	June 1909	Slackness . . .	26	Confectionery labourer (1), engine cleaner (2)	27	,,
Iron turner . . .	28	July 1908	Inefficiency . . .	43	Errand boy (3) . .	45	,,
Groom	6	Jan. 1910	To better himself .	21	Engine boy (2) . .	21	,,
Butcher . . .	4 or 5	1909	?	23	?	24	Weak
Steam lurry driver .	1½	Oct. 1909	Drink and consequent inefficiency	31	Fitter (13), motor-driver (2)	32	Good
Whitesmith . . .	3	March 1910	Slackness . . .	29	Whitesmith (12) .	29	,,
Grocer's assistant . .	1¼	Jan. 31, 1910	,, . . .	32	Grocer (17) . .	32	,,
Brush-hand and window cleaner	3	Nov. 1909	,, . . .	21	Confectioner's labourer (5)	22	Poor
Optical instrument maker	8½	Jan. 31, 1910	Inefficiency . . .	23	Errand boy (½) . .	23	Good
Grocer's assistant. .	5	,,	Displaced by younger lad	29	Errand boy (2), grocer's assistant (8)	29	,,
Water buffer (comb works)	2	Apr. 30, 1910	To better himself .	20	Errand boy (2), opti-cian's labourer (2)	20	,,
Confectioner's labourer	15	March 1910	Bankruptcy of firm .	32	? (2)	32	,,
,, ,,	40	,,	,, ,, .	53	....	53	,,
,, ,,	9	,,	,, ,, .	26	? (3)	26	,,
Printer's labourer .	5	Dec. 1909	Slackness . . .	22	Errand boy (3), sugar boiler (1)	23	Very good
Steam and hot-water engineer	17	Apr. 26, 1910	,, . . .	40	Plumber (7) . .	40	Not capable of heavy work
Confectioner's labourer	7½	April 1910	Inefficiency . . .	21	....	21	Strong .

[1] Number of years in brackets.   [2] Member of Trade Union.   [3] Including all regular pensions, poor relief, etc.

WORK (291 IN NUMBER)—*continued*

Present Condition. — Character.	Nature of Temporary Occupations.	Nature of Permanent Occupations sought.	Apparent Personal Handicaps in Search for Regular Work.	Average Weekly Casual Earnings.[3]	Average Weekly Income of Rest of Household.[3]	Number of Persons in Household. — Adults.	Children (under 16).	Is Family under Poverty Line?[5]
Excellent	Designer (for private customers)	Draughtsman[2]	None	..	53/-	4	..	No
,,	Bricklayer's labourer and catch jobs	Factory labourer	,,	?	17/6	3	..	,,
Fair, lost place as policeman through drink	....	Any	Age	..	25/-	3	2	,,
Very good	Corporation watchman	,,	,,	?	15/-	3	2	?
,,	....	Police force or tram conductor	None	..	3/-	2	..	Yes
Good	Telegraph linesman (6 months), soap works labourer (2 months)	Fitter	,,	?	55/-	4	1	No
Excellent	....	Groom, gardener, or milkman	,,	..	67/-	5	2	,,
Good	Casual factory porter and catch work	General labourer	,,	15/-	30/-	4	2	,,
Doubtful, good reference	Post office auxiliary, school cleaning, gardener	Any	Age	?	25/-	3	..	,,
Lazy and careless	Groom (1 week)	Any	On down grade	..	62/8	6	1	,,
Good references	Butcher's assistant (4 months)	,,	Not looking for regular work	..	6/6	3	..	No has savings.
Lost several places through drink	....	Fitter	Intemperance	..	63/-	4	..	No
Excellent	Own trade (1 week)	Own trade	None	..	59/-	5	..	,,
Good	....	Clerk	,,	..	..	3	1	Yes
Good	Gasworks labourer	Temporary work only	Delicate health	?	53/8	5	3	No
Steady	....	Instrument-maker	Partly inefficiency	..	34/6	5	..	,,
Good	....	?	None	13/-[4]	?	3	..	,,
Subject to bad moral influences at home, inclined to loaf	....	General labourer	On down grade	..	24/-	3	..	,,
Very good	Farm work (few days)	Any suitable	None	?	7/-	2	2	Yes
,,	,, ,,	Any	Age	10/-	Over 30/-	5	1	No
,,	Bricklayer's labourer, factory porter	,,	None	?	Over 35/-	5	1	,,
,,	Bill distributor (2 weeks)	Printer	,,	10/-	45/-	6	2	,,
,,	....	Any light labour	Ill-health	..	..	..	..	Yes
Lazy	Furniture removing, hotel waiting (1 week), at fried fish shop (1 week)	General labourer	Laziness	?	34/-	4	3	No

but not occasional gifts or savings.   4 In receipt of Trade Union benefit.   5 See note, p. 61.

MEN WHO HAVE BEEN IN REGULAR

Last Regular Employment.					Previous Regular Employments.¹	Present Age.	Present Condition. Physique.
Nature.	Dura-tion (years).	Date of Leaving.	Cause of Leaving.	Age at date of Leaving.			
Confectioner's labourer	5	Jan. 1910	Slackness	23	Confectioner's labourer (4)	24	Good
Blacksmith's striker	3	June 1908	Displaced by machinery	26	Glass blower (3), confectioner's labourer (1), smith's striker (6)	28	,,
Sawyer	12	March 1910	To better himself	27	Errand boy (2)	27	,,
Keel captain	1½	Feb. 1910	End of voyage	65 or 66	Keelman (58) (no school education)	66	,,
Boilersmith	7	June 1908	Reduction of staff	23	Boilersmith (2)	25	Healthy
Fitter's apprentice	7	Jan. 1910	End of apprenticeship	21	....	22	,,
Motor lurry driver	2	April 1910	Strike	24	Clerk (5), motor fitter (3)	24	Good
Engineer	5½	March 1910	Drink	32	Stoker (10½)	32	,,
Hairdresser's apprentice	6	June 1909	End of apprenticeship	21	....	22	Hunchback
Butcher	6	,,	Inefficiency due to drink	29	Glass grinder (2 months), butcher (7)	30	Good
Publican	9	Dec. 1909	"Did not sell enough beer"	34 or 35	Grocer (7), barman (4)	35	Fair
Waiter	4	Oct. 1909	Bad feet	18	....	19	Good
Upholsterer	10	May 1910	Inefficiency	24	....	24	Bad eyesight, mentally defective
Kitchen help, hotel	2	,,	Ill-health	23	Cabinetmaker (2), carter (3), farm labourer (2)	28	?
Gardener's labourer	?	March 1910	?	?	Errand boy (3), railway labourer (7)	48	Strong
Engine-driver	4	May 1910	Slackness	21	Confectioner's labourer	21	Healthy
Confectioner's labourer	20	Dec. 1909	Bankruptcy of employer	30	(Left school age 11)	31	Consumptive
Shop cleaner	1½	Apr. 11, 1910	Nervousness	21	Errand boy (4)	21	Deformed
Station porter	21	Mar. 24, 1910	Petty thefts	41	Foundry labourer (1)	41	Good
Bus conductor	2	July 30, 1908	Route discontinued	20	Farm boy, engine cleaner (3)	22	Healthy
Fitter's labourer	22	July 14, 1909	Inefficiency	47	Errand boy (2), engine-driver (2), errand boy (2)	48	Strong
Carriage builder, railway	11	March 1910	Ill-health	38	Clerk (3), joiner (10)	38	Fair, cannot do heavy work
Traveller	1½	Feb. 17, 1910	Drink	33-34	Paper-maker (16)	34	Good
Optician's apprentice	6½	Dec. 1908	Inefficiency	21	....	23	,,
Club steward	2	May 10, 1910	Theft	35	Photographer (18), traveller (1)	35	,,
Cabinetmaker	18	May 1908	"Short-sightedness"	58	Cabinetmaker	60	Fair
Warehouseman	1	Jan. 1909	Inefficiency	19	Confectioner's labourer (4)	20	?

¹ Number of years in brackets. ² Including all regular pensions, poor relief, etc.

WORK (291 IN NUMBER)—*continued*

Present Condition. Character.	Nature of Temporary Occupations.	Nature of Permanent Occupations sought.	Apparent Personal Handicaps in Search for Regular Work.	Average Weekly Casual Earnings.[2]	Average Weekly Income of Rest of Household.[2]	Adults.	Children (under 16).	Is Family under Poverty Line?[3]
Very good	Distress Committee relief work (1 month)	Any	None	?	26/-	4	1	No
,,	Distress Committee relief work (2 months), manure mixing (twice 3 months)	Factory labourer	,,	?	..	2	4	Yes
Very good and efficient	....	Sawyer or labourer	,,	..	1/6	2	2	,,
	....	Captainship	Age	..	?	?	?	No
Quiet and decent	Station tout and other catch jobs	Own trade	On down grade	14/-	?	3	..	,,
Good	....	None		..	20/-	2	..	,,
,,	....	Chauffeur or motor mechanic	,,	..	80/-	6	..	,,
Lost several jobs through drink	Bicycle repairing and furniture removing (odd days)	Own trade	On down grade	4/6	..	2	4	Yes
Good	....	,,	Deformity	..	60/-	?	?	No
Lost several chances through drink	....	,,	Drink	..	Over 60/-	?	?	,,
Probably fair	....	Public house manager	None	..	..	2	2	Yes
Good, won't do hard work	Waiter, seasonal	Any light work	,,	20/-	36/6	4	7	No
Willing worker	Nil	Any	Physical and mental unfitness	..	38/-	5	1	,,
,,	,,	,,	Physically below normal	..	22/-	3	1	,,
Indifferent	,,	Labourer	Probably laziness and age	..	18/-	2	..	,,
Good worker	Five weeks casually, old employer	,,	None	?	22/-	3	2	,,
,,	Railway goods warehouse porter	Only casual	Ill-health	5/6	2/-	2	3	Yes
,,	Distributing bills and samples	Any	Deformity	?	?	?	?	No
Dishonest, but good worker	Temporary factory porter	Labourer	Bad record	?	15/-	4	2	?
Betting	Probably bookmaker's tout	,,	On the down grade	?	?	?	?	No
Good	None	,,	Age	?	16/-	?	?	?
,,	Joiner's work on own account (14 days)	Joiner	None	?	..	2	1	?
Given to drink	Nil	Own trade	,,	..	..	2	2	Yes
Satisfactory, good time-keeper	Own trade (3 weeks)	Labourer	Inefficiency at own trade	?	47/-	4	..	No
Dishonest	None	Caretaker	Bad record	..	..	2	2	Yes
Good	Jobbing gardener	Own trade	Age	5/-	?	?	?	No
,,	Odd jobs on Polo ground, etc.	Any	On the down grade	?	?	?	?	,,

but not occasional gifts or savings.   3 See note, p. 61.

MEN WHO HAVE BEEN IN REGULAR

Last Regular Employment.				Age at date of Leaving.	Previous Regular Employments.[1]	Present Age.	Present Condition.
Nature.	Dura-tion (years).	Date of Leaving.	Cause of Leaving.				Physique.
Engineer's labourer	3	May 1, 1909	Insubordination	23	Fitter's labourer (6)	24	Good
Platelayer	4	,,	Own account (? why)	22	Farm lad (4)	23	,,
Insurance agent	1	Mar. 9, 1909	Dispute about commission	21	Grocer's assistant (5), waiter and billiard marker	22	Too weak for hard work
Engineer's labourer	4	May 1, 1910	To better himself	21	Confectioner's labourer (4)	21	Strong
Groom	2	Apr. 30, 1910	Horses sold at end of hunting season	45	Jockey and groom	45	Good
Messenger	12½	April 1909	Reduction of staff	26	Wood carver	27	Very strong
Groom	5	1909	Horses sold	31	Groom	32	Good
Electric wireman	4	June 1909	Inefficiency	24	Ironmonger's apprentice (5)	25	,,
Railway clerk	9	Nov. 1909	?	29	Clerk (3)	30	Weak
Grocer's assistant	1	1909	Difference with manager	23	Errand boy, grocer's assistant (8)	24	Good
Brass-finisher	7	June 1908	Slackness of trade	21	....	23	,,
Gardener and chauffeur	1½	March 1910	Car sold	21	Grocer's apprentice (4½)	21	,,
Shoemaker	5	June 2, 1909	To better himself	32	Shoemaker	33	,,
Hotel waiter	2	April 1910	Inefficiency and bad conduct	39	Page, waiter	39	Healthy
Joiner and waggon repairer	16	May 1910	Theft	49	Joiner	49	Good;
Tram conductor	7	Oct. 1909	Intemperance	20	....	21	,,
Draper's assistant	35	1908	Bad trade	47	....	50	Delicate
Errand boy	3	June 1908	Ill-health	18	At home (2)	20	Abscesses and subject to fits
Ropemaker	3	Mar. 25, 1910	Displaced by machinery	35	Errand boy (½), ropemaker (17)	35	Moderate
Tram conductor	1½	Dec. 1909	Negligence	22	Errand boy (½), vanman (5)	23	Healthy
Blacksmith's apprentice	1½	July 1908	To better himself	19	Confectioner's labourer (4)	21	Good
Saddler	1¾	Oct. 1909	End of apprenticeship	20	Errand boy (1), sadler (3)	21	,,
Coal carrier	9	April 1910	To better himself	29	Glass worker (6)	29	,,
Comb works labourer	1½	,,	?	20	Factory labourer	20	Fair
Platelayer	2½	,,	"Slackness"	33	Taker-in (3), nipper (1), confectioner's labourer (9), platelayer (3), fireman (2)	33	Good
Glass sorter and packer	18½	Dec. 1908	Bad time-keeping	33	Comb works — half-timer (3), errand boy (2)	35	,,
Farm labourer	1	June 1909	Retirement of employer	44	Hawker (5), coal carter (2), carter(22)	45	,,
Brakesman	17	Jan. 1910	? (own fault)	32	Errand boy (1)	33	,,
Printer's feeder	7	June 4, 1910	Slackness of trade	21	....	21	,,
Accountant and cashier	16	March 1909	Failure of firm	36	Carpenter(1), draughtsman (2), timekeeper (3)	37	,,

[1] Number of years in brackets.   [2] Including all regular pensions, poor relief, etc.

WORK (291 IN NUMBER)—*continued*

Present Condition. Character.	Nature of Temporary Occupations.	Nature of Permanent Occupations sought.	Apparent Personal Handicaps in Search for Regular Work.	Average Weekly Casual Earnings.[2]	Average Weekly Income of Rest of Household.[2]	Adults.	Children (under 16).	Is Family under Poverty Line?[3]
Industrious .	Catch jobs (rare) . .	Any	None . .	29/-	?	?		No
?	Possibly bookmaking .	,, ...	Doubtful . .	60/-	5		..	,,
Very good .	Great variety of catch work	Grocer's assistant .	Probably becoming casual	10/-	..	2	1	Yes
Excellent .	Temporarily on trams (2 days)	Labourer . . .	None . .	20/-	3		..	No
,, .	At horse auctions . .	Casually with horses	Age . . .	6/-	10/-	2	2	Yes
,, . .	Catch jobs only . .	Summer porter .	Drifting . .	?		2	4	,,
Addicted to drink .	Cleaning cattle wagons	Any	Deteriorating .	9/-	..	2	3	,,
Good . . .	Two months at own trade, helps in shop	Own trade .. .	Inefficiency .	?	?	4	..	No
,, . .	Waiter at camp and canteen 3 and 8 weeks	Clerk or anything .	Probably consumptive	?	12/-	3	2	?
,, . .	Several temporary jobs as grocer's assistant	Any	Inefficiency, drifting	?	27/-	4	..	No
,, . .	Flour-mill labourer and catch work	Own trade or labouring	None . .	?	40/-	4	1	,,
Excellent .	Nil	Any	,, . . .	..	60/6	5	2	,,
,, .	Temporarily managing grocer's shop	Own trade or any .	,, . . .	15/-	..	2	2	Yes
Not good .	Temporary waiter . .	Waiter . . .	Getting casual	?	13/-	4	3	?
Dishonest .	Nil	Any	Age . . .	..	29/-	4	..	No
Good . . .	,, ...	Carter or labourer .	None . .	..	53/6	5	2	,,
Excellent . .	Rent collector (until 4 months ago)	Light work . .	Infirmity . .	..	24/-	4	2	Yes
Intelligent and good	. . . .	Boots or kitchen boy	Ill-health .	..	48/-	5	3	No
Willing but inefficient	Farm work (1 month), parish relief	Labourer . . .	Partly inefficiency	?	3/6	2	5	Yes
Willing and industrious	Carter	Carter . . .	None . .	21/6	..	2	1	No
Good . . .	Factory and railway porter	General labourer .	,, . . .	?	39/6	5	3	,,
Slow, lazy, bad time-keeper	General labourer . .	Own trade or labourer	Inefficiency .	18/-	61/6	5	..	,,
Good worker . .	Gas works, wharf, and railway labourer	Any	None . .	?	..	2	2	Yes
Doubtful character	. . . .	,, . . .	Doubtful character	..	..	1	..	,,
,, ,,	. . . .	,, . . .	Probably becoming casual	..	..	2	3	,,
Drinker . . .	Cattle market, chopping firewood, helping in lodging-house	,, . . .	Drink, and becoming casual	5/-	..	1	..	,,
Heavy drinker .	Farm work (casual)	,, . . .	,, ,,	10/-	..	1	..	No
?	Unloading boats, navvying	Warehouse porter .	?	7/-	5/-	3	..	Yes
Excellent .	Fixing tents . . .	Printer . . .	None . .	?	?	4	..	?
,, .	Salesman, clerk . .	Clerk or cashier .	,, . . .	?	..	2	1	No

but not occasional gifts or savings.   [3] See note, p. 61.

MEN WHO HAVE BEEN IN REGULAR

Last Regular Employment.				Age at date of Leaving.	Previous Regular Employments.[1]	Present Age.	Present Condition.
Nature.	Dura-tion (years).	Date of Leaving.	Cause of Leaving.				Physique.
Deal carrier . . .	2	May 7, 1910	To better himself .	21	Errand boy (5) . .	21	Good . .
Confectioner's labourer	18	Feb. 1910	Failure of firm . .	40	Errand boy (9), shop assistant (1), confectioner's labourer(2)	40	Very good .
,, ,,	3	March 1910	,, ,, . .	20	Errand boy (3). .	20	Healthy . .
Plateman (Hotel). .	5	Oct. 1909	To better himself .	23	Errand boy (1), confectioner's labourer (1), brickyard and ironmonger's labourer (3)	24	,, . .
Confectioner's packer .	6	April 1910	Failure of firm . .	22	Brewer's labourer (2)	22	,, . .
Beer bottler . . .	2	Jan. 1910	To better himself .	22 or 23	Various (1), brewer's labourer (3), factory labourer (¼), along with casual work	23	Not strong .
Confectioner's labourer	Over 20	Dec. 1908	Slack trade . . .	50	Confectioner's labourer (14)	52	Excellent .
Bottle packer . .	5	Feb. 1909	Drink and bad time-keeping	42	Glass works labourer (16)	43	Not good .
Smith's striker . .	18	Oct. 1909	To better himself .	38	Sawyer's labourer (3), taker-in (glass works) (5)	39	Good .
Cattle dealer's stock keeper	7	Dec. 1908	Bad time-keeping .	34	Page (3), farmer's labourer (11)	36	Not strong .
Wetter-off (glass works)	4	March 1910	Strike for better wages	19	....	19	Not strong and undersized
Timber wagoner . .	20	Dec. 1908	Retirement of employer	38 or 39	Confectioner's labourer	40	Good . .
Cab washer (night work)	14 (on and off)	Oct. 1909	Dispute with foreman	41	Errand boy, cab-driver (16)	42	Strong . .
Confectioner's labourer	9	Dec. 1908	Failure of firm . .	48 or 49	Farm labourer (3), brewer's labourer (11)	50	Good, but weak ankle
Confectioner. . .	1	March 1910	Slackness . . .	34	Errand boy, confectioner	34	Weak eyes .
Flour-mill labourer .	9	1909	"Bad trade" (?). .	31	Cleaner (1), taker-in (5), hoistman (1), iron-moulder (3)	32	Underfed .
Sawyer's labourer .	29	Feb. 1910	Winding-up of firm .	60	Confectioner's labourer (3), smith (13), timber carrier (after 14 months' unemployment) (4)	60	Good .
Boilersmith . . .	1½	Dec. 1908	?	44 or 45	Van boy (3), boiler-smith	46	Not good .
Grocer's assistant. .	6	June 1909	Insubordination . .	20	....	21	Moderate .
Engineer's labourer .	2	April 1910	To remove to York .	25	At colliery, copper works, and brickyards	25	Good .
At oil works. . .	4	May 28, 1910	To better himself .	21	Errand boy, confectioner's labourer, workhouse, farm-work, unemployment (1)	21	Fairly good .
Glass blower . .	8	1908	?	44	"Taker-in" at glass works (2), glass blower (12)	46	Good . .

1 Number of years in brackets.   2 Member of Trade Union.

WORK (291 IN NUMBER)—*continued*

Present Condition. Character.	Nature of Temporary Occupations.	Nature of Permanent Occupations sought.	Apparent Personal Handicaps in Search for Regular Work.	Average Weekly Casual Earnings.[3]	Average Weekly Income of Rest of Household.[3]	Adults.	Children (under 16).	Is Family under Poverty Line?[4]
Good worker, probably gambler	Bandsman . . .	Labourer . . .	None . .	6/-	?	5		.. No
Exemplary . .	Builder's labourer, navvy, relief work	,, . . .	,, . .	5/-	1/-	2	1	Yes
Good . . .	Seed mixing (10 days) .	Any	,, . . .	..	14/-	3	..	,,
,, . . .	....	Kitchen or factory porter	,, . . .	..	12/-	3	..	,,
,, . . .	....	Factory labourer .	,, . . .	..	15/-	4	1	,,
,, . . .	Cattle market, catch jobs	Carter or any . .	Many changes, drifting	2/-	?	4	..	No
,, . . .	....	Confectioner . .	Age	..	18/-	3	3	Yes
Drinker and unreliable	Florist's labourer . .	Gardener or labourer	Age and bad record	5/-	5/6	3	..	,,
Good . . .	Farm work, relief work .	Striker or any . .	None . .	?	15/-	3	..	No
Fair . . .	Cattle market, catch jobs	Farm or garden work	Probably becoming casual	6/-	..	2	..	Yes
?	,, ,,	Any	Poor home, on down grade	1/6	?	2	1	,,
Good . . .	Casual railway goods porter	,, ...	Becoming casual	?	?	3	..	?
Not reliable, previous good record	Navvy, catch jobs (rare)	,, ...	Bad reputation	?	8/6	4	3	Yes
Very good . .	Malting, relief work .	,, ...	Age . . .	?	6/6	3	2	?
,, . .	Timber carrying . .	Confectioner . .	None . .	?	?	?	?	?
,, . .	Bandsman, unloading boats, catch jobs, relief work	Any	,, . .	..	7/-	3/-	2	4 Yes
,, . .	Ostler (3 weeks) . .	,, ...	Age . . .	..	?	6	..	?
?	Chopping wood, catch jobs	Own trade[2] . .	,, . . .	5/-	?	6	3	?
Good . . .	Chopping wood . .	Grocer's assistant .	None . .	10/-	?	6	3	?
Probably drinker .	? Catch jobs . .	Any	Bad reputation	?	..	2	1	?
Industrious, but unintelligent	....	Any	Very bad home, drifting	..	14/-	2	1	Yes
Drinker . . .	Farm labourer and relief work	,, ...	Bad record .	?	?	5	2	?

[3] Including all regular pensions, poor relief, etc., but not occasional gifts or savings.   [4] See note, p. 61.

MEN WHO HAVE BEEN IN REGULAR

Last Regular Employment.				Age at date of Leaving.	Previous Regular Employments.[1]	Present Age.	Present Condition.
Nature.	Dura-tion (years).	Date of Leaving.	Cause of Leaving.				Physique.
Glass packer . . .	2	May 1909	To better himself .	32	Shop assistant (1), clerk (2), shop assistant (1), in hay business (10), catch work (2)	33	Healthy . .
Carriage cleaner . .	2	Sept. 1909	Bad time-keeping .	27	Branding corks (1), comb works (1), catch jobs (2), brewer's labourer (1), bottler (1), brickmaker (1), casual railway worker (4)	28	Strong . .
Box-maker's labourer .	4½	Oct. 1909	Failure of firm . .	18 or 19	. . . .	19	Healthy . .
Glassblower's apprentice	9	Dec. 1908	Insubordination . .	24	Confectioner's labourer (1)	25	,, . .
Moulder . . .	5	May 1909	Slackness . . .	29	Moulder's apprentice, moulder	30	,, . .
Coke filler (colliery) .	4	?	To remove to York .	?	Errand boy, confectioner's labourer	29	Strong .
Farm labourer . .	5	Nov. 1909	Replaced by younger boy	22	Grocer's assistant (2)	23	,, . .
Cab-driver . . .	1	April 1910	Bad trade (due to trams)	28	Milkman, errand boy, labourer, coachman	28	,, . .
Carter	11	Jan. 1910	Closing of works .	49	Farm labourer (7), carter (13)	49	Very good .
,, ...	12	March 1910	Quarrel with father .	26	. . . .	26	Good .
Confectioner's labourer	7	June 1909	Slackness . . .	23	Errand boy (1), in brickyard (1)	24	,, .
Aerated water maker .	8	Oct. 1909	,, . . .	23	. . . .	24	,, . .
Laundry machineman .	2	Sept. 1909	,, . . .	26	Bricklayer's labourer	27	,, .
Brewery foreman . .	8	May 1909	Insubordination . .	36	Engineer's labourer .	37	Strong .
Bus conductor . .	4	1909	?	24	Errand boy, boots (½) bus conductor (⅓)	25	Delicate .
Foundry foreman . .	?	1908	Failure of firm . .	33	Errand boy, foundry labourer (7)	35	Strong .
Farm labourer . .	1 or 2	1909	To better himself .	18	Shop assistant (1), farm servant (1)	19	Good .
Gunsmith . . .	1½	1908	Bad health . . .	abt. 66	Shop assistant (7), gunsmith (46)	nly. 70	Fairly good .
Tin plate worker . .	11	Dec. 1908	Slackness . . .	38 or 39	Ironmonger, tin plate worker	40	Good .
Grocer's apprentice .	6	April 6, 1910	Inefficiency . . .	21	Errand boy (1) . .	21	,, . .
Brass turner . . .	2 or 3	1909	To better himself .	18	Bookbinder's apprentice (1), brass turner's apprentice (1), brass turner's improver (1)	19	,, . .
Flour-mill labourer .	9	April 1910	Bad time-keeping .	32	Farm lad (3), catch jobs (6)	32	,, . .

[1] Number of years in brackets.   [2] Member of Trade Union.

WORK (291 IN NUMBER)—*continued*

Present Condition. Character.	Nature of Temporary Occupations.	Nature of Permanent Occupations sought.	Apparent Personal Handicaps in Search for Regular work.	Average Weekly Casual Earnings.3	Average Weekly Income of Rest of Household.3	No. of Persons in House-hold.		Is Family under Poverty Line?4
						Adults.	Children (under 16).	
Inefficient, but good character	Furniture remover, glass packer, and catch jobs	Light work in warehouse	Inefficiency	15/-	..	2	1	Yes
Good on the whole	Butcher's assistant, at brickyards	Any	None	5/-	54/-	5	..	No
Good	Catch jobs only (rare)	„	„	?	?	5	5	?
Good worker	Catch jobs at glass work, railway, and other	„	„	8/-	39/-	6	..	No
Good	Labouring (5 weeks)	Own trade	„	?	36/-	5	3	„
„	....	Any	„	..	..	2	3	Yes
„	....	Farm work	„	..	over 45/-	4	1	No
Good worker, but drinker and dishonest	Catch jobs	Any	„	?	..	2	1	?
Very good	Carting, navvying, relief work	Carting	Age	9/-	32/-	4	1	No
Good	Manure mixing, railway goods porter	Any	None	5/-	4/-	2	1	Yes
„	Builder's labourer, brickyard (nil for 1 month)	„	„	..	22/6	8	1	No
Excellent	Cattle market, and other catch work	Any "suitable"	„	2/-	23/-	4	2	„
Satisfactory worker	Laundry work (temporary)	„	„	?	18/-	3	..	„
Excellent	Cattle driving	„	„	?	..	2	1	Yes
Good	....	Any light work	Ill-health	..	39/-	4	2	No
First rate worker, all round hand	Temporary at planing machine	At foundry	None	?	28/-	3	..	„
Good	Farm work (6 months)	Factory work	„	..	62/-	7	..	„
„	Night watchman	Night watchman	Age	7/1½	..	3	..	Yes
Excellent	Catch work (after illness)	Own trade2	None	?	..	2	3	?
Good character, but inefficient	....	Any	Perhaps inefficiency	..	37/-	4	..	No
Good	Temporarily at own trade (7 months)	Own trade	None	..	33/-	4	2	„
Inveterate gambler	Farm work (1 day).	Any	On down grade	..	..	2	..	Yes

3 Including all regular pensions, poor relief, etc., but not occasional gifts or savings.   4 See note, p. 61.

MEN WHO HAVE BEEN IN REGULAR

Last Regular Employment.					Previous Regular Employments.[1]	Present Condition.	
Nature.	Duration (years).	Date of Leaving.	Cause of Leaving.	Age at date of Leaving.		Present Age.	Physique.
Taker-in (glass works) .	1½	Dec. 1908	To better himself	17	Confectioner's labourer (½)	19	Strong
Confectioner's packer .	9	March 1909	Dispute	38	Pot maker (2), carter	39	Good
Cab-driver . . .	18	March 1910	Age	64	Groom	64	,,
Coppersmith : lastly coil bender	?	?	Fluctuation of trade .	37 or 38	Coppersmith	39	,,
Wetter-off . . .	6	June 1909	Age	20	....	21	,,
Waiter	3	Nov. 1909	" Reduction of staff " .	27	Page (7), waiter (3) .	28	Good, but undersized
Glass worker . .	7	,,	Inefficiency . .	21	....	22	Very good
Bandsman . . .	5 or 6	Jan. 1910	" No opening " .	20 or 21	....	21	,,
Waterman . . .	4	March 1910	No boat on hand .	25	Ropemaker (8), confectioner's labourer (3), bottler (1)	25	Good
Flour sack cleaner .	6	June 1909	Work too hard . .	34	Confectioner's labourer, builder's labourer (1)	35	Underfed.
Factory labourer . .	1	Aug. 1909	Bad time-keeping	18	Errand boy (2), cobbler (1)	19	Strong
Carpet printer . .	12	June 1909	To better himself	26	Confectioner's labourer (1½)	27	,,
Confectioner's labourer	5	,,	,, .	20	....	21	Good
,, ,,	10	1903	Illness . . .	23	Errand boy (½) . .	30	Was ill for 6 years; now fair
Sawyer and small holder	30	?	To come to York	?	Farm labourer ; then in Canada (30)	53	Good, except for deafness
Driller	18	1908	Works closed . .	37	Gardener (2), confectioner's labourer (3)	39	Good
Office manager . .	10	1899	To start poultry farming	43	Clerk (17) . . .	54	Vigorous .
Gardener . . .	1	Nov. 1909	Ill-health . . .	58	Farm service, coachman (5)	59	Healthy .
Engineer's labourer .	2	June 1909	,, . . .	18	Sugar boiler(1), errand boy (2)	19	Discharged from sanatorium as cured
Butler	9	April 1908	Change in administration	43	Errand boy (3), fitter (18)	45	Healthy .
Publican . . .	4	Oct. 1908	Closing of house .	63	Farmer, publican, insurance agent	65	Fair .
Coach-builder . .	4½	1906	Accident . . .	19	....	23	Poor
Greengrocer (on own account)	6	Feb. 1910	Series of misfortunes .	40	Pupil teacher (1), butcher (10), salesman (8)	40	Good
Cellar and barman .	30	Oct. 1908	Age	68	Wood turner (7), own business (5), asylum attendant (7), barman (5)	70	Very good

1 Number of years in brackets.

WORK (291 IN NUMBER)—*continued*

Character	Nature of Temporary Occupations.	Nature of Permanent Occupations sought.	Apparent Personal Handicaps in Search for Regular Work.	Average Weekly Casual Earnings.²	Average Weekly Income of Rest of Household.³	Adults.	Children (under 16).	Is Family under Poverty Line?³
Doubtful	Glass and water works .	Any . . .	On down grade	7/6	?	3	1	No
Good	Cleaning boots, builder's and joiner's labourer, factory porter, and other	,, ...	None	25/-	..	2	2	,,
,,	....	Cab-driver or any .	Age . . .	..	44/-	4	..	,,
Excellent	....	Own trade . .	None . .	..	53/-	6	2	,,
Good	Shop assistant (1 week) .	Any . . .	,, . .	..	29/-	4	..	,,
,,	Ostler, waiter, and other catch jobs	Waiter . . .	,, . .	4/-	33/-	4	1	,,
Thoroughly spoilt and lazy	At home at own trade .	Factory labourer .	Laziness . .	..	21/-	3	..	,,
Good	At soap works (1 month) motor driving (2 weeks)	Any . . .	None . .	?	48/-	5	1	,,
,,	Illness ; recently unloading boats	Mate on lighter .	,, . .	6/-	..	2	..	Yes
,,	Potato setting and catch jobs	Farm labourer or any	,, . .	15/-	3/-	2	3	,,
Dishonest	Shoe cobbling (with father)	Any . . .	Bad record .	?	24/-	3	..	No
Respectable	?, gas works (2 weeks) .	,, ...	?	?	7/-	2	2	?
Inefficient and lazy, gambler	....	,, ...	Bad character and inefficiency	..	?	?	?	Yes
Good	....	(Since 1909) confectioner's labourer	Unemployment through prolonged illness	..	20/-	2	?	No
,,	....	Sawyer or labourer .	Age . . .	..	..	1	..	Yes
,,	?	Driller, or any .	None . .	..	63/-	5	..	No
Excellent	Poultry farming, keeping boarding house	Clerk or secretaryship	Age . . .	..	?	5	..	,,
Good	Labourer and farm hand	Any . . .	,, . . .	?	15/-	3	..	?
,,	Shop assistant . .	,, ...	None .	4/-	33/-	4	1	No
Excellent	Caretaker (twice 6 months)	Caretaker . .	,, . .	?	?	2	..	?
Honest and energetic	Clerk	Light work . .	Age . . .	?	..	2	..	Yes
Very good	....	,, . .	Ill-health .	..	28/-	4	3	No
Good	Hawking . . .	Labouring or bookkeeping (?)	None .	10/-	12/3	2	3	,,
,,	....	Any light work .	Age . . .	..	30/-	3	..	,,

² Including all regular pensions, poor relief, etc., but not occasional gifts or savings.   ³ See note, p. 61.

E

MEN WHO HAVE BEEN IN REGULAR

Last Regular Employment.					Previous Regular Employments.[1]		Present Condition.
Nature.	Dura-tion (years).	Date of Leaving.	Cause of Leaving.	Age at date of Leaving.		Present Age.	Physique.
Fitter	45	1905	Removal of works .	58	Errand boy . .	63	Vigorous . .
Clerk	45	Dec. 1909	Age	66	Farm work . .	67	Good . .
Checker (railway). .	45	,,	,, ...	65	Butcher (6) . .	66	Robust . .
Sawyer	19	Dec. 1905	Business sold . .	62	Confectioner's labourer (3), errand boy (1), sawyer (29)	67	Good . .
Coal hawker . . .	½	Dec. 1909	Illness	67	Farm. work, striker (23), coal hawker (18)	68	,,
Whitesmith . . .	Over 50	1909	Accident . . .	70	....	71	,, . .
Gardener . . .	5	1904	Illness	57	Farming and garden-ing	68	Suffering from chest com-plaint
Caterer	25	1902	Age	64	Stonemason (4), striker (21)	72	Not strong .
Fitter's labourer . .	30	1903	,, ...	59	Farm work (2), tailor (4), postman (2½)	66	Good . .
Mess-room attendant .	3	Feb. 1910	Failing sight . .	65	Railway guard (47) .	65	Suffering from gout
Joiner	29	Oct. 1907	Stroke	68	Cabinetmaker and joiner	66	Weak . .
Signalman . . .	42	Nov. 1909	Age	65	Gamekeeper (8) . .	66	?

[1] Number of years in brackets.   [2] Including all regular pensions, poor relief, etc.

are these men unemployed? In order to answer it satisfactorily, we must not only know why they lost their employment, but what prevents them from finding work at present. Indeed, it is the latter question which really constitutes the problem of unemployment. The answer to the first will doubtless, in many cases, be the answer to the second; as, for instance, when dismissal was due to dishonesty, or incompetence, or ill-health. Often, however, they will differ entirely. Thus a man may, through the failure of a firm, lose his work when he is 45 years old. He did not lose it on account of his age, but

WORK (291 IN NUMBER)—*continued*

Present Condition. Character.	Nature of Temporary Occupations.	Nature of Permanent Occupations sought.	Apparent Personal Handicaps in Search for Regular Work.	Average Weekly Casual Earnings.²	Average Weekly Income of Rest of Household.²	Adults.	Children (under 16).	Is Family under Poverty Line?³
Excellent	....	Own trade . .	Age . . .	..	55/-	5	..	No
,,	Works sewing machine for wife	Light work . .	,, . . .	7/-	2/6	2	..	Yes
,,	....		,, . . .	13/-	..	2	..	No
,,	....	Own trade . .	,, . . .	5/-	26/6	4	..	,,
Good . .	Catch jobs . .	Light work . .	,, . . .	?	?	?	?	?
Very respectable	....		,, . . .	5/-	..	2	..	Yes
Very good .	Gardening jobs (rare) .	Gardening . .	,, . . .	..	Over 80/-	7	..	No
Good . .	Kitchen porter .	Light work . .	,, . . .	12/6	..	2	..	,,
,, . .	Relief work . .	Gardener, brush-hand	,, . . .	?	26/-	4	..	,,
,, . .	....	Light work . .	,, . . .	..	22/-	3	1	,,
Very good .	Own trade (rare) .	Caretaker or rent collector	,, . . .	6/-	?	3	1	,,
Good . .	Road mending .	Light work or caretaker	,, . . .	7/-	37/-	5	..	,,

but not occasional gifts or savings.   ³ See note, p. 61.

this may render it difficult for him to secure further permanent work.

As the whole problem is both so important and so complicated, it will be worth while to give a few particulars about each of the men in the class, which will enable the reader to form his own conclusions on some of the matters discussed, and also throw light on certain questions which we do not raise. It should be pointed out, however, that the details here given only represent a small part of the information contained in our case papers. Much of this was necessarily omitted, and sometimes occupations could only be defined in general terms to avoid identification. The particulars were obtained from the men themselves or members of their families, and checked in nearly all cases by reference to the previous employer or some other person having special knowledge of the circumstances. Thus any opinion expressed as, for instance, that a man is inefficient or that his character is satisfactory, is not the result of a hasty impression, but of statements carefully sifted.

Working on the information contained in the preceding pages, we are now able to answer in a large measure the question why these men are unemployed. First it may be noted that in many cases inability to secure further permanent work is due not to one, but to several causes; for instance, a somewhat advanced age combined with some moral defect. Possibly neither factor taken alone might have sufficed, but together they afford the explanation.

If, however, to avoid bewildering complexity, we select in each case what seems to be the principal cause rendering the search for work unsuccessful, we find that personal and purely economic causes operate in proportions which are roughly equal. Thus in 51 per cent of the cases there is apparently no personal disqualification for work; in 23 per cent age is a handicap; in 7 per cent there is some physical drawback and in 15 per cent some fault of character, while in 3 per cent both are evident.

Men Handicapped by Age (68 cases = 23·3 per

Present Age	Army Service		Last Employment Previous to Service				Last Regular Work since Service			
	Duration (years).	Date of Leaving.	Nature.	Duration (years).	Age at Leaving.	Was it Preceded by Regular Work?	Nature.	Duration (years).	Date of Leaving.	Cause of Leaving.
29	?	?	Butcher	A few	?	No	Dairyman	3	May 1907	Refused to sign 'radius agreement
29	8	Nov. 1907	Printer	2 or 3	18	,,	Window cleaner	2	Jan. 1910	Work too hard
26	8	Easter 1910	Confectioner's labourer	4 or 5	18	,,	Nil	..	..	....
32	3	?	Millwright	..	..	..	Millwright	7½	May 1910	Disagreement with employer
25	1½	1903	Apprentice to plumber	2	16 or 17	No	Miner	1	Dec. 1909	To return to England
22	3½	March 1910	Confectioner's labourer	abt. 3	about 17	,,	Nil	..	..	....
34	?	?	Farming	?	?	,,	Stone merchant's labourer	1	June 1909	To better himself
34	8	1909	Photographer	2 or 3	25	Yes	None	.-	..	
40	21	?	None	..	..	..	Butler	10	1909	During last part of army service. Had to leave
26	8	Oct. 1909	Solicitor's clerk	3	18	No	Nil	..	..	....
30	navy 14	Nov. 1909	Errand boy	?	?	,,	,,	..	..	....
26	8	Feb. 1910	Groom	1 or 2	17	,,	,,	..	..	....
24	8	June 1910	Optician	8	16	,,	Nil	..	..	....
52	7	1886	Errand boy	?	22 (?)	,,	Storekeeper	4½	Feb. 1910	Bankruptcy
36	18	April 1910	Fireman	1	19	Yes	Nil	..	..	....
27	8	Dec. 1907	Printer	3	19	No	Flour-mill labourer	1	April 1910	To better himself
30	8	1909	Fitter's apprentice	7	21	,,	Nil	..	..	....
32	8	May 1910	Shoesmith	9	24	Yes	..	..	..	....
44	18	1906	Railway clerk	6 or 7	21 or 22	No	Bank messenger	1	Nov. 1909	"Not suitable"
46	3	1883	None	..	..	..	Railway carriage cleaner	24	1908	Theft
25	6	1907	Hurrier (mine)	3	16	No	Keel captain's mate	7	1909	Assault affair arising from drink
45	7	?	Farm labourer	?	?	,,	Farm labour	11	June 1909	"Quarrel with employer"
46	19	?	Breaking cinders	4	?	,,	Timber carrier	3	March 1909	"Quarrel with employer. Dispute regarding wages
30	12	May or June 1910	Barman	8	18	,,	Nil	..	..	....
48	8	1889	In colliery	9	19 (?)	,,	Unloading boats	4	June 1909	Displaced by machine
25	5	Feb. 1908	Probably farm work	?	?	?	Drayman	2	May 1910	"Reduction of staff"
27	8	March 1910	Glass works labourer	1 or 2	19	Yes	Nil	..	..	....
27	8	May 1910	Carter	3 or 4	19	,,	..	..	..	....
62	12	1882	Farm labourer	over 20	34	No	Glass works labourer	26	Early 1909	Age
25	?	?	Moulder's apprentice	2	17	Yes	Farm labourer	1	Nov. 1909	Inefficiency
44	4	1881	Errand boy	3	17	No	Piano wire stretcher	8½	May 1910	Displaced by machine
32	12	April 1910	Confectioner's labourer	6 or 7	20 or 21	,,	Nil	..	..	....
35	12	End 1909	Terra-cotta presser	11	22 (?)	,,	,,	..	..	....
28	8	April 1909	Pony driver	3	18	Yes	,,	..	..	....

EX-ARMY MEN

Nature of Temporary Work done since.	Nature of Occupations sought.	Present Condition.		Apparent Personal Handicaps in Search for Regular Work.	Average Weekly Casual Earnings.[1]	Average Weekly Income of Rest of Household.[1]	No. of Persons in Household.		Is Family under Poverty Line.[2]
		Physique.	Character.				Adults.	Children (under 16).	
Had shop which did not pay.	Dairyman or any	?	Very respectable	None	..	?	2	2	?
Window cleaner and catch jobs	Any	Good	Good	Has become casual	9/-	..	2	2	Yes
	...	?	Excellent	None	3/6	?	5	1	?
None	Own trade or any	Good		,,	..	?	?	?	?
Catch jobs	Navvy or any	Strong	Good, but somewhat adventurous	,,	..	?	4	1	No
....	Confectioner's labourer	Was invalided; now fit	Good	Apparently too limited search	..	?	?	?	?
With a baker and at laundry	Any	Strong	Good worker, but shiftless	None	?	9/-	2	1	?
Railway porter (8 months)	Labourer		Very good	,,	12/-	12/-	2	?	?
Two months soap-maker's labourer	Butler or any	Healthy	Good	Seems too well off with pension and lodgers to care greatly for hard work	10/-	48/-	6	?	No
Temporary clerk	Clerk or any	,,	Very good	None	10/-	35/-	3	..	,,
Painting..	Sailor			,,	?		1	..	?
Railway porter	Labourer	Mentally affected, otherwise good	?(Discharge "fair")	Mental disorder	18/6		1	..	No
None	Platelayer	Good	Good	None	?	22/-	3	1	,,
	Warehouseman	Begins to fail	Very good	Age	5/-	23/-	3	4	,,
None	Clerk or any	Strong	Good	Poor education	12/-		2	1	Yes
Cleaning cattle waggons	Printer	,,		None	3/6		2	..	,,
	Labourer	,,	Very good	,,	?	16/-	3	1	?
	Policeman, asylum attendant	Robust		,,	3/6	20/-	3	..	No
Farm work, then parish relief work	Any	Healthy	Good army discharge, but seems to have deteriorated	Age	17/4		2	5	Yes
Fitter's labourer, relief work.	Any casual	,,	Must have been good worker, but dishonest	,,	?	?	?	..	?
Casual jobs on river	Skipper or mate	,,	On the whole good	None	?	?	5	3	?
Casual jobs on farms	Corporation labourer or any	,,	?	,,	10/-	8/-	2	5	Yes
Sells old things, Labour Bureau relief work and other catch work	Slater's or bricklayer's labourer	,,	Drinks heavily	Drink	10/-		2	1	,,
One day's waiting	Any	,,	Good	None	?	..	2	2	,,
Catch jobs, unloading boats	Navvy or any	,,	?Wife left him, lives with other woman	Age	5/-	17/-	3	1	No
None	Labourer	,,	Good army discharge	None	?	..	2	1	Yes
....	Any "suitable"	,,	Good	,,	3/6	?	?	?	?
	Factory labourer	,,		,,	3/6	62/-	7	..	No
Occasionally night watchman	Watchman	,,	Excellent	Age	9/-	12/-	3	..	,,
Whitewashing, milker	Labourer	,,	Said to be inclined to loaf	Shiftlessness	?	35/-	3	2	,,
Musician	Musician	,,	Good	None	21/3	5/-	2	7	Yes
	Labourer		Very good	,,			1	..	,,
Temporary railway porter	Any	Very good	"Fair," "ordinary casual"	,,	?		2	1	?
Licensed pedlar	Groom	Good	"Very good, sober, and reliable"	,,	3/6	?	?	?	?

[1] Including all regular pensions, poor relief, etc., but not occasional gifts or savings.

[2] See note, p. 61.

cent).—It will be noted that in nearly one-fourth of
the cases age is a primary factor, rendering difficult
re-entry into the ranks of permanently employed
workers. In about a third of these some other
factor is present, but apparently is only secondary.
It is unfortunately indisputable that when an unskilled worker gets past 40 he finds it very difficult
to meet with an employer who is willing to give him
regular work. He may be able to work quite as well
as a younger man, but in a labour market where the
supply of unskilled labour almost invariably exceeds
the demand, an employer having to choose between
a younger and an older man not unnaturally chooses
the younger; and though it may sound paradoxical,
the more considerate he is for his men, the more
likely is he to adopt this course. There are, as a
matter of fact, few employers who take no interest
whatever in their men, and who will dismiss any one
who has been with them for five or ten years as soon
as his powers begin to fail, with no anxiety as to
what is to become of him. For this very reason,
most of them hesitate to put on their permanent
staff men who have reached middle life and who,
though for the next ten years or so they might hold
their own absolutely against younger men, would
then probably begin to flag. It is, of course, much
more difficult for an unskilled than for a skilled
worker to find regular employment when past middle
life, for he is probably at his best earlier on. A
skilled worker, however, should gain in knowledge

and experience as the years go by ; and very often a
man of 40 or 45 will, on this account, be more
useful to an employer than one of 25 or 30. We
note that of the 68 men who are unemployed
primarily on account of their age, only 18 belong
to skilled trades, while the remaining 50 are either
entirely or partially unskilled. It may be remarked,
however, in passing, that 14 of these 50 men have
at one time of their career been engaged in skilled
occupations, but for some reason have dropped out
of them.

Men Physically Handicapped (21 cases = 7·2 per
cent).—The 21 men who are in some way physically
disqualified consist of 2 who are more or less mentally
defective, 3 consumptive, 2 deformed, 1 subject to
fits, and 13 who are merely returned as " not strong "
and " unable to undertake hard work." With four
exceptions all could probably retain employment
permanently if it were suited to their capacities, but
those capacities are so limited as to constitute a great
handicap. The four excepted, being consumptive or
subject to fits, are liable at any moment to be laid
aside by their ailments, and will find it difficult to
secure situations with employers to whom their
condition is known.

Men Handicapped by Faults of Character (45
cases = 15·5 per cent).—The majority of the men in
this section are returned as lazy and inefficient, others
as drinkers or confirmed gamblers. It is probable
that in applying for work some of them may be

more successful in hiding their defects than men suffering from physical weakness; but to judge by their record, it is to be feared that many, even if they find a job which promises to be permanent, may soon lose it. Still it is a hopeful fact that many of them are quite young, 20 under 25 years old, while 21 are between 25 and 35, and only 4 over the latter age; and probably through one influence or another not a few of them will succeed in leaving the slippery down-hill path upon which they have entered. If not, they will in a few years be ranked among the loafers and unemployables, for they have taken the first step in that direction. Our inquiry shows that their present condition— possibly with a few exceptions—is not due to the demoralising influence of a long period of unemployment, as is the case with a number of those now found in the casual class.

Men Handicapped by Physique and Character (9 cases = 3·1 per cent).—Nine men, representing 3 per cent of the whole class, were defective both in physique and character, and it was difficult to say which defect was the more serious from the point of view of finding fresh employment. Obviously, however, they were doubly handicapped.

Satisfactory Men (148 cases = 50·9 per cent).— So far we have dealt with 49 per cent of the men in this class. The remainder consists of those whose physique and character both seemed to be satisfactory. The causes of their unemployment are

purely economic, and do not call for discussion at
this stage. We shall therefore proceed to consider
certain questions affecting the whole class.

It may be said that the 291 men in this class
represent a reserve of workers varying greatly in
efficiency, who are not at the moment required in
their various industries. We must now examine the
constitution of this reserve, and see whether it is
made up of small reserves for a large number of
trades and occupations, or whether some trades are
carrying an extravagantly large reserve.

The question first arises whether we should regard
the workers as a reserve for the industries which
they have left, or for those which they seek to enter.
Although there is something to be said for each
course, probably we shall come nearer the truth
if we regard them as forming a reserve for the
industries upon which they were last engaged. Very
few would refuse to re-enter them if they got the
chance; and their statements as to the industries
they desire to enter, especially in the case of unskilled workers, are usually too vague to make
classification possible. The following is a list of
the last occupations held by the men, with the
number engaged in each.

Industry

Electricians . . . 2	Brewery foreman . . 1
Coppersmiths . . . 2	Beer bottlers . . . 2
Boilersmiths . . . 3	Aerated water maker's
Fitters 5	labourer . . . 1
Fitter's labourers . . 3	Ropemaker . . . 1
Strikers 4	Confectioners . . . 2
Turners 2	Confectioner's labourers . 20
Moulders 4	Flour-mill labourers . . 13
Mechanical Engineers . . 5	Other mill and factory
Blacksmiths . . . 3	labourers . . . 3
Millwright . . . 1	Boxmakers . . . 3
Driller 1	Water buffers (comb works) . 2
Planer (foundry) . . 1	Shoemaker . . . 1
Machineman (laundry) . 1	Saddler 1
Engineer's labourers . . 4	Opticians 2
Machinists (engine) . . 2	Bookbinder . . . 1
Whitesmiths . . . 3	Lithographer . . . 1
Draughtsman . . . 1	Printer's labourer . . 1
Wire-stretcher . . . 1	Printer's feeder . . . 1
Brass-finisher . . . 1	Wetter-off (glass) . . 1
Brass-turner . . . 1	Taker-in (glass) . . . 1
Piano-action fitter . . 1	Glass engraver . . . 1
Gunsmith 1	„ polisher . . . 1
Carpet printer . . . 1	„ picker . . . 1
Pad weaver (oil) . . 1	„ sorter . . . 1
Engine-driver . . . 1	„ blowers . . . 2
Silver miner . . . 1	Bottle packers . . . 4
Stone merchant's labourer . 1	Coke filler . . . 1
Spokeshaver . . . 1	Deal carriers . . . 2
Sawyers 4	Paper buyer . . . 1
Sawyer's labourers . . 2	Warehouseman (in factory) . 1
French polisher . . . 1	Coach-builder . . . 1
Cabinetmakers . . . 2	
Upholsterer . . . 1	Total . . 142
	(= 48·9 per cent)

Transport

Railway wagon builders	2	Fireman	1
Railway wagon repairers	1	Wireman (on railway)	1
Platelayers	2	Carriage cleaners	2
Station porter (regular)	1	Railway labourers	4
Brakesman	1	Coal carriers	2
Loader	1	Checker (on railway)	1
Shunter	1	Signalman	1
Van driver	1	Cab cleaner	1
Draymen	2	Unloading boats (regular)	1
Carters	5	Wagoners	2
Bus conductors	2	Lightermen	3
Tram conductors	2	Steam lurry drivers	3
Cab-drivers	3		

Total . . 46
(= 15·8 per cent)

Distribution and Retail Trade

Shop porters	5	Insurance agents	3
Butchers	2	Dairymen	2
Bakers	2	Draper's assistant	1
Hairdresser	1	Grocer's assistants	10
Clerks	4	Grocers (own business)	2
Messengers	3	Shop cleaner	1
Errand boys	3	Accountant	1
Publican	2	Window cleaners	2
Greengrocer (own business)	1	Warehousemen	3
Cellarman	1	Musician	1
Caterer	1		
Mess-room attendant	1	Total	52

(= 17·8 per cent)

Agriculture

Farm labourers	6	Cattle storekeeper	1

Total . . 7
(= 2·4 per cent)

Domestic Service

Coachman	1	Butlers	2
Grooms	7	School caretakers	2

Chauffeur and gardener	. 1	Kitchen porter .	. . 1
Gardeners . . .	. 4	Plateman (hotel)	. . 1
Club steward . .	. 1	Waiters . .	. . 3
Groom and coachman .	. 2	Barmen . .	. . 2
Groom and gardeners .	. 2		—

Total . . 29
(= 10·0 per cent)

Last employment in Army; previously

Confectioner's labourers	. 2	Optician . .	. . 1
Terra-cotta presser	. . 1	Groom . .	. . 1
Shoesmith . .	. . 1	Photographer .	. . 1
Carter . .	. . 1	Fireman . .	. . 1
Confectioner .	. . 1	Glass-worker's labourer	. 1
Barman . .	. . 1	Clerk . .	. . 1
Fitter . .	. . 1		—

Total . . 14

Last employment in Navy; previously

Errand boy . . . 1
(= 5·1 per cent)

It will be noted that the unemployed of this class
are distributed over an amazing variety of occupations.
Only about one-half of them were engaged in industry
proper, distribution and retail trade claiming 18 per
cent, transport 16 per cent, agricultural pursuits 2½
per cent, and domestic service 10 per cent, while
5 per cent have been unable to regain permanent
situations after leaving army or navy.

Analysing a little more closely, we find that the
largest group of men last engaged in one occupation
is that of confectioner's labourers with 20, followed
by flour-mill labourers with 13. Next are grocer's
assistants with 10, grooms with 7, and agricultural

labourers with 6 ; while in none of the other groups are there more than 5, and 66 occupations, not counting those who have last been in the army, show a reserve of only one man each.

As apparently no single industry has a large special reserve of labour, all these men, except those disqualified by age or some serious personal defect, will probably sooner or later be reabsorbed in their own previous occupation or in some other; but it is possible, especially in times of trade depression, that such reabsorption will not occur until the demoralisation so often consequent on unemployment has begun its deadly work. We recognise immediately in the case of youths how mischievous a period of unemployment is, and, speaking generally, it is no less mischievous to adults. Even men of strong character tell us how exceedingly difficult it is to resist this demoralisation, which is partly due to psychical and partly to physical causes. They suffer psychically because of the depression, often amounting to acute despair, which comes after days and weeks spent in tramping the streets and meeting with nothing but disappointments and refusals—the latter, unfortunately, often couched in language neither kindly nor courteous ; and physically, because unemployment is so frequently accompanied by an insufficient supply of nutritious food and the other necessaries of life. Thus the health is rapidly undermined, and with it the power to resist demoralising influences and the determination to maintain a high standard of living.[1] Reference to the table on pp. 30 to 51 will show that approximately one-third of this class (74 out of 217) are living under the poverty line,[2] the rest being raised above

[1] A friend of one of the writers recently gave him rather striking evidence of the demoralisation resulting from malnutrition. When he was a medical student he once put a sovereign in his pocket and determined to live upon this in the East End of London for a month, at the rate of 5s. a week. He took a small room in a squalid part of Whitechapel, for which he paid half a crown a week, leaving the other half-crown for food and other necessary expenditure. He said that by the end of a fortnight he definitely felt his power of resistance going. He was becoming careless in matters of cleanliness, and generally slipping down to the level of those among whom he was living. By the end of the month these effects were yet more marked, and he realised that if life under such conditions were to be continued he would very rapidly deteriorate, not only in physique, but *morale.* He attributed this slackening of moral fibre, and inability to rise above his environment, largely to the loss of physical vitality, consequent on malnutrition and unhealthy surroundings.

[2] In establishing the poverty line it is estimated that the following minimum sums are necessary for the maintenance of physical efficiency, and that any family whose total income from all sources, including the total earnings of all the children, falls below this minimum, is below the poverty line.

		s.	d.	
Food—				
Adults .	. . . . .	3	0	per week.
Children	. . . .	2	3	,, ,,
Clothing—				
Adults .	. . . . .	0	6	,, ,,
Children	. . . .	0	5	,, ,,
Fuel .	. . . . .	1	10	,, family per week.
All other sundries .	. . .	0	2	,, head per week.
Rent .	. . .	The sum actually paid by the family.		

This works out to 21s. 8d. for a family of two adults and three children, paying 4s. for rent. These figures are not put forward as representing the amount which a family of this kind *ought* to get, *but the minimum upon which it is possible to maintain physical efficiency.* No expenditure is allowed in this estimate which does not come under that heading. The above calculation was made in 1900 when food prices were lower than now. It may therefore be regarded as a very moderate estimate. (See *Poverty : A Study of Town Life,* by B. Seebohm Rowntree, chap. iv., " The Poverty Line.")

It should be noted that the family earnings given in the table are only approximate ; for while every care was taken to obtain accurate figures from the families themselves, the information was not verified by reference to

it through the earnings of other members of the
family, and to a smaller extent through the proceeds
of their own temporary work. The proportion under
the poverty line would have been much higher but
for the fact that so many of the unemployed are
young men living with their parents.

That many men in this class are in serious danger
of complete deterioration will be seen from the
following table, which shows in the case of 269
individuals, the length of time which had elapsed
since they lost their last regular employment.

PERIOD OF UNEMPLOYMENT (PREVIOUS TO DATE OF INQUIRY)
OF 269 CASES

	Number.	Per cent of total.
Less than one week	3	1·1
One to two weeks	4	1·5
Two to four weeks	21	7·8
Four to six weeks	17	6·3
Six to eight weeks	19	7·1
Eight to twelve weeks	39	14·5
About four months	12	4·5
About five months	19	7·1
About six months	16	5·9
About seven to nine months . . .	31	11·5
About ten to twelve months . . .	26	9·6
About thirteen to eighteen months .	24	8·9
About nineteen to twenty-four months .	23	8·6
Over two years	15	5·6
Total . . .	269	100·0

The above table shows that nearly two-thirds of
the number had been without regular work for four

employers, although it was often possible to check it by our personal knowledge of the wages paid in York for different classes of labour.

months or more, and one-half for six months or more, while nearly one-quarter of them had had no regular employment for over a year. It is obvious, therefore, that we are here confronted with a grave problem.[1]

Of course, almost all the men had done temporary jobs while looking for regular work—and in a few exceptional cases these were of considerable duration —but, as we point out in the next chapter, such work, though much better than none at all, has special dangers of its own, tending permanently to degrade men from the ranks of regular to those of casual workers. The following itinerary, supplied by an unemployed grocer's assistant, aged 22, illustrates these dangers, and shows how disheartening may be the search for regular work, and how comparatively easy it is for an energetic and intelligent young fellow to pick up a living by casual jobs.

Monday.—Called on . . . (grocer) in answer to an advertisement. Was told I had been too long out of the trade. Then searched advertisements in the Library.

Tuesday.—Got job of digging up sand at boat landing-place (having drawn owner's attention to need for the job).

Wednesday.—Same.

Thursday.—Worked for boat owner. Earned 3s. 6d.

Friday.—Library for advertisements.

Saturday.—Applied for work at stores and for horse clipping at . . . without success. Spent afternoon outside the town looking for a job haymaking.

Monday.—Started at 4 A.M. seeking haymaking job at three villages (named): got work at 9 A.M. Came home early owing to rain. Earned 3s.

---

[1] It must, however, be remembered that the 5·6 per cent out of work for over two years are partly composed of men unlikely, on account of their age, to regain regular employment.

Tuesday.—Applied for investigation work.[1] Did six cases.

Wednesday.—3.30 to 7.30 unloading London boat. Earned 3s. Spent rest of morning waiting for fine weather to unload other cargo.

Thursday.—Loading boat with flour. There all day, but owing to rain had to stand off for several hours. Was on spot from 6 A.M. to 7 P.M. Earned 3s. 6d.

Friday.—Finished investigation cases : rest of day at Library.

Saturday.—Delivered case papers. Earned 3s. 9d. Applied for carting job at . . . without success.

We do not put forward the above case as typical, our impression being that the energy of this man and his range of application for permanent or temporary jobs are somewhat exceptional.[2]

Even if men escape the danger of degenerating into casuals, there is a very real risk that, in order to avoid a protracted period of unemployment, they will accept work inferior to that which they have previously done, thus, in all probability, permanently lowering their standard of living. That this is not mere theory, but is constantly occurring, is demonstrated by the fact that of 49 men who were undoubtedly skilled workers,[3] and who were unemployed, 23 stated to our investigators that they would be willing to accept a permanent job, even though unskilled.[4]

[1] This refers to certain investigations connected with this volume.

[2] See also diary given on p. 232.

[3] Their trades were as follows : electrician, coppersmith, boilersmith, millwright, mechanical engineer, blacksmith, brass-finisher, draughtsman, carpet printer, wire stretcher, gunsmith, piano-action fitter, glass engraver, glass polisher, glass blower, lithographer, bookbinder, instrument-maker, optician, saddler, shoemaker, wireman, steam lurry driver, butcher, baker, hairdresser, upholsterer, paper-buyer, accountant, shoesmith, French polisher, photographer, engine-driver, cabinetmaker, whitesmith.

[4] Only 3 of the 49 men seek light unskilled occupations on account of age or infirmity.

A couple of illustrations taken from those given on p. 30 *et seq.*, and somewhat amplified from our case papers, may here be given.

No. 726, age 25, was apprenticed to a boilersmith, and has worked at his trade for nine years, being last employed continuously for eighteen months at a wage of thirty-four shillings per week. He lost this situation through slackness of trade in October 1909, and has since taken work as a bricklayer's labourer for three months, at an average wage of twenty shillings per week. He is a man of excellent physique and good character. At the time of inquiry he had looked for work as a general labourer at nearly all the larger factories in York, and hoped to be taken on temporarily as a casual goods porter at one of them.

No. 1508, age 37, had for eight years held a good position as foreman in a brewery, which he resigned in May 1909, in consequence of differences with one of the managers. Very respectable and of robust physique, he has nevertheless been quite unable to obtain work suitable to his ability. He told the investigator that he had done nothing since losing his place, but we have learnt that he has since been reduced to cattle driving. He is still searching for "any suitable position," and has applied personally at many firms.

The facts set forth above indicate the urgent need not only of reducing periods of unemployment, but of lessening the danger of demoralisation while they last. Certain proposals in this connection will be made later. The importance of the matter is emphasised when we realise what a large number of young men are included among the 291 men in this class. The following table gives the particulars of their ages.

[TABLE.

F

AGES OF MEN IN THIS CLASS

Age.	Number.	Percentage of Total Number.	Percentage of all Men of these Ages living in York.
19 to 20	23	7·9	1·2
21 „ 25	88	30·2	2·0
26 „ 30	44	15·1	1·2
31 „ 35	37	12·7	1·2
36 „ 40	23	7·9	0·9
41 „ 50	41	14·1	1·0
51 „ 60	16	5·5	0·6
61 „ 70	17	5·9	1·0
Over 70	2	0·7	0·2
Total . .	291	100·0	average 1·2

It will be seen that the age of these unemployed workers is low, over half of them (53·2 per cent) being under 30 years, and 88 per cent being under 50.[1]

It is a serious thing to expose so large a number of young men, with their industrial careers before them, to conditions which we know to be in a high degree demoralising. The part which some form of

[1] It is of interest to find that nearly one-third of the men in this class are between 21 and 25 years of age, a time of life, one would imagine, at which they would find it easy to secure work. Our suggested explanation of this phenomenon is threefold : Firstly, before 25, men are less competent and skilled than during the next two decades, and are liable to be dismissed in times of slackness before workers of greater experience. Secondly, they have not established the same claim on their employers as older hands, and so would be dismissed before, say men of 35 or 40. Thirdly, most of them are unmarried, and are more liable to throw up their employment on slight provocation, and to become indifferent in their time-keeping and in their work generally, than men with family responsibilities. There is, however, no adequate explanation of the fact that the percentage of unemployed workers is much larger between 31 and 35 than between 36 and 40, and the numbers here dealt with are, perhaps, too small to permit of trustworthy deductions. The percentage of the unemployed between 19 and 20 is high, but we must remember that many of these young workers have not yet found a definite trade or occupation, and others are in the transition between boys' and men's employments.

insurance could play in mitigating the evils of unemployment is discussed in a later chapter, but it
may be pointed out that this unemployed reserve is
distributed so evenly over a great variety of trades,
that its insurance should not lay an insupportable
burden on any of them. Indeed, as a rule, it was
unnecessary to make a prolonged inquiry into the
probable number of men actually engaged in a
particular occupation, because it was at once obvious
that its reserve at the time of our inquiry could hardly
have been smaller, although, as the reader will remember, trade in York in June 1910 was somewhat
depressed.

Now, with the facts disclosed by our inquiry
before us, we are in a position to discuss measures
of reform. But, perhaps, before doing so, it will be
well to refresh our memories by summarising very
briefly what has been said. We are here dealing, it
will be remembered, with men who have been engaged
in regular work within the last two years, and who
are still looking for it.

Half of them, we found, were satisfactory, both as
regards efficiency and character. The rest were more
or less disqualified in their search for work by age,
or by defects of physique or character, the number
affected by these handicaps being 68, 21, and 45
respectively, while 9 men were disqualified both
physically and morally. It must not be inferred for
a moment that the men were in any sense unemployable. Probably, on the average, they would compare

satisfactorily with not a few of those in regular work. On the other hand, many of them have entered upon a dangerous course, and unless brought under reformative agencies, may degenerate into loafers.

A large proportion of the men in this class are still young, and should be quite amenable to restorative measures of the right kind.

Many had been without regular work for so long as to run a serious risk from continued exposure to the demoralising influences which, under existing conditions, almost invariably accompany extended periods of unemployment.

Finally, we have seen that the unemployed are not drawn principally from one or two industries, but from an astonishing variety of trades and occupations.

To what reforms do the facts point? Obviously in answering this question we must strictly limit our field of inquiry, or it would open out a discussion of almost every subject involved in the social problem. For the evil of unemployment is but one symptom of the fatal anomaly of our social system—a system in which the material desires of very few are realised and the material needs of millions are not met, while society allows all the factors necessary to remedy this state of things to spoil for want of use. None will dispute that in this country great quantities of the three factors on which the creation of all wealth depends—land, labour, and capital—are either lying idle, or being but partially used, and that until they

are brought together the problem of unemployment
cannot be solved.

But while recognising that far-reaching reforms
are essential for the better adjustment of these three
factors, we need not refuse to deal with a specific
result of social maladjustment such as unemployment,
so long as the treatment adopted is such as will
further and not hinder fundamental reforms.

Coming, then, to measures advocated for the
immediate relief of unemployment, these will best
be considered under two heads : first, those which
propose to reduce the amount of the evil, and second,
those intended to mitigate its effects. As the latter
measures apply not to any particular section of unemployed men, but to practically all, they will be
considered in a later chapter.

PROPOSED MEANS OF INCREASING THE VOLUME OF EMPLOYMENT

A. *Labour Exchanges.*—We will deal first with
Labour Exchanges, which, since this inquiry was
made, have become an established part of the
machinery for grappling with the problem ;[1] and ask
how far, in the light of the facts before us, they may
be expected to reduce the volume of unemployment.

The methods by which masters sought men and
men sought work, which were revealed in the course
of our inquiry, showed great lack of co-ordination.

---

[1] The York Labour Exchange was opened in September 1910.

The man's method was usually "going all round," or "hearing of a vacant job from a pal," or sometimes answering advertisements; while the masters in each trade got to know of unemployed men by advertisement, or, more often, through other workmen, or selected them from among personal applicants in a most haphazard manner. In spite, however, of the lack of system, York is a sufficiently small place for such rough and ready methods to have proved fairly effective, *in the case of men seeking regular work,* and it is to be doubted whether any appreciable number of posts suited to York men have, in the past, remained long vacant merely on account of the absence of an official centre for bringing together supply and demand. We believe, therefore, that the function of the Exchange in this city will be principally to enlarge the labour market for its workers, advising them of vacancies in other towns when none exist in York. As a matter of fact, since its inauguration the York Exchange has, to our knowledge, been of service in placing men in situations at a distance, thus reducing the volume of unemployment in York itself. Probably the most important work of the Exchanges will be to organise the casual labour market. This is of the greatest moment, and if well done would in itself fully justify their existence, but it is a subject for discussion in the next chapter.

B. *Regulation of Public Employment.*—It has been pointed out by various writers how considerable is the proportion of the total industry of the country which is directly controlled by public authorities, either national or local, and that to a large extent this work could be so regulated that it should be withheld when the general trade of the country is active, and pushed forward in periods of seasonal or cyclical trade depression. But the total number of men in York who are engaged on Government work is exceedingly small. Any help, therefore, to be derived from the regulation of Government orders would, for the most part, come indirectly through its steadying influence on the trade of the country generally. It is impossible to estimate the extent of this indirect influence on York's industry. The figures given in Mr. and Mrs. Webb's book, *The Prevention of Destitution*,[1] which are based upon calculations made by Professor Bowley, suggest, however, that a great deal might be done to smooth out cyclical and, to a lesser extent, seasonal fluctuations in the volume of business. While there is no doubt that such a policy could do much to improve matters at times of general trade depression, it must be remembered that periods of depression and activity in different localities do not always synchronise; for instance, we have shown that when our census was taken, trade in York was rather depressed, although more than usually active in the country generally. Under such circumstances the local problem would not have been helped by the regularisation of Government orders. This consideration emphasises

[1] Longmans & Co., 1911, p. 110 *et seq.*

the need for the regularisation of municipal work, by
means of which it is certain that more might be done
directly to reduce the volume of unemployment in
the city. It may be urged that since, at present,
there is little or no evidence that work done for the
municipality in times of general trade activity entails
either much overtime or the introduction of outside
workers, no advantage is really to be gained by
postponing it to times of trade depression. If, it
may be said, men are to be found unemployed even
when trade is active, you are doing as much to reduce
the volume of unemployment by giving the work to
these men during a time of trade activity as you
would do by giving it out when trade was depressed.
One day's work does not grow into two by being
thus withheld! At first sight this would appear to
be a valid criticism, but the answer to it is, that men
are tempted to enter any industry in numbers
sufficient to cope with its demands in times of trade
activity. By increasing the demand for labour at
such times, more men are tempted to enter the trade,
and consequently the number unemployed in that
trade in a time of depression will be greater. Action
tending to regulate the demand for labour in any
industry will eventually tend to lessen unemployment.

In the case of municipal, as of national work, we
are without the data necessary to estimate just how
much relief a policy of regularisation would afford;
but whether it be great or small it would certainly

be in the right direction. It carries with it no
danger of pauperising or of weakening personal
effort, and is in every way to be strongly commended.

C. *The Creation of New Industries.*—We recognise
the accuracy of the view that, paradoxical though
it may seem, the problem of unemployment cannot
be solved by the creation of new industries. If it
could, unemployment would be unknown, or, at any
rate, reduced to a minimum, in towns where a number
of new industries had recently been started. This,
however, is not the case, the fact being that each
industry introduced soon attracts its own reserve
of labour, and is marked by the same variations
in the demand for workers as the old-established
ones.

(*a*) *Forestry.*— But while this holds good of
ordinary industries, *i.e.* those whose activity at any
given moment is determined by the current demand
for the goods produced, it is not true of certain other
undertakings, notably that connected with the growing of timber, an industry which in this country
has been strangely neglected. The reason why the
general rule just considered does not apply to it, is
that the process of producing timber is so slow that,
so far as the greater portion of the labour involved
is concerned, it is a matter of little moment whether
this is applied at one time or another within the
limits of a few years. The planting of trees, for
instance, can be held back or pressed forward at will,

so can the labour involved in felling them, since it does not very much matter whether a tree is cut down when it is, say, eighty years old, or left until it is eighty-three or -four. This means that the bulk of the labour can be applied in times of trade depression and held back when trade is active. And further, the greater part of it is comparatively unskilled in character, though it must always, of course, be conducted under the direction of highly skilled foresters. There is good evidence that afforestation can be made to pay, and it should be undertaken with this object, so that the unskilled workers who are temporarily engaged upon it may never consider themselves as occupied in mere "relief work." They must be employed on strictly business lines—selected on account of their special fitness for the work, and dismissed if they prove unfit.

Let us try and measure the extent to which such an enterprise would help to solve the problem of unemployment. According to the *Report of the Royal Commission on Afforestation*[1] there are in Great Britain $8\frac{1}{2}$ million acres suitable for afforestation. Of course a forest does not provide its maximum amount of labour until the work of felling and carting away the timber has commenced. How long this will be after the planting will depend upon the kind of tree grown; whether conifers, which mature in

[1] Vol. II. part i., 1909 (Cd. 4460), p. 32. For the other details here given also see this volume, and *Land and Labour: Lessons from Belgium,* by B. S. Rowntree (Macmillan, 1910), chap. xiii.

about forty years, or broad-leaved trees, which require
about eighty. The selection of trees would depend
largely on the situation, but it may be assumed that
one-third would be conifers and two-thirds broad-
leaved. If one-sixtieth of the total area were planted
annually (the proportion mentioned by the Commission to give ultimately a sustained timber yield), it
is estimated that 25,500 men would be required
during four winter months each year, in addition to
a permanent staff of skilled foresters, and that about
an equal number would derive indirect employment
in connection with the incidental and subsidiary
occupations connected with forestry, such as road-
making, fencing, etc. This demand for labour would
materially increase as soon as the first important
thinnings took place, in about twenty years, and
again at the end of forty years, when the conifers
were ready for felling, and it would reach its
maximum when the broad-leaved trees began to
mature, at the end of eighty years. From that time
onward, the labour provided by the forests would be
equivalent to one man per 100 acres working all the
year round, or 85,000 men in all.

But if afforestation is to be of service in providing
work for unemployed men, the labour must be so
organised that it may be largely performed by
temporary workers—as is done in Belgium, where,
not counting officials, nine-tenths of the men are
employed for four months annually, and only one-
tenth are regular workers. If a similar arrangement

were made in Britain, this would mean that 21,250
men would be employed permanently, and 191,250
for four months each year.

York's share in the national afforestation scheme,
pro rata with her population, would be 17,000 acres,
and this would at first provide work for about 50
men for four months each winter in planting, and
approximately another 50 in subsidiary forest work,
making about 100 in all. These numbers, as we
have seen, would materially increase as the first
thinnings began to be made in twenty years, and
again when the conifers began to mature at the end
of forty years. At the end of eighty years, when
the whole forest reached maturity, 42 men would
be permanently employed, and 382 for four months
each winter.

The total capital cost of afforestation is estimated
by the Royal Commission at £13 : 6 : 8 per acre,[1] and
the annual outlay for administrative purposes at 4s.
per acre. The total cost of buying and planting 285
acres annually[2] would therefore be about £3800.
Assuming the money were borrowed at 3 per cent
(the rate allowed for by the Royal Commission on
Afforestation), the loss to the city would be £180 the
first year, rising to a maximum of £5953 in the fortieth
year. Then the timber-felling would begin, and the
loss would be gradually changed into a profit. After
the eighty-first year the annual profit should be about

[1] Land, £6 : 10s. ; planting, £6 : 10s. ; contingencies, 6s. 8d.
[2] *I.e.* one-sixtieth of 17,000 acres, which on a *pro rata* with population
basis would be York's share of the whole area.

£33,000, or 3¾ per cent compound interest on the capital invested.[1]

It may be urged that the period which must elapse before a scheme of afforestation becomes profitable is long, but, on the other hand, the advantages to be gained are very great. It would substantially help to solve the problem of unemployment in York if

[1] Net Annual Deficit or Surplus

(Calculated from Table given in Cd. 4460)

Year.	Acres Afforested.	Deficit (-) or Surplus (+).
1	285	− £171
2	570	− 342
6	855	− 513
10	2850	− 1711
11	3135	− 1882
20	5700	− 3422
21	5985	− 3555
30	8550	− 5097
31	8835	− 4413
40	11,400	− 5953
41	11,685	+ 102
50	14,260	− 1437
51	14,545	+ 102
60	17,113	− 1437
61	17,113	+ 856
70	17,113	+ 856
71	17,113	+ 3992
80	17,113	+ 3992
81	17,113	+ 41,021 *

* This revenue is not constant in each succeeding year, and will be decreased very largely during the twenty years succeeding the hundred and fortieth year. It may be represented by an approximate equalised annual revenue of £33,100.

Note.—The variations in returns from the fortieth to the sixtieth year, are due to the proceeds from thinning.

year by year a number of men, rising gradually from
about 100 to nearly 400, could be drawn from the
labour market for four months each winter—especially
when it is remembered that this number could be
increased or reduced according to the amount of
unemployment in the city.[1]

(b) *Other Enterprises.*—We have discussed
afforestation as probably the most important exception to the general rule that the mere creation
of new industries will not solve the unemployed
problem. Obviously, however, any industry in which
the number of persons engaged can be modified
without regard to the immediate state of trade,
will fall into the same category. The reclamation
of waste lands and of foreshores is usually mentioned
in this connection, and other works of national
importance may from time to time suggest themselves. Something has already been done at times
of trade depression by many local authorities in the
direction of pressing forward road improvements,
river embankments, the laying out of parks, and
the like. But whatever the nature of the enterprise, it is essential that it should be undertaken
because the work is needed, and should be conducted
on business principles and not as relief work. The
best men available should be selected for the task,

---

[1] It should perhaps be stated that in a volume published in 1910 (*The
Development of British Forestry*), Mr. A. C. Forbes, F.H.A.S., states that he
considers the report of the Royal Commission on Afforestation takes too
optimistic a view of the financial aspects of forestry. We have not the expert knowledge necessary to estimate the value of this criticism.

and they should be dismissed if not satisfactory—since men engaged upon ordinary relief work, whether offered by a Board of Guardians or by a municipal Distress Committee, regard their employment as a kind of charity, and seldom put forward their best effort. Moreover, although the remuneration is usually too small to maintain them in physical efficiency, the cost of the work done proves to be enormous.

Of course, work such as is here contemplated will only directly relieve the unemployment of a certain class of workers, for those unused to heavy labour could not undertake it. But undoubtedly the temporary absorption in afforestation or other work of some hundreds of men who were competing for every unskilled job, whether light or heavy, would improve the prospects of those who were left.

D. *Short Time.*—Something might be done to avoid distress consequent on a lessening in the demand for labour in any particular industry by working all the men short time instead of dismissing some and keeping the rest on full time. But an examination of the particulars on pp. 30 to 51 shows how limited is the extent to which such a policy could be adopted. First it would only apply to those men who lost their last job through slackness of trade, and they were only a small minority, while even all the members of this minority could not be included. Again, the extent to which the distress arising from periods of trade depression can wisely be met by working short time can never be great, since, in all except highly paid trades, any reduction made in the hours of labour, and consequently in the wages, must, or should be, very small. It is undoubtedly a very dangerous policy—first, because it places the whole burden of meeting the difficulty upon the workers, regardless of their individual ability to bear it; and second, because it conceals the evil of unemployment, while doing nothing to lessen it. It is better that the community should actually face and overcome the difficulty which arises from the entire unemployment of a comparatively small number of men, than that the income of a large number should for any length of time fall seriously below the minimum required for the maintenance of physical efficiency. There is a great risk that the standard of living of the workers might be permanently lowered if the policy of working short time during protracted periods of trade depression were generally adopted.

E. *Emigration.* — The question may be asked whether, among the men here considered, there are many who, with their families, might with advantage emigrate to countries where the demand for labour is greater than at home. We may at once rule out the 19 per cent of the total number whose age interferes with their prospects at home, and who cannot be expected to adapt themselves to an entirely fresh environment abroad. We may also exclude nearly all who suffer from physical disqualifi-

cations, and could not undertake the heavy work
which is generally required of immigrants into new
countries, and most of those who are out of work
on account of defects of character. These together
amount to half the men in this class. Of the
remaining half, undoubtedly many would succeed
if they emigrated, but as regards the problem of
unemployment, would the money enabling them
to do so be well spent? The men and families who
emigrated during a period of bad trade would not
return when times improved, and their work would
be lost to the mother country. All unused labour,
like unused land or capital, is potential wealth and
a national asset; to reject it because, through some
maladjustment of our industrial system, it is left
momentarily idle, is like giving away machinery
because for a time the supply of fuel has run short.
Until there is evidence of a shortage of land and
capital in the country, the emigration of labour—
the third factor in the production of all wealth—
must be regarded as a confession of failure on the
part of the community to organise these three factors.
The remedy is not to dispense with one of them, but
to co-ordinate them aright.[1]

F. *The Training of Youths.*—Before concluding
this chapter, we may remind the reader of the proposals
made in Chapter I. for the better training of youths,
which, if rightly given, and accompanied by the

---

[1] We are here, of course, only discussing emigration from the point of
view of unemployment.

personal help and guidance of Advisory Committees, would not only increase their general intelligence, physical powers and industrial efficiency, but strengthen their whole moral fibre. Our review of the various factors which have directly led to the unemployment of the men, and handicap them in their search for work, has shown how great is the need for such help, and how important would be its consequences in diminishing adult unemployment. We are confident that some such scheme as we have outlined in Chapter I. must find a place in any adequate attempt to grapple with this problem.

The conclusions here arrived at on the probable efficacy of various proposed methods of decreasing unemployment among those who have, within the last two years, been engaged in and are still seeking regular work, may briefly be summarised as follows :—

A. That the usefulness of the Labour Exchange will lie rather in the direction of advising York workers of vacancies in other towns than in filling local vacancies which would not previously have been filled.

B. That the policy of regulating the work given out by public bodies according to the state of the labour market is thoroughly sound ; and its effect in reducing the volume of unemployment in times of trade depression would be considerable.

C. (a) That if the nation fully developed a scheme

for the afforestation of waste lands, York's share in the demand for labour created might be expected at first to average 100 men for four months a year, which number would gradually increase to nearly 400 as the forests became established, and the work of felling timber commenced. The average demand for labour could be modified according to the state of trade.

(b) That other similar enterprises undertaken by the Government or by the Local Authority, might likewise prove useful in this direction, but only if managed on strictly business lines, and not on those of what is commonly understood as " relief work."

D. That the extent to which the evil of unemployment could wisely be met by working shorter time is small.

E. That emigration is an unnecessary and undesirable method of dealing with the unemployment of the vast majority of the men in this class.

F. That no scheme for reducing unemployment among adults is likely to succeed which neglects the training of youths between the ages, say, of 14 and 19, and that much may be hoped from wisely directed and systematic efforts in this direction.

We have been led to these conclusions by our study of the facts, and it is clear that while none of the proposals considered would solve the problem, i.e. create a machinery by which any temporary surplus of labour would be automatically absorbed, some of them would go far in this direction, especially if the suggestions made at the end of the previous chapter were fully acted upon.

It is, as a matter of fact, neither possible nor desirable that there should *never* be any reserve of workers, any more than that there should never be a reserve of land or capital, available for the development of fresh business enterprise, or for meeting the constantly changing calls made by the nation's industries. But just as land and capital, when for the moment no opportunity occurs for putting them to their fullest uses, are put to uses of secondary importance, or at any rate taken care of, even at the cost of current expenditure, so, if only from the economic standpoint, labour which at the moment is not required, should be taken care of so that it may be at once available in an efficient condition when wanted. It is in the highest degree wasteful to allow this essential factor in the creation of wealth to deteriorate when it is not in actual use. An employer who adopted such a course with his machines, or a farmer who thus farmed his land, would be held up to derision as incompetent. Once it is recognised that unemployed labour should be treated as carefully as unemployed land or capital, a great step forward will have been taken; and we can then address ourselves whole-heartedly to determining on whom the responsibility for its preservation shall rest, and the methods likely to achieve the desired end.

CHAPTER III

In this chapter we shall consider those casual workers, out of work on June 7, 1910, who are permanently under-employed, but are, as far as we could ascertain, more or less earnestly seeking for work. The class includes a great variety of types : (1) the man who depends principally upon a particular industrial firm or group of trades for intermittent employment ; (2) the man who interchanges two or more seasonal employments in a more or less regular succession ; (3) the outdoor labourer ; (4) the porter with a connection of his own ; and (5) a large number of men who are willing to turn their hand to any work, indoor or out. It also includes (6) a small number who, at one time in their career, have been skilled workmen. The only characteristic which these types have in common, which justifies their being grouped into one class, is that they have all for at least two years depended for their livelihood upon temporary employment. We here definitely exclude from consideration casual workers who are connected with the building trades, whether skilled workmen, such as bricklayers, carpenters, or painters, or unskilled labourers, who rely entirely or principally on the building trades for their living.

The questions which we shall seek to answer are the following :—

> *First.*—What is the probable number of casual workers, as here defined, in York ?
>
> *Second.*—How is it that these men are employed in casual and not in regular work ? Is it due, for instance, (*a*) to their home training, or (*b*) to personal failings, either of physique, or character, or (*c*) to industrial and economic conditions, of which they are the victims, but for which they are not responsible ?
>
> *Third.*—How many men have never been regularly employed, and how many were regularly employed at one time, but have since become casuals ? In the latter case, what has made them casuals, and what prevents them from resuming regular work ?
>
> *Fourth.*—Are their lives on the whole fairly satisfactory, or is there marked evidence of demoralisation and degradation ? In a word, does this class consist of " unemployables " in the making ?

These questions, with a few remarks on the methods which the facts suggest for remedying some of the evils connected with casual labour, will form the principal subject-matter of this chapter.

The class of casual workers is a large one, consisting of 441 men, but it must be remembered that we deal in this chapter only with those who happened to be out of work on June 7, 1910, and the total number of men in York who depend upon casual employment for their livelihood is considerably greater. We have no means of knowing what that total number is, but, judging from such information as we have, it can hardly be less than 700, and may very possibly be more. Still, it may be taken as practically certain that, whatever it be, the main characteristics of the individuals composing it are identical with those of the men here described in detail.

The class may be divided at the outset into two groups : viz. those who have, and those who have not, been engaged at some time or other in regular work, that is, in continuous work for one employer, lasting over at least a year.[1]

MEN WHO HAVE NEVER WORKED REGULARLY

(83 IN NUMBER)

This group is a comparatively small one, and can soon be disposed of. In order to help the reader better to picture the men it includes, we give on pp. 88 to 91 certain extracts from our investigators' note-books with regard to each of them.

[1] Eighteen doubtful cases have been added to those who probably have been engaged in regular work.

CASUAL WORKERS WHO HAVE NEVER BEEN IN REGULAR WORK (83 IN NUMBER)

Present Age	Present Condition. Physique.	Character.	Nature of Casual Occupations.	Nature of Permanent Occupation said to be desired.	Apparent Personal Handicaps in Search for Regular Work.	Average Weekly Casual Earnings.[1]	Average Weekly Income of Rest of Household.[1]	No. of Persons in Household, Adults	Children (under 16).	Is Family under Poverty Line?[1]
26, 22, 19	Good ? ?	Bad / Good	Cattle drover	Joiner	? ?	? ?	? ? ?	2 2 0	1 1	? ? No
32	Strong	"	Brickyard in summer, joiner's labourer in winter	Any	None	18/-	18/-	2		"
28, 67	Excellent / One arm crippled, subject to fits	Excellent / Very bad	Cab-driver, canvasser, farm labourer, navvy		"	18/6		1 2	2	" : "
66	Feeble	Good	Carter, ostler, navvy / Was a cab-driver, occasionally with horse dealer	Carter or navvy	" Age	10/- ?	?	2	?	?
67, 34	Good / Robust	Drinker of low type ?	Formerly farm work and jobbing gardener		"	?	? ?	2 8		? No
54	Good	Superior type of navvy	Porter, hawker, fruit dealer / Farm labourer, bricklayer's labourer, wool trade		"	14/-		2		Yes
32	Good, but rather deaf	Doubtful	Builder's and general labourer, toll collector, navvy		Age	6/-	3/-	3		No
49	Good	Good average worker	(Army 6 years to 1902), gardener, engineer's and bricklayer's labourer	Any		?	18/-	4	1	" Yes
30	"	Very good	Bricklayer's and farm labourer				Over 20/-	3		?
28	"	Good	Bricklayer's labourer and furniture remover				12/-	2	1	No
48	Mentally deficient	Gambler and drinker	Gas worker, summer porter, builder's labourer	General labourer	Mental deficiency	?		2	2	"
26	Good	One of worst families in York	(Army 6 years, 1883-1889), unloading boats, mixing putty, carrying coals			17/-		2	1	No
31	Excellent	Good discharge, drinker	Navvy and general labourer (Army 8 years to 1908), railway porter		Reserve pay	3/6		2		Yes

Age	Physical	Character	Occupation and work history		Remarks							Yes/No
29	"	Good discharge	(Army 3 years to 1907), farm labourer, hawker, general labourer		"	13/6			2	2		"
33	?	Drinker	(Army 7 years), dealer in old iron, farm work		"	11/6			2	3		"
28 / 40	Strong / Good	Exemplary discharge / Good	(Army to Feb. 1910), railway porter / Navvy, boot repairer, rag and bone gatherer	Any	"	6/6 / 4/-			1 2	: 4		? / Yes
24 or 25	Fit	Respectable family, allowed to loaf	With milkman one day per week		Probably giving help in father's shop	?	5/-		3	1		No
33 / 33 / 23	Good, but dense / Delicate / Mentally and physically below par	Good / Steady / Inclined to loaf	Farm labourer, navvy, gardener / Painter's labourer, sales porter / (Army 2½ years), looking after horses, window cleaning	Any	Infirmity / Living on sisters	9/- / 10/- / 3/-			2 2 6	2 6 :		Yes / ? / ?
38	Good	Bad	(Army 13 years to 1906), railway porter, painter, unloading boats	?	"Utterly casual family"	15/-	5/-		2	2	5/-	No
22	Strong	Good	Started in brickyard, brewer's labourer, vanman, tout			?	10/6		2	2	10/6	?
19	Good	Inclined to loaf, but good worker	Confectioner's labourer, cattle drover, seed, etc., mixing			3/-	48/6		4	5	48/6	No
23	Strong	Unreliable	(Army 1906-1909, 3 years), cattle drover, seed merchant's labourer		Reserve pay	?	7/-		6		7/-	Yes
46	Healthy	Respectable	Brickmaker, farm labourer		Probably almost always in work / Lowest type of worker	18/-			8	2		No
28	Strong	Ignorant and coarse, heavy drinker	Farm labourer and cattle drover		Bad reputation / Nearly always employed	? / 8/-			2	2		? / No
42 / 28	" / ?	Drinker and gambler / Quite unreliable	Last 5 years sales porter, navvy / Carter, unloading boats, farm labourer		Probably reserve pay / Bad reputation				1 1			?
29	Strong	Drinker, unreliable	(Army 3 years, 1899-1906), waiter, window cleaner, and general labourer			?	8/-		1		8/-	Yes
49	Strong	Drinker, quite unreliable	(Army 3 years, 1899-1901), carter and catch jobs, navvy	Any	Reserve pay	? / ?			8	:		No / ?
23 / 27	Good / Strong	Fair (poor home) / Good worker	Railway and factory porter / (Army 1903-1906), brickyard, gas works, cattle market, auctions			? / ?			1	:		? / ?
24	Mostly working, good		Brickyard until 5 years ago, cattle market, bill delivering			5/6			5	4		?
27	Drinker, rowdy, police case		Farm labourer, bricklayer's labourer, painter		Just been in prison	?	?			2		?
36	Good	Good	Was comb worker (irregular), now cattle drover, brickyard and farm labourer		Nearly always employed	10/-	18/-		4		18/-	Yes
36 / 28	Strong / Healthy	Appears good / Fair	Brickyard labourer and cattle drover / Ostler, paper-hanger, cattle drover, whitewasher, grocer's assistant, farm labourer			5/6 / 4/-	42/-		4 5	: 1	42/-	No / "

1 Including all regular pensions, poor relief, etc., but not occasional gifts or savings.

2 See note, p. 61.

CASUAL WORKERS WHO HAVE NEVER BEEN IN REGULAR WORK (83 IN NUMBER)—continued

Present Age.	Present Condition — Physique.	Character.	Nature of Casual Occupations.	Nature of Permanent Occupation said to be desired.	Apparent Personal Handicaps in Search for Regular Work.	Average Weekly Casual Earnings.1	Average Weekly Income of Rest of Household.1	No. of Persons in Household.1 — Adults.	Children (under 16).	Is Family under Poverty Line?2
29	Healthy	Good discharge	(Army 8 years to 1908), carter, railway carriage works and general labourer	Any	Reserve pay	8/6	..	2	2	Yes
43	Good	Very lazy	Wood chopping	....	....		6/-	2	8	,,
31	,,	Respectable .	Cattle drover	....	....	8/6	..	2	8	,,
21	,,	Gambler, but good worker	Carter, farm labourer	....	....	10/-	?	1	..	No
25	Strong	Drinker .	Winter—gas works, hawker, brickyard labourer	....	....	?	?	4	..	Yes
32	Mentally defective		Snow shovelling and other catch work (very little)	Any	Mental deficiency	?	?	5	1	?
43	Underfed	,,	Saw-mill, corporation labourer, navvy and general labourer	,,		?	?	?	?	?
27	Big and strong	Fair .	Cattle drover	....		4/-	4/-	2	1	Yes
48	Healthy ?	Respectable ?	Bandsman, factory labourer	General labourer	Partly relies on wife's earnings	?	?	6	..	?
41			Painter's labourer	....	Age Probably good average earnings as painter's labourer	?	..	1	..	?
25	Poor	Gambler, was in reformatory school for theft.	Farm work, selling papers, general labouring, snow shovelling	Any	....	?	?	?	?	?
28	Good	Good .	(Army 3 years), cattle market and auctions. Winter—gas works	Any	....	6/6	?	?	?	?
24	,,	Inclined to loaf	(Army 2 years, 14-16), casual railway porter and tout	....	....	?	?	?	?	?
30	,,	?	(Army 8 years to 1907), farm labourer, navvy, general labourer	Any	....	8/-	4/-	2	2	Yes
85	Flabby	Decent .	(Army 12 years), railway porter, farm labourer, navvy, general labourer	Bricklayer's or general labourer	....	10/-	..	2	..	,,
22	Strong and healthy	Good discharge	(Army 6 years, age 14-22), not yet had time. Builder's and general labourer	Any	Reserve pay	?	5/-	8	8	?

Age	Physique	Character	Occupations	Fit for	Cause						
23	Healthy	Lazy	Brickmaker, glass worker, pedlar, selling papers			9/-			2		Yes
21	"	Respectable	Helping at home in milk trade	Any	None	?	61/-		5	1	No?
30	Good	"	Navvying, auction sales			4/-			2	2	?
29	"	Shiftless	Cabman, brickyard labourer, ostler, cattle drover, painter, etc.						2	3	Yes
45	"	Doubtful, probably drinker	(Army 6 years), farm labourer, cobbler, navvy	Any		10/-	1/-		2	5	Yes
35	Very good	Not anxious for permanent work	Cattle drover, cab-driver, farm labourer			?	?		2	2	?
21	Good	Lazy, bad stock	Cattle drover, farm labourer, wood hawker			?	?		3	1	Yes
31	Undersized	Gambler	Hawker, farm labourer, cattle drover			?	?		?	2	?
32		Shiftless, but not bad character	Furniture porter, shop porter, window cleaner, bill distributor			7/6			2	2	Yes
21	Moderately strong	Probably betting, fairly good	Selling papers, casual warehouseman	General labourer	Does not want regular work	?	42/-		?	?	?
19	Good	Good army discharge	Selling papers, 2 months with printer	Any	Poor worker	5/-	8/-		3	1	Yes
85	?		(Joined army at 16, for 12 years), general labourer, goods porter	"	Typical slumster	7/-			2	3	?
80	Robust	Good	Nipper, brick works, builder's labourer, farm work, sorting potatoes			?	?		2	1	?
21	Healthy	Lazy	Cattle drover for 6 months, butcher's boy		Unwillingness to work regularly	9/-	36/-		6	1	No
43	"	Shiftless	For 12 years pigman, field work, cattle drover		Unwillingness to work regularly	10/-	12/-		4	8	Yes
86	Very good	Good	Jobbing gardener	Gardener	None	10/-	18/-		2	?	?
58	Very stout	Fairly good	Markets, navvy, farm labourer		Age	8/-			1	:	?
61	Good	Bad lot, drinker	Brickyard labourer, hay-making and other farm work		Age and bad reputation	13/6	18/-		6	:	?
61 or 65	Not robust	Drinker, often in prison	General labourer, contract work		Age		5/-		2	2	?
19	Good, but underfed		Farm labourer, gas works labourer		"	?			1	:	No
20	Very strong, probably weak mentally	Good	Confectioner's labourer (rare)		Probably mental dullness		87/6		4	1	?
	Not strong		Farm work, organ-grinding		Delicate health	3/-			4	1	?
19	Robust	Good	Hawker		Family of hawkers	?	Over 30/-		3	2	?
19	Good	?	Cattle drover		Bad home influences	6/-			?	?	?
19	?	?	Glass-works labourer, selling papers		Bad home influences	?			?	?	?

¹ Including all regular pensions, poor relief, etc., but not occasional gifts or savings.   ² See note, p. 61.

We only give here a comparatively small part of the information gained regarding each case, partly from exigencies of space, and partly because much of the information was given on the understanding that it would not be published in such a form as might lead to the identification of the persons concerned.[1] It will be noted that the ages of the men in this group vary from 19 to 67.[2] It is notoriously difficult to get any exact information with regard to the upbringing of men of this class, but such data as we have gathered confirm what was a natural supposition, that the great majority come from unsatisfactory slum homes, and have never really had a chance to become good workers.

The existence of this group points to the import-

[1] It will be readily understood that, in many instances, a casual worker could not, if he would, give accurate information as to his average earnings ; and hence the figures regarding them must be looked upon as merely approximate. Nevertheless, they serve to show whether the earnings are substantial or slight. The statements of the earnings of other members of the family are more accurate, since in the majority of cases they refer to regular employment. We have not submitted them to the employers, but have checked them to a certain extent from our knowledge of the wages current in York in different occupations.

[2]

Age.	Number.	Per cent.
19 to 25	26	31·3
26 ,, 30	19	22·9
31 ,, 35	14	16·9
36 ,, 40	5	6·0
41 ,, 45	6	7·3
46 ,, 50	5	6·0
51 ,, 55	1	1·2
56 ,, 60	1	1·2
61 ,, 65	3	3·6
Over 65	3	3·6
	83	100·0

ance of compulsory training for all unemployed lads. It is not unlikely that if these 83 men had undergone such training, and if, associated with it, there had been the personal help and friendship that is given in connection with Care Committees, not a few of them might have entered the ranks of the regular workers. It would be a mistake to suppose that they are nearly all of unsatisfactory character or physique. On the contrary, 38 appeared to be fully up to the average of unskilled workers, both physically and mentally. Nothing was known against their characters, and many of them worked well in their temporary jobs; probably lack of training alone is responsible for their never having been engaged in regular work. Twenty-eight of the group appeared to be physically strong, but of unsatisfactory character, but to what extent their characters have deteriorated as a result of casual work we cannot say. Only 17 showed definite signs of physical weakness, and here again we do not know how far it is a cause and how far a consequence of their irregular manner of life.[1]

In passing, it may be remarked that 20 men in this group have been in the army. Possibly they entered because they were not a success in the industrial world, but the fact that after leaving they

---

[1]   Of the 83 men, 38 were of good health and good character.

    9 ,, ,, poor ,, ,, good ,,
    28 ,, ,, good ,, ,, bad ,,
    8 ,, ,, poor ,, ,, bad ,,

The term " poor health ' includes mental deficiencies.

still remain casual workers, suggests the advisability
of so training men while they are with the colours,
that they may become efficient and regular workers
when they re-enter industrial life.

MEN WHO HAVE ONCE BEEN IN REGULAR EMPLOYMENT
(358 IN NUMBER)

The main interest in this chapter centres in those
who have once worked regularly. It is of the utmost
importance to know why they have ceased to do so,
and the detailed particulars given in the following
pages will help us to answer this question.[1]

Ages.—Dealing first with the ages of men in this
group, which we know for 349 of them, it will be
noted that they vary from 19 to 76, classified as
follows :—

Age.	No.	Per cent.	Per cent of all Men of these Ages living in York.
19 to 25	75	21·5	1·4
26 „ 30	68	19·5	1·9
31 „ 35	36	10·3	1·2
36 „ 40	32	9·2	1·2
41 „ 45	32	9·2	1·5
46 „ 50	37	10·6	1·9
51 „ 55	29	8·3	1·8
56 „ 60	14	4·0	1·2
61 „ 65	18	5·1	1·7
66 „ 70	7	2·0	1·0
Over 70	1	0·3	0·1
	349	100·0	Average 1·4

It is an unsatisfactory feature that so many young

[1] See footnote, p. 92.

men should only be casually employed. It will be
noted that over half the members of this group are
under 36 years of age.

Proportion of Skilled Workers.—Only 68 have
been skilled workers.[1] This fact indicates the comparative security which the possession of a trade
gives a man. It will not protect him from recurring
periods of unemployment at times of trade depression ;
but judging from the present analysis it generally
secures him against sinking down, through long-
continued inability to find regular work, to the level
of a " casual."

Reasons why last Regular Employment was lost.—
We have taken considerable pains to ascertain, wherever
possible, the reasons why the last regular employment
of these men was lost. The information obtained from
the workers themselves in the first instance was
checked, where at all possible, by reference to other
persons, usually their previous employers. Setting
aside 93 cases where the statistics seemed of doubtful
value,[2] we are able to report on 265 cases.

[1] The figure cannot be stated with absolute accuracy, as in many cases
the particulars given regarding occupations followed were too indefinite to
enable us to say with certainty whether they were skilled or not. We refer
to such descriptions as "comb worker," "cement worker," etc. Our estimate
of 70 as the number of once skilled workers is probably an outside one.
In addition to these there are 41 who followed partially skilled trades,
i.e. trades skilled in their higher, but not in their lower branches, *e.g.*
engine-driver, gardener, etc. The presumption is that the men found in
this class followed the lower branches of these occupations.

[2] This number includes many cases of alleged "slackness of trade"
(entered in the table in quotation marks) which could not be verified.

CASUAL WORKERS WHO HAVE BEEN

| | Last Regular Employment. | | | | | | Present Condition. |
Nature.	Dura-tion (years).	Was it preceded by an industrial career indicating power to retain permanent work ?	Date of Leaving.	Cause of Leaving.	Age at time of Leaving.	Present Age.	Physique.
Confectioner's labourer	8	Yes	April 1905	Illness (barber's rash)	24	29	Smart. Bad foot .
Confectioner . . .	4	,,	1907	Bad time-keeping, ill-health	25	28	Looks consumptive
Flour-mill labourer .	1½	,,	Aug. 1909	Ill-health . . .	30	31	Consumptive
Iron-moulder . .	20	,,	1899	?	32	43	Defective sight .
Coach fitter . . .	7	,,	?	Illness	44	45	Poor health . . .
Farm servant . .	¼	,.	June 1910	Skin eruption . .	25	25	Strong, but temporarily suffering from skin trouble
Carriage washer . .	3	,,	May 1904	Ill-health (lumbago) .	41	47	Good . . . .
Chocolate moulder .	1	No	1907	Illness . . .	18	21	Very weakly .
Wood sawyer . .	24	Yes	1902	Failing sight . .	44	52	Fairly good .
Saddler	13	,,	1905	Slackness (motors ruining trade)	28	33	Good . . . .
Engineer's labourer .	5	,,	March 1903	Failure of firm .	33	40	Strong . . . .
Cowboy . . .	6	?	1890	Inherited money .	20	40	Healthy . . .
Iron-moulder . .	7	Yes	?	Slackness of trade .	22	22	,, . . .
Furniture salesman .	½	,,	Oct. 1909	Ill-health . . .	32	33	Moderate . . .
Gardener . . .	13	,,	Aug. 1905	Intemperance . .	38	43	Weak . . . .
Joiner	4	No	?	Finish of contract .	25	26	Crippled . . .
,, ...	?	Yes	?	Slackness of work .	?	30	Strong . . . .
Poultry dealer . .	5	,,	1900	Ill-health . . .	34	44	Good . . . .
Circular sawyer . .	24	,,	April 1908	Death of Employer .	53	55	,, ...
Groom	4	,,	1895	Dispute with Employer	45	60	Not good . . .
Cabinetmaker . .	29	,,	1900	Retirement of Employer	50	60	Very good . . .
Confectioner's labourer	7	,,	1906	Dispute with foreman	21	25	Good . . . .
Engineer's labourer .	35	,,	1902	Failure of firm . .	54	62	,, . . .
Warehouseman . .	25	,,	1906	?	64	68	,, . . .
Packer	10	,,	?	?	?	70	Very good . . .
Confectioner's labourer	About 50	No	1905	Age	65	70	Healthy . . .
Engineer's labourer .	22	Yes	Oct. 1903	Closing of Works .	39	46	Underfed . . .
Ironfounder's labourer .	1 or less	No	1887	To enlist . . .	16	39	Good . . . .
Brickworks labourer .	1	Yes	?	Slackness . . .	26	27	,, ...
Labourer at barracks .	2	,,	1906	Regiment left York .	45	49	,, ...

IN REGULAR WORK (358 IN NUMBER)

Present Condition. Character.	Nature of Casual Occupations.	Nature of Permanent Occupations sought.	Apparent Personal Handicaps in Search for Regular Work.	Average Weekly Casual Earnings.[1]	Average Weekly Income of Rest of Household.[1]	Adults.	Children (under 16).	Is Family under Poverty Line?[2]
?	?	Any	Temporary damage to foot	?	..	..	..	?
Rather doubtful	Casual labourer	Labourer . . .	Delicate health	3/-	5/-	2	2	Yes
?	Any odd jobs . . .	Any	,,	1/-	15/-	3	1	,,
Good . . .	Boot repairing, 2nd hand. Clothing shop. Farm work	Labourer . . .	Bad eyesight .	15/-	?	2	4	?
Respectable .	Nil	Jobbing work .	Rheumatism and sciatica	..	20/-	2	2	No
Good . .	,, ...	Farm work . . .	Skin trouble and mental deficiency	15/-	88/-	8	..	,,
,, . . .	Hawker of soaps . .	Labourer . . .	None . .	7/6	4/-	2	1	Yes
Fairly good .	Labourer . . .	,, ...	Ill-health .	3/-	..	2	1	,,
Good . .	Casual goods porter .	Any	Defective sight .	15/-	..	2	..	No
,, . .	Insurance collecting and keeps little grocery shop, etc.	,, ...	None . .	6/2	?	2	3	?
,, . .	Glazing and odd plumbing	,, ...	Deafness . .	7/-	7/-	2	7	Yes
Spendthrift .	Labourer . . .	Labourer . . .	?	5/-	?	2	1	No
Good . .	Own trade. 1, 2 or 3 days per week	Own trade . .	None . .	?	?	?	?	,,
?	Nil	Draper's assistant, salesman or clerk	Delicate health	?	?	?	?	,,
Unreliable .	Working in his own garden and odd jobs	Gardening . . .	Intemperance .	?	37/6	5	..	,,
Good . .	Painting, gardening, odd jobs, whitewashing	Own trade . . .	Diseased hip, one short leg	8/6	70/-	4	..	,,
,, . .	Joinering, labouring, etc.	,, ...	None . .	?	?	?	?	?
,, . .	Works 2 days a week for employer, and attends market	,, ...	,, . .	6/-	?	?	?	?
,, . .	Nil for 2 years . .	Any	Age . . .	..	8/-	4	1	Yes
,, . .	Coachman . . .	Groom	,, . . .	?	?	3	..	No
Doubtful .	Own trade . . .	Any	,, . . .	?	?	?	?	?
Good . .	Catch jobs, nil for 3 months	,, ...	None . .	..	8/-	4	1	Yes
,, . .	Collecting mushrooms, berries, etc., relief work	Gardening or any .	Age . . .	1/-	35/6	5	1	No
Exemplary .	Farm labourer, watchman	Farm work or any .	,, . . .	8/-	15/6	3	..	,,
Very good .	Gardening, whitewashing	Painter or builder's labourer	,, . . .	1/6	14/-	3	..	Yes
Respectable .	Cleaning cattle pens .	Any	,, . . .	?	?	2	..	?
Excellent .	Window cleaner, pallbearer, bill distributor	General labourer .	Lack of intelligence	9/-	..	1	..	No
Good . .	(In army 8 years), chiefly builder's labourer	. . . .	None . .	..	..	2	3	Yes
,, . .	Cattle drover, catch work with butcher and milk dealer	General labourer .	,, . .	8/-	27/-	5	..	No
,, . .	Builder's labourer and whitewasher	. . . .	Age . . .	10/-	36/-	5	1	,,

[1] Including all regular pensions, poor relief, etc., but not occasional gifts or savings.   [2] See note, p. 61.

H

CASUAL WORKERS WHO HAVE BEEN

		Last Regular Employment.				Present Condition.	
Nature.	Dura-tion (years).	Was it preceded by an industrial career indicating power to retain permanent work?	Date of Leaving.	Cause of Leaving.	Age at time of Leaving.	Present Age.	Physique.
Packing-case maker .	2	Yes	1902	Insubordination . .	27	35	Good . . . .
Joiner's labourer . .	5	,,	1904	Closing of works. .	20	26	,, ...
Smith's labourer . .	3	,,	1904 or 1905	Dismissed (why?) .	32 or 33	38	,, ...
Canteen waiter . .	4	,,	1907	Canteen taken over by contractors	34	37	,, ...
Cab-driver . . .	1½	,,	?	Retirement of pro-prietor	?	47	,, ...
Machine attendant .	33	,,	1904	Closing of works. .	47	53	,, ...
?	?	?	?	?	?	33	Excellent . . .
?	?	?	?	?	?	25	Strong . . . .
Cab-driver . . .	2 or 3	?	Jan. 1908	?	37	39	Excellent . . .
Farm labourer . .	?	Yes	1910	Work seasonal . .	45	45	Robust . . . .
Coal porter . . .	3	,,	1907	?	22	25	,, ...
Carter	2	,,	1904	Objected to jobs given him	37	43	,, ...
Farm labourer and quarryman	11	?	1906	Retirement of em-ployer	37	41	Strong . . . .
"Taker-in"(glass works)	4	No	1904	To better himself .	17	23	Good . . . .
Flour-mill labourer .	1	Yes	Feb. 1910	Only temporary . .	22	23	Strong . . . .
Navvy on public works	2	,,	?	End of contract . .	?	41	Robust . . . .
Flour packer . .	4	,,	Sept. 1906	To better himself .	22	26	,, ...
Ostler	3	,,	1892	,, ,, .	20	38	Excellent . . .
?	?	?	?	?	?	40	Strong . . . .
Groom	4	Yes	?	To better himself .	?	50	Healthy . . .
Sawyer	1½	,,	1902	Bankruptcy of firm .	32	40	,, ...
Drilling machinist .	26	,,	1900	To better himself .	42	52	Fairly good . .
Drayman . . .	14	,,	Aug. 1905	Inefficiency . .	42	47	,, ...
Coal carter . . .	7	,,	1905	Death of employer .	39	44	,, ...
Striker	11	,,	,,	Illness	45	50	,, ...
Carter	2½	,,	,,	"Slackness" . .	26	29	Undersized . . .
Joiner	31	,,	1901	?	57	66	Fair . . . .

IN REGULAR WORK (358 IN NUMBER)—*continued*

Present Condition. Character.	Nature of Casual Occupations.	Nature of Permanent Occupations sought.	Apparent Personal Handicaps in search for Regular Work.	Average Weekly Casual Earnings.[1]	Average Weekly Income of Rest of Household.[1]	Adults.	Children (under 16).	Is Family under Poverty Line?[2]
Good	Cattle auctions, hawking, trading in old iron	....	None	16/-	..	2	3	No
,,	Hotel porter in summer, club waiter in winter	Hotel porter or waiter	,,	7/-	34/-	6	..	,,
,,	Cattle market and auctions, unloading boats	Any	?	7/-	..	2	..	Yes
,,	Canteen waiter, railway porter	Waiter or railway porter	None	?	..	2	5	,,
,,	Waiter	Cab-driver	Age	7/6	3/6	3	..	,,
,,	Labourer, sand yard, etc.	....	,,	3/-	..	1	..	,,
Excellent	Gardener and other casual work	Any	None	..	1/-	2	3	,,
,,	Engineer's and general labourer	,,	,,	?	?	2	..	?
,,	General labourer, hawker	,,	,,	13/-	9/-	3	3	Yes
Good	Seasonal farm work, sorting wool, unloading boats, general labourer	,,	,,	10/-	13/-	3	2	No
,,	Bricklayer's labourer, markets, furniture remover	,,	,,	..	..	1	..	Yes
Excellent	Farm work, unloading coal, carting, navvying	,,	,,	12/-	6/-	3	5	,,
Industrious	Builder's labourer, carting, gardening, and other	,,	,,	5/6	..	1	..	No
Good	Farm work, engine cleaner, builder's labourer, navvy	,,	,,	8/	3/6	3	1	Yes
Excellent	Farm work, carting	None	,,	20/-	..	3	3	,,
Good	Navvy on public works, farm work	Navvying	,,	15/-	17/6	3	6	,,
,,	Coal porter	Any	,,	7/-	Say 22/-	5	3	,,
Excellent	(Army 1892 to 1902). General labourer, wool sorter	,,	,,	7/6	..	2	..	,,
Good worker	Coal porter and carter	Carting or any	,,	10/-	10/-	2	5	,,
Good	Groom and gardener	Groom or gardener	Age	..	?	?	?	?
,,	Unloading boats	Any	None	8/-	5/-	3	1	Yes
,,	Coal yard and general labourer	,,	Age	5/-	10/-	4	2	No
,,	Coal yard labourer	....	None	22/-	..	2	3	,,
,,	Unloading boats and on river craft	On river craft	,,	10/-	56/-	2	6	No
Very good	Very little, painter's model and odd jobs	....	Age	..	20/-	3	..	,,
?	Cattle fairs, rag and bone sorting, unloading boats	....	Lack of intelligence	15/-	..	2	2	Yes
Heavy drinker, but good references	Bill delivering	....	Age	10/-	10/-	3	..	No

[1] Including all regular pensions, poor relief, etc., but not occasional gifts or savings.　　　　[2] See note, p. 61.

CASUAL WORKERS WHO HAVE BEEN

	Last Regular Employment.						Present Condition.	
Nature.	Dura-tion (years).	Was it preceded by an industrial career indicating power to retain permanent work?	Date of Leaving.	Cause of Leaving.	Age at time of Leaving.	Present Age.	Physique.	
Machine attendant	25	Yes	1902	Closing of works	61	69	Excellent	
Butcher	5	?	1880	To start for himself	30	60	?	
Gamekeeper	7	Yes	1897	To better himself	63	76	Strong	
Carter	15	,,	1903	Sickness	48	55	Lame with rheumatism	
Engine-driver	15	,,	1905	Intemperance	50	55	Good	
Glass-blower's apprentice	3	No	1906	Finger cut off	16	20	Healthy	
Engineer's labourer	11	,,	1899	Closing of works	24	35	Good	
Labourer on public works	2	,,	1904	Finish of contract	36	42	Strong	
Forge hand	5	,,	1903	Closing of works	21	28	Very strong	
Brickyard labourer	About 1	,,	1886	Failure of employer	15	39	Good	
Labourer	1½	Yes	1909	?	37	38	Healthy	
French polisher	About 1	,,	1906	Removal of employer	16	20	Strong	
Engineer's labourer	Abt. 4 (doubtf'l whether regular)	,,	1909	"Slackness"[1]	32	33	Good	
Flour-mill labourer	3	,,	1907	Sickness	26	29	Strong	
Forgeman	35	,,	1904	Closing of works	47	53	Good	
Groom and gardener	2	,,	1900	To enlist	18	28	,,	
Carriage painter's apprentice	7	No	,,	,,	18	28	,,	
Labourer	2	,,	?	End of contract	?	49	Strong	
Confectioner's or builder's labourer	2 or 3	Yes	1907	"Slackness"[1]	20	23	Good	
Errand boy	,,	No	About 1894	?	16 or 17	31	Exceptionally robust dull,	
Builder's labourer	2	,,	1896	Intemperance	39	53	Healthy	
Billposter	7	,,	1906	Firm changed hands	24	28	Strong	
Coal hugger	3	Yes	,,	Displacement by machinery	53	57	Good	
Engineer's labourer	6	,,	1909	?	44	45	Fair	
Bottle washer	7	No	1903	To better himself	23	30	Moderate	
Confectioner's labourer	2¼	,,	1907	Dismissed (reason unknown)	16	19	Not strong	
Engine-driver	25	Yes	Sept. 1905	Inefficiency	43	48	"Capable of work"	

[1] Reason given not checked. [2] Including all regular pensions, poor relief, etc.

IN REGULAR WORK (358 IN NUMBER)—*continued*

Present Condition. Character.	Nature of Casual Occupations.	Nature of Permanent Occupations Sought.	Apparent Personal Handicaps in Search for Regular Work.	Average Weekly Casual Earnings.2	Average Weekly Income of Rest of Household.2	No of Persons in Household. Adults.	Children (under 16).	Is Family under Poverty Line?3
Good . . .	Coopering and manure labourer	....	Age . . .	4/-	5/-	2	..	Yes
Sober . . .	Ostler, cattle drover .	....	,, . . .	8/-	5/-	1	2	,,
Excellent . .	Gardener, painter, white-washer	....	,, . . .	?	..	1	..	?
Reformed character	Gardener . . .	....	,, . . .	5/-	24/-	4	4	Yes
Confirmed drunkard	Platelayer and in brick-yard	....	,, . . .	?	4/-	2	..	?
Gambler and inclined to loaf	Farm work, bricklayer's labourer	Any	Poor character	10/-	33/-	4	3	No
Drinker and waster	Pickpocket, bricklayer's and joiner's labourer	,, ...	,,	?	..	2	3	?
Drinker . . .	Farm work, bricklayer's labourer	....	,,	12/-	..	1	..	No
Hard-working and respectable	Iron and steel worker, builder's labourer	....	None . .	12/-	..	2	5	Yes
Low type . .	Builder's labourer, cattle drover	....	Not trained to regular work	?	..	2	2	,,
Good . . .	Labourer, cleaner . .	....	None . .	4/-	13/-	3	4	,,
Doubtful, inclined to loaf	Carter and own trade .	Any	Shiftless . .	..	62/-	4	..	No
Drinker . . .	(8 years army, to 1906), navvy, builder's labourer	,, ...	Reserve pay and laziness	16/-	..	2	2	Yes
Very decent . .	Bricklayer's and general labourer	,, ...	None . .	17/-	8/-	2	4	No
Very good . .	Farm work, bricklayer's and general labourer	....	Age . . .	1/-	31/6	7	1	Yes
Good . . .	(Army 3 years, to 1902), groom, gardener, bricklayer's labourer	Groom or gardener .	None . .	18/6	..	1	..	No
,, . . .	(Army 8 years, to 1908), painter, bricklayer's labourer, hawker	Any	,, .	10/6	..	1	..	,,
Hard worker . .	General and farm labourer	,, ...	Not trained to regular work	10/-	6/-	3	1	Yes
Very good . .	Bottler and general labourer	General labourer .	None . .	..	28/-	5	..	No
Good . . .	Carter	General labourer or carter	Mental density	..	?	?	?	?
Drinker, been in prison	Hawker, cattle drover, etc.	....	None . .	12/-	3/-	2	1	Yes
Steady and hard-working	Travelling with picture show, billposter	....	,, . .	..	10/-	2	1	,,
Very fair . .	Navvy and builder's labourer	....	Age . . .	?	?	?	?	?
Drunkard and callous	Cattle drover, holds horses, market porter	....	Bad appearance and reputation	6/-	..	1	..	?
Inclined to loaf, otherwise good	Railway summer porter, canvasser, waiter, furniture remover	Light work . .	Delicate health	?	12/-	3	..	No
Does not want steady work	Unloading boats . .	Any	Bad home .	7/-	21/-	4	1	,,
Probably loafing .	Navvy, post office and general labourer	....	Age . . .	3/-	22/-	4	3	Yes

but not occasional gifts or savings.

3 See note, p. 61.

CASUAL WORKERS WHO HAVE BEEN

			Last Regular Employment.				Present Condition.
Nature.	Dura-tion (years).	Was it preceded by an industrial career indicating power to retain permanent work?	Date of Leaving.	Cause of Leaving.	Age at time of Leaving.	Present Age.	Physique.
Railway carriage cleaner	3	Yes	1907	Probably laziness .	19	22	Weak eyesight . .
Confectioner's labourer	2	,,	1899	To enlist (army 8 years)	17	28	Damaged eye . .
Barman (with father) .	4 or 5	,,	1908	?	24	26	Crushed finger . .
Confectioner's labourer	3	No	1905	Inefficiency . . .	17	22	Very dense, "practically unemployable"
? (Army 3 years, to 1905)	?	?	?	?	?	27	Good . . . .
Chimney sweep . .	?	..	?	?	?	Over 50	Deaf and mentally deficient
"Taker-in" (glass works)	2	Yes	1907	?	22	25	Mentally deficient .
Confectioner's labourer	About 20	No	1905	?	36	41	Poor . . . .
,, ,,	Say 32	,,	1902 or 1903	Inefficiency . . .	43	50	Mentally deficient .
,, ,,	2 or 3	,,	1901	Had an accident . .	17	26	Good . . . .
Glassworks labourer .	2	,,	1906	?	16	20	?
Railway labourer (locomotive department)	3	,,	1904	Removal of works .	23	29	Good . . . .
Salesman . . .	5½	Yes	1905	Theft, or similar offence	25	30	Destroyed by drink .
Foundry labourer .	9	,,	189?	"Slackness" . .	24	41	Corpulent . . .
Comb worker . .	6	No	1898	Closing of works .	abt. 19	31	Fairly healthy . .
Coal hawker . . .	24	Yes	1903	Retirement of employer	44	51	Underfed . . .
Sawyer	7	,,	1905	Bad sight accelerated by drink	35	40	Bad . . . .
Coach - builder's apprentice	8	No	1885	"To better himself " .	17	42	Healthy . . .
Shipyard labourer .	4	Yes	1901	To enlist (army to 1909)	26	35	,, . . .
Bottle washer . .	2 or 3	No	1890	To enlist (army 13 years, to 1904)	10	36	Strong . . . .
School caretaker . .	4 or 5	Yes	1904	Gave up post rashly .	31	37	Moderate . . .
Confectioner's labourer	3	,,	1899	To better himself .	20	31	Excellent . . .
Stableman . . .	4½	No	1888	To enlist (army to 1899)	16	38	?
? (Army 1902-1910) .	?	?	?	?	?	29	?
Engineer's labourer .	14	No	1899	"Slackness" . .	28	30	?
Confectioner's labourer	6	Yes	1908	Slackness . . .	19	21	Good . . . . .
Tinsmith's apprentice .	?	?	?	?	?	49	Bad eyesight, liable to giddiness

IN REGULAR WORK (358 IN NUMBER)—*continued*

Present Condition. Character.	Nature of Casual Occupations.	Nature of Permanent Occupations Sought.	Apparent Personal Handicaps in search for Regular Work.	Average Weekly Casual Earnings.[1]	Average Weekly Income of Rest of Household.[1]	No. of Persons in Household. Adults	Children (under 16)	Is Family under Poverty Line?[2]
Gambling and drinking, lazy	Cattle drover, tout	....	Loafing	5/6	..	1	..	?
Good discharge, but lazy	Casual goods porter	Groom, asylum attendant, or any	Low type	12/6	35/6	4	..	No
Lazy and shiftless	Timber carrier and odd jobs	....	,,	6/8	?	8	1	?
No energy	Selling papers	....	No energy of muscle or thought	5/-	28/-	4	1	No
Bad timekeeper	Gas works, navvy	....	None	22/6	..	2	2	,,
?	Charitable employment as sweep and general labourer	....	Inefficiency	?	..	1	..	?
Bad	Chops and hawks wood	....	Mental deficiency	8/-	?	?	?	?
Respectable	Organ-blower, boot-black	....	Ill-health	3/-	?	5	..	No
Respectable, sober	Coal carrier	....	Mental deficiency and age	?	?	5	2	?
"Black sheep"	Brickyard, sorting rags	....	No record as a worker	..	Over 50/-	5	2	No
Slumster	Keelman and other odd jobs	....	Since joined army	?	?	?	?	?
Fairly decent (slum family)	Bricklayer's labourer, factory porter	....	Inclined to loafing	16/-	..	1	..	No
Very bad record, drinker	Temporary clerk	Clerk	Bad appearance, no references	..	37/-	4	..	,,
Lazy, loafing blackguard	Cattle drover, striker, navvy, mill labourer, unloading boats	....	Quite demoralised	8/-	Over 16/-	3	1	,,
Drinker, been in prison	Cattle drover	....	Bad home	11/-	34/-	6	..	,,
Drinker, dissolute	Station tout	....	Age	10/-	8/-	3	1	Yes
Bad	Unloading boats, cattle drover, relief work	....	Bad reputation	12/-	..	2	4	,,
Good worker, but drinker	(Army 12 years 1885-1897), unloading boats	....	Practically always been casual	5/-	12/-	3	3	,,
Good discharge, steady	Firewood hawker, cattle drover	Any	Reserve pay	9/6	..	1	..	No
Contradictory	Coal filler, bill poster	....	Pension commuted?	10/-	10/-	3	..	,,
"Black sheep of family"	Painter, other catch work	....	Waiting for heritage	..	..	2	5	Yes
Exemplary discharge	(Army 8 years, to 1909), railway porter	Groom	Reserve pay	15/6	32/6	4	..	No
?	Farm labourer, bricklayer's labourer	....	,, ,,	?	?	5	..	,,
?	Factory porter	Coachman	,, ,,	?	..	1	..	?
Drinker, bad worker	Unloading boats, tillage, and other casual work	....	Inclined to loafing	10/-	5/-	3	..	No
Good	General labourer	Any	None	10/-	?	?	?	?
Given to drink	Chiefly unloading boats, also general labourer	....	Infirmity	3/-	8/-	2	..	Yes

[1] Including all regular pensions, poor relief, etc., but not occasional gifts or savings. [2] See note, p. 61.

CASUAL WORKERS WHO HAVE BEEN

Nature.	Dura-tion (years).	Was it preceded by an industrial career indicating power to retain permanent work?	Date of Leaving.	Cause of Leaving.	Age at time of Leaving.	Present Age.	Physique.
?	?	?	?	?	?	?	?
? ?	? ?	? ?	? ?	? ?	? ?	? ?	? ?
? ? (Ex-army) ? . . .	? ? ?	? ? ?	? ? ?	? ? ?	? ? ?	? ? ?	? ? ?
?	?	?	?	?	?	?	?
?	?	?	?	?	?	?	?
Packer	1½	Yes	June 1907	To better himself .	24	27	Good . . . .
Fireman . . .	14	,,	1907	Failure of firm . .	29	32	,, ...
Engine driller . .	7	,,	Dec. 1907	To enlist (army only 6 months)	26	29	Very good . . .
Confectioner's labourer	?	?	?	Failure of firm . .	?	24	Undersized . . .
Errand boy . . .	1⅛	No	1908	To better himself .	17	19	Alert, small . . .
Telegraph messenger .	1	,,	1907	Could not pass medical test	16	19	Underfed and neglected
?	?	?	Not later than 1899	?	?	36	?
Ostler	1	No	1908	?	25	27	?
Postman . . .	4 or 5	,,	1902	Intemperance . .	30	38	Healthy . . .
Commercial traveller .	1⅛	Yes	1908	,, . .	48	50	Good . . . .
Fitter	30	,,	1904	Closing of works .	47	53	Healthy . . .
Confectioner's labourer	15	No	1906	Intemperance . .	29	33	Fairly healthy . .
Labourer . . .	4	Yes	,,	Theft and imprison-ment	25	29	Poor . . . .
? (Ex-army) . . .	?	?	?	?	?	48	Lost one eye . . .
Sawyer	2	?	?	Retirement of em-ployer	?	26	Underfed and feeble .
Instrument-maker .	25	Yes	1907	Intemperance . .	40	43	Good . . . .
Box-maker . . .	7	,,	1906	Death of employer .	33	37	Slender, but healthy .
Furniture remover .	8	,,	,,	Intemperance . .	31	35	Fairly good . . .
Grocer's assistant .	6	,,	1904	To better himself .	24	abt. 30	Seems strong . . .

IN REGULAR WORK (358 IN NUMBER)—continued

Character.	Nature of Casual Occupations.	Nature of Permanent Occupations Sought.	Apparent Personal Handicaps in search for Regular Work.	Average Weekly Casual Earnings.[1]	Average Weekly Income of Rest of Household.[1]	Adults.	Children (under 16).	Is Family under Poverty Line?[2]
Drinker . . .	Farm work, cattle drover	....	Not trained to regular work	?	?	?	?	?
?	,, ,, ,,	....	,, ,,	?	..	1	..	?
Good worker, but hard drinker	Miller's labourer, loading boats	....	,, ,,	8/-	9/-	2	1	No
Respectable family	Waterman . . .	....	,, ,,	?	?	?	?	?
Lazy . . .	Station tout . . .	....	,, ,,	?	?	?	?	?
Steady and industrious	Painter	....	? ,,	?	?	?	?	?
Won't take regular work	Glass worker . . .	....	Not trained to regular work	?	?	?	?	?
Roving poacher .	Corporation labourer .	....	,, ,,	?	?	?	?	?
Good worker, steady	Bath-chairman, gardener	Any	None . .	?	?	3	..	?
Very respectable .	Carpet-beater, porter .	,, . . .	,, . . .	?	?	2	..	?
Bad stock, unreliable	Navvy, gravel pit, railway porter	Own trade . .	Bad reputation	10/-	?	?	?	?
Good . . .	Bill distributor . .	....	Dullness . .	6/-	48/4	5	..	No
Shiftless and drinker	Station tout . . .	....	Never kept work for long, bad reputation	6/-	..	1	..	?
Bad home life, but bright and willing	Farm and other casual labourer	Any	Bad home .	5/-	15/-	4	1	Yes
?	Carter, farm labourer .	....	Not trained to regular work	?	..	1	..	?
Good . . .	Mineral water bottler, boots, navvy	....	Practically always casual because looking after egoistic and ignorant invalid father	?	5/-	?	?	?
Drinker . . .	Labourer, "odd jobs," bricklayer's labourer	....	Intemperance .	?	?	4	..	?
Heavy drinker and unreliable	Shop assistant, canvasser	Work in clothing trade	,, .	6/-	36/-	4	2	No
?	Cattle drover, station tout	....	Age . . .	?	..	1	..	?
Fairly good worker, but heavy drinker	Hawker	....	Skin affection (through drink)	7/-	..	2	4	Yes
Drinker, and very lazy	Farm labourer, rag and bone collector	....	Imprisonment .	5/-	..	2	3	,,
Heavy drinker .	?	....	Bad reputation	?	?	?	?	?
Was in prison for theft, heavy drinker	Chopping wood and other philanthropic employment	Any	,, ,,	?	32/-	4	2	No
Good worker, but heavy drinker	Bill distributor, rag gatherer, sandwichman	....	Shady character partly maintained by wife	10/-	10/6	2	4	Yes
(Theft) and drinker	Box-maker, carter, general labourer	....	Been in prison, bad record	16/-	5/-	2	4	,,
Good workman, but drinker	Furniture remover . .	....	None . .	?	?	2	..	?
Drinker and bad lot (theft)	Waiter, insurance agent, traveller. At one time had his own shop	....	Bad record .	?	..	2	2	?

[1] Including all regular pensions, poor relief, etc., but not occasional gifts or savings.   [2] See note, p. 61.

CASUAL WORKERS WHO HAVE BEEN

Last Regular Employment.							Present Condition.
Nature.	Dura-tion (years).	Was it preceded by an industrial career indicating power to retain permanent work?	Date of Leaving.	Cause of Leaving.	Age at time of Leaving.	Present Age.	Physique.
Confectioner's labourer	12	No	1904	Pilfering . . .	26	32	Strong, stammers. .
Shop porter . . .	3	,,	1907	Drunkenness and in-attention	26	29	Very good . . .
Hoistman . . .	1⅛	Yes	,,	Illness	19	22	Good . . . .
Compositor . . .	7	No	1897	"Quarrel with fore-man"	21 or 22	35	Strong . . . .
Groom	1¼	Yes	1904	"End of hunting season"	23	29	Robust . . . .
Box-maker . . .	6	No	1908	To better himself .	19	21	Strong . . . .
Engineer's labourer .	9	Yes	,,	Intemperance . .	39	41	Good . . . .
Bricklayer's apprentice	2	No	1901	Failure of master .	16	25	,, ...
Mason's apprentice .	?	,,	?	?	?	24	Healthy . . .
Coal carter . . .	2	,,	1907	"Quarrel with fore-man"	41	44	Very good . . .
Flour-mill labourer .	Nearly 2	Yes	June 1909	?	29	30	Healthy . . .
Farm labourer . .	? (as boy)	No	?	?	?	36	,, . . .
Confectioner's labourer	4	,,	Christmas 1908	Bad timekeeping .	18	20	,, . . .
Farm labourer . .	5	Yes	1907	To better himself .	19	22	Weak heart . . .
Engineer . . .	25	,,	,,	Breaking time . .	49	52	Rheumatic . . .
On fishing trawler .	7	,,	?	Out of time . . .	?	27	Good . . . .
Engine-driver . .	9 or 10	,,	1907	Accident . . .	47	50	,, ...
Groom	5	No	?	Sale of horses by em-ployer	?	24	,, ...
Confectioner's labourer	3	,,	1904	?	17	22	Healthy, but slender .
,, ,,	8 or 9	,,	1902	To enlist . . .	20	28	Good . . . .
Steelworks labourer .	1¼	,,	1908	Strike	28	30	,, ...
Confectioner's labourer	3½	,,	1902	To enlist . . .	20	28	Strong . . . .

IN REGULAR WORK (358 IN NUMBER)—*continued*

Present Condition. Character.	Nature of Casual Occupations.	Nature of Permanent Occupations Sought.	Apparent Personal Handicaps in search for Regular Work.	Average Weekly Casual Earnings.¹	Average Weekly Income of Rest of Household.¹	No. of Persons in Household. Adults	Children (under 16).	Is Family under Poverty Line?²
Good worker, but now drinker	Gardener and farm labourer, loafing	....	Case of rapid deterioration after dismissal for theft	8/-	?	2	..	?
Reformatory school, then casual, worthless	Labouring, whitewashing, etc.	....	Not trained to regular work	7/-	..	2	1	Yes
Good . . .	Window cleaner (own account)	Any	None . .	15/-	..	2	1	No
Heavy drinker .	Hawker, auction porter, cattle drover	....	Intemperance .	6/-	2/6	2	1	Yes
Good . . .	Cattle drover. . .	....	Good earnings at casual work	18/-	..	2	..	No
Very good . .	Sawyer	Any	None . .	..	..	2	1	Yes
Good worker, but drinker, unreliable	Navvy and general labourer	,, ...	Intemperance and bad record	7/-	5/6	2	2	,,
Good man . .	Gardener's labourer, and general labourer	,, ...	None . .	9/-	32/-	4	2	No
Incompetent worker, good character	Sculptor, whitewasher, hawker	Sculptor, or any .	Incompetency at his trade	7/6	..	2	1	Yes
Good . . .	Always been more or less casual. Carter, navvy, gardener, farm labourer	....	Not trained to regular work	9/-	4/6	2	..	No
Good references .	Confectioner's labourer, unloading coals	Any	None . .	10/-	15/-	2	4	,,
Excellent . .	Drayman, farm labourer	Carter or navvy .	,, . .	7/-	12/-	3	1	Yes
?	Painter	Any	?	?	?	?	?	?
?	(Army 2 years, to April 1910), carter, unloading boats	Carter, groom, farm work	None . .	7/-	..	2	..	?
Lazy and drinker .	Odd jobs, low class casual	Night watchman .	Infirmity and intemperance	4/6	..	1	..	Yes
Good . . .	On vessels and saw-mills	Any	None . .	?	16/-	3	1	,,
Energetic . .	Keeps fried fish shop, boilerman, navvy	....	Age . . .	?	?	2	1	?
Very good . .	Groom in hunting season, summer porter	....	Good alternate employments	?	45/-	6	..	No
Very good, but rough	Bricklayer's labourer, and brick-works labourer	Any . . .	Good wages in summer	10/-	?	3	1	?
Very good . .	(Army 8 years, to March 24,1910), factory porter	Confectioner's or miller's labourer	None . .	19/6	27/-	5	..	No
Not very steady .	Outdoor labourer, cab-driver, and general labourer (for 6 or 7 years)	Any	Bad record as a worker	13/-	4/-	3	4	Yes
Good worker . .	(Army 1902-1906), carter, general labourer, mills, etc.	,, ...	Pension . .	?	..	2	1	,,

¹ Including all regular pensions, poor relief, etc., but not occasional gifts or savings.   ² See note, p. 61.

CASUAL WORKERS WHO HAVE BEEN

Last Regular Employment.						Present Condition.	
Nature.	Dura-tion (years).	Was it preceded by an industrial career indicating power to retain permanent work.	Date of Leaving.	Cause of Leaving.	Age at time of Leaving.	Present Age.	Physique.
Gardener . . .	1	Yes	March 1908	Finish of contract .	30	32	Good . . . .
?	?	?	?	?	?	25	,, ...
Engineer's labourer .	8	Yes	Oct. 1906	Winding-up of firm .	30	34	,, ...
Shoemaker . . .	4	No	1901	?	18	27	,, ...
Engineer's labourer .	About 8	Yes	1904 or 1905	Winding-up of firm .	23 or 24	29	Lost one eye . . .
Confectioner's labourer	2 or 3	,,	1904	Illness	27	33	Good . . . .
Rope-maker . . .	6	,,	1898	Slackness . . .	35	47	,, ...
Shop porter . . .	2	,,	1908	?	41	43	,, ...
Flour packer . .	3	,,	June 1904	Could not stand dust .	20	26	,, ...
Confectioner's labourer	2 or 3	No	1904	Ill-health . . .	16	22	,, ...
Tallow chandler . .	4 or 5	,,	· 1899	To better himself .	18	29	,, ...
Farm labourer . .	1	Yes	1907	To get married . .	23	26	,, ...
Joiner's apprentice .	7	No	1906	End of apprenticeship	21	25	,, ...
"Taker - in" (glass works)	2 or 3	Yes	1905	Death of employer .	22	27	,, ...
Sign painter (own account)	?	?	?	Slackness of trade .	?	? 39 or 44	Flabby . . . . .
Boilersmith . . .	4	Yes	1904	Closing of works . .	34	40	Good . . . . .
Glassworks labourer .	5	No	1905	To better himself .	19	24	,, ...
Carter (own account) .	5	Yes	1907	Retirement . . .	52	55	,, ...
Clerk (with father) .	9	No	1899	Father disposed of business	25	36	,, ...
Telegraph line man .	5	Yes	Feb. 1907	To emigrate . .	27	31	Healthy . . .
Hurrier (coal mine) .	3	,,	1893	Strike	19	36	Good . . . .
Confectioner's labourer	4	,,	About 1903	Closing of works . .	41	48	,, ...
Railway carriage works labourer	8	,,	1901	Insubordination . .	44	53	,, ...
Chain-maker . . .	Over 30	,,	1904	Closing of works .	48	54	,, ...

IN REGULAR WORK (358 IN NUMBER)—continued

Present Condition. Character.	Nature of Casual Occupations.	Nature of Permanent Occupations Sought.	Apparent Personal Handicaps in search for Regular Work.	Average Weekly Casual Earnings.[1]	Average Weekly Income of Rest of Household.[1]	No. of Persons in Household.		Is Family under Poverty Line?[2]
						Adults.	Children (under 16).	
Decent . . .	Farm work . . .	Any	Not trained to regular work	8/-	4/-	2	..	No
Good . . .	Summer porter . .	....	None (maintained by respectable family)	..	20/-	3	..	,,
Good, steady . .	Railway porter . .	Any	None . .	?	11/-	3	..	,,
Good references .	Confectioner's labourer, painter, navvy	Painter or any . .	,, . .	?	6/-	3	3	Yes
Good . . .	Keelman, and unloading boats	Any	?	7/-	35/-	6	1	No
Steady . . .	Chopping and hawking sticks, paper selling, furniture portering	Any . . .	Seems to have given up hope	8/-	?	3	1	?
Good . . .	Cattle drover, tout .	,, . . .	Age . . .	4/6	..	2	..	Yes
Sober and industrious	Farm work, navvy, gardener, casual porter	General labourer .	Probably good casual earnings	?	3/-	2	..	?
Good ,, . .	Railway porter . .	Any	None . .	15/-	..	1	..	No
Good	Labourer in hide factory, builder's labourer	,, ...	,, . .	7/-	Over 80/-	4	3	,,
Respectable . .	Ice-cream maker, odd jobs	....	Illiteracy (not been at school)	4/-	..	1	..	Yes
Industrious . .	Farm work . . .	Carting or farm work .	Always been more or less casual	?	?	2	..	?
Good . . .	Railway outdoor labourer, unloading boats	....	Almost fully employed	14/6	?	?	?	?
Good worker . .	Carter, farm work, cattle drover	....	Poor home .	2/-	28/6	5	1	No
Good, trustworthy	Sign writer and general labourer	....	Hardly any education	?	?	?	?	?
Good worker . .	Toolsmith, pipe - layer, own trade	....	None . .	?	10/-	2	3	?
Good . . .	Mill labourer, navvy, general labourer, coal carrier	....	,, . .	5/-	?	2	1	?
,, . . .	Factory porter . .	....	Age . . .	?	..	2	2	No
,, . . .	? (probably bookmaker)	Messenger . . .	Family has means	4/-	14/-	3	4	Yes
Unintelligent, very good	Bricklayer's labourer, navvy, plumber	Any	Somewhat adventurous, good casual earnings	?	6/3	2	2	?
Reliable . . .	Farm labourer, builder's labourer	Carter or labourer .	None . .	9/-	..	2	4	Yes
Excellent . .	Ticket collector (rare), Christmas P.O. (very little)	Storekeeper or night watchman	Age, too long out of work	6d.	17/-	5	1	,,
Good . . .	Navvy, gardener, farm labourer, timber and coal carrier	....	Age . . .	5/-	15/-	8	7	,,
Seems steady . .	Waiter, general labourer (very little)	Any	,, . . .	?	?	?	?	?

[1] Including all regular pensions, poor relief, etc., but not occasional gifts or savings.   [2] See note, p. 61.

CASUAL WORKERS WHO HAVE BEEN

Nature.	Duration (years).	Was it preceded by an industrial career indicating power to retain permanent work.	Date of Leaving.	Cause of Leaving.	Age at time of Leaving.	Present Age.	Physique.
Bottler . . .	2 or 3	Yes	1908	Bankruptcy of firm .	20	22	Mentally inferior, good health
Carter . . .	1	No	1900 or 1902	" Left for no particular reason "	38 or 40	48	Good . . . .
Coal hawker . .	2 or 3	Yes	1898	Business given up .	18	30	,, ...
Carter . . .	8	,,	1908	Slackness . . .	24	26	Healthy . . .
General labourer .	2	,,	1907	,, . . .	45	48	Good . . . .
Railway porter .	1	No	March 1906	To join family in York	19	23	,, ...
Plumber . . .	28	Yes	Aug. 1904	Bad timekeeping .	40	46	Fairly strong . .
Match-maker . .	4 or 5	Yes (army 1884-1891)	1884	To enlist . . .	21	47	Healthy . . .
Mineral water bottler .	1	No	1908	Business changed hands	32	34	,, . . .
Labourer, comb factory	3	Yes	1904	Removal of firm . .	35	41	,, . . .
Plumber's apprentice .	4	No	1876 (army 10 years)	To enlist . . .	17	51	, . . .
Grocer's assistant .	1	Yes	1904	End of temporary job.	28	34	Was twice in lunatic asylum
Railway spring-smith .	20	No	1902	Removal of works .	41	49	Too stout . . .
Packer	6½	Yes	April 1907	Bad time-keeping .	33	36	Very strong . .
Shop assistant and traveller	9	,,	1907	Intemperance . .	30	33	Ruined health through drink
Grocer's packer . .	?	?	?	?	?	50	?
Grocer's assistant .	4	No	1895	Ill-health . . .	33	48	Fairly healthy . .
Furniture remover .	1½	Yes	1902	Put on irregular work	24	32	Delicate . . .
Railway labourer (carriage works)	?	,,	1908	Probably bad time-keeping	20	22	?
Comb worker . .	Some	?	1904	Removal of firm . .	35	41	Good . . . .
Engineer's labourer .	14	Yes	May 9, 1908	?	40	42	?
Farm servant . .	1	,, (1 year)	1908	End of service . .	19	21	?
Moulder's apprentice .	?	No	?	?	?	32	Strong . . .
Confectioner's labourer	About 5	,,	1907	Bad time-keeping .	17	21	,, ...
Fitter's labourer . .	3	Yes	1900	?	40	50	,, ...

IN REGULAR WORK (358 IN NUMBER)—continued

Present Condition. Character.	Nature of Casual Occupations.	Nature of Permanent Occupations Sought.	Apparent Personal Handicaps in search for Regular Work.	Average Weekly Casual Earnings.¹	Average Weekly Income of Rest of Household.¹	No. of Persons in House-hold. — Adults.	Children (under 16).	Is Family under Poverty Line?
Gambler, often loafs	First temporary as bottler, now general labourer	....	Mental inferiority and unsteady	?	Over 40/-	4	1	No
Disreputable . .	Waterman and other catch work	....	Age, and casual career from beginning	?	12/-	4	4	Yes
Drinker . . .	Electric light fitter, general labourer, navvy	....	Fair earnings by casual work	?	..	2	1	,,
Moderate (drinker)	Brickyards and general labourer	....	,, ,,	16/-	..	2	1	No
Good . . .	Painter, unloading boats, timber carrier	....	Age . . .	8/-	3/-	3	1	Yes
Good, but inclined to loaf	Hawker, market porter .	....	Supported by wife's earnings (7s.)	3/-	9/-	2	..	,,
Drinker . . .	Glazier, casual carter .	....	Appearance of loafer	?	12/-	4	..	?
,, . . .	Unloading coal . .	....	Fair earnings by casual work, supplemented by wife's earnings	15/-	10/-	2	..	No
Drinker, been in gaol for theft	Cattle drover, hawker .	....	Not trained to regular work	10/-	5/-	3	..	,,
Heavy drinker .	Cattle drover and unloading boats	....	Bad reputation	7/-	4/-	2	4	Yes
Drinker . . .	Plumber, French polisher, farm work	....	Age . . .	6/-	8/-	2	2	,,
Used to drink, now all right	Catch work, snow shovelling, timber carrier	Grocer's assistant .	Regular cadger	?	4/-	3	2	?
Drinker . . .	Pall - bearer, market porter	Any	Age . . .	11/-	6/-	3	1	Yes
,, . . .	Carter and labourer .	,, ...	Bad reputation and record	?	..	2	1	?
Heavy drinker .	Milkman and various catch jobs	Shop assistant or any	Bad appearance and reputation	?	24/-	3	..	No
Good . . . ?	Had own shop, which failed, waiter (rare)	?	Age . . .	?	?	?	?	?
,, . . . ?	? Catch work . . .	....	,, . . .	..	20/6	4	4	Yes
?	Factory porter . .	Any	Ill-health .	8/-	4/-	2	1	,,
			?	?	?	?	?	?
Good worker .	Joiner and general labourer	?	?	?	?	1	..	?
?	Oil works and other labouring	General labourer .	None . .	?	?	4	2	?
Gambler . . .	Tallow works and farm work	....	Not trained to regular work	?	..	1	..	?
Bad (assaults police)	Railway porter, postman (Christmas), etc.	....	Possibly shirker	?	..	1	..	?
Drinker and loafer	Cattle drover, stableman, railway porter	....	Bad home influences	?	?	5	1	No
Drinker (been in prison)	Coachbuilder's labourer, workhouses, sandwichman	....	Age, unreliability	6/-	..	8	1	Yes

¹ Including all regular pensions, poor relief, etc., but not occasional gifts or savings.   ² See note, p. 61.

CASUAL WORKERS WHO HAVE BEEN

	Last Regular Employment.					Present Condition.	
Nature.	Dura-tion (years).	Was it preceded by an industrial career indicating power to retain permanent work ?	Date of Leaving.	Cause of Leaving.	Age at time of Leaving.	Present Age.	Physique.
Confectioner's labourer	2	No	1903	Theft	16	23	Big and strong . .
Gasfitter's apprentice .	8	,,	1908	Insubordination . .	24	26	Healthy . . .
Gardener . . .	?	?	?	?	?	55	,, . . .
Farm servant . .	2	No	1908	Retirement of employer	18	20	,, . . .
Wine merchant's labourer	3	,,	1899	To enlist (army 8 years)	17	28	Underfed . . .
Newspaper machine-room labourer	16	,,	May 1908	Discharged . . .	33	35	Very stout . . .
Fitter	6½	Yes	"Long ago"	To better himself .	Long ago	47	Rheumatic . . .
Bookmaker's clerk .	Over 5	,,	June 1908	Imprisonment for assault	32	34	Degenerate type . .
Canteen waiter . .	2	No (enlisted at 14)	1904	Removal of regiment .	36	42	Fairly strong . .
Labourer (railway signal department)	2¼	Yes	1906	Reduction of staff .	27	31	Underfed . . .
Wagoner . . .	1½ or 2	,,	1892	End of temporary engagement	20	38	Lumbago . . .
Railway clerk . .	21	,,	1903	Illness	42	49	For long time ill with asthma and bronchitis
Police constable . .	7	,,	1902	,, ...	42	50	Moderate . . .
Flour-mill labourer .	3 (army 1901-1907)	,,	1901	?	21	30	Good . . . .
Railway carriage works labourer	2 or 3	,,	1900	Slackness . . .	44	54	
Comb worker's apprentice	5 or 6 (army 19 years)	No	1881 (army to 1906)	To enlist . . .	19 or 20	43	Good . . . .
Smith's striker . .	1	No (4 firms in 4 or 5 years)	1900	,, ...	18	28	,, ...
Foundry labourer . .	2 or 3	Yes	1902	,, ...	18	26	,, . . .
Machinist . . .	About 20	Yes	1905	Failure of firm . .	48	53	Strong . . . .
Comb worker . .	8	,,	1898	Closing of works .	21	33	Healthy . . .
Striker	About 40	No	1904	,, ,, .	48	54	.. . . .

IN REGULAR WORK (358 IN NUMBER)—*continued*

Present Condition. Character.	Nature of Casual Occupations.	Nature of Permanent Occupations Sought.	Apparent Personal Handicaps in Search for Regular Work.	Average Weekly Casual Earnings.[1]	Average Weekly Income of Rest of Household.[1]	No. of Persons in Household. Adults.	Children (under 16).	Is Family under Poverty Line?[2]
Fair	Brickyard, factory porter, footballer	....	Gambling habits	?	..	2	..	?
Ill-tempered, poor worker	Cattle driving, painter's labourer, shovelling snow, cleaning windows, plumbing, etc.	Gasfitting or any	None	12/-	35/6	4	..	No
Good	Gardening and odd jobs	Gardener	Looks very old, kept by daughters	?	18/6	3	..	?
Industrial school education, gambler	Field work	....	Probably prefers casual work	?	?	?	?	?
Inclined to loaf	Bookmaker and odd jobs	....	Army pension, not strong	?	10/-	2	2	?
Drinker and gambler	Hawker and bookmaker	....	Sufficient earnings	12/6	6/-	2	5	Yes
Drinker, untrustworthy	Canvasser (rare)	....	Looks very old, no impression of a worker	?	..	2	2	?
Not energetic	Cattle drover, general labourer, toll collector, tent erector	....	Maintained in excellent comfort by wife	5/-	?	3	3	No
Heavy drinker and bad time-keeper	Telegraph Department G.P.O., theatre attendant	....	Good earnings and army pension	22/-	..	2	3	,,
Good and fairly respectable	Joiner, railway porter	Any	None, before deteriorated by unemployment	?	?	?	?	?
Trustworthy	Bricklayer's labourer, carter	Carting or any	Ill-health	?	?	2	..	Yes
Very respectable	Gardening, loading boats	....	Age, has been very unfortunate	?	9/-	3	..	,,
Very good	Only odd jobs, very little	....	Pensioner	10/9	9/-	3	5	,,
Good army discharge, but little known	Mill labourer, casual farm work	Any	Not looking for permanency	8/-	..	1	..	No
Good reputation	Joiner's and builder's labourer	,,	Age	?	?	2	..	?
Probably not energetic	" Any work " (rare)	....	Pensioner, wife earning, bad appearance	9/-	16/-	2	6	Yes
?	Market and other rare and casual jobs (army 8 years)	....	Reserve pay, low type	?	?	3	3	?
?	(Army), brewer's labourer, general labourer	Any	Reserve pay, good earnings of relatives	?	..	1	..	?
Good	Loading boats, farm work, navvying	General labourer	Age and inefficiency	7/-	35/-	6	1	No
Intemperate	Bricklayer's labourer, coal carter, unloading boats, selling papers	Any	Gets fair amount casual work	7/-	4/6	2	7	Yes
Good	Deal carrier, navvy, farm labourer	,,	Age, maintained by children	?	43/-	4	..	No

1 Including all regular pensions, poor relief, etc., but not occasional gifts or savings.   2 See note, p. 61.

I

CASUAL WORKERS WHO HAVE BEEN

	Last Regular Employment.						Present Condition.
Nature.	Dura-tion (years).	Was it preceded by an industrial career indicating power to retain permanent work?	Date of Leaving.	Cause of Leaving.	Age at time of Leaving.	Present Age.	Physique.
Fitter's labourer . .	1	Yes	1898	?	26	38	Short, but healthy .
Railway fireman . .	12	,,	Dec. 1906	Inefficiency . . .	26 or 27	80	Good . . . .
Railway wagon works labourer	4	,,	1888	"Slackness" . .	29	51	?
Glass-blower . . .	?	No	?	?	?	43	Stout . . . .
Cement worker . .	8	,,	1907	Ill-health . . .	30	33	?
?	?	?	?	?	?	21	Very good . . .
Railway fitter's apprentice	?	?	?	?	?	23	Good . . . .
Waiter	2	Yes	1906	To better himself .	19	23	Healthy . . .
Confectioner's labourer	1½	,,	Nov. 1905	Says illness, but probably preferred casual work	16	21	Healthy, not muscularly strong
Goods porter . .	1	,,	June 1902	Ill-health through exposure	21	29	Good . . . .
Hotel servant . .	2	,,	1906	?	24	28	,, ...
Turner	10	,,	1908	Drink and disorderly conduct	31	33	,, ...
Wagon-builder . .	2 or 3	,,	1906	Slackness . . .	17	21	,, ...
Errand boy . . .	7	No	1909	Displaced by younger boy	21	21	?
Bellows-maker . .	?	?	?	?	as a boy 38	54	Good . . . .
Manure merchant's labourer	19	Yes	1898	Work too hard . .	38	50	,, ...
Confectioner's labourer	8	,,	1908	Closing of works .	19	21	Apparently good .
Railway clerk . .	3½	No	?	Disliked confinement and frequent removal	?	22	?
Crane-driver . . .	27	,,	1903	Winding-up of firm .	46	58	Fairly strong . . .
Confectioner's labourer	?	?	,,	To better himself .	18	25	Good . . . .
Flour-mill labourer .	2	Yes	1905	Bad time-keeping .	23	28	,, ...
Striker	12	No	1903	Closing of works .	31	38	.. . . . .

IN REGULAR WORK (358 IN NUMBER)—continued

Present Condition. Character.	Nature of Casual Occupations.	Nature of Permanent Occupations sought.	Apparent personal Handicaps in Search for Regular Work.	Average Weekly Casual Earnings.1	Average Weekly Income of Rest of Household.1	Adults	Children (under 16).	Is Family under Poverty Line?2
Drinker, low type	Loading boats	....	Lack of intelligence, intemperance	10/-	..	2	..	Yes
Good	Railway and general labourer	Any	Good earnings at casual work	?	..	2	..	?
Drinker and gambler	General labourer	,,	Age	10/-	?	3	..	?
Drinker	Glassworks labourer, timber carrier, navvy and general labourer	Glass-blower or any	Appearance of drinker	8/-	..	1	..	No
,,	Rag and bone collector, hardware hawker, farm labourer, cattle drover	....	Low type, hardly ever worked regularly	?	..	2	6	Yes
Never stuck to any occupation, of which had many	Jobbing carter	....	Shiftlessness, indulgent mother	?	49/-	5	..	No
Lazy and unintelligent	Furniture porter, fitter's labourer	Fitter or any	Lack of intelligence	8/-	..	1	..	,,
Lazy	Casual porter and general labourer	....	Apparently demoralised through dismissal from last job for theft or similar offence	?	81/-	5	3	,,
Good	Goods porter (rare), selling papers	....	Makes sufficient living by casual work	7/-	42/-	4	4	,,
Shirker	Bricklayer's and farm labourer	....	Shirker	2/6	30/-	7	1	Yes
Bad reputation	Canvasser, officer's servant, waiter	....	Very bad home, unstable	?	31/6	6	..	No
Bad reputation, drinker	Platelayer, general labourer	....	Appearance of loafer	?	16/-	5	..	,,
Appears respectable	General labourer, railway porter, navvy	General labourer	Poor record	?	50/-	4	..	,,
?	Summer porter (railway)	"Light labour"	?	..	?	?	?	?
Fairly good	Farmer's and market gardener's labourer	....	Age, trade died out	4/6	..	1	..	Yes
Bad appearance	Hawker	Any	Good earnings as hawker	15/-	24/-	3	6	No
?	General labouring (very little)	?	?	?	?	6	..	?
Shiftless	Goods porter	Regular railway porter	Mother has private income, probably loafing	?	?	4	..	?
Good	Electrician's labourer	General labourer	Age	?	..	1	..	?
,,	Flour-mill labourer, goods porter, grocer's assistant (army reserve)	,,	Stammers, illiteracy	?	..	1	..	No
,,	Catch jobs (very little)	Any	Kept by brothers	1/-	35/-	5	..	,,
Respectable	Navvying, hawking wood, sand boats, etc.	Any, own trade if possible	Maintained by relatives	?	?	2	4	?

1 Including all regular pensions, poor relief, etc., but not occasional gifts or savings. 2 See note, p. 61.

CASUAL WORKERS WHO HAVE BEEN

Last Regular Employment.					Present Condition.		
Nature.	Dura-tion (years).	Was it preceded by an industrial career indicating power to retain permanent work?	Date of Leaving.	Cause of Leaving.	Age at time of Leaving.	Present Age.	Physique.
Joiner's labourer . .	3	No	1905	Bad time-keeping .	17	22	Good . . . .
Railway labourer . .	5	Yes	July 1906	?	'37	41	,, ...
Groom	1 or 2	,,	1906	?	27	31	,, ...
Errand boy . . .	3	No	1901	Preferred cattle driving	17	26	,, ...
Warehouseman . .	3½	,,	Aug. 1907	To better himself .	17	20	Strong . . . .
,, . .	2 or 3	Yes	1903	?	17	24	Good . . . .
Oiler (railway) . .	,,	,,	,,	Made a mistake . .	19	26	Robust . . . .
Waiter	2	,,	1905	To better himself .	25	30	,, ...
Shoeing and general smith	Over 12	,,	1908	Displaced by steam traction	45	47	Fairly good . . .
General labourer . .	2	,,	1907	Work getting too hard	45	48	Fair , . . .
?	?	?	?	?	?	22	?
Dyer's apprentice. .	6	Yes	1900	To work for same firm in Hull	21	31	Undersized, but good physique
Carter	4	?	?	To better himself . .	..	abt. 55	Looks old . . .
Carriage-builder's labourer	1	No	1908	Inefficiency . . .	26	28	Healthy . . .
Goods porter . .	3	,,	1906	To better himself .	19	23	Good . . . .
Tinsmith . . .	1¼	(Was apprenticed 7 years)	June 1908	Discharged, reason unknown	23	25	,, ...
Iron-moulder . .	8	First employment	1902	Worked elsewhere at own trade till age	27	29	,, ...
Packer	9	?	1907	Bad time-keeping .	26	29	,, ...
Bricklayer's labourer .	1	No	1908	End of contract . .	25	27	,, ...
Beer bottler . . .	4	?	May 1908	Removal to York .	23	25	Weak . . . .
Navvy	1½	Yes (to 1896)	1909	End of contract . .	33	34	,, ...
Joiner's apprentice .	2	No	1880	Left because did not learn trade	17	47	Good . . . .
Farm servant . .	2½	Yes	1906	To better himself .	19	23	Underfed, ruptured .
Comb worker . .	?	No	?	?	As boy 25	28	Good . . . .
Match-maker . .	12	,,	(Army 1898-1908) 1891	Closing of works . .	25	44	,, ...
Laundry vanman . .	4	Yes	March 1908	To better himself .	28	30	Undersized, not strong

IN REGULAR WORK (358 IN NUMBER)—*continued*

Present Condition. Character.	Nature of Casual Occupations.	Nature of Permanent Occupations sought.	Apparent Personal Handicaps in Search for Regular Work.	Average Weekly Casual Earnings.[1]	Average Weekly Income of Rest of Household.[1]	No. of Persons in Household.[1]		Is Family under Poverty Line?[2]
						Adults.	Children (under 16).	
Steady . . .	Cleaning barracks . .	Any	Bad upbringing	?	?	3	..	?
Good references .	General labourer . .	,, ...	?	10/-	..	1		No
Respectable and steady	Railway porter, unloading boats, gardener, navvy	,, ...	?	4/-	26/-	3	3.	,,
Shiftless .	Cattle drover, rag and bone gatherer, odd jobs	....	Bad home .	10/-	..	1	..	,,
Respectable appearance	Engine cleaner (good record)	Motor trade . .	None . .	11/-	35/-	3	2	,,
,, ,,	General labourer, goods porter	Any	,, . .	?	?	7	1	?
Excellent . .	Painter, cattle drover, general labourer	Painter and paperhanger	,, . .	5/-	29/-	5	..	No
Good . . .	Waiter (rare) . . .	Waiter or caretaker .	Maintained by relatives	15/-	8/-	?	?	?
Excellent record .	General labourer . .	Any	Age . . .	?	..	3	5	Yes
Gambler. . .	Groom, labourer, chiefly among horses	Groom	,, . .	15/-	..	1	..	No
?	Hawker	....	All family are hawkers	?	?	?	?	?
Good . . .	Coal porter, carter . .	Dyer or labourer .	None . .	7/-	..	1	..	?
Probably drinker .	Groom, painting, paperhanging, whitewashing, navvying, etc.	....	Age and bad record	?	1/6	2	..	Yes
Good . . .	Coal hawker, painter, paperhanger, whitewasher, and other jobs	Any	?	6/-	24/-	4	..	No
Lazy . . .	Navvy and general labourer	,, ...	Inefficiency .	?	39/6	5	3	,,
Apparently lazy .	Painting, navvying, laying cable	Any but heavy work .	None . .	?	..	2	1	Yes
?	Hawker	Own work . . .	Good earnings as hawker	17/-	4/-	2	3	No
Lazy, not bad character	Timber yard, unloading boats, cattle market, field work	Any	Wife's regular earnings	8/-	9/-	2	3	Yes
Poacher, drinker .	Footballer, cattle drover, odd jobs	....	Kept by family	12/6	?	?	?	?
Respectable .	Casual railway porter, general labourer	Any	Obviously weak, unsuitable	?	38/-	4	..	No
No initiative .	Casual gardening, field work	,, ...	Typical slumster	?	..	2	1	Yes
Good . . .	Station tout (after casual career)	....	Age . . .	?	..	1	..	No
Not energetic .	Unloading boats and general labourer	General labourer. .	Ill-health .	?	1/-	2	2	?
Bad, probably betting, but sober	Cattle drover, field work	....	Good earnings at casual work	?	3/-	2	..	?
Bad reputation .	Asphalting, field work, mixing tillage, wool packing	....	Drunkard, probably likes tramping	10/-	..	1	..	No
Excellent . .	Goods warehouseman, snow shovelling, farm work	General labourer. .	None . .	8/-	13/-	3	4	Yes

[1] Including all regular pensions, poor relief, etc., but not occasional gifts or savings.   [2] See note, p. 61.

CASUAL WORKERS WHO HAVE BEEN

	Last Regular Employment.						Present Condition.
Nature.	Dura-tion (years).	Was it preceded by an industrial career indicating power to retain permanent work?	Date of Leaving.	Cause of Leaving.	Age at time of Leaving.	Present Age.	Physique.
Rope righter (mine) .	36	No	1904	Defective eyesight .	48	54	Lost one eye, otherwise good
Confectioner's labourer	3	Yes	1906	Illness	17	21	Weedy . . . .
Scavenger . . .	9	,,	1904	Quarrel with foreman	34	40	Underfed . . .
Groom	1¾	,,	1908	?	26	28	Slender, good health .
Porter	1½	No	,,	Ill-health . . .	21	23	Good . . . .
Sand catcher . .	2½	Yes	1905	Retirement of employer	33	38	Robust . . . .
Farm labourer . .	1½	No	1901 or 1902	,, ,,	45	54	Looks older than he is.
Fitter's labourer . .	8	Yes	1908	Intemperance . .	32	34	Good, stammers . .
Glasshouse boy . .	4	No	1906	To better himself .	18	22	Good . . . .
Farm labourer . .	5	Yes	1905	To enlist . . .	20	25	Healthy . . .
Box-maker . . .	2	No	1904	To work casually .	16	22	,, . . .
Messenger . . .	1	Yes	1907	To better himself .	18	21	Good . . . .
Confectioner's labourer	4½	No	March 1908	Inefficiency . . .	18	20	,, ...
Fireman . . .	1½	Yes	1907	Bad character and insubordination	23	26	Strong . . . .
Page	?	,,	1909	?	23	24	Good . . . .
Railway porter . .	2½	,,	Jan. 1907	To better himself .	18	21	Strong . . . .
Horsebreaker . .	1	,,	June 1908	"Slackness" . .	51	53	Healthy . . .
Cab-driver . . .	9	,,	1902	Sickness . . .	30	38	,, . . .
Printer	?	,,	?	To better himself .	?	19	,, . . .
Groom	?	?	?	?	?	21	Strong . . . .
Gardener . . .	2	No	Dec. 1907	Reduction of staff .	23	26	Healthy . . .
Tinsmith . . .	16	Yes	1904	Slackness . . .	49	55	Not strong . . .
,, . . .	1	,,	,,	,, . . .	24	30	Rather delicate . .
Polisher's apprentice .	?	No	?	End of apprenticeship	?	27	Rather delicate and inert, mentally below normal
Horsebreaker . .	? (In army 21 yrs., to 1906)	?	?	?	?	44	Good . . . .

IN REGULAR WORK (358 IN NUMBER)—continued

Present Condition. Character.	Nature of Casual Occupations.	Nature of Permanent Occupations sought.	Apparent Personal Handicaps in Search for Regular Work.	Average Weekly Casual Earnings.[1]	Average Weekly Income of Rest of Household.[1]	No. of Persons in Household. Adults.	No. of Persons in Household. Children (under 16).	Is Family under Poverty Line?[2]
Excellent	Wool sorting, farm work, mixing tillage	General labourer.	Age and defective sight	9/-	8/-	3	..	No
Bad home	Farm work, hawking firewood	,, ,,	Weedy, and unkempt appearance	1/-	21/6	4	8	Yes
Good	Window cleaner, general labourer	,, ,,	None	?	6/-	2	4	,,
Good, respectable	Ostler in different inns	Any	Becoming demoralised	5/-	..	1	..	?
Good	Selling papers, kept paper shop for 10 months	,,	Not trained to regular work	8/-	5/-	3	1	Yes
Drinker, poor worker, and untrustworthy	Navvying, unloading boats, hawking, general labourer	....	Bad reputation	?	?	8	5	?
Gambler	Field work (rare)	....	Age and bad record, always been more or less casual	?	7/-	?	?	?
Very poor	Hawker, general labourer	....	"Absolutely impossible"	4/6	19/-	6	3	Yes
Good	Goods porter, officer's servant	Billiard marker, asylum attendant, or waiter	Inclined to loaf	2/-	31/6	6	..	No
,,	(In army 1905-1908), cattle drover	Any	Maintained partly by wife's earnings, reserve pay	6/6	..	1	..	?
Lazy	Unloading boats and similar work	....	Unwillingness to work regularly	5/-	20/-	3	3	Yes
Good	?	General labourer	None	?	?	?	?	?
,,	Gardener	,, ,,	,,	6/-	34/6	5	6	No
"Bad lot"	Railway goods porter	Fireman or general labourer	No references	14/-	?	?	?	?
Excellent	Bath-chairman, farm labourer, waiter	Servant or waiter	None	10/-	11/-	4	..	Yes
Good	(Army Aug. 1907 to Aug. 1909), blacksmith's striker	Groom or valet	,,	..	17/-	?	?	?
Heavy drinker	Cab-driver, groom	Groom	Intemperance	?	7/-	2	..	?
Good	Cab-driver, catch jobs	General labourer	None	9/-	..	2	4	Yes
Good, but somewhat shiftless	Own trade	Own trade	,,	?	22/-	3	1	No
?	Groom, never long at one stable	Groom	None	..	40/-	5	4	,,
Very good	Casual gardener and labourer	Gardener	,,	?	25/-	8	..	,,
Heavy drinker	At his own trade	Own trade	Age	12/-	10/-	3	..	,,
Good	At his own trade and bandsman	,,	None	12/-	12/-	2	..	,,
Drinker and loafer	At his own trade	,,	Bad reputation	?	..	3	..	?
Discharge not good	Waiter and officer's servant	Waiter or officer's servant	Bad reputation and age	?	..	2	..	?

1 Including all regular pensions, poor relief, etc., but not occasional gifts or savings.　　2 See note, p. 61.

CASUAL WORKERS WHO HAVE BEEN

Last Regular Employment.						Present Condition.	
Nature.	Dura-tion (years).	Was it preceded by an industrial career indicating power to retain permanent work?	Date of Leaving.	Cause of Leaving.	Age at time of Leaving.	Present Age.	Physique.
Glassworks labourer .	1 (In army 22 yrs., to 1906)	No	1884	To enlist . . .	14½	41	Good . . . .
Saddler	?	?	?	?	?	47	Strong . . . .
?	?	?	?	?	?	48	Healthy . . .
Fitter	1	Yes	1908	Inefficiency . . .	36	38	Mentally below normal, otherwise healthy
Groom	?	?	?	?	?	60	Good . . .
Waterman . . .	Several	?	?	?	?	50	?
Boatman . . .	1	Yes	?	?	?	25	Strong . . . .
Farm labourer . .	?	?	?	?	?	26	,, ...
Warehouseman . .	4	Yes	Dec. 1906	Inefficiency . . .	21	25	Healthy . . .
Glass-blower . . .	11¾	,,	1905	Closing of works .	42	47	,, . . .
Carter	?	?	?	?	?	35	Subject to bronchitis, unintelligent
Grocer (own account) .	11	Yes	1902	Illness	44	52	Crippled with gout .
Publican . . .	6	,,	1908	Could not make it pay	43	45	?
Compositor . . .	?	?	?	?	?	47	Good . . . .
,, . . .	?	?	?	?	?	42	Strong . . . .
Printer	2	Yes	?	Failure of firm . .	?	40	Good . . . .
Cab-driver . . .	?	?	?	?	?	63	,, ...
,, . . .	?	?	?	?	?	43	Chronic indigestion .
French polisher . .	2	Yes	Dec. 1907	?	46	49	Good . . . .
Milkman's assistant .	4	,,	1902	Displaced by younger lad	20	28	,, ...
Confectioner's labourer	4 or 5	No	1899 or 1900	Insubordination . .	18 or 19	29	,, ...
Tailor	1	Yes	1906	Slackness . . .	49	53	Fairly good . . .
? (Army 10 years) . .	?	?	?	?	?	24	Good . . . .
Engineer's labourer .	28	Yes	1902	Winding-up of firm .	52	60	,, ...
Boot repairer . .	17	,,	1907	?	53	56	Fair . . . .
Butcher . . .	11	No	1887	Death of employer .	36	59	Ruptured . . .
Platelayer and signal-man	22	Yes	1895	Error	42	58	Good . . . .
Painter	25	,,	1902	Death of employer .	48	56	,, ...
Engineer's labourer .	4	?	,,	?	48	56	Strong . . . .
Tramway labourer .	11	Yes	1906	Displaced by younger man	55	59	Healthy . . .

IN REGULAR WORK (358 IN NUMBER)—continued

Present Condition. Character.	Nature of Casual Occupations.	Nature of Permanent Occupations sought.	Apparent Personal Handicaps in Search for Regular Work.	Average Weekly Casual Earnings.[1]	Average Weekly Income of Rest of Household.[1]	Adults.	Children (under 10).	Is Family under Poverty Line?[2]
Good . . .	Waiter since 1906 . .	....	Not trained to regular work	7/6	..	2	..	Yes
Good at his trade, but drinks	Always casually at own trade, also harvesting	Own trade, or any suitable occupation	Intemperance .	?	12/6	2	1	?
Drinker and quite immoral	Carter	Carter. . . .	Bad record .	?	?	2	..	No
Good references .	Own trade, groom, gardener	Own trade or any .	Inefficiency .	10/-	?	4	..	?
Good . . .	Officer's servant . .	Groom . . .	Age . . .	7/-	?	2	..	No
,, . . .	Keel captain, short voyages	Own trade . . .	None . .	?	24/-	3	4	?
Good worker, but heavy drinker	Boatman, unloading boats	Any	Intemperance .	?	6/-	2	2	?
Very good .	Farm labourer and carter	Farm labourer and carter	None . .	?	..	1	..	No
Rather lazy .	Warehouseman . .	Warehouseman or any	Laziness . .	5/-	24/-	3	..	,,
Good . . .	Glass-blower . .	Any	Age . . .	5/-	11/-	3	2	Yes
,, . . .	Carter	Carter or any . .	None . .	10/-	2/-	2	1	,,
Very energetic, good	,, ...	Carter. . . .	Age and ill-health	?	50/6	6	..	No
?	Debt collector, club steward	Any suitable casual work	Age. . .	?	..	2	4	?
Excellent .	Reporter, sub-editor, etc., latterly printer	Printer . . .	,, . . .	?	24/-	3	2	No
Good worker, but drinker	Own trade . . .	Own trade (T.U.) .	None . .	?	18/-	4	5	Yes
Drinker . . .	,, . . .	Own trade . . .	,, . . .	?	..	1	..	?
Unsatisfactory .	,, . . .	Own trade or any .	Age and bad record	3/-	5/-	3	1	Yes
Good . . .	,, . . .	Own trade or cook .	?	12/-	9d.	2	..	,,
Drinker, bad timekeeper, lazy	,, . . .	Own trade . . .	Age and bad reputation	?	21/-	4	3	?
Good . . .	Goods porter . . .	....	Regular work several days a week	16/-	52/-	4	..	No
Fair . . .	Seasonal brewer's labourer, bill distributor, snow shovelling, etc.	....	Satisfied, gets 18s. regular in summer	?	2/-	3	1	Yes
Good . . .	Repairing, cleaning club	Own trade or any .	Age . . .	5/-	16/6	4	2	,,
Inclined to loaf .	Navvy, relief work, railway labourer to 1908	....	Not trained to regular work	10/-	10/-	2	5	,,
Good Record . .	General labourer . .	....	Age . . .	15/-	..	1	..	No
Poor Record . .	Boot-repairing and workhouse	....	,, . . .	?	..	2	4	Yes
Fair . . .	Billposter and sandwichman	....	,, . . .	12/-	..	1	..	No
Good . . .	Gardening 3 days per week	....	,, . . .	12/-	..	2	1	Yes
Excellent .	Whitewasher, cab-driver, hawker	....	,, . . .	5/-	8/-	3	1	,,
Well-known poacher	Navvy and general labourer	....	,, . . :	10/-	?	3	..	?
Fair . . .	Almost in regular work as navvy and general labourer	....	,, . . .	?	?	?	?	?

[1] Including all regular pensions, poor relief, etc., but not occasional gifts or savings.   [2] See note, p. 61.

CASUAL WORKERS WHO HAVE BEEN

Last Regular Employment.							Present Condition.
Nature.	Dura-tion (years).	Was it preceded by an industrial career indicating power to retain permanent work?	Date of Leaving.	Cause of Leaving.	Age at time of Leaving.	Present Age.	Physique.
Gardener . . .	13	Yes	1907	Dismissal on trivial grounds	57	60	Good . . . .
Carriage trimmer . .	19	,,	1899	Death of employer .	49	60	,, ...
Furnaceman . .	20	,,	1903	Slackness . . .	54	61	,, ...
Tram-driver . . .	7	,,	1901	To better himself .	52	61	Fair . . . .
Builder's labourer .	16	,,	1905	?		63	68	Very good . . .
Glass-blower. . .	2 or 3	,,	1906	Slackness . . .	57	61	Frail . . . .
Goods porter . .	34	,,	1904	Intemperance . .	58	64	Good . . . .
Farm labourer . .	All his life	,,	1908	Removal of employer .	63	65	Able-bodied . . .
Boiler fireman . .	10	,,	1893	Reduction of wages .	45	62	Bronchitis . . .
Machiner and despatcher (newspaper)	30	,,	1907	Age	60	63	Fair . . . .
Sawyer and carter .	11	,,	1904	Premises destroyed by fire	59	65	Good . . . .
Builder's labourer .	All his life	,,	?	End of contract . .	?	62	,, ...
Corporation labourer .	20	,,	1892	To better himself .	43	61	Bronchitis . . .
Tanner	5	,,	1900	Closing of tannery .	55	65	Fairly strong . .
Telephone labourer .	2	,,	Dec. 1905	Resigned owing to introduction of new codes	56	61	Spine affected . .
Stone carver . . .	?	,,	About 1892	?	43	61	Very good . . .
Forgeman . . .	36	,,	1901	Closing of works .	53	62	Good . . . .
Railway labourer . .	12	,,	1886	Bad time-keeping .	41	65	?
Bricklayer's labourer .	2	,,	1873	?	29	66	Weak leg . . .
Fitter's apprentice .	½½	,,	July 1908	Illness	17	19	Delicate . . .
"Taker-in" (glass-works)	1	No	1907	Strike for higher wages	17	20	Good . . . .
Agricultural labourer .	?	?	?	?	?	?	?
Taker-in (glassworks) .	2	No	1907	Strike for higher wages	16	19	?
,, ,, .	1	Yes	1906	Slackness (?) . .	16	20	Healthy . . .
Warehouseman . .	2	,,	1907	Work too heavy . .	16	19	Good . . . .

IN REGULAR WORK (358 IN NUMBER)—*continued*

Present Condition. Character.	Nature of Casual Occupations.	Nature of Permanent Occupation sought.	Apparent Personal Handicaps in Search for Regular Work.	Average Weekly Casual Earnings.[1]	Average Weekly Income of Rest of Household.[1]	Adults.	Children (under 16).	Is Family under Poverty Line?[2]
Honest and willing	Gardener . . .	....	Age . . .	?	..	2	..	?
Good . . .	Coach trimmer and amongst cab owners	....	,, . . .	7/-	5/-	2	..	No
,, . . .	General labourer and market	....	,, . . .	5/-	?	8	..	,,
Apparently good .	Relief driver, vanman, unloading boats, G.P.O.	....	,, . . .	3/-	6/-	2	..	Yes
Drinker . . .	Labourer on farm and building work	....	,, . . .	6/-	..	1	..	?
Good repute . .	Navvy (very little). .	....	,, . . .	1/-	8/-	3	..	Yes
"Drunken, dirty fellow"	Corporation watchman .	....	Age, bad reputation	?	?	2	..	?
Excellent . .	Painter's and general labourer	....	Age . . .	18/-	2/6	3	..	No
Loafer, sometimes drunk	Gas worker, general labourer	....	Age, and bad reputation	10/-	15/-	3	1	,,
Very respectable .	Sandwichman and mendicant	....	Age . . .	?	..	1	..	Yes
Very good . .	Farm labourer, gardener	....	,, . . .	6/-	38/-	4	..	No
Drinker, good worker	Cattle drover . . .	....	,, . . .	?	24/6	4	..	?
Good record . .	Timberman's, corporation, and builder's labourer, farm labourer	....	,, . . .	4/-	5/-	2	..	Yes
Steady and respectable	Selling rags and odd jobs	....	,, . . .	?	?	2	..	,,
Excellent . .	Post office at Christmas, bailiff, builder's labourer and other jobs	....	,, . . .	?	5/-	3	1	?
Very good . .	First own trade, now gardening and whitewashing	....	,, . . .	8/-	?	?	..	No
Good . . .	Gardener and general labourer	....	,, . . .	?	29/-	4	1	,,
Fair . . .	Farm work and casual jobs	....	,, . . .	?	?	5	..	?
Drunkard . .	Hawker and auction porter	....	,, . . .	8/-	..	..	..	No
Good . . .	Bandsman and other (?)	Carter or any . .	Ill-health .	2/6	20/-	3	..	,,
?	Farm and catch work .	Any	Bad home influences	?	?	?	?	?
?	Farm work, cattle driving, etc.	?	?	?	..	1	..	?
?	Packer, farm work, and catch jobs	Any labouring . .	?	4/-	8/-	4	..	Yes
Good worker and time-keeper	In army (1907-1908, 20 months), confectioner's labourer, cab cleaning and catch work	,, . .	None . .	5/-	10/-	3	..	,,
Good . . .	Rink attendant (8 months)	,, . .	,, . .	..	43/6	5	2	No

[1] Including all regular pensions, poor relief, etc., but not occasional gifts or savings.   [2] See note, p. 61.

REASONS WHY 265 MEN IN THIS CLASS LOST THEIR LAST
REGULAR EMPLOYMENT

Faults of Character.		Other Personal Reasons.		Reasons other than Personal.	
Intemperance	15	Age	2	Superseded by younger labour	3
Inefficiency	10	Ill-health	28	Superseded by machinery	3
Laziness	1	Accident	3	Removal of employer	9
Theft	4	To better their positions	53	Death of employer	7
Bad time-keeping	10	To enlist	18	Winding-up of business	37
Imprisonment	1	Dispute with employer	5	Failure of business	11
		Insubordination	5	Slackness of business	17
		To remove	2	End of Contract	9
		End of apprenticeship.	3	Business changed hands	4
				Work only temporary.	5
	41		119		105

It will be seen that 119, or nearly one-half, left
through personal causes indicating no fault of character. The majority of them gave in their own notice.
Five lost their work through insubordination, a reason
which, although personal, does not adequately explain
the failure of the worker to establish himself in a
permanent position. Next, 41, or 15 per cent of
those for whom reliable information was available,
were dismissed for faults of character. The remaining
105, 40 per cent of the number, lost their work
through circumstances for which they were in no way
responsible, such as the winding-up of the business,
the replacement of hand-power by mechanical power,
and the like.

Theoretically, those who are squeezed out of
employment as the demand for labour lessens, will
be the most inferior workmen; but this is by no
means always the case, especially in small work-
shops, or wherever there is some personal touch
between employer and worker. Thus, an employer
will often dismiss a man whom he has recently
engaged, while retaining an old employee, although
he may be less efficient than the one dismissed. This
personal element must not be lost sight of in considering the various problems of unemployment, and
though while, taken as a whole, the men dismissed
were doubtless inferior to those retained, it is pretty
certain that many of the former would compare
favourably with many of the latter.

Apart from those dismissed for personal failings,
or who left their work through illness, it may be said
that these men, when dismissed, had proved their
ability to undertake regular work, and there was no
personal reason why they should not have continued
to do so.

Before inquiring why they did not, let us briefly
summarise the result of our analysis of the class up
to the present point.

The broad fact is that four-fifths of the men who
are now casuals have, at one time or another, been
regularly employed. Analysing the reasons why
they left their regular jobs, we find that about
8 per cent left through illness, about 15 per
cent through misconduct or inefficiency, and about

78 per cent through no fault of their own, or, at any rate, none which explained their inability to secure regular work afresh.[1] In connection with those who left through illness or accident, we must point out that although they could not continue the heavy or trying work they were doing, such as flour-milling, they could all have done regular work of a lighter kind had they been able to find it. Men rendered totally unemployable through illness have been entirely excluded from our analysis.[2]

REASONS WHY MEN ONCE REGULAR WORKERS HAVE BECOME CASUALS

Since then this large class of men who are now casuals have, at one time, formed a useful section, even if not the *most* useful, of the great body of regular workers, let us ask what prevents them from re-entering it.

The reasons why the 41 men dismissed for personal failings could not obtain work are obvious from the particulars given on pp. 96-123. Nor need we linger over the 33 who lost their posts through ill-health, age, and accident, further than to repeat that all of them might have been usefully and regularly employed in lighter work, could such have been found for them.

---

[1] It should be noted that in calculating these percentages it has been assumed that for the 68 cases where no reliable information was available, the proportion of dismissals falling under the different heads was the same as in the cases where reliable information was obtained.

[2] See p. xiv.

The severity of competition in the unskilled labour market explains, however, their inability to find it. Passing, then, to the 110 men who left their last regular job through no fault, or at any rate no serious fault, of their own, let us inquire why they have never resumed regular work. First, we note that the class includes 42 men who were over 40 when they were thrown out of their situations. Under the present industrial conditions this fact alone explains their drifting into casuals.

We have already pointed out (p. 53) why men become " too old at forty," and need not here dwell further on the matter. But after eliminating those who were dismissed for personal failings, and those who have reached middle life, there still remain a large number of men who have been engaged in regular employment, but have failed to re-establish themselves in it for a period of at least two years. Why is this ? As stated above, it is probable that many of them, even if they are not definitely inferior, could not be described as workmen of the first quality. At the same time it would certainly be doing them an injustice to say that they could only be employed in periods of trade boom. The length of time for which many of them have held previous positions disproves such a hypothesis.[1]

[1] Of 304 men for whom the information was available, the following gives the period during which they held their last regular job :—

[Table.

The class undoubtedly comprises some distinctly inferior men, but it also comprises a number who, at the time of their dismissal, were fully equal to the average workman retained. It is possible that some of them were lacking in the push and enterprise necessary to force themselves upon the notice of employers. Others, again, might create a poor impression at an interview with an employer, although they might be good and steady workmen. But undoubtedly many of them are now casuals simply because, when dismissed, they had no financial reserve to enable them to hold out till a fresh post was found.

It must be remembered that almost all the men in this class were unskilled labourers, and one of the present writers has demonstrated elsewhere that the wages of unskilled labour in England allow men with families dependent upon them no margin for saving.[1] Immediately they fell out of work it became absolutely incumbent upon them to obtain a living in some way.

	Number.	Per cent.
For less than 1 year*	4	1·3
,, 1 year	41	13·5
,, 2 years	54	17·8
,, 3 ,,	38	12·5
,, 4 ,,	30	9·9
,, 5 ,,	20	6·6
,, 5 to 10 years	50	16·4
,, 10 ,, 15 ,,	24	7·9
,, 15 ,, 20 ,,	12	3·9
More than 20 years	31	10·2
	304	100·0

* Included as regular work because preceded by other employment of a regular character.

[1] See *Poverty: A Study of Town Life* (Macmillan), p. 303.

If, in their search for regular work, they heard of
some casual employment, they were compelled to take
it, and when it came to an end the process was
repeated again and again. There are, in the present
disorganised state of industry, many more casual jobs
to be had than permanent ones, and unless a man
can afford, when he is out of work, to let them go by,
determined to wait until he can get a permanent one,
there is great danger that he will gradually slip into
the ranks of casual labour. For while he is temporarily occupied he cannot be keenly on the look-out
for regular employment, chances of which he often
lets slip. There is little doubt that if these men had
been able to wait, a large number of them would still
have been among the ranks of regular workers. The
advantage of this to the community would undoubtedly be very great.

To suggest that an unskilled worker who has
always been used to regular work should, when
unemployed, refuse casual jobs is not unreasonable.
The principle is the same as that which prevents
trade unionists from accepting work under conditions
which may lead to a permanent lowering of their
industrial position.

How long Workers once regular have been casually employed

Perhaps at this point it may be well to state the
periods which have elapsed since the men in this
group were regularly employed. It gives some

indication of the probability of their re-entering the group of regular workers, for when a man has been a casual worker for a number of years, say four or five, the chance of his again taking up regular work is slight. The following table gives these particulars for 297 of the men for whom they are known.

TIME WHICH HAS ELAPSED SINCE CASUAL WORKERS HAD
REGULAR WORK

	Number.	Per cent.
Under 1 year [1] . . .	5	1·8
1 year [1]	11	3·8
2 years	40	13·4
3 ,, ...	42	14·1
4 ,, ...	34	11·4
5 ,, ...	28	9·4
6 to 10 years . . .	89	29·8
11 to 15 ,, . . .	23	7·8
16 to 20 ,, . . .	12	4·1
Over 20 ,, . . .	13	4·4
	297	100·0

The above table shows that out of the 297 men who have, at one time or other, been in regular employment, over 55 per cent have been at casual work for five years or more. While, of course, it cannot be stated definitely that none of these will ever rejoin the ranks of the regular workers, this is a fairly safe assumption in the majority of cases. On the other hand, it is to be hoped that a considerable number of those who have only recently sunk to the

[1] These 16 cases are included here and not in Class I., because they have definitely ceased searching for permanent work.

status of casual workers may yet become permanently employed once again. It is to be noted that one-fifth of the men have been engaged on casual work for less than three years.

The kind of work done by the men in this class is exceedingly various. Of the 430 workers who supplied information under this head (see tables pp. 96 to 123), 111 seemed to rely on one kind of employment, though most of them were willing to take other odd jobs. One hundred and ten relied mainly on two occupations, first seeking it in one, and falling back, if that failed, upon the other. The remaining 209 men appeared to take unskilled work of almost any description, without expressing preference for one kind over another. Of the 111 who usually rely on one kind of employment, 12 find work as casual goods or seasonal passenger porters for the railway company, 4 as goods porters for other firms, 7 in waterside work, such as unloading keels, etc., 10 in connection with the cattle market, 7 rely on hawking firewood, vegetables, and other goods, 6 principally on gardening, 5 on farm work, and 5 on carting, while there are 4 waiters, 4 grooms, and 4 station touts. The rest are engaged in a great variety of other occupations.[1]

---

[1] Printers, brush-hands (3 each) ; cab-drivers, bill distributors, polishers, newspaper vendors, coal carriers, milk dealers' assistants (2 each) ; con-

Of the 110 men who rely principally on two occupations, 29 find them in seasonal sequence, usually farm work during the summer, and carting, navvying, asphalting, etc., in the winter, while the other 81 rely on two occupations which they seem to have selected simply by chance. No useful purpose will be served by giving detailed information with regard to the selection of employments made.

The 209 men, who did not express preference for any particular kind of work, have, among them, and at one time or other of their casual careers, been engaged upon a bewildering list of occupations, among others, navvying, farm work, unloading boats and occasional trips on keels, attending the cattle market, rough painting, hawking, gardening, labouring for bricklayers, work at the goods station, carting, delivering bills, station touting, chopping firewood, working at brickyards, glassworks, and gasworks, acting as boilermen, salesmen, packers, painters' models, ostlers, cobblers, cab-drivers, window cleaners, whitewashers, joiners, sign writers, ice-cream makers, canvassers, officers' servants, waiters, bill-posters, rag and bone gatherers, second-hand goods dealers, auction porters, sandwichmen, plumbers and glaziers, ticket collectors, fellmongers, tailors, indoor cleaners, scene shifters, grave-diggers, plate-layers, cable-layers,

---

fectioner's labourer, plumber, moulder, poultry dealer, cabinetmaker, gas worker, clerk, watchman, navvy, glass-blower, glassworks labourer, keel captain, tinsmith, warehouseman, scavenger, furniture remover, window cleaner, sawyer, canvasser, electrician's labourer, cleaner, engine cleaner, ostler, striker (1 each).

stablemen, carriage cleaners, coach-builders' fitters, extra post office hands, potato sorters, tillage mixers, newspaper sellers, etc. Yet, even within this group, men do not go quite indifferently from one occupation to another. In the case of those who informed us that they were looking for " any kind of work " we usually found, on further investigation, that their field of inquiry was restricted, though almost all were willing to accept *any* casual work within their powers. Generally, and this is especially true of those who have been casuals for some time, they had a prescribed circle when looking for work, and only went outside it when they failed to secure the minimum amount of employment necessary to maintain them in their accustomed standard of living. This circle, however, is largely the outcome of routine, and the fact remains that, for the most part, this great class of casual workers, except that small minority who have once been more or less skilled artisans, constitutes an unspecialised labour reserve, ready to enter any industry requiring such services as they could offer.

An examination of the details given on pp. 96 to 123 shows, however, that the majority of the men who are now seeking work as unspecialised unskilled labourers have been associated with particular industries for a sufficient length of time to be considered members of them,[1] and hence might be regarded, when unemployed, as a reserve of labour for those industries.

[1] See also table on p. 128.

We mention this fact in view of proposals which have been made, that each industry should be able to insure its own reserve from unemployment arising out of fluctuations of trade. Before passing to other matters, we may mention that, in connection with the problem of casual labour in York, we have sought to ascertain how far the number of casual workers is swollen by the fact that they consist of a number of separate bodies, each constituting a reserve for a particular employer; whether, in fact, the same conditions obtain in York, on a small scale, as those at the London Docks. There does not, however, appear to be much evidence that this is the case. York is a comparatively small place, and the labour market is fairly homogeneous. This is no argument against the need for decasualising the labour market, for there is very little doubt that all the demand for casual labour could be supplied by a much smaller number of men than those who now scramble for their share of the available work.

We now pass to consider the present condition of the men of this class. Is there evidence that the casual nature of their employment is demoralising them, physically or morally?

PHYSICAL AND MORAL CONDITION OF CASUAL WORKERS

It is difficult to state with anything approaching statistical accuracy the number of men who are, and who are not, physically strong and of satisfactory character. The terms are so indefinite, and the gradations separating one class from another are so fine, that in many cases classification must be more or less tentative. But with this qualification we may refer to the notes on the physique and character of the casual workers given on pp. 96 to 123. An examination of the facts there given shows that of the 317 men who have once worked regularly and for whom the information is available :

156, or 49 per cent, are satisfactory both in physique and character, *i.e.* are in both respects not markedly different from the average standard of unskilled workers who are in employment.

86, or 27 per cent, are of satisfactory physique, but unsatisfactory character.

39, or 12½ per cent, are of satisfactory character, but unsatisfactory physique.

36, or 11½ per cent, are unsatisfactory both in physique and character.

That is to say, half of them are satisfactory in both respects, and half unsatisfactory in one or both.

It is impossible to measure accurately the extent to which these men have deteriorated since they left regular work, as in many cases a number of years have elapsed. But when it is remembered that only 28 per cent left work through physical or moral unfitness, and that now 51 per cent are either physically or morally unfit, it is obvious, even if we under-estimate rather than exaggerate the value of the figures, that strong adverse influences have been at work, and almost all the men in this class are undergoing a more or less rapid process of deterioration. Some are still anxiously looking for permanent

work, and could hold it if they got it. A few, no
doubt, will ultimately get it. Others would be willing
to take it if it came their way, but although at one
time they may have been eager for it, they are now
becoming resigned to the life of a casual worker. A
third group, again, are not looking for regular work,
nor would they keep it long if it were given them.
Although at one time regular workers, they have
now come to prefer the life of the casual. In their
case the process of deterioration has made considerable
advance. Its final stage lands the men in the " work-
shy " class described in Chapter V.

That physical deterioration must be going on
among the members of this class is evidenced by the
facts obtained regarding the total family earnings of
its members. Although, as previously stated, the
information concerning these is only approximate, it
points to the probability that nearly one-half of those
in this class are living under the poverty line.[1]

This is a serious fact, especially when we remember
how many children are involved.

Suggested Remedies

That the community should do something to
check this deterioration of its workers is clear. Let
us consider what remedies would best overcome the
evils we have been describing.

[1] Information concerning the family earnings was obtained for 297
of the 441 cases ; of these 48·5 per cent had an income insufficient to
maintain physical efficiency.

Decasualisation of the Labour Market.—Undoubtedly the first step is so to reorganise industry that more work is carried out by permanent and less by casual workers. At present an employer frequently relies on having a large proportion of his work done by the latter, but this is not necessarily because his demand for workers is so variable that he could not possibly give permanent work to any of those casually employed. Very often he might, by a little modification of his arrangements, guarantee permanent work to a certain proportion of those now employed casually, and thus reduce the fringe of casual workers. One of the writers when recently going into this matter in his own factory, found that it had become the custom in certain departments to carry out a portion of the work by casual labour. Some of these departments were busy in summer and others in winter, and it was found possible so to dovetail the casual occupations that permanent employment could be offered to a number of the men. In other departments it was ascertained that over a period of years the number of men casually employed never fell below a given figure, and it was obviously possible, therefore, to place this minimum number on the permanent staff. This illustration merely shows that individual employers may, by giving the matter attention, sometimes do not a little to reduce the evils inseparably connected with casual work. But even if they all did their utmost in this direction, there would remain a considerable

margin of casual workers, and in dealing with these
the newly established Labour Exchanges must play
an essential part. It is earnestly to be hoped that
employers will support these Exchanges by engaging
all labour through them. Just in so far as this is
done it will be possible to organise the casual labour
market, which hitherto has remained in a state
bordering on chaos. It has been a slough into which
all sorts and conditions of workers have fallen, and
in which they are scrambling for scraps of work.
Such a dismal swamp offers no firm foothold or
guarantee of adequate maintenance, and yet, as we
have seen, many of the casual workers engulfed in
it are men of good character, physique, and ability.
Moreover, they are performing valuable service in the
field of industry by meeting those temporary and
often sudden demands for extra labour, which almost
every employer is compelled to make from time to
time. We need not here enter fully into the methods
by which the Exchanges could organise casual labour,
the matter having been dealt with so admirably in
Mr. Beveridge's book on Unemployment.[1] Briefly,

[1] *Unemployment: a Problem of Industry*, p. 201 *et seq.* One method
of decasualisation which has been adopted with considerable success among
dock labourers and other classes of casual workers is that of registration.
Its application, however, is limited to aggregations of casual workers
employed in varying numbers by a large number of employers, since the
varying demands for labour of large employers could, of course, best be
satisfied by immediate and direct application to a Labour Exchange. In
York the cattle market seems to us to offer a field of necessarily casual
employment which can best be supplied by the method of registration,
since the demand arises at short notice and must be satisfied on the spot.
We have seen how large a number of men are occasionally employed as
cattle drovers and at odd jobs about the cattle market and auctions. The

however, their endeavour would be so to dovetail the demands for labour which they had to meet, that the best men would get practically permanent employment, although possibly for a constantly changing list of employers. This would, of course, mean that a certain number of men would be squeezed out. Instead of an arrangement whereby all casual workers got some work, but nearly all were under-employed, a certain proportion of them would get constant work and the rest none at all. This is what is meant by "decasualisation." It obviously carries with it the necessity for dealing in some way with those who are squeezed out. What proportion that would be we cannot say. We have suggested that all the casual work in York might possibly be done by little more than half the workers, but this is merely a guess, and possibly two-thirds would be required. But if the labour market in York were thoroughly decasualised it is almost certain that between 150

---

suggestion was made at a meeting of the York Distress Committee (Report of Monthly Meeting, December 5, 1910) "that there are always hanging about two or three times the number of men necessary for the needs of the market, and that the value of the employment could be increased, to the benefit of the labourers and their employers, by only permitting registered men being employed for such work. It would make the job worth having and consequently looked after ; it would lessen the attendance of the 'out-of-works' of the loafing order ; it would cause the men to be more humane in their treatment of the animals ; it would enable the users of the market to identify their men ; it would enable the police and R.S.P.C.A. men more easily to regulate the traffic ; it would subject to a certain amount of control an otherwise uncontrolled section of the community ; and it would most likely cause a gradual and permanent migration of surplus labour." To us this proposal and the reasons advanced in support of it appear admirable, and we regret that the Markets Committee found it inexpedient to act upon it.

and 300 men would be squeezed out altogether, and these would, of course, be the inferior workers. What, it may be asked, could be done with them? Obviously they could not be left to starve, but must be adequately provided for in some way. The first thing would be to classify them, and see what kind of work they were capable of doing. In so far as they were efficient workers, the problem would be simply one of providing them with employment, but the inefficient, whether physically, mentally, or morally defective, would confront us with other problems. It is possible that some of those who were morally defective should, after conviction by a magistrate, be dealt with in penal labour colonies, where reformative measures could be applied. Others, who were suffering from physical or mental weakness, would require such treatment as would restore them to the ranks of efficient workers, or if this were impossible, maintenance sufficient to prevent those dependent on them from being seriously handicapped in their training and development. Questions of this kind were dealt with at length by the Royal Commission on the Poor Laws, which has thrown much light upon their solution. It is, however, important to remember that much of the inefficiency which marks these casual workers is the direct result of unemployment, and to reduce unemployment is to reduce inefficiency.

Coming now to the efficient workers who are squeezed out, it would lead us into a very long discus-

sion to describe in detail all the methods which might
be adopted to absorb them. We believe that no single
method would be adequate, and that the problem
must be approached from many standpoints. Mr.
and Mrs. Webb, in their recent book on the *Prevention of Destitution*,[1] express the view that the
surplus could be entirely absorbed if three reforms,
which they hold to be desirable in themselves,
were carried out. The first is a reduction in the
hours of railway, tramway, and omnibus employees,
which would lead to the employment of many
additional thousands of men ; the second is that all
young persons over school age and under 18 should
spend half their time only in industrial employment,
and the other half " at some continuation school or
technical institute." This great reduction in the
supply of juvenile labour would lead to the employment of an increased number of adults. The third,
only dealing with women workers, is that no widows
having young children dependent on them should be
forced to go out to work, but should be maintained
by the State. Whether Mr. and Mrs. Webb are
correct in thinking that these industrial changes, if
carried out, would absorb the whole of the surplus
labour, is a point upon which we cannot express an
opinion, not having the necessary data. But it is
clear that the absorption of a permanent surplus of
efficient, even though unskilled labour, cannot be an
insoluble problem unless there is a shortage of one or

[1] Longmans, p. 133 *et seq.*

both of the other two factors in the production of wealth, viz. land and capital. As there is no such shortage in England to-day it must be possible for statesmanship to bring unemployed labour into union with unemployed land and capital, and so absorb any surplus which might result from decasualisation.

In so far as reforms may take the form of developing agriculture, the objection will probably be urged that the men squeezed out would not be suitable for labour on the land. This is true; but it is not at all essential that *these particular men* should be sent to work on the land. If the necessary facilities were given, some men now engaged in industrial pursuits would quit these for agriculture or horticulture, and the vacancies thus created might, either directly or indirectly, be filled from the squeezed-out surplus of casual workers.

The Provision of a Financial Reserve.—So far we have dealt with the men who have already become casual workers, but evidently one of the tasks confronting us is to prevent men who are in regular employment from becoming casual workers at all. If we are to do this, it is imperative that some system should be adopted which would give unskilled men, who have never earned high wages, the power to wait for some time after losing regular employment before they are driven to accept casual work. Some readers will, no doubt, argue that if working-men were more thrifty they could themselves set aside a fund which would carry them through such waiting periods.

We should like, however, to ask such critics to try
to realise how very small is the margin left to an
unskilled labourer with a family, after supplying the
bare needs of physical efficiency—if, indeed, such a
margin exists at all. We do not, of course, forget
for a moment the large sums spent annually by
the working classes on drink, gambling, tobacco, and
various amusements, but we would remind those who
accuse them of gross want of thrift, that since they
have the same inclinations and weaknesses as their
wealthier brethren, it is unreasonable to demand from
them a higher standard of austerity than is found
among other classes. Indeed, when the extreme
monotony of much of their work, the limitation of
their intellectual interests, and the confined character
of their homes are remembered, their expenditure
on such luxuries is more excusable than the extravagance of those whose lives are full of variety.

How can these men be supplied with a financial
reserve sufficient to enable them to stand out for a
job as good as the one they have lost, instead of
being forced, as they are at present, to take the first
job that offers, whether it be casual or permanent?
There are two ways :—

Insurance against Unemployment.—First by some
method of unemployment insurance such as that
proposed in the Unemployment Insurance Bill
introduced in Parliament in May 1911. In connection
with any such measure, however, even if it were made
general, the conditions to be observed in order to

obtain benefits must necessarily be strict, and there would always be a considerable number of workers who would fail to observe them. For instance, all those who lost their employment through any fault, such as quarrelling with their employer, etc., would be ruled out of benefit. A further limitation of any scheme of insurance, perhaps even more important, is that the payment of insurance benefits would only partially lessen that serious deterioration of physique and *morale*, which so rapidly affects a workman when he has nothing to do but walk the streets or sit in the office of a Labour Exchange waiting for a job to turn up. These limitations do not constitute an argument against unemployment insurance, but merely indicate that it must be supported by other reforms.

A Second Way of creating a Financial Reserve.— A second way in which men might be furnished with the financial reserve necessary to enable them to tide over periods of unemployment, would be to enable industrial workmen to live in the country, although continuing to work in the towns. Such a policy is widely adopted in Belgium, where it is found that the crops grown on the land attached to the houses, along with the produce from live-stock, just supply that reserve of wealth necessary to prevent men from becoming destitute directly they are unemployed. This method of meeting the difficulty is dealt with at length in Chapter VIII., and here we need merely point out that it not only provides a financial reserve, but gives unemployed men a healthy occupation, preventing that demoralisation which almost invariably accompanies unemployment in the towns.

In conclusion, if any readers shrink from supporting these schemes, merely because they involve much reorganisation of the labour market, and extensive economic changes, let them remember that the evil to be remedied is very great, that its social consequences are disastrous, and that it will not be possible to arrest it by half - hearted or timid measures.

CHAPTER IV

MEN ENGAGED IN THE BUILDING TRADE
(173 in number)

ALTHOUGH most of the men engaged in the building trade are, in a sense, casual workers, since they do not expect to be permanently employed at one place or by one employer, they differ in so many respects from the ordinary casual workers that they must be considered apart.

Really good workmen in the building trade, even if seldom out of employment, may, unless they become foremen, remain casual workers all their lives, moving not only from job to job, but from employer to employer. Certainly those contractors who always have work in hand in one town, will keep their best men so long that they may virtually be looked on as regular workers. This is most frequently the case with joiners and plumbers, less often with bricklayers and painters, and still less often with the other trades. But, in spite of these exceptions, the great majority of workers in the building trade are casually employed. They are engaged at the begin-

ning of a contract and dismissed at its close, unless
the contractor happens to have further work in hand
in the same locality, when they will probably be
transferred to the new job. Again, it may happen,
during the construction of a building, that the
different trades do not all progress at the same
pace, and then the men most in advance must stand
off until the others catch up with them. Or delay
may occur in the delivery of materials, making it
necessary for men to stand off until they are forthcoming. Such breaks, which may last for a week or
two, are by no means infrequent. These conditions
differentiate the building trades from all others, and
have important economic and industrial consequences.
As most men engaged on new buildings are subject
only to an hour's notice, no careful inquiry, as a rule,
is made when a man is set on. If he looks likely he
is tried, without being asked for a reference, and if
he works well he stays on so long as the job lasts.
Thus a good moral character does not materially help
him, nor a bad one hamper him, in getting work.
The only question is that of his ability as a workman.
Poor workmen are soon weeded out, and, in a town
of the size of York, they come to be known to the
employers, who of course always give the preference
to more capable workers. But since a bad moral
character is no handicap, the unskilled branches of
the building trade come to be looked on as a possible
source of employment by those whose records make
it difficult to secure permanent work elsewhere, and

thus men of good character are in these trades
subjected to especially severe competition. Another
consequence of the casual nature of the building
trades is the comparative ease with which old men,
whether skilled or unskilled, find work there, so long
as they are physically efficient. There is no question
of a man's being " too old at forty," as is so often the
case when he is seeking permanent work. As we
pointed out in Chapter II., employers hesitate to
add to their permanent staff men who have reached
middle life, not because they are, at the time, incapable
of doing good work, but because it may be difficult to
get rid of them when they begin to fail. But in the
building trades a man of 60 or even more, if he is
a good worker, stands as good a chance of getting
ordinary work as a younger man; his present value
is the only question considered. We say " ordinary
work," because it might be thought unadvisable to
employ an old man on very high buildings, but this
is not a serious handicap.

With these preliminary remarks let us examine
the problem of unemployment as it affected the
members of the building trade in York on June 7,
1910. Altogether, we found 173 men unemployed,
but in order to understand the significance of this
figure we must know approximately the total number
of men in York who follow the trade. There are no
means by which this information can be obtained
with absolute accuracy; but by questioning trade
union secretaries, and others having special know-

ledge, we are able to give in the following table,
figures which are substantially correct :—

	Unemployed.		Approximate Total.
Bricklayers. . . .	. 35	out of	150
Builder's labourers . .	. 57	,,	400
Painters (all grades) [1] . .	. 25	,,	400
Joiners	. 34	,,	500
Plasterers	. 7	,,	40
Plumbers	. 9	,,	80
Stone-masons . . .	. 6	,,	70
	173		1640

These figures show that at the time of our inquiry
the unemployed constituted much more than a small
reserve for the different trades. As it cannot be
supposed that such a condition of things is permanent,
we are led to the conclusion that the building trade
generally was abnormally depressed. It may be
asked, however, might not these unemployed men
constitute, not one undifferentiated reserve for all the
employers in the city, but a number of separate
reserves, none of them large in relation to the particular firm with which it was connected, but together
forming an unduly large reserve for the maximum
demand likely to be made on one day by all the
masters in the city. But, as a rule, men will only

[1] Although there is, of course, a world-wide difference between a highly
skilled painter and decorator, who has served his seven years' apprenticeship, and the brush-hand who has had no special training, the gradations
which separate these extremes are so fine that we cannot draw a broad line
of demarcation. All men engaged in the trade actually handle brushes, and
thus there is no such distinction as exists between a bricklayer and his
labourer, where the latter only fetches and carries for the former. As
June is the busy time for painters, it may safely be assumed, however, that
the men unemployed were at best but partially skilled.

continue under one employer so long as he gives
fairly regular work. When that ceases they go elsewhere; and though, when this inquiry was made, no
Labour Exchange existed, the number of employers
was so small and the knowledge of available jobs so
easy to obtain, that the city may be said to have consisted of one labour market. We are therefore forced
back upon our first conclusion, that the building trade
in York on June 7, 1910, was unusually depressed.

Although the figures published by the Board of
Trade show that by June 1910 employment in the
building trade had greatly improved in the country
generally after the depression which had lasted for
two years,[1] this improvement had not been felt in
York at the time of our census, though it has come
since. For seven years prior to 1910, the building
trade in York had been depressed, and the depression
was especially severe because there had previously
been a great boom, and York had become overbuilt.[2]
Moreover, the census of population made in April
1911 shows that the population of the city, which,
during the preceding three decades, increased by 13·09

[1] The official figures refer to carpenters and plumbers only, but the
variations in their employment no doubt reflect fairly accurately those for
the whole of the building trades. The following are the percentages of
unemployed carpenters and plumbers in the month of June in each year
since 1901.

1901.	1902.	1903.	1904.	1905.	1906.	1907.	1908.	1909.	1910.
3·3	3·4	4·2	6·7	7·2	5·9	6·1	9·7	10·9	6·8

[2] According to the Report of the Medical Officer of Health for 1910,
the number of empty houses in York was on March 31,

1905.	1906.	1907.	1908.	1909.	1910.
564	796	855	711	611	543

per cent, 8·44 per cent, and 14·52 per cent respectively, only increased during the last ten years by 5·26 per cent. The rapid growth of the ferro-concrete system of construction is affecting stone-masons and bricklayers unfavourably, for it employs fewer of them and a larger proportion of labourers and carpenters.

On p. 152 *et seq.* we give certain particulars of each of the men in this class.[1] For reasons already stated, examination of personal details is of less moment in the case of men in the building trades than elsewhere, but attention may be drawn to a few points. Although many of the skilled workers followed an unskilled occupation after leaving school, they soon settled down to their apprenticeships, but the unskilled workers have, for the most part, followed, and frequently still follow, an extraordinarily wide range of different occupations, so that it has sometimes been difficult to say whether certain individuals should be included in this class or among the miscellaneous casual workers. This is, perhaps, especially true of the " brush-hands," who only find work in connection with the painting trade for a few months each spring and summer, and turn to other work for the rest of the year.

An examination of the columns dealing with the physique and character of the men shows that a very

[1] We do not in this table give the wages earned in the particular cases, because in the building trade all the masters pay the standard rates, viz.

	Pence per hour.			Pence per hour.
Bricklayers	9	Plasterers		9
Bricklayer's Labourers .	6	Masons		9
Joiners	8¼	Slaters		9
Painters (see footnote, p. 149)	5 to 7	Plumbers		8

MEN ENGAGED IN THE

Age.	At what Age did he enter the Trade?	Member of Trade Union?	Previous Occupations.	Makeshift Occupations while not working at own Trade.
			BRICKLAYERS	
26	14¼	No	As a boy, confectioner's labourer (6 months); army, 18 months (to 1904)	....
49	19	Yes	On brickfields (age 14-19)	....
55	14	No	....	....
25	14	,,	....	....
28	15	Yes, but run out	Apprentice to painting (age 14-15) . .	Painting and foundry labouring
36	14	No	....	....
54	14	Yes	Errand boy (few months)	....
25	13	No	,, (age 12-13)	....
57	16	,,	,, (age 11-16)	....
31	16	Yes, but run out	Half-timer (age 11-12), brickyard labourer (age 12-16)	In country, fruit - hawking (probably in nature of holiday)
24	14	No	....	....
55	?	Yes	Errand boy (?)	....
25	15	,,	Confectioner's labourer (1899-1900) . .	....
32	14	No	....	Casual carting . .
30	14	Yes, but run out	Milkman (a few months in 1894) . .	....
50	16	Yes	Page-boy (age 10-12)	Navvying, concreting . .
33	15	,,	Errand boy (1 month), carriage trimmer (1 year)	....
53	14	No	....	....
26	?	,,	Bricklayer's labourer (army 3 years, to 1908)	....
28	14	,,	....	Relief work . . .
55	Boyhood	Yes	Farm work (as a boy)	....
61	14	No	....	....
50	12	Yes, but run out	....	....
35	14	No	....	....
22	14	,,	Errand boy (3 months 1902), labourer (6 months 1902)	Haymaking, labourer . .
40	?	Yes	?	....
64	12	,,	....	Labourer, pall-bearer, wheeling invalid
21	14	No	Confectioner's labourer (age 12-14) . .	....
29	14	,,	....	....
48	22	Yes, but run out	Coach-building (as a boy)	Labourer . . . .
45	?	Yes	Comb works	....
27	16	No	Apprenticed to grocery (age 14-16) . .	....
29	?	,,	?	....
50	14¼	,,	In sawmill (as a boy)	Labourer . . . .
41	14	,,	....	Musician (probably on tramp)

BUILDING TRADE (173 IN NUMBER)

If looking for Occupations other than own Trade, which?	Present Condition. Physique.	Character.	Apparent Personal Handicaps in Search for Work.	No. of Persons in Family. Adults.	Children (under 16).	Average Weekly Income of Family, excluding Casual Earnings of Unemployed.[1]
....	Good	Good	None	2	1	..
....	Robust	,,	,,	6	1	?
....	Bad sight, healthy	,,	,,	3	1	4/-
....	Good	,,	,,	4	2	67/-
Painting or labouring	Healthy	,,	,,	4		9/6
....	Robust	,,	,,	2	4	..
....	Very good	,,	,,	2	1	..
....	Good	,,	,,	3	1	23/6
....	Fairly good	Fond of drink	,,	4	..	Over 30/-
....	Very good	Good	,,	4	..	49/9
....	Good	,,	,,	1	..	..
....	Healthy	Very respectable, but slow worker	Slowness	2	..	..
....	,,	Good	None	7	1	?
....	,,	,,	,,	2	3	2/-
....	,,	Excellent	,,	5	1	38/-
Any in building trade	Strong	Heavy drinker	Bad reputation	5	..	?
....	,,	Excellent	None	2	1	..
....	,,	Good	,,	5	3	28/-
....	,,	,,	,,	3	..	17/6
....	,,	Good, but slow worker	Slowness	2	3	..
....	Good	Good worker, fond of drink	,,	2	..	..
....	,,	Excellent	None	3	1	?
....	,,	Good	,,	2	..	10/-
....	,,	,,	,,	2	..	..
....	,,	,,	,,	6	2	55/-
....	,,	Respectable, but slow worker	Slowness	2	3	..
Any light labouring	Healthy	Very good, but slow worker	None	2	..	?
....	,,	,, ,,	,,	5	..	?
....	Good	Good	,,	6	..	84/-
....	Good	Slow worker, drinker	Slowness	4	5	10/-
....	,,	Good character, slow	,,	?	?	?
....	.,	Good	None	2	3	..
....	,,	Probably lazy	,,	?	?	?
....	.,	Fairly efficient, good	,,	?	?	23/-
....	,,	Frequently loafing, has often been in workhouse	Bad reputation	1	..	..

1 Including pensions, poor relief, etc., but not occasional gifts or savings.

Age.	At what Age did he enter the Trade?	Member of Trade Union?	Previous Occupations.	Makeshift Occupations while not working at own Trade.
			STONE-MASONS	
44	14	Yes	....	....
46	?	,,	?	....
42	14	No	Errand boy (age 11-14)	....
41	16	Yes	Grocer's assistant (age 13-16)	....
28	13	No	Errand boy (few weeks)	Navvy (rarely)
38	14	,,	....	General labourer, whitewasher
			PLUMBERS	
31	16	Yes, but dropped out	Moulder's apprentice (age 14-16)	....
27	14	No	....	....
55	15	,,	....	General labourer
23	14	,,	....	....
49	Boyhood	,,	Railway telegraph clerk (as a boy)	Casual painting
25	14	?	....	....
24	13	No	....	....
29	Boyhood	Yes	Lithographer's feeder (as a boy)	....
48	14	No	....	....
			PLASTERERS	
28	14	No	....	....
24	14	Yes	....	....
60	Boyhood	,,	Errand boy (from age 11)	Plasterer's and general labourer
27	15	No	,, (age 11-15)	Painter
26	14	Yes	....	....
47	15	No	....	....
23	14	,,	....	Labourer (rare)
			JOINERS	
20	14	No	....	Labourer (rare)
19	14	,,	....	Eight months labourer on Tramway

BUILDING TRADE (173 IN NUMBER)—continued

If looking for Occupations other than own Trade, which?	Present Condition.		Apparent Personal Handicaps in Search for Work.	No. of Persons in Family.		Average Weekly Income of Family, excluding Casual Earnings of Unemployed.[1]
	Physique.	Character.		Adults.	Children (under 16).	
....	Good	Very superior.	None	2	1	4/-
....	,,	Good ,,	,,	?	?	?
....	Robust	Good	,,	2	2	..
....	Good	First rate	,,	2	3	?
Any labouring	,,	Very good character	,,	2	3	..
Stone-mason's labourer	Very good	Probably drinker, poor worker	Inefficiency	1	..	..
....	Good	Good	None	2	1	..
....	?	Lazy and inefficient	Very casual, constantly receiving poor relief and other help, inefficiency	2	4	..
"Any," own trade preferred	Strong	Good	None	4	..	22/-
....	Good	Excellent	,,	5	1	?
"Any," own trade or painting preferred	,,	Good	,,	2	3	5/-
Plays with idea of emigration	,,	,,	,,	?	?	?
....	,,	,, (good worker)	,,	4	..	?
....	,,	,, ,,	"Permanent places are by preference given to the older and more experienced men"	2	2	?
....	,,	,,	None	5	3	over 35/-
....	Good	Good	None	2	..	..
....	,,	,,	,,	3	5	?
....	Feeling age	Fair worker	,,	3	3	18/-
....	Healthy	Good	,,	2	1	..
....	,,	,,	,,	3	5	?
....	Strong	,, (fair worker)	,,	3	..	15/-
....	,,	,,	,,	3	..	21/-
....	Healthy	Good	None	3	..	25/-
....	,,	,,	Apprenticeship not finished	?	?	?

1 Including pensions, poor relief, etc., but not occasional gifts or savings.

MEN ENGAGED IN THE

Age.	At what Age did he enter the Trade?	Member of Trade Union?	Previous Occupations.	Makeshift Occupations while not working at own Trade.
21	16	No	Clerk (age 14-16)	....
50	14	,,	....	Labourer, and catch jobs .
32	Probably 23	,,	Post office messenger, cab-driver . .	Cab-driver, and catch jobs .
41	?	Not now	Errand boy	Labourer . . . . .
56	13	No	,, (age 10-13)	....
59	14	,,	....	....
49	15	,,	....	....
63	Boyhood	,,	Among farmers (as a boy)	....
45	14	,,	....	....
22	14	,,	....	....
38	?	,,	Errand boy	....
55	14	Yes	....	....
37	14	No	....	....
47	14	,,	....	....
40	14	,,	....	Labouring . . . .
?	?	?	?	?
34	14	Yes	....	....
32	14	No	....	....
25	14	Yes	Errand boy (age 13-14)	" Depression in his trade only cause of his casual labour." Timber carrier several years on and off
56	14	No	Confectioner's labourer (age 10-14) . .	....
56	14	,,	Publican (1879-1899)	....
48	14	Yes	....	....
22	14	,,	....	....
41	14	No	....	....
31	15	,,	Errand boy (age 14-15), in brickyard for one season (age 15), casual painting between 1900-1903	Painter . . . . .
45	15	,,	....	Musician, insurance agent .
30	14	Not now	....	....
28	18	No	Errand boy (6 months), apprentice sanitary engineer (4 years)	....
53	15	Yes	Errand boy (age 14-15)	....
50	?	No	?	....
27	14	,,	....	....
60	14	,,	....	....

JOINER'S LABOURER

| 30 | 25 | No | Brickyard, farm work, railway labourer, general builder's labourer | Only expects to find temporary work |

SLATER'S LABOURER

| 48 | 32 | No | Comb works, farm work, general labourer | Only expects to find temporary work, general labourer |

BUILDING TRADE (173 in Number)—*continued*

If looking for Occupations other than own Trade, which?	Present Condition.		Apparent Personal Handicaps in Search for Work.	No. of Persons in Family.		Average Weekly Income of Family, excluding Casual Earnings of Unemployed.[1]
	Physique.	Character.		Adults.	Children (under 16).	
....	Healthy	Good	None	5	1	44/-
....	"	Bad ?	?	3	2	5/-
....	Strong	?	Too long out of trade	3	..	23/6
....	Good	Good, moderate hand	None, except perhaps inefficiency	2	?	3/6
Any	Strong	Good	None	3	4	26/6
....	"	Very good	"	4	..	?
....	Good	"	"	3	1	18/-
....	Fairly good	Good	"	2	1	..
....	"	"	"	4	..	40/-
....	Good	"	"	3	2	42/-
....	Strong	Given to drink	Probably inefficiency	3	..	25/-
....	?	Good	None	2	..	10/-
....	Healthy	"	"	2	6	..
....	Delicate	Not anxious for regular work	Delicate health	3	2	?
Own trade or any	Healthy	Good	None	3	4	..
?	?	?	?	1	..	..
....	Healthy	Incompetent, good character	Inefficiency	7	..	71/-
....	"	Incompetent	"	7	..	81/-
Joiner or labourer	"	Very good	" ?	2	2	..
....	"	Excellent	None	5	2	48/-
Public-house manager	"	Very respectable	"	6	..	Over 40/-
....	"	Good	"	3	7	13/-
....	"	"	" ?	?	?	?
....	"	"	"	3	2	..
Joiner or labourer	Consumptive	"	Ill-health	2	7	..
....	Strong	"	None	1	..	
....	"	"	"	5	..	39/6
....	Delicate	"	Delicate health	2	3	..
....	Good	"	None	3	1	33/-
Joiner or wheelwright	"	"	"	4	..	9/-
....	"	"	"	2	2	..
....	Very good	Excellent	"	3	..	..
Builder's labourer	Very good	Good	None]	4	..	?
Any labouring	Good	"Average"	None	4	2	?

[1] Including pensions, poor relief, etc., but not occasional gifts or savings.

MEN ENGAGED IN THE

Age.	At what Age did he enter the Trade?	Member of Trade Union?	Previous Occupations.	Makeshift Occupations while not working at own Trade.
			PLASTERER'S LABOURERS	
45	19	Yes, out of benefit	Cotton-mill half-timer (age 11-13), nipper (age 13-16), farm work (age 15-19)	Only expects to find temporary work, general labourer, relief work
60	Boyhood	No	Farm service (4½ years)	....
			PAINTERS (AND PAINTER'S LABOURERS)	
48	?	No	Jam boiler (as a boy), summer painting, winter—gas works (30 years)	Gas works labourer . .
40	?	,,	?	Whitewashing, paper-hanging
45	Probably 28	,,	Foundry labourer (age 14-28) . . .	....
33	?	,,	....	Coal carrier, pig-sty cleaner .
25	Probably 16	,,	Errand boy (age 13-14), box-maker (age 14-16), bill-poster (age 16-17)	Snow shovelling, paper-hanging, station touting
37	Before 30	,,	Box-maker	Catch jobs . . . .
36	,,	,,	Errand boy, bill-poster, 4 years . .	....
22	17	,,	Errand boy (from age 12), confectioner's labourer (age 16-17)	....
34	13	,,	....	....
30	?	?	?	?
21	15	No	Box-maker (age 14-15).	....
20	Boyhood	,,	Golf caddie	....
29	14	,,	....	General labourer . . .
25	14	,,	....	....
51	14	,,	....	....
60	Boyhood	?	Army (12 years)	....
42	24	No	Tallow chandler (to age 24) . . .	Firewood hawker, farm labourer
38	14	,,	....	....
50	14	,,	....	....
21	15	,,	Errand boy (age 12-15) . . .	....
50	22	,,	"Gentleman's service" (age 14-22) . .	Catch jobs . . . .
48	Before 28	,,	?	Navvy (relief work) . .
24	21	,,	Groom (age 13-21)	....
28	14	,,	....	....
35	31	,,	Printer's labourer (age 12-16), labourer (age 16-21), army (age 21-26), flour-mill labourer (casual to age 31)	General labourer, bill distributor

BUILDING TRADE (173 IN NUMBER)—continued

If looking for Occupations other than own Trade, which?	Present Condition. Physique.	Character.	Apparent Personal Handicaps in Search for Work.	Adults	Children (under 16)	Average Weekly Income of Family, excluding Casual Earnings of Unemployed.[1]
Builder's labourer . .	Good . . .	Heavy drinker .	Bad reputation	1	..	..
....	Seems strong. .	Good . . .	None . .	1	..	..
....	Healthy . . .	Respectable . .	None . .	?	?	?
Any	,, . . .	,, . .	,, . .	2	4	..
Painter's labourer . .	,, . . .	Inefficient . .	Inefficiency .	?	?	?
Any but painting . .	Suffering from painter's colic	Good . . .	Ill-health .	?	?	?
Any	Healthy . . .	Drinker . . .	Inefficiency .	3	..	..
,, ...	Fairly good . .	Intemperate and untrustworthy	Bad reputation	2	6	12/-
....	Strong . . .	Bad upbringing, poor type	Inefficiency .	2	2	..
....	Healthy . . .	Very good . .	None . .	2	2	..
....	Not strong . .	Good . . .	Ill-health, which prevented him from getting regular occupation	2	2	..
? Painting or any . .	? Good . . .	? Good . . .	? Possibly laziness	? 4	? 4	? 60/-
,, ,, . .	Rheumatic . .	Slow, but steady .	Possibly ill-health	?	?	?
,, ,, . .	Healthy . . .	Good . . .	None . .	7	3	43/-
,, ,, . .	,, . . .	,, . .	,, . .	7	3	51/6
,, ,, . .	,, ? . .	,, ? .	Lack of energy	7	3	55/-
....			None . .	2	..	4/-
Any	Healthy . ? .	Good ? . .	Probably laziness	1	..	..
....	Poor . . .	Fair . . .	Delicate health	2	2	5/-
....	Fair . . .	Very lazy and inefficient	Inefficiency .	4	..	?
....	Good . . .	Slow and inefficient	,, .	2	1	6/6
Any	Healthy . . .	Very respectable .	None . .	3	2	8/-
,, ...	Suffering from painter's colic	Good . . .	Ill-health .	4	1	?
,, ...	Good . . .	Lazy . . .	Inefficiency and laziness	6	3	48/-
....	,, . . .	Good worker . .	None . .	3	..	20/-
Any	Strong . . .	Bad character .	Intemperance and inefficiency	2	4	..

1 Including pensions, poor relief, etc., but not occasional gifts or savings.

MEN ENGAGED IN THE

BUILDER'S LABOURERS

Age.	At what Age did he enter the Trade?	Member of Trade Union?	Previous Occupations.	Makeshift Occupations while not working at own Trade.
40	?	No	Coal miner (from age 12)	General labourer
48	About 25	,,	Rivet heater (age 10-13)	Gas works in winter, 4 months
45	27	,,	Glass works labourer (age 14-16), saw-mill labourer (age 16-21), army (age 21-27)	Cattle drover
47	12	,,	....	Farm work and other catch jobs
24	22½	,,	Farm service (age 14-17), confectioner's labourer (age 17-21), flour-mill labourer (age 21-22½)	Casual goods porter and other catch work
23	13	,,	....	?
32	?	,,	Box-maker (age 12-14).	Cattle drover, relief work
44	14	,,	Army (age 33-41)	Casual labourer
58	?	,,	?	Catch jobs (since 1890)
65	15	,,	?	Hawking, farm work, begging
35	Before 25	,,	Confectioner's labourer (from age 12)	Cattle drover
32	23	,,	Errand boy, dock labourer (age 17-21), general labourer (age 21-23)	Hawking peas
35	19	,,	Confectioner's labourer (age 14-16), engine cleaner (age 16-17), labourer in carriage works (age 17-19), in timber yard (age 29-34)	....
35	?	Yes	Glass works labourer .	....
35	?	No	Gardener (as a boy), railway labourer (age 24-26)	....
25	21	,,	Confectioner's labourer (age 14-16), nipper, 6 months (age 17), army (age 18-21)	General labourer, relief work
38	?	,,	Glass works labourer (as a boy)	....
33	?	,,	Dock labourer (4 years)	Help in small shop.
56	41	Was years ago	Farm hand (age 11½-22), brickmaker (age 22-31), farm labourer (age 31-33), engineer's labourer (age 33-40)	Farm labourer
30	14	No	Brewer's labourer (9 months)	Footballer
65	Boyhood	Yes	Errand boy (age 12-?) .	....
48	14	No	....	Haymaking, relief work
49	20	,,	Agricultural labourer (age 14-17), in brick-yard (age 17-20)	....
46	23	Yes	Glass works labourer (age 10-21), engineer's labourer (age 21-23)	Seed mixing (rare)
57	18	No	Errand boy (age 13-15), catch jobs, farm labourer (age 15-18)	Workhouse, farm work, catch jobs, relief work
50	?	Yes	Farm labourer (age 12-19), general labourer	Farm work, relief work, catch jobs
25	21	No	Errand boy (age 14-15), bricklayer's labourer (age 15-21)	Unloading boats, help in lodging-house
28	19	Yes (out of benefit)	Stone-mason (age 14), sawyer (age 14-16), forge labourer (age 16-19)	Scavenger, general labourer
55	27	No	Foundry labourer (age 10-27)	....
34	15	,,	Confectioner's labourer (age 13-15)	Farm work, manure mixing, catch jobs (in hospital 33 weeks)

BUILDING TRADE (173 IN NUMBER)—*continued*

If looking for Occupations other than own Trade, which?	Present Condition.		Apparent Personal Handicaps in Search for Work.	Adults.	Children (under 16).	Average Weekly Income of Family excluding Casual Earnings of Unemployed.[1]
	Physique.	Character.				
....	Strong . . .	Respectable . .	None . .	1	..	..
....	Looks very old .	Drinker, but good worker	Old appearance	1	3	3/6
Farm or cattle work .	Very good . .	Good . . .	None . .	1	..	..
....	Good . . .	Good average worker	„ . .	1	..	..
....	?	Very bad stock, betting, and low lodging-house type	Probably laziness	1	..	..
Any	?	?	?	2	2	..
„	Good . . .	?	Probably laziness	1	..	..
„ . . ? . .	„ . . .	?	None . .	2	..	9/-
		Drinker . . .	„ . .	3	3	..
Any	Suffering from bronchitis	Bad . . .	Bad reputation	3	3	?
„	Underfed . .	Unsatisfactory .	Inefficiency .	1	..	..
„	Good . . .	Average labourer .	None . .	2	5	..
„	Strong . . .	Average labourer, bad character	„ . .	2	1	..
....		Very good . .	„ . .	3	?	20/-
....	Weakly . . .	Good . . .	Delicate health	2	1	..
....	Robust . . .	Excellent . .	None . .	2	1	..
....	Good . . .	Good . . .	„ . .	2	8	..
....	„ . . .	Fairly good . .	„ . .	6	..	Over 30/-
....	„ . . .	Good . . .	„ . .	7	1	63/-
Any	Weak . . .	Spoilt by sport .	Poor health .	1	..	..
„	Strong . . .	Drinker . . .	None . .	?	?	27/6
„	„ . . .	Good . . .	„ . .	2	5	9/6
„	„ . . .	Drinker . . .	Bad reputation	3	1	..
....	Ill-health . .	Lazy . . .	Ill-health and bad reputation	3	1	21/-
....	Good . . .	Drinker . . .	Bad record .	5	3	5/-
Any	Very good . .	Excellent . .	None . .	2	1	4/-
„	„ . .	Good . . .	„ . .	4	1	?
Own trade or any .	Good . . .	Good "average" .	„ . .	2	3	..
Any	„ . . .	„ . . .	„ . .	4	1	14/6
„	Good, except eyesight	„ . .	„ . .	2	..	..

1 Including pensions, poor relief, etc., but not occasional gifts or savings.

M

MEN ENGAGED IN THE

Age.	At what Age did he enter the Trade?	Member of Trade Union?	Previous Occupations.	Makeshift Occupations while not working at own Trade.
29	21	No	Taker-in (age 11-15), chain-maker (age 15-16), general labourer (age 16-17), army (age 17-21)	Barman, cattle fairs, catch jobs, boxing
35	25	?	Comb works labourer (age 12-23), navvy (age 24-25), brickyard (age 25)	Farm work . . . .
36	17	Yes, but run out	Box-maker (age 14-17), pipelayer, etc. .	. . . .
?	?	?	?	Cattle driving . . . .
22	16	No	Errand boy (age 14-15), confectioner's and glass works labourer (age 15-16)	. . . .
40	?	,,	Comb works labourer (half-timer) (age 9-10), farm labourer	Farm work and catch jobs .
40	?	,,	Farm labourer	?
45	?	,,	Comb works labourer (from age 11), farm work, navvy, army (6 years)	Navvy . . . . .
27	?	,,	Farm labourer (as a boy)	Farm work, catch jobs . .
40	Casually since 23	,,	Engineer's labourer (age 14-23) . . .	Cattle market, station touting, furniture sales, farm work
48	Boyhood	,,	"Taker-in" at glass works (from age 11) .	Hawking firewood, relief work
48	?	,,	Farm labourer	Farm and other catch work .
26	?	,,	Wagoner (as a boy), warehouseman . .	Unloading boats and other catch work
26	Boyhood	,,	Railway labourer (as a boy) . . .	Cattle market, brickfield labourer
60	?	?	?	. . . .
60	?	?	?	
47	Probably 33	Yes	Bottle washer (age 14-20); turner (age 22-33), navvy	Catch jobs . . . .
61	About 40	No	Carter (age 17-18, 19-21), shunter (age 18-19), platelayer (age 21-23), driver (age 23-25), litter's labourer (age 25-26), mason's labourer (age 26-28), sand catcher (age 28-31), miner (age 31-32), etc.	Hawking, unloading boats, relief work
34	18 (off and on)	,,	Comb works labourer (age 12), glass works labourer (age 14-16), general labourer (age 18-20)	Unloading boats and catch jobs
60	?	,,	Fitter (age 14-21).	Railway porter (rare) . .
50	?	,,	Farm work (from age 12), market gardener, army (age 17-20)	Market gardener . . .
53	31	Yes (out of benefit)	Farm service (age 16-31)	Managing lodging-house .
66	?	?	Cattle droving and catch jobs . . .	Catch jobs . . . .

BUILDING TRADE (173 IN NUMBER)—continued

If looking for Occupations other than own Trade, which?	Present Condition.		Apparent Personal Handicaps in Search for Work.	No. of Persons in Family.		Average weekly Income of Family, excluding Casual Earnings of Unemployed.[1]
	Physique.	Character.		Adults.	Children (under 16).	
....	Robust . . .	Excellent . .	None . .	2	4	..
....	,, . . .	Fair labourer . .	,, . .	2	..	6/-
....	Good . . .	Good . . .	,, . .	4	..	?
?	?	Drinker . . .	Bad reputation	?	?	?
Any	Good . . .	,, . . .	None . .	3	4	23/-
,, ...	,, . . .	Average labourer, bad time-keeper, drinker	Laziness and bad record	3	..	14/-
,, ...	,, . . .	Only moderate worker	Inefficiency .	1	..	..
,, ...	Strong . . .	Good . . .	None . .	3	..	?
,, ...	?	,, . . .	,, . .	3	3	?
,, ...	Good . . .	,, . . .	,, . .	2	6	..
,, ...	Robust . . .	Bad time-keeper on account of drink	Bad reputation	5	4	?
,, ...	Fairly good . .	? probably bad .	Probably bad reputation	4	4	20/-
,, ...	Strong . . .	Respectable . .	None . .	4	..	33/-
,, ...	Healthy . . .	?	,, . .	3	..	?
?	?	Drinker . .	,, . .	?	?	?
?	?	Respectable . .	,, . .	2	..	?
....	Good . . .	Good . . .	,, . .	3	..	7/-
Any	,, . . .	Bad . . .	,, . .	3	4	17/-
,, ...	Robust, but deaf .	Drinker . . .	,, . .	3	4	14/-
,, ...	Good . . .	,, . . .	,, . .	3	..	24/-
,, ...	Fairly good . .	,, . . .	,, . .	4	..	20/-
....	Healthy . . .	Respectable, hard-working	Possesses property, and probably does not seek work assiduously	5	1	?
Any	Ageing . . .	"Hard-working all his life."	Age . .	1	..	?

1 Including pensions, poor relief, etc., but not occasional gifts or savings.

large proportion of the skilled workers [1] have a satis-factory record.

77 per cent are satisfactory in both respects,
2 „ „ „ in character, but have poor health,
17 „ „ „ physically, but not in character,
and only 2 „ „ „ neither in physique nor in character.

Study of the cases shows that since the faults of character are by no means always such as to interfere with a man's technical ability, economic and not personal reasons account for the unemployment of almost all these men.

With unskilled workers the record is not so good, a fact not to be wondered at when it is remembered that these occupations offer a means of livelihood to many who, from one cause or another, have lost other employment.

52 per cent are satisfactory in character and physique,
26 „ „ „ physique, but not character,
8 „ „ „ character, but not physique,
while 14 „ „ „ neither character nor physique.

REMEDIES

Let us now consider to what reforms the facts under review point.

Labour Exchanges.—We have seen that for some time previous to our census the building trades in York had been suffering from an unusual depression, due not only to general, but to local causes. They are, of course, from their nature, especially liable to such fluctuations, and therefore should benefit greatly from

[1] We include all "painters" among the unskilled, for reasons given in the footnote to p. 149.

a national system of Labour Exchanges, informing men residing in a locality where the building trades are dull, of vacancies in other places. At the time of our inquiry, such information was only available for men in York to a very limited extent through their trade unions and through newspaper advertisements.

Decasualisation of Labour.—Labour Exchanges may also help to reduce unemployment in the building trades by decasualising the labour as far as possible. They might first suggest to the principal employers the social importance of so regulating the work of their own staffs as to secure the great advantage of permanent work to the greatest possible number of men. Most employers have a certain minimum number below which their staff never falls. It is advisable that this minimum should always consist of the same men, who would thus be removed from the ranks of casual workers. There is no doubt that this might be done to a much greater extent than at present, and the Labour Exchange might usefully encourage such action. But even when that was accomplished, the great majority of men in this class would still remain casual workers, working first for one and then another employer, and subject to frequent periods of unemployment.

Another step towards remedying this state of things will have been taken when, through the action of the Labour Exchange, regular work is secured, as far as possible, to the best of these casual workers. This would be done by a process of decasualisation, as outlined in the previous chapter. In the case of the building trades it would involve having a list of men arranged in groups, according to efficiency— A, B, C, D. Whenever a demand for workers came in, all those in group A would be sent before any in the other groups were called up, and similarly all in group B would be sent before C and D were called up. Thus the best workmen would be employed much more continuously than at present, and in their case the evils arising from casual work would be reduced to a minimum.

If the total number of men engaged in the building trade in York is not excessive, the men in all the groups would get enough work to make it worth their while to continue to depend on it for a livelihood ; but if the above process of decasualisation showed that men in class D, for example, were scarcely ever called on, it would be clear that the total number of those who at present seek work in the building trade is in excess of the true demand, and they would either move to another town with better prospects, or change their occupation. It may be said that such a process would tell very heavily on the lowest group. That is true, but it is not an argument against decasualisation, but in favour of some supplementary measure dealing with those "squeezed out." Moreover, when once the decasualisation of labour in the building trades is accomplished it will not, under normal conditions, and to any serious extent, have to be repeated. At present nearly all the men engaged in these trades suffer constantly from uncertainty of employment, and frequently from unemployment itself, a state of things which it is worth making a strenuous effort to alter.

Of course, though the help of the Labour Exchange is essential to complete the suggested process of decasualisation, the desired end is, in practice, already realised to a considerable extent, since, as we saw, the best and most reliable workmen become known to employers, and get a better chance of securing whatever work is going than the inferior men.

After the reforms above indicated are carried out, viz. the sending of labour to other towns when the local trade is temporarily depressed, and the de-casualisation of the workers, there will still remain much irregularity of employment—the outcome of conditions inherent in the building trades. How can this evil be dealt with? Two methods are practicable. One, the provision of an alternative employment, which could be taken up or laid down readily, according to the demand for labour in the building trades, and the other, insurance against unemployment. Possibly the two methods could be combined.

The Provision of an Alternative Employment.— So far as the first is concerned we have already shown (p. 76) that if the nation afforested all the areas which the Committee on Afforestation and Coast Erosion considered suitable, it might be expected that about 100 York men would immediately find

work in the forests for four months each year, and
that this number would ultimately rise to about
400 when the forest was established. The work,
although carried out under highly skilled supervision,
would be unskilled in character. It would be well
suited to a number of men in the building trades,
especially to bricklayer's labourers, and as it could be
developed or held back according to the number of
men unemployed, it would prove a most valuable
means of dealing with the difficulty. Moreover, it
should be financially profitable. Obviously, once a
man was selected for afforestation work, he would
have to stay at it for some months, for the under-
taking could not be made to pay if the men were
constantly coming and going. But this condition is
no drawback, and would fit in well with any scheme
of decasualisation such as we have described.

What is true of afforestation holds good also of
other works, such as the construction of repair of
roads, laying out of parks, etc., which may be undertaken by local bodies and which we suggested should
be carried on as far as possible when the number of
unemployed workers was large.

So many national, as well as municipal, works
consist of construction either of buildings or roads,
that their regularisation, according to the state of the
labour market, would very materially improve the
conditions of the building trade.

Insurance.—We now pass to a question which has
become a very living one since the introduction of a

Government Bill providing for the insurance of
workers in the building trade.

There is no doubt that workers so precariously
occupied as those in the building trades must save
money regularly when employed, unless they are to
be plunged into recurring periods of distress. But,
being human, they find it exceedingly difficult to do
this, a difficulty increased by the fact that, except in
the most highly skilled branches of the trade, their
wages, even in full work, do not allow any large
margin for thrift if a reasonable standard of living is
to be maintained. At present most of the saving
is " done backwards," debts being incurred in periods
of unemployment and paid off when work is found.
Some scheme of insurance, therefore, should be a
distinct boon to the members of this class.

Turning to the Government proposals, we cannot
state exactly how many of the men whose unemployment we have here been considering, would have
been eligible for benefit at the time of our census,
because we did not obtain full particulars of the
number of weeks in which they had been unemployed
during the last twelve months, our information being
limited to the length of time which had elapsed
since their last considerable job. A number of the
men had, in the meantime, done little repairing jobs,
both on their own account and for contractors, and
probably few of those who had worked very irregularly,
could have told us exactly to how many weeks their
total unemployment amounted during the year. But

from such information as we have, it is evident that a considerable number of them, possibly one-half, would have run out of benefit at the time of our census. It is unfortunately a condition attached to any scheme of unemployment insurance, that its aid can only continue for a limited period, and of course the men whose unemployment extends beyond that period are just those who stand most in need of financial help. This is especially noticeable where the benefit has been comparatively small, as in the case of the six shillings a week proposed in the Government measure. That sum, if it be the sole income of the family, although much better than nothing, would only go a little way towards meeting the minimum requirements of existence, let alone of physical efficiency; and families whose income had been limited to it for some weeks would not only have suffered from privation, but run into considerable debt. Undoubtedly, however, if the proposals made above for reducing unemployment in the building trades were adopted, its total amount would be less, and its periods less protracted for the individual. In that case benefits might be increased without increasing premiums, and the number of workers who would run out of benefit would be much smaller. If the insurance proposals of the Government are regarded, as they are by those who have framed them,[1] as one

---

[1] Mr. Lloyd George, when introducing the National Insurance Bill in the House of Commons, said, "I do not pretend that this is a complete remedy. . . . Before you get a complete remedy for social evils you will have to cut deeper."

instalment only of a widely conceived scheme for reducing unemployment, or mitigating its results, they should prove of great value; but we hope that a realisation of their inevitable limitations will prevent the public from lulling itself into the belief that once the Bill is made law, the hardships due to unemployment will cease.[1]

There is one important aspect of the Government Bill which should be noted, viz. the financial inducement offered to employers to decasualise their own workers, i.e. to reduce to a minimum the proportion of work done by casual hands. As it would be impossible to enforce such action by direct legislation, this indirect method of securing it is especially valuable.

Before turning from the question of insurance, reference must be made to a proposal, set forth at length in Chapter VII., that we in this country

[1] Among these limitations, the following may perhaps be mentioned: One of the writers has had considerable experience in connection with the building trade in York, which has taught him that it would often be very difficult to determine whether the cause for which a man loses his work is or is not such as to render him eligible for benefit. So much depends on the opinion of the person who dismissed him. It is, unfortunately, not a very rare occurrence for men to "treat" foremen in order to keep in their good books, and those who refused to do this might find it hard to establish their claim to benefit in the face of a strongly unfavourable report from their foreman. Again, it is suggested in the Bill that the test whether a man is or is not unemployed shall be his willingness to accept suitable work offered through the Labour Exchange. It would, however, often be very hard to determine whether a man might reasonably be expected to accept a given piece of work or not. For instance, if any one quite unused to afforestation were offered employment in connection with it at a distance, and preferred the insurance money at home, he could make some excuse for refusing which it would be very difficult to dispute; although he might willingly have accepted had no benefit been forthcoming as a possible alternative.

might wisely follow the example of Belgium, in giving to working-men the necessary facilities for living in the country although working in the towns. Bricklayers and others in Belgium find this arrangement an inestimable boon, for they have a plot of land attached to their houses which they cultivate when not working at their trades, and the produce from which helps to tide over recurring periods of unemployment. It forms an insurance fund, the amount of which each man can regulate according to his needs, and which can be drawn on regardless of the cause of unemployment, and as long as the necessity lasts. The scheme offers other advantages, which are described in Chapter VII.

CHAPTER V

(105 in number)

As this book deals solely with unemployment as a problem to be solved, we have not taken any account of those who were unemployable either because of age or illness. Some account must, however, be taken of the work-shy—men whose inefficiency, or unwillingness to work, is not due to age, illness, or any other physical disqualification, but primarily to infirmity of character. Thus we deal with mendicants and with persons who are so lazy that they will only work as a last resource, preferring an inexpressibly low standard of comfort to the effort involved in toil. We also deal with men who live in comparative ease on the labour of their parents, wives, children, or other members of their families.

The number of men here considered is 105, but it is probable that the total number of such men in the city is far greater, because in our census the investigators inquired whether there were any persons

in the household who were without work and *desirous
to obtain it*, and only those who could at least
strain their imagination sufficiently to answer such a
question in the affirmative would be enumerated.
The line of division separating some of the men
included in this group from the casual worker proper
is a very fine one—a little more evidence of desire
to find work would have placed them on the other
side of it, and closer knowledge of the facts might
possibly have shifted it slightly one way or another.
But the alteration would have been unimportant.
The real fact is that among a number of casual
workers a process of gradual deterioration is going
on.   Many of them, as we saw, began as regular
workers, and for a time they continued to look for
regular work till, very gradually, the search for it
ceased, and they resigned themselves to relying
entirely on casual jobs for a living.   Then the search
for casual jobs became less and less keen.   All
employment requiring serious effort of any kind
grew distasteful, and if any other possible mode of
existence presented itself, such as reliance on the
labour of parents, wife, or children, the systematic
search for work ceased entirely.   The men who have
reached this stage usually call forth our strong
condemnation, but they do not always deserve it.
Their state of mind is often the result of external
conditions beyond their control.
    It must be remembered that the casual worker,
especially if not very successful in securing jobs, is

generally underfed. This does not necessarily mean that he is hungry—any more than a horse fed on green meat is hungry—but he is physically unfitted to undertake hard work for a sustained period. Add to this physical disability the mental despondency due to continued failure to find employment, and the deteriorating influence of the environment in which he and his fellows, as a rule, are obliged to live—an influence which there is no physical vigour to resist —and you have a perfect machine for the manufacture of " unemployables."

As we have held our melancholy review of the unemployed army in York, and traced the industrial records of its members, we have been forcibly impressed with the deadly efficiency of this machine, acting, as it often does, on men who for long years have been engaged in regular work which they have lost for no fault, and we have felt that in such cases the blame rested rather upon the social and industrial machine itself than upon the products of its operations.

Of course there are many work-shy men for whom no such excuses can be made, but if we eliminate from among them those whose early training has been unsatisfactory, the proportion of the whole class which the remainder would represent would, we believe, be small.

It is on this account that the interest of this chapter will chiefly centre in a study of the past history of the members of the class, and an examination

THE WORK-

Last Regular Employment.						
Its Nature.	Duration (years).	Was it preceded by an industrial record showing power to retain permanent post?	Date of Leaving	Cause of Leaving.	Age at time of Leaving.	Present Age.
Warehouseman	10	Yes	1904	To better himself . .	41	47
Wood sawyer	2	No	1909	?	28	29
Hotel waiter	15	Yes	1895	Intemperance	37	52
Wire worker	2½	No	About 1890	Death of employer . .	20	40
Railway clerk ?	? 7	Yes	? 1904	? To avoid removal . .	? 27	50 33
Instrument-maker's apprentice .	6	No	1906	Bad time-keeping (due to drink and bad company)	21	24
Confectionery works . . .	4	(In army 1894-1906), No	1894	Slackness	17	33
Keelman	5	No	?	?	?	22
.... (army 7 years) . .	..	,,	..	....	..	40
Farm labourer	?	,,	?	?	As a boy	31
Iron worker (foundry) . .	8	?	1905	?	35	40
Box-maker	4	No	1904	To enlist	18	24
Railway labourer (army 24 years) .... (army 1 year)	8 or 9 ..	,, ..	,, ..	?	42 ..	48 19
Probably nil	..	..	..	....	..	? 22
Railway fireman	1½	No	1907	Intemperance . . .	17	20
Glass works labourer . . .	2	,,	1905	To work casually . .	17	22
Groom	2	,,	1907	Ran away . . .	19	22
Confectioner's labourer . .	3 or 4	(In army 1888-1902), Yes	1888	To enlist	18	40
....	..	..	..	....	..	35
Labourer	4	No	1907	Too old for boy's job .	19	22
Printer's labourer . . .	½	(In army 1883-1897), No	1908	Intemperance . . .	43	45
Engineer's labourer . . .	2¼	No	1905	Closing of works . .	29	34
Confectioner's labourer . .	About 1	Yes	About 1900	Larking	17	27

SHY (105 IN NUMBER)

Physique.	Character.	Nature of Casual Occupations.	How is Unemployed Supported?	Adults.	Children (under 16).
			Present Condition.	No. of Persons in Family.	
Delicate, suffering from bronchitis	Betting man . . .	Election canvasser, book-maker's runner	Wife earns 10s. . . .	2	..
Good . . .	Probably betting man .	Election canvasser . .	By family	?	?
Good, but rather stout	Quite demoralised .	Waiter	By wife and children . .	3	..
Good . . .	Deteriorated from casual labouring to station tout, thence pauper, probably been in gaol for theft	Station tout . . .	Own work	..	..
Fair . . .	Content to loaf . .				
Not energetic .	Drinker, gambler, and altogether demoralised	Clerk," butcher's assistant .	Partly by parents . .	2	2
Weak (now) . .	Ruined and depraved by drink, very lazy	Nil for about 2 years . .	By parents	3	..
Strong . . .	Lazy, gambler . .	Farm work	Reserve pay and by family	..	..
Fair (bad stock) .	Lazy and dishonest, never trained to decent habits	Sometimes hawker and attending sales	Theft, betting, etc. . .	?	?
Good . . .	Very neglected and quite demoralised	Hawker and attending sales	Own work and occasional poor relief	2	6
Bad . . .	Heavy drinker, dishonest, lazy	Farm labourer, carter, navvy	By catch work . . .	2	2
Very strong .	Heavy drinker, dirty, lazy	Navvy	By poor relief and catch work	2	3
Rejected recruit .	Very lazy . . .	Gardener, bricklayer's labourer, and catch jobs	By mother, charity, poor relief	2	2
Good . . .	Very lazy, cadger . .	Gardener (rare), catch jobs .	By wife, often poor relief .	2	4
Strong . . .	From industrial school, never has worked	Racing tout . . .	By brother-in-law . .	2	1
?	Drinker, bad character	Station tout . . .	?	2	2
Slender, but healthy	Gambler . . .	Wool packer (6 years ago), selling papers	By family	?	?
Strong . . .	Drinker, fighter, cadger	Railway goods porter . .	By parents	4	..
„ . . .	Detests work . .	Betting tout, sometimes brickyard labourer	Betting	..	..
Healthy . . .	Racing man (wanted to be a jockey)	Groom	By parents	4	1
„ . . .	Heavy drinker . .	Railway porter, timber carrier	By wife and catch jobs .	2	3
?	Drinker, gambler, cadger	Bricklayer's labourer (rare)	Cadging	?	?
Strong . . .	Lazy and restless, but clever	Occasionally carter . .	By family	5	1
?	Stubborn type . .	Nil	Mother's old age pension .	?	?
Mentally dull (bad stock)	?	Sandwichman (practically nil)	Cadging	3	1
Fair . . .	Lazy	Station tout . . .	By father	5	..

N

THE WORK-

Last Regular Employment.						
Its Nature.	Dura-tion (years).	Was it preceded by an industrial record showing power to retain permanent post?	Date of Leaving.	Cause of Leaving.	Age at time of Leaving.	Present Age.
Railway fitter	8½	No	1905	Removal of works	22	27
Railway cleaner	2 or 3	,,	1904	,, ,,	16	22
Boiler-maker	18	,,	1902	Bad time-keeping	32	40
Bricklayer	7	,,	1908	End of apprenticeship	20	22
? ?	? ?	? ?	? ?	? ?	? ?	? ?
Groundsman	5	Yes	1907	?	39	42
Moulder	?	?	1880	?	21	51
Publican	4	Yes	1906	Illness	38	42
.... (Workhouse 2 years)	..	..	..	....	..	About 50
....1	..	..	..	....	..	About 20
Engineer's labourer	21	No	1902	Works changed hands	40	48
....	..	..	..	....	..	23
....	..	..	..	....	..	23
....	..	..	..	....	..	59
Engineer's labourer	11	No	1901	Slackness	27	36
Maltster	5	Yes	1902	Removal of firm	39	47
Telegraph messenger	5	(3 years in army) no	1906	To enlist	20	24
Boiler cleaner	2	No	1907	Unsatisfactory conduct	20	23
Railway machinist	¾	Yes	1908	Laziness	23	25
French polisher	10	,,	1907	,,	34	37
Railway labourer (on permanent way)	¾	No	,,	Completion of work	24	27
Rulley lad	½	Yes	1910	Illness	21	21
Glass-blower	2½	?	?	?	?	?
Probably nil	..	..	..	....	..	Young
,,	..	..	..	....	..	,,
?						?
Newspaper vendor	8	Yes (errand boy)	1902	Failure of employer	17	25
....	..	..	..	....	..	27
Probably nil	..	..	..	....	..	?
,,	..	..	..	....	..	?
?	..	..	..	....	..	About 53
(Brought up to street music)	..	..	..	....	..	36

1 Son of preceding case.

SHY (105 IN NUMBER)—*continued*

Physique	Character	Nature of Casual Occupations	How is Unemployed Supported?	Adults	Children (under 16)
Strong . . .	Loafer (very bad family)	Gardener, porter . . .	By family	4	..
,, . . .	,, ,,	Porter	,, ...	?	?
,, . . .	Very lazy . . .	Catch jobs	Parents	5	..
Healthy . . .	,, ...	Whitewasher, bricklayer's labourer	By parents	5	..
?	Heavy drinker, prodigal	Nil	Wife's heritage . . .	?	?
?	Immoral house, since removed	?	?	?	?
Good . . .	Had a good job, lost through drink and bad time-keeping	Nil, except catch jobs .	By wife	?	?
,, . . .	Drinker and very lazy .	Auctioneer's porter and trade in second-hand goods	,, ...	2	..
Suffering from indigestion	Drinker and lazy . .	Waiter (rare) . . .	By stepfather . . .	3	..
?	Very lazy . . .	Practically nil . .	By wife and excellent cadging	?	?
?	,, ...	?	?	?	?
Able-bodied . .	Quite demoralised .	Station tout . . .	By wife and family . .	4	1
Good . . .	Well known at police court, "born tired"	Sand catcher . . .	Catch jobs	..	..
,, . . .	,, ,,	Cattle drover, timber carrier	,, ...	..	..
,, . . .	Never trained to work, incorrigibly lazy	Rag gathering . . .	Partly by wife's earnings .	2	..
Sallow and undersized	Drinker, "carries on" .	Out porter, station tout .	By stepmother . . .	4	..
Good . . .	Street corner loafer .	Ostler and carter . .	Catch jobs	..	..
Very good . .	Loafer and gambler .	Timber carrier, bricklayer's labourer	Catch jobs and by family .	6	..
Poor . . .	Very lazy . . .	Nil	By parents	5	..
Good . . .	,, ...	,, ...	?	2	1
,, . . .	Ejected for keeping disorderly house	Station tout, railway porter, relief work	?	2	1
,, . . .	Drinker and loafer .	Delivering newspapers .	By parents	8	..
,, . . .	Shiftless and loafer .	Since last work, nil . .	,, ...	5	1
?	Gambler and drunkard	Glass works labourer, relief work	Partly by wife and children	2	5
?	Often in police court .	Cattle drover . . .	?	?	?
?	Often in police court, heavy drinker and fighter	Poacher	?	?	?
?	Gaol bird . . .	?	?	?	..
Good . . .	Loafer and gambler .	Newspaper seller . .	By parents	5	..
Excellent . .	Constantly in gaol for all sorts of offences, never worked	Three months in army, turned out on account of dishonesty, occasionally drover	Chiefly prison, theft, etc. .	3	..
?	Fighter and drinker .	Cattle drover . . .	?	?	?
?	Drinker and thoroughly bad lot	"Sometimes engaged by mistake as brush-hand"	Mendicity	?	?
?	Drinker and gambler .	First hawker, then station tout	?	?	?
Good . . .	Never worked in his life	General labourer, organ grinder, unloading boats	By sons	3	7

Last Regular Employment.						
Its Nature.	Dura-tion (years).	Was it preceded by an industrial record showing power to retain permanent post?	Date of Leaving.	Cause of Leaving.	Age at time of Leaving.	Present Age.
Packer	1	No	?	?	?	22
....	..	..	..	....	..	52
Box-mill labourer . .	3	Yes (errand boy)	1902	?	18	26
Probably nil	..	..	..	....	..	About 40
....	..	..	..	....	..	20
....	..	..	..	....	..	42
....1	..	..	..	....	..	30
Crane man	13	Yes	1902	To enlist	28	36
Garden labourer . . .	4½	No	1906	Closing of business . . .	24	28
....	..	..	..	....	..	50
Sailor (various lines) . .	14 or 15	No	Many years ago	Laziness	?	38
Baker	½	Probably yes	1907	Intemperance	?	?
Cook	7	Yes	1906	Bad time-. ?eping and careless-ness	25	29
Carter 1	4	,,	1905	To enlist (did not come off) .	17	22
.... (Army 1899-1904) .	..	..	..	....	..	26
....	..	..	..	....	..	37
....	..	..	..	....	..	28
....?	..	..	..	....	..	30 60
?	?	?	?	?	?	Over 50
?2 ?2	? ?	? ?	? ?	? ?	? ?	? ?
Cab cleaner	3	No	As a boy	?	17	50
Motor-driver . . .	7	Yes	1907	Defective eyesight . . .	33	36
Laundry labourer . . .	5	,,	1890	?	27	47

1 Brother of preceding case.　　　　2 Sons of preceding case.

SHY (105 IN NUMBER)—*continued*

Present Condition.				No. of Persons in Family.	
Physique.	Character.	Nature of Casual Occupations.	How is Unemployed Supported?	Adults.	Children (under 16).
Strong . . .	Probably been in gaol, gambler	Nil	By sisters and parents .	6	..
Fair . . .	Never known to have worked	Furniture porter and sale porter	Catch jobs and cadging .	8	1
Healthy . . .	Drinks gallons, been up for stealing, well known to police	Cattle drover, hawker (was in Militia for 2 years and was turned out when had 11 convictions against him)	Living immorally with woman who probably supports him	2	2
?	Drinker and waster .	Checker of newspaper sellers	?	?	?
Very healthy . .	Tried to get into army under false pretences, probably never worked	Cattle drover, practically nil for 2 years	By father	4	2
Healthy . . .	" Always been busy propping up one of the city bars "	Farm work, wool sorter .	Own catch jobs and brothers'	8	..
Not good . . .	Always lived by cadging	(In South Africa 1½ year), hawker, cattle drover	Mendicity and small army pension	8 ?	.. ?
Fair . . .	Apparently tramp .	Probably tramp . . .	Wife's earnings and mendicity	?	?
Big and strong .	Not worked for many years, several times had up for poaching	Nil (formerly navvy) . .	Poaching	?	?
Strong . . .	Probably gaol-bird .	Nil	Probably immoral earnings of wife	?	?
?	Drinker, often locked up	Hawked pastry on own account, but neglected this	?	2	8
Strong . . .	Utterly careless, lost many chances	Nil for 12 months . .	By father	4	..
Not very strong .	Never worked vigorously	Cattle drover, etc. (practically nil)	„	4	..
Good . . .	Has been in trouble with police, drinker and loafer	Cattle drover . . .	„	5	2
„ . . .	Not been brought up to work, racing man	Bookmaker's tout, cattle drover	Own earnings . . .	?	?
Not very strong .	Heavy drinker, never known to work	Casual labourer (railway relief work, etc.)	Chiefly cadging and immoral earnings of wife	2	4
Fair . . .	Never did work . .	Tramp	By mother and sister . .	8	..
?	Heavy drinker, occasionally working, mostly loafing	Farm work	Cadging	?	?
?	Heavy drinker . .	?		?	?
? ?	Have been in gaol more than once for drinking and fighting, loafers and gamblers, probably never been in regular work	? ?	Slum home, probably earn enough between them, daughter in regular work	? ?	? ?
Big and strong .	Loafer and mendicant .	Painter in summer, firewood hawker in winter	Partly by wife and daughter	?	?
Strong . . .	Loafer	" Keeping house " . .	Sisters	?	?
?	Heavy drinker, loafer .	Unloading boats . . .	In lodgings, earns enough for his keep	..	..

Its Nature.	Duration (years).	Was it preceded by an industrial record showing power to retain permanent post?	Date of Leaving.	Cause of Leaving.	Age at time of Leaving.	Present Age.
....	..	..	..	....	..	40
....	..	..	..	....	..	40
Wood turner	A few	No	As a boy	Ran away	As a boy	50
Farm labourer	Prob-ably a few	,,	,,	,, ...	,,	45
Errand boy and groom . .	,,	,,	,,	?	,,	56
.... (Army 1893-1905) . .	..	..	..	....	..	33
?	?	?	?	?	?	44
Newspaper vendor . . .	?	?	?	?	?	?
Labourer	?	?	?	?	?	?
Bicycle repairer	?	?	?	?	?	?
.... (In navy 10 years) . .	..	?	(1909)	? (Discharge very good) . .	(27)	28
Glass packer	2	No	1902	Ill-health	23	31
Labourer	?	?	?	Intemperance	?	?
Plumber	8	?	1904	,, ...	44	50
Carriage cleaner . . .	3	Yes	1905	To better himself . . .	18	23
Labourer	4	?	May 1908	Ill-health	48	50
,, ...	7	?	1895	,, ...	47	62
Stoker	½	No	1904	,, ...	24	30
Railway labourer . . .	20	?	,,	Closing of works . . .	52	58
Gardener	1½	Yes	June 1906	Intemperance	51	55
Fellmonger	?	?	About 1890	,, ...	34	54

of the preventive measures which such a study may suggest. It is of much greater importance that we should cease to manufacture shirkers than that we should learn how best to deal with them after they have been manufactured.

As in the preceding chapters, a table giving certain particulars regarding each member of this class will form the best introduction to our study.

SHY (105 IN NUMBER)—*continued*

Present Condition.		Nature of Casual Occupations.	How is Unemployed Supported?	No. of Persons in Family.	
Physique.	Character.			Adults	Children (under 16).
Fairly good . .	Workhouse child . .	Always been mendicant .	Mendicity	..	..
„ . .	„ ? „ . .	„ „ .	„	..	..
„ . .	„ ?	„ „ .	„	..	..
Good . . .	Was sent out to sell matches as a child	Been a mendicant since youth	„	..	..
„ . . .	?	Station tout, been a mendicant for 16 years	„	..	..
Underfed . .	Used to work casually and to hawk, degenerated into tramp	Occasional farm work, tramps with family	„	2	3
?	"Drunk 6 days out of 7"	Rag and bone gatherer, cattle drover	„	?	?
?	"Props up one of city bars"	Paper selling . . .	Father working, mother begs	?	?
Undersized . .	Cadger	Begging . . .	By begging	?	?
?	Bad (probably bookmaker)	Bookmaker	By wife	?	?
Healthy . . .	Recently 12 months in gaol	Cadging	Begging	?	?
Not strong, mentally dull	Lazy, gambler . .	Field work	By sister	?	?
?	Refuses work when offered, drinker	Ice - cream selling, occasionally	By wife	?	?
?	Lazy	Does not look for any .	By family	5	..
Healthy	„	Bookmaking . . .	„	5	2
Delicate . . .	?	Parcel carrying . .	„	3	..
Now invalid . .	Sponger, loafer, drunkard	?	„ ?	?	?
Good . . .	Cadger, when not working	Potato digging, brickyard, erecting market stalls	Catch work	3	2
Bronchial . .	"Has lived without much work"	Wife takes nurse children .	By family	4	1
Poor . . .	Drunkard . . .	„ „ .	„	6	1
?	Drunkard and immoral	Nothing . . .	„	?	?

The first point that arises from our examination of the table is that of the 105 members of this class, 55, or rather more than half, have, to our knowledge, once been engaged in regular work. Thirty-two have, apparently, never worked regularly. Of the remaining 18, 3 have served in the army and 1 in the navy, and for the rest we could obtain no reliable information.

RECORDS OF MEN WHO ONCE WORKED REGULARLY (55)

Of those who had once worked regularly, 9 held their last regular situation for less than two years, 28 from two to five years, 11 from five to ten years, and 7 for over ten years. Such records do not point to anything approaching to serious incompetence.[1] They indicate that once, at any rate, a large number of these men were capable of sustained effort. But if we inquire why they are now unemployed, it becomes apparent that demoralising influences have been at work among some of them for a long time. Only of 44 could we learn why they left their situations, and 21 of these left for satisfactory reasons —or 26, if we add 5 who enlisted. Fifteen were dismissed for misconduct or incompetence, and 3 ran away.

Perhaps we shall not be far wrong in assuming that roughly one-half of those once in regular employment had a fairly satisfactory record. Nearly all of them were young men when they fell out of work. Ten were actually under 20, 9 were between 20 and 30, and 3 between 30 and 40, and only 4 were over 40.

Obviously they were not of the stuff from which heroes are made, or they would have found regular work again. They were probably somewhat inferior

[1] While we have checked the information obtained, by reference to past employers where possible, this could not be done in the case of those who left their last regular employment several years ago ; and so possibly some of the statements as to the length of time for which the last regular employment lasted, and the causes of leaving, may be incorrect.

workmen who, though they could, apparently, keep
work when they got it, would find it difficult, once
unemployed, to compete for it successfully against
better men. They were just the people to fall into
the clutches of the fell machine which so rapidly
turns workers into unemployables; and such men
most of all need protection from circumstances and
from themselves.

Turning to the men who lost their last regular
work for unsatisfactory reasons, we find that these
reasons are miscellaneous, though " drink " heads the
list. They need not occupy us long. Such men are
found in all classes of society, and the problem of
their reform is primarily a moral one,—though not
entirely ; for the conditions which govern the work
and lives of many working-men tend to encourage
carelessness and intemperance. Indeed, we often
wonder if those of us who are apt to stand apart and
judge thriftless drunkards with but little sympathy
would, under similar conditions, have done better
than they ! Born often of a poor stock, and growing up amid a degrading environment, with a slum
street for an unguarded playground, receiving the
legal minimum of education with no encouragement
from their parents, sent into the world at 13 or 14
to drift into whatever occupation comes their way,
then, whether single or married, living in a poor
house and dingy street, and returning to it night by
night after nine or ten hours of unskilled work, which
rouses neither interest nor ambition, with minds

untrained to serious thought, and a horizon on which the marvels of art and science and literature have never dawned—what wonder if, in their effort to introduce some colour into the drab monotony of their lives, they fall victims to the allurements of the bookmaker or publican, or lose heart and join the ranks of those who have ceased to strive?

However, whatever may have been the ultimate cause of the downfall of the men now especially under observation, the immediate one is principally moral. The list contains a fair proportion of men who were once skilled workers, but it is important to note that almost all of them lost their work when they were quite young,[1] a fact which points clearly to the need for effective help during the critical period between leaving school and manhood.

MEN WHO HAVE NEVER WORKED REGULARLY (32)

Now we pass to the 32 men of whom we know that they have never worked regularly. Theirs is a sad record, and little will here be gained by analysing it closely. Drink, gambling, cadging, crime, and incorrigible laziness are words which often occur in the investigators' notebooks. The present age of the men is very various: the youngest is 19, and the oldest 59.

These men, like all the members of the work-

[1] Information as to their ages when their last regular job was lost, was only available for 16 of the 18 men. Of these, 5 were under 19, 2 between 19 and 21, 3 between 21 and 25, and 5 between 26 and 44, while one was 51.

shy class, are either living under conditions which
represent an excessively low standard of comfort, or
by the work of other members of their families.
Apparently in about one-half of the cases, one of the
family, more frequently a parent, is working, and
thus the home is maintained.

Not all members of the work-shy class are degraded.
Some are quite reputable in their way ; they are not
drunkards or gamblers or dishonest, but merely lazy,
preferring a life of idleness to one of work, especially
if their material needs can be supplied through the
efforts of wife or parent.[1] They often adopt the
savage point of view—a low standard of comfort, and
women to do the work. But the bulk of the class,
whatever they may once have been, are now, or are
in process of becoming, thoroughly degraded members
of the lowest class of society.

Perhaps, as our whole treatment of this class has
been somewhat slight, it may be worth while to give
a few extracts from the investigators' notebooks which
will help the reader to realise the human material of
which it is composed.

[1] The following story, told us by one of our investigators, illustrates this
type :—
    A young man, rather smartly dressed, living in a respectable working-
class district, who was known to follow no regular occupation, was recently
asked how he managed to live. "You always seem to be better dressed
than any of us," said an acquaintance, "can't you give us the tip how you
do it?" After some hesitation, the young man said, "If you will give me
threepence for a glass of beer, I will tell you." When this amount had
been grudgingly produced, the oracle answered as follows : "Well, Arthur,
it is a very poor street in which you cannot get twopence. I go round sing-
ing, and I can easily do forty streets in a day." "Why," said his friend,
after a rapid calculation, "that comes to 6s. 8d." "Yes," he replied, "and
that's more than ever you will earn in a day."

. . . is a York man. He never had any schooling, never knew his parents, but was early in life adopted by some one who sent him into the streets to sell matches. Having become accustomed to an easy mode of earning money, it is not surprising to learn that when sent to a farm later on he found the work too hard, and returned, to settle down to a life of mendicity. He is now 45 years old, and except for an occasional day's haymaking, lives on the proceeds of light jobs at the market, and of begging.

Another man, aged 44, and the head of a family, gave in his name as "unemployed" and desirous of employment for some reason best known to himself. He has succeeded for many years in scraping through with rare and very brief intervals of work, chiefly rag and bone gathering, and jobs at the cattle fair. He was visited several times in connection with this inquiry, but was always found too drunk to give precise information. His neighbours say that he drinks six days out of every seven.

The next man, aged 52, is known at furniture sales in the city, where he obtains fair average earnings as a porter. He has also worked spasmodically at a local factory, but never for more than a week at a time. He has two children, one of whom, aged 16, helps to support the home. The wife is physically handicapped, and cannot, therefore, contribute to the earnings. The family last had poor relief in 1904 during her confinement. The house, situated in one of the worst slums of the city and consisting of two rooms, is unspeakably squalid and dirty, and nearly bare. The family seems to be reconciled to its present condition, never having known a better one, and is unwilling to face exertion for the sake of a higher level of well-being.

The next case, a man of 59 years of age, may perhaps be considered too old to justify his inclusion in this class. But against this involuntary disability must be set his notorious objection to working for more than a day or two per week. He is helped by the earnings of his wife, aged 49, who is herself content with one day's charing per week, and by their combined effort they somehow maintain a four-roomed house at a rental of half a crown. They receive parish relief when ill. The man is illiterate, and started his industrial career, if it can be so named, at a very tender age, as errand boy, an employment very soon exchanged for potato-picking and other temporary work. He has never done any regular work, and now earns a maximum of 6s. per week, the proceeds of rag-gathering.

In more respectable circumstances we find a man, aged 37, who lives with his parents and seems to contribute to the household expenses by acting as tout to a bookmaker. Occasionally he works at cattle fairs, but his earnings never exceed a few shillings per week. He has never done more serious work in his life.

Two other men live in a common lodging-house. They are only 23 years of age. One of them began his career as soon as he left school with "sand-catching" on the river, and has not tried his hand at any other job. He is well known to the police, and has the reputation of being an incorrigible loafer. The other earns about 4s. per week as a casual labourer on a timber-wharf and occasionally as a cattle drover, and is described as a hardened case, without inclination to work, and well known to the police. He, too, began this irregular career immediately after leaving school, at the age of 13.

More promising was the start of another young man, aged 24, who at 13 became an errand boy for a York tradesman, and afterwards seems to have been in regular employment for three or four years with one firm of manufacturers. At the age of 18 he enlisted, but came back in ten weeks with heart disease (?) and an outfit of new clothes. For a few years he worked temporarily as a labourer for his former employers, and at a flour-mill. But his work became more and more intermittent. In 1909 he was a bricklayer's labourer for three months, and since then he has chiefly done odd gardening and field jobs. He was for seven consecutive months without any work at all. The man's story, as related by him, sounds plausible and suggests great hardship arising from causes over which he had no control. But the impression of his character received from other sources is very different. The family is known to the Poor Law Authorities, who have relieved it once for the sake of the wife, who did her best to help her husband, and who, apparently, has left him since the first inquiry was made. He simply "won't have work" though it was offered him by the Guardians. They live in a house of two rooms, let at half a crown, in a respectable court. The wife is 22 years old, and has been married for one and a half years. One child died, aged nine months, one is living, and four months old. Her mother, living in the same court, has helped them from time to time, parting with pieces of furniture for their sake, but unable to save them from destitution of the worst kind.

The case of another young man, aged 25, is of interest. He was apprenticed to a trade, but is included in this class because since his apprenticeship he has not worked at his trade at all, but only at temporary unskilled jobs, separated from each other by intervals of idleness. His last comparatively long period of employment was for nine months, ending June 1908, with the Railway Company, when he was discharged for inefficiency and laziness. The Company had previously given him temporary employment for three months, and has taken him on again since the inquiry was made. But whereas he previously earned 25s. 4d. per week, he now only earns 18s. The explanation of this young man's career must be found, we believe, in the fact that on the completion of his apprenticeship he was for three years in the army, and there, unfortunately, did not acquire attainments and habits which might have compensated him for the inevitable loss of skill in his former industry. He is married and has a young child, and as the household occupies a four-roomed house in a respectable street, one is left to assume that it cannot be entirely dependent on his earnings.

Here is the case of another man who has fallen from a higher social position. He was apprenticed clerk to a company, and won several prizes for shorthand. He continued in this employment for six or seven years, but lost it in 1904 because he refused to submit to a system of fines which then came into vogue, and which, as his wife says, " would have robbed him of all his wages." Once thrown out of regular employment he became rapidly demoralised. His work since 1904 has consisted chiefly of odd errands, and occasional jobs for his father. In 1908 he obtained a temporary appointment as a clerk, but lost it after seven weeks through some misconduct. Now he spends most of his time in loafing, has become a confirmed gambler and a heavy drinker, and in the opinion of his relatives has lost all hope of obtaining work —for which he no longer looks. In the first instance, his indolence seems to have been encouraged by the ready help given him by his own and his wife's relatives for the mere asking. The little family now lives in a small four-roomed house, which is devoid of furniture, and for which his mother pays half the rent. Two children attend school, but get no material assistance there, as their mother keeps them clean and respectably dressed. They look, however, distinctly underfed.

Demoralisation often sets in later in life through home circumstances which have nothing to do with a worker's industrial capacity, as is illustrated by the story of another man, 49 years of age. He began his industrial career at the age of 9 in a Leeds factory. Later, he was a stone-sawyer, and a bricklayer's labourer. For twenty-one years, if one may believe a story which it was impossible to verify, he was a labourer for one firm in York, which was wound up eight years ago. Since then he has only done outside portering, especially for commercial travellers, earning four or five shillings per week at the best of times. His downfall seems to be closely connected with the misconduct of his wife, who has been twice in prison for being drunk and disorderly, and for wandering abroad without any visible means of support. Still, although physically fit for work, the man now depends almost entirely on the combined earnings of his wife—about 3s. per week—and of two sons aged 18 and 16, who earn 9s. and 6s. per week respectively. Another son is still at school. The home, consisting of three rooms, is not altogether without comfort, though situated in one of the poorest courts in the city.

Another man, aged 51, is a skilled worker who has not worked at his trade for the past thirty years. He is employed by an auctioneer for one half-day each week, and does a little trading in second-hand things on his own account. He rarely obtains other jobs, although he has the reputation of being honest and reliable when not under the influence of drink. His chief employer believes that he would not only refuse permanent work, but even occasional work lasting over a whole day. He is supported principally by the earnings of his wife. There are no children.

Different, again, is the case of another man, aged 40, who was originally apprenticed to a trade, but left after only two and a half years work, owing, as he says, to trade depression. He has done no work since, apart from occasional odd jobs at the railway station and in the streets. He has undergone a term of imprisonment for theft, and is said to have become completely reckless, having drifted to the lowest possible stage at which he can maintain himself.

It is difficult to account for the downfall of another man, aged 33, who worked as a labourer in a factory for four or five years after leaving school, then entered the army, in which he only remained one year, and now seems to have lost all incentive to work, being employed in jobs of a very casual nature, chiefly on farms. Although living in a lodging-house, he receives some support from a sister who is married to a respectable working-man. Apparently his relatives have failed entirely to prevent him from loafing about and to persuade him to look energetically for employment. He is strong and healthy, but would probably take no regular work, or even temporary work of any duration, if it were offered him.

Another case of deterioration is that of a man, aged 47, who now belongs to the street corner type of loafer. He was brought up in the country and employed in farm service for a number of years. In 1902 he lost his last permanent situation in a brewery, and since then has only obtained temporary employment as ostler and as carter. He has been married and has a son in regular employment, though not at home with him. Those who know this man say that he has become thoroughly demoralised by unemployment, aided, perhaps, by drink. He does not now look for more work than will suffice to keep him at a low-class lodging-house.

A few more histories of very young loafers may here be given, to illustrate the composition of this class.

One, aged 22, was in regular employment until 1905, when he started labouring casually in a brickyard,—work which, for the majority of those employed, only lasts for six months in the year. He spends a good deal of time, and picks up occasional earnings, by acting as tout to a bookmaker. He is strong and healthy, but of very lazy habits and generally unsatisfactory character. Although returning himself as "unemployed," he could give no evidence of any active search for work during the last few years.

Another youth, also of excellent physique, probably certain of at least casual employment if he were really anxious to get it, and only 22 years of age, was an errand boy for a short time after leaving school, and then worked for two or three years as a railway labourer. After four months' unemployment in 1904, he went to a flour-mill, but left very soon "because the work did not suit him." For the same reason he lost a temporary engagement with another firm in the city, where he refused to unload coal. Since then he has hardly looked for employment, but spent his time loafing in the streets. In this case, father and sister are in regular work, and the total income of the family averages 28s. per week.

We will close our review with two cases which illustrate the danger arising from a bad start immediately after leaving school.

One young man, aged 20, left school at the age of 13, and began his career by selling evening papers. In 1905 he got employment as fireman, but this only lasted for eighteen months, since, in 1907, he refused to go back to it after having been fined for drunkenness. He soon found casual work at a warehouse, usually for two or three days per week, earning on the average 8s. 6d. per week. In this case, the household is unsatisfactory, the father frequently out of work, and one brother given to drink and loafing like the youth under review. Both are said to be content with idling in the streets and depending for their livelihood on their parents.

The other, aged 22, was irregularly employed as errand boy, and at a brickwork when he left school. He managed, however, to keep one post for four years, and only left it in 1907, through the engagement of a younger boy by the firm. He is said to be a clever lad, sometimes working "like a nigger" for a week, but soon tiring, and not really determined to find employment. He spends much of his time at the street corner, and seems to acquiesce in being supported by his father and brothers, who are in regular employment. He is a strong, fine lad, and there is no apparent reason why his family should be so indulgent to him.

Such, then, are a few typical examples of this work-shy class. Not very hopeful material, we fear, to work on *now*! But was it once hopeful? Could the entry of the men into this class have been prevented, entirely or in part, if the right kind of help had been given at the right moment? And when and how should this have been done?

Our inquiry has shown us that probably about 30 per cent of the class once worked regularly, and left their last regular employment for satisfactory reasons. Another 30 per cent also worked regularly, but left for reasons which, as far as could be ascertained, were unsatisfactory, and about 40 per cent have never done any regular work.

PROPOSALS FOR REFORM

Dealing with preventive measures, we would once again draw attention to the proposals made in Chapter I., when discussing the unemployment of youths. There can be no doubt that if they were adopted they would go far, farther, perhaps, than any other single measure of reform, to reduce the number of work-shy men. Especially would they lessen the ranks of those who have never learnt to work regularly. It will be remembered that these proposals included a wide extension of the present system of Care Committees, consisting of voluntary workers, probably in the larger towns assisted by a paid secretary. The members of these Committees would give especial care to school children whose homes were not satisfactory, each worker supervising three or four homes only, so that considerable attention might be devoted to each case. Such workers could do much to counteract evil home influences, and could, if necessary, take steps for the removal of children from thoroughly bad homes. Then, as the time came for lads to begin industrial life, the Care Committees, acting in conjunction with an Advisory Committee concerning itself especially with such matters, would seek to prevent them from entering blind-alley occupations. Moreover, lads up to the age of 19 would be obliged to spend all their periods of unemployment in training schools, in which mental and manual training were combined with a liberal measure of physical exercise. Under existing conditions those members of the work-shy class who have never done any regular work, have spent the five precious formative years between 14 and 19, when they were not engaged on casual jobs of no educational value whatever, in hanging about the streets. Scarcely any better system for producing a class of loafers could be devised, and there is little hope of effecting any satisfactory reduction in the number of the work-shy, unless strong influences are brought to bear upon them in the critical years after they leave school.

We pointed out in Chapter I. that the creation of training schools and the compulsory attendance at them of every unemployed lad up to the age of 19 was a first step, and one which we believe could be taken immediately. But we recognise that as soon as the country is ready for such a reform it would be advisable to insist that *all* boy workers should spend a considerable portion of their time in undergoing training which would develop their physical and mental resources, and increase their manual dexterity and powers of adaptability. Possibly, as an intermediate stage, such a regulation might be made to apply only to certain scheduled trades which are recognised as constituting blind-alley occupations. We also believe that boys whose homes are unsatisfactory, and possibly many others, should remain under the personal influence of members of the Care Committees until they are 19. Many of them lack character, and at this formative period of their lives greatly need that moral support which is not always forthcoming in their homes. We recognise that for the Care Committees to give it, would involve a large amount of self-sacrificing voluntary work, but it is work which does not demand any extraordinary qualifications. There are very many men and women belonging to the more leisured classes, who are fully competent to render such help, and if they could once realise its vital importance in building up a strong nation, we believe that they would respond to the call made upon them.

As we have studied the life histories of men in this and other classes of the unemployed workers in York, we have been increasingly impressed by the belief that the comradeship and help of men and women of strong moral fibre, given, not mechanically to large numbers, but intensively to three or four persons related to them by bonds of sympathy and mutual understanding, are essential if we are to remedy those industrial evils which are due to moral defects on the part of the workers. Organisation and machinery can do much, but divorced from personal effort they will fall far short in important respects.

We believe, then, that a scheme on the lines indicated above, and explained in greater detail in Chapter I., is the best that can be devised for arresting at its source the stream of work-shy men who have never been in regular work. But it is obvious that it will also help materially in reducing the other sections of the work-shy class, especially that section consisting of men who have once been regular workers but have left for unsatisfactory reasons. We have seen what these reasons were—drink is the chief one; others are gambling, inefficiency, laziness, and so forth.

It is not unreasonable to suppose that with the better start which the system outlined above would have given these men, not a few of them might have been prevented from falling victims to their own weakness. But we must, of course, recognise that many men fail morally who have had a good start; and the reforms here needed are such as develop conscience and self-control. No mere piece of industrial or economic machinery can help a man who has fallen a victim to drink: both the causes and the remedies lie deeper. These, however, are questions which lie outside our present inquiry.

We pass then to the 30 per cent of the unemployable class who once worked regularly and lost their work through no apparent fault of their own. We have seen the forces reducing these men from regular workers to unemployables—how when they first lost their work they sought anxiously for other regular work, but were unable to obtain it, how circumstances compelled them to take the first casual job which offered, and the next, and the next, till their energy was diverted from the search for a regular job into the channel of casual work; then how, in many instances, even the effort to secure casual jobs became less and less active, until it almost ceased, leaving

them idle dependents upon the labour of others, or,
it may be, living on the verge of destitution on
their own intermittent earnings.

Here the reforms needed affect our industrial
machinery. They have already been indicated in
previous chapters, and comprise all those measures
which increase a man's chance of getting work and
which improve his condition when unemployed, and
reduce the likelihood of demoralisation. The regulation of industry through the action of public bodies,
spreading work more evenly over good and bad years,
the provision of additional work in connection with
afforestation, or other schemes which could be rapidly
developed or held in abeyance according to the state
of trade, the decentralisation of town-dwellers so that,
although continuing to work in towns, many of them
might reside in the country and find employment on
their holdings when industrial work failed them, the
decasualisation of the labour market, by means of the
Labour Exchanges—those and the other reforms dealt
with at length in the preceding pages, are necessary
to prevent men from sinking into the work-shy state
through inability to secure regular work, and it is
by such measures that the 30 per cent now under
consideration might have been retained in the ranks
of the regular workers.

But while we believe that if such schemes were
carried out the number of unemployables would be
enormously reduced, a residuum of unemployed men
would still exist.

We do not propose to enter in detail into the treatment which they should receive. It would, no doubt, be treatment in some form of Labour Colony suited to men unfit to support themselves under the ordinary conditions of industry. While, of course, it is important that careful thought should be given to the elaboration of methods suited to the needs of these men, it is obviously more important that we should cease to manufacture an unemployable class. The community should be made to realise that its existence and its magnitude is a serious blot upon the face of the nation, a blot which not only should be, but must be, wiped out.

CHAPTER VI

WOMEN AND GIRLS
(139 in number)

NOT a few women returned themselves unemployed when we took our census, who, as further inquiry showed, could not be so described, for although quite willing to do an odd day's work of one kind or another, they were not really seeking it, or dependent on it. We have, however, eventually included 139 women and girls in the class, but 12 of these, to whom we shall not refer again, had only just left school, and though they are included here for the sake of completeness, they had hardly yet had time to inquire for suitable openings. The remaining 127 may be divided into two clearly defined groups— first girls and unmarried women ; second, widows and deserted wives, or wives whose husbands from one cause or another are unable to earn money.[1] We will consider these groups in the order named.

GROUP 1

This group consists of 82 persons. Certain

---

[1] Two unmarried women, with illegitimate children, are included in this group.

particulars with regard to each of them will be found
on p. 202 *et seq.*, an examination of which will show
that almost all were young, 54 of them being under
21 years of age, 14 between 21 and 25, and only 10
over the latter age, while the ages of 4 could not be
ascertained. With 3 exceptions, all were looking
for permanent situations, 35 as domestic servants,
and the rest in connection with a great variety of
occupations. It is evident that the problem of
unemployment does not very seriously affect this
group of workers. In fact, there is a dearth of
juvenile female labour in York, and at the time of
our inquiry there were vacancies in the city which
could not be filled, for some hundreds of girls aged
between 14 and 17. It may therefore be said that
any respectable young girl who is in good health and
of average capacity can readily find employment in
connection with one industry or another. After the
age of 17 such openings are much less numerous,
since the chief firms absorbing female labour in York
do not employ married women, and therefore do not
set on girls who, in all probability, will no sooner
have become proficient than they will leave to be
married. On the other hand, respectable girls of
17 or over can, if of average capacity, easily obtain
employment as domestic servants, although the
purchase of the necessary outfit of clothes sometimes
presents a difficulty. As a matter of fact, the unemployment of domestic servants noted in our census
was for the most part merely a short break between

GIRLS AND UNMARRIED

Age	Nature.	Duration.	When Left.	Why Left.	How Long Unemployed?	Any Casual Work while Unemployed?
			Last Occupation.			
?	Dressmaking	..	..	....	..	....
?	Domestic service .	..	..	....	..	....
?	,, ,,	..	..	....	..	....
14	General servant .	1 month	May 1910	Work too heavy .	A few weeks	....
14	Scholar . . .	..	1 week ago	....	..	....
15	Confectionery packer .	7 weeks	Easter 1910	Dishonesty . .	Since Easter	....
15	....	..	..	....	Left school at age of 11 !	....
15	Scholar . . .	..	1 year ago	....	1 year	....
15	....	..	..	....	..	....
16	General servant .	8 months	June 1910	To better herself .	1 week	....
16	Domestic service .	16 months	June 1909	To live with sister.	1 year	....
16	,, . .	,,	May 30, 1910	Removal of employer	1 week	....
16	,, . .	10 months	June 1, 1910	?	,,	Charing . . .
16	Laundress . . .	12 months	May 20, 1910	To better herself .	3 weeks	....
16	Bookbinding . .	4 months	June 2, 1910	?	1 week	....
17	Errand girl . . .	2½ years	March 10, 1910	Dirty girl and bad time-keeper	3 months	....
17	Saleswoman . . .	5 months	?	To better herself .	?	....
17	Housemaid . . .	,,	May 31, 1910	Quarrel . . .	1 week	Cooking . . .
17	Confectionery operative	9 months	June 1908	To assist at home .	2 years	....
17	Confectionery packer .	3 years	May 24, 1910	Misconduct and theft, dismissed	2 weeks	....
17	Day-girl . . .	10 months	Feb. 10, 1910	To better herself .	4 months	....
18	Housemaid at hotel .	6 months	April 15, 1910	A love affair . .	2 months	....
18	Barmaid . . .	3 weeks	May 29, 1910	Too small . .	3 weeks	....
18	Domestic service .	2 months	March 31, 1910	To keep home .	2 months	....
18	Confectionery operative	3 years	Oct. 1909	Poor health and bad time-keeping	8 months	At confectionery works
18	Confectionery packer .	2½ years	April 1909	Inefficiency . .	13 months	General servant .
18	Cardboard-box maker .	2½ years	18 months ago	Ill-health . .	18 months	Farm work . .
18	Pea sorter and packer .	6 months	?	Temporary work .	?	....
18	General servant .	3 months	May 1910	To better herself .	1 month	....
18	Laundress . . .	3½ years	,,	Quarrel . . .	,,	....
18	Clerk	3 months	Dec. 31, 1909	Laziness? . .	5 months	....
19	Domestic service .	12 months	April 30, 1910	To better herself .	1 month	Day servant . .
19	Confectionery operative	9 months	Dec. 1909	Slackness . .	6 months	....

¹ Sixpence per day has been added to earnings of charwomen as estimated value of food received.

WOMEN (82 IN NUMBER)

What Occupation Sought?	Apparent Personal Handicaps in Search for Work.	Home Circumstances.	No. of Members of Household.		Average Casual Earnings per Week.[1]	Average Weekly Income of Rest of Household.[2]	Is Family under Poverty Line?[3]	Remarks.
			Adults.	Children (under 16).				
....	....	?	?	?	?	?	?	....
....	....	?	?	?	?	?	?	....
....	....	?	?	?	?	?	?	....
General servant	None	Widowed mother	3	3	..	20/-	Yes	....
Factory work	Bad sight.	,, ,,	1	2	..	9/-	,,	Sons allow 2s.
Laundress	None	Poor	2	3	..	25/-	No	Slum home
Printer	Weakness.	Widowed mother	2	6	..	20/-	Yes	....
Factory work	Poor physique.	Fair	3	3	..	over 30/-	No	Brother unemployed
Any agreeable work	Not looking energetically for it	?	?	?	..	?	?	....
Domestic servant	None	Deserted mother	?	?	..	?	?	Slum home
Domestic servant or factory work	Disagreeable habits and weakness	Widowed mother	4	..	..	14/-	Yes	Married son allows 6s.
Domestic servant	None	Poor	3	5	..	19/-	,,	Low wages of father
Laundry or factory work	Anæmia	Family of unsatisfactory character, girl has already had 4 places	3	3	2/6	..	,,	Father unemployed, he is a bad character
Domestic service	None	Poor	3	2	..	6/-	,,	Father and brother unemployed
Domestic service or own trade	,,	,,	?	?	..	?	No	Living with grandparents
Factory work	Weakness	Poor, drink-sodden	4	1	..	?	?	....
Shop work	Anæmia	Good	4	..	..	53/-	No	Father and sister in bad health
Domestic service	None	Poor, but respectable	3	4	?	23/2	Yes	Low wages of father
Confectionery work	,,	Good	4	4	..	55/4	No	Was temporarily required at home
Factory work	,,	Widowed mother	2	..	..	17/-	,,	Savings
Domestic service or shop	,,	Poor	3	1	..	20/-	,,	Father in casual employment
Housemaid at hotel	,,	,,	5	5	..	21/-	Yes	Father bad character, brother unemployed
Domestic service	,,	Good	5	3	..	81/-	No	....
,, ,,	,,	Poor	3	1	..	22/-	,,	....
Confectionery operative	Poor health	,,	3	3	5/-	18/-	Yes	Low wages of father
Domestic service	Dullness	Good	5	1	..	34/-	No	....
Factory work	Unsuited for factory life	Poor	3	2	7/-	16/-	,,	Father and sister under-employed
Domestic service or any	None	Widowed mother	3	..	..	8/6	Yes	Sister unemployed
,, ,,	,,	Good	5	4	..	33/-	,,	Brother unemployed
Domestic service	,,	,,	1	..	..	..	,,	Slum lodgings
Clerk	Inefficiency	,,	6	2	..	40/-	No	....
Domestic service	None	Poor	3	2	7/-	19/-	,,	Mother intemperate, low wages of father
Confectionery work	,,	Good	4	4	..	46/-	,,	....

[2] Including pensions, poor relief, etc., but not including occasional gifts or savings. [3] See footnote, p. 61.

GIRLS AND UNMARRIED

Age.	Last Occupation.				How Long Unemployed?	Any Casual Work while Unemployed?
	Nature.	Duration.	When Left.	Why Left.		
19	Typist	4 years	Feb. 19, 1910	Removal of firm .	4 months	....
20	Domestic service . .	?	?	?	?	....
20	Shop assistant . .	4 months	March 1910	Ill-health . .	2 months	....
20	Dressmaker . . .	3 years	1908	Employer married.	2 years	....
21	,, . . .	1½ years	1907	Slackness . .	2 or 3 years	Dressmaking . .
21	Clerk	3 years	Dec. 31, 1909	Ill-health . .	5 months	....
22	Milliner . . .	5 years	Feb. 28, 1910	End of apprenticeship	4 months	....
24	Domestic service . .	1¾ years	Nov. 20, 1909	Employer removed	6 months	....
24	Cleaning . . .	11 months	May 1910	To better herself .	1 month	....
24	Cooking . . .	14 months	March 1910	Overwork . .	3 months	....
24	Domestic service . .	3 months	May 1910	Run down . .	1 month	....
26	Confectionery operative	10 years	Summer 1908	Failure of firm .	1½ years	Charing and field work
27	Barmaid . . .	15 months	June 1909	Bad trade . .	1 year	Casually as kitchen maid
30	Dressmaker . . .	1 year	,,	Slackness . .	,,	Dressmaker . .
21	Hair frame worker .	6 weeks	May 15, 1910	,, . .	3 weeks	....
14	Confectionery operative	,,	Dec. 1909	Ill-health . .	5 months	
14	....	..	..	....	..	Cleaning . . .
15	Nurse	5 weeks	?	?	?	
15	....	..	..	....	..	10 weeks as confectionery operative
15	Confectionery operative	1 year	?	?	?	2 months as confectionery operative
15	Printer's inserter . .	4 months	?	Employment temporary	?	....
15	Confectionery operative	3 months	April 24, 1910	Inefficiency . .	1 month	....
16	,, ,,	4 months	Dec. 1909	,, . .	5 months	
16	Laundress . . .	1 month	June 2, 1910	?	1 week	....
16	,, . . .	6 months	? 1910	To better herself .	?	....
16	....	..	..	....	..	....
16	Confectionery operative	8 months	?	Weakness and bad time-keeping	?	....
17	,, ,,	3 months	Dec. 1909	Employment was temporary	5 months	
18	Bookbinder . . .	3 or 4 years	June 2, 1910	,, ,,	1 week	....
21	At dye works . .	2 years	1905	To better herself .	5 years	....
21	Cleaner and dyer . .	1 month	May 1910	Employment only temporary	1 month	Barmaid . . .
29	Office cleaner . .	5 months	April 1910	Temporary work .	5 weeks	Charing . . .
29	,, . .	3 months	?	Inefficiency . .	?	....
30	....	..	..	....	..	Charing . . .

¹ Sixpence per day has been added to earnings of charwomen as estimated value of food received.

WOMEN (82 IN NUMBER)—continued

What Occupation Sought?	Apparent Personal Handicaps in Search for Work.	Home Circumstances.	No. of Members of Household.		Average Casual Earnings per Week.[1]	Average Weekly Income of Rest of Household.[2]	Is Family under Poverty Line?[3]	Remarks.
			Adults.	Children (under 16).				
Clerk	None	Good	3	..	..	42/-	No	....
Domestic service	,,	,,	3	..	..	?	,,	....
Shop assistant	Ill-health	Poor	5	..	..	35/-	,,	Father casual, mother ill
Waitress	,,	Good	3	..	..	30/-	,,	....
Dressmaker	None	,,	4	1	5/-	43/-	,,	....
Clerk	,,	,,	6	2	..	40/-	,,	....
Milliner	,,	,,	7	2	..	46/-	,,	....
Domestic service	Delicate health	,,	4	..	..	42/-	,,	....
Charing	Delicate health and unsatisfactory character	,,	5	2	..	43/-	,,	....
Cooking	None	,,	4	2	..	42/-	,,	....
Domestic service	Delicate health	,,	7	3	..	67/-	,,	Brother unemployed
Laundry work	Anæmia and having young illegitimate child	Widowed mother	2	2	.	5/-	Yes	Widowed mother, sister and illegitimate child
Barmaid	None	Good	3	2	3/-	29/-	No	....
Dressmaker	,,	Widowed mother	2	..	10/-	5/-	,,	Old age pension
General servant	,,	Poor	?	..	..	?	?	Lives with married sister
Daily nurse	Delicate health	....	4	6	..	45/-	No	....
Domestic service	None	Widowed mother	1	8	..	9/6	Yes	Poor relief 9s. 6d.
Any	,,	....	4	5	..	34/-	,,	Father casual, and a bad character
Domestic service	,,	....	2	2	..	15/-	,,	Living with widowed aunt, cousin unemployed
Factory work	Probably inefficiency	Poor	?	..	?	?	?	Slum home
,,	,, ,,	Very poor	?	..	..	?	?	....
Factory work or laundry work	Somewhat loose character	....	2	4	..	24/-	Yes	....
Any	Inefficiency and poor health	....	3	4	..	24/-	,,	....
Factory or laundry work	None	Poor	?	..	..	?	,,	Two male members of the family unemployed
Factory work	,,	....	4	3	..	31/-	No	....
Any suitable	Lack of energy	....	5	..	..	36/-	,,	Widowed mother
Domestic service	Bad health	....	3	4	..	30/-	,,	....
?	None	....	4	6	..	40/-	,,	....
Bookbinding	,,	....	7	..	..	78/-	,,	....
Housemaid at hotel	,,	....	?	..	..	?	?	....
Domestic service	Delicate health	....	3	..	2/6	25/-	No	....
Charing or laundry work	None	Widowed mother	3	2	7/6	16/-	Yes	Widowed mother and widowed sister
Domestic service or charing	Inefficiency and slowness	,, ,,	6	1	..	37/-	No	....
Charing	Weakness	Poor type	4	..	?	?	?	Maintained by father, one brother mentally defective

[2] Including pensions, poor relief, etc., but not including occasional gifts or savings.   [3] See footnote, p. 61.

GIRLS AND UNMARRIED

Age.	Last Occupation.				How Long Unemployed?	Any Casual Work while Unemployed?
	Nature.	Duration.	When Left.	Why Left.		
31	Confectionery operative	9 years	1904	To get married .	6 years	Cleaning and washing
41	Farm service . .	3 years	1907	To better herself .	3 years	Charing . . .
?	Teacher	?	?	?	?	
24	Domestic service . .	9 months	Nov. 1909	' ?		?
26	Nursemaid . . .	4 years	1902	Illness . . .	6 months	....
					?	Dressmaking and
18	Domestic service . .	,,	May 6, 1910	Overwork . . .	1 month	upholstering
25	,, . .	1 year	Dec. 1908	To join her family .	1½ year	....
						Domestic service (day
15	....	..	..	....	..	work)
						....
23	General servant . .	4 years	May 1909	Employer's removal	1 year	....
19	?	?	?	?	?	
						....
16	....	..	..	....	..	....
16	....					
18	Confectionery operative	½ year	1907	Dismissed . .	3 years	Sempstress 2½ years
23	Domestic service . .	,,	Dec. 1909	Illness . . .	½ year	....
26	Nursemaid . . .	?	?	?	?	?

1 Sixpence per day has been added to earnings of charwomen as estimated value of food received.

two posts, the time being spent at home. Those cases of unemployment, whether industrial or domestic, which had lasted for a long time were, as pointed out in the previous pages, almost invariably due to ill-health or to home ties.

With a view to showing the importance of the earnings of persons in this group, we give approximately in the table on p. 202 *et seq.* the total earnings of the other members of the families to which they belong, and show in one of the columns whether, without any contribution from the unemployed member, the families are or are not above the poverty line.[1] It

[1] See p. 61.

WOMEN (82 in Number)—continued

What Occupation Sought?	Apparent Personal Handicaps in Search for Work.	Home Circumstances.	No. of Members of Household.		Average Casual Earnings per Week.[1]	Average Weekly Income of Rest of Household.[2]	Is Family under Poverty Line?[3]	Remarks.
			Adults.	Children (under 16).				
Cleaning . . .	....	Widowed mother	2	..	8/-	10/-	No	Already earns 8s.
Cleaning or charing	....	,, ,,	2	..	2/6	3/-	Yes	Average earnings 2s., poor relief, 3s.
Teaching . . .	None . .	....	1	..	?	..	?	In lodgings
Packing in factory .	?	....	1	..	..	..	?	,,
Dressmaking or upholstering	Delicate health	Poor . . .	?	?	?	?	?	Respectable home
Domestic service .	None . . .	,, . . .	3	3	..	22/-	Yes	....
,, ,, (day work)	,, . . .	Well-off . .	4	..	?	46/-	No	....
Domestic service .	Family of bad reputation	Unsatisfactory home	3	..	..	27/-	,,	Drunken parents
Domestic service (days only)	None . . .	Good . . .	5	..	..	52/-	,,	Mother invalid
Laundry work . .	,, . . .	Poor . . .	2	4	..	?	Yes	Mother dead, father army pensioner
Domestic service .	,, . . .	?	?	?	..	?	?	
Confectionery service	,, . . .	?	?	?	?	?	?	Mother dead
Any	Weakness. . .	Well-off . .	5	1	4/6	47/6	No	....
Domestic service .	Bad reference .	,, . .	6	..	..	76/-	,,	....
Nurse . . .	?	....	1	..	..	..	Yes	In lodgings

[2] Including pensions, poor relief, etc., but not including occasional gifts or savings.   [3] See footnote, p. 61.

will be noted that of the 65 cases for which information was obtained, 25 are below and 41 above it. Of the former, 13 were seeking posts as domestic servants, 11 in laundries or factories (2 of these had not good characters), and 1 older one wanted additional charing. Seven were handicapped in their search for situations by ill-health. Bearing in mind the great dearth of domestic servants, it is clear that the problem of unemployment among unmarried women in York is not serious—indeed the facts disclosed by our inquiry chiefly point to the need of measures for the physical improvement of some of the workers, and their maintenance when, through ill-health, they are unable to work. No doubt the proposals contained in the Government Insurance Bill will largely meet these needs.

GROUP 2 : WIDOWS, DESERTED WIVES, AND MARRIED
      WOMEN WHOSE HUSBANDS FROM ONE CAUSE OR
      ANOTHER ARE UNABLE TO EARN MONEY

The number of persons in this group is 45, particulars regarding whom are given on p. 210 *et seq.* It will be noted that the group is made up of 30 widows, 6 wives deserted by their husbands, 1 who has left her husband, 3 whose husbands were unemployed or under-employed, 2 whose husbands were ill, and 1 whose husband was a drunkard. Two are unmarried, with illegitimate children depending on them. About two-thirds of them are over 40 years of age,[1] and with five exceptions they are all casual workers who are not looking for regular work. All but 4 had been in work of some kind prior to their marriage ; 15 as domestic servants. Many have been depending for years on their own earnings, 2 of them for 28 and 30 years respectively, 10 are handicapped in their search for work by age and ill-health, and 5 either by moral defects or both moral and physical defects. On the other hand, in 24 cases there appear to be no personal reasons to . prevent their finding regular work, but the fact is that nearly all of them are

---

[1] 3 are between 21 and 25   10 are between 41 and 50
  2 ,,   ,,   26 ,, 30   12 ,,   ,,   51 ,, 60
  7 :,   ,,   31 ,, 35   4 ,,   ,,   61 ,, 70
  5 ,,   ,,   36 ,, 40   1 is over   70
          and the age of 1 is unknown.

seeking unskilled work—usually charing or washing
—and the supply of labour of this kind is in excess
of the demand.

There is no doubt that the families in this group,
although comparatively few in number, are often
living in a state of destitution which has serious
consequences—nearly all of them, and 38 out of 45
children, below the poverty line.   Their need may be
gauged from a glance at the column on p. 211 *et seq.*
giving their total earnings, and showing how important it is that these unemployed women should
secure regular incomes.

It must further be borne in mind that the total
number of widows and other married women in York
who are in the condition here described, is considerably in excess of the 45 enumerated in our census,
possibly two or three times as large, for evidently
such women rely almost exclusively on casual work
for a livelihood, and we only counted those who were
unemployed on a particular day.   The total volume
of destitution must, therefore, be considerable, and
since it involves the malnutrition of a large number
of children, it becomes especially necessary to consider
remedial measures.

The first fact that emerges from a careful examination of the case papers, is that the problem of giving
the right kind of help is more complex than that of
helping efficiently any other class which has come
under our observation in this inquiry.   Each case
must be considered carefully in relation to its own

P

WIDOWS, DESERTED WIVES,

Married or Widow.	Age.	Last Regular Employment.					How long unemployed and dependent on Earnings?	Casual Occupation now followed.
		Nature.	Duration (years).	When Left.	Why Left.	Left Since or Before Marriage.		
W	34	Nursing	¾	1908	?	?	2 years at least	Washing, charing, etc.
W	34	Confectionery operative	10	1896	Unfit for work	Before	5 ,, ,,	Cleaning.
W	33	Setter-up (comb factory)	6	About 1899	Removal of firm	?	A few months	Washing.
W	33	Weaver	4	1901	To marry	Before	?	Charing.
W	38	....	..	..	....	..	8 years	,,
W	37	....	..	..	....	..	4 years	,,
W	43	Domestic service	7	1887	To marry	Before	?	,,
W	47	....	..	..	....	..	Since Oct. 1909	,,
W	44	....	..	..	....	..	Recently	....
W	47	Sewing woman	¼	1909	Employment was only temporary	Since	?	Sewing and dressmaking
W	50	Domestic service	5	1880	To live with father	,,	?	Cooking.
W	62	,,	2 or ?	1865	To marry	Before	Since Oct. 1907	Nursing and field work
W	51	Shop assistant	11	1882	,,	,,	14 years	Waiting.
W	55	Workhouse laundress	1¾	May 1909	To better herself	Since	1 year	....
W	54	Laundress	¼	1908	Ill-health	,,	2 years	Charing.
W	52	Workhouse charing	¼	Feb. 1910	Employment was only temporary	,,	4 months	Field work
W	56	Domestic service	?	?	?	Before	?	Charing.
W	61	,,	7	1867	To marry	,,	....	,,
M	24	Ironer	2	1904	Ill-health	Since	6 years	,,
M	48	?	?	?	?	?	?	,,
M	30	Waitress	¼	1905	Employment was seasonal	Since	5 years	....
M	31	?	?	?	?	?	?	Washing, cleaning.
M	23	Domestic service (day)	2	Dec. 1909	Quarrel with employer	Since	5 months	....
M	32	Confectionery operative	3	?	To marry	Before	?	Charing.
M	45	Domestic service	?	?	,,	,,	?	,,
M	45	....	..	..	....	..	....	Farm work
...	40	Cleaning	1	June 1909	Ill-health	Since	1 year	Charing.
W	56	Domestic service	½	1880	To marry	Before	30 years	Dressmaking.
W	54	,,	3	March 1910	Ill-health	Since	3 months	....
W	53	,,	12	1882	To better herself	Before	28 years	Charing.
W	52	Machinist	2¾	Jan. 1910	Dispute re overtime	Since	5 months	....
W	42	Housekeeping	2¾	Dec. 1909	To attend to sick child	,,	,,	Charing.

¹ Sixpence per day has been added to earnings of charwomen as estimated value of food received.

AND MARRIED WOMEN (45 IN NUMBER)

Occupation sought. Nature.	Casual or Regular.	Apparent Personal Handicaps in Search for Work.	No. of Members of Household. Adults.	Children (under 16).	Average Casual Earnings per Week.[1]	Average Weekly Income of Rest of Household.[2]	Is Family under Poverty Line?[3]	Remarks.
Sewing, washing, etc. .	Casual	None	1	1	10/-	..	Yes	....
Cleaning or any . .	,,	,, ...	1	2	8/6	6/-	,,	Poor relief, 6s.
Laundry work . .	Regular	,, ...	1	2	7/-	5/-	,,	,, 5s.
Laundry, washing, cleaning	Either	Delicate health . .	2	1	8/6	12/-	No	....
Washing and charing .	Casual	,, . . .	2	1	3/-	1/-	Yes	....
,, ,, .	,,	Ill-repute . . .	1	3	3/6	9/6	,,	Aliment, 5s.
Washing . . .	,,	None	1	..	8/-	..	No	....
Cleaning . . .	,,	,, ...	3	3	5/-	Over 30/-	,,	....
Any	,,	,, ...	2	2	..	?	?	Married son pays rent, unmarried son maintains rest of family
Sewing and dressmaking	,,	,, . . .	1	..	Say 5/-	..	Yes	....
Cooking . . .	,,	,, ...	2	..	Over 20/-	?	No	....
Nursing or field work .	,,	Age and ill-health .	1	1	7/-	2/-	Yes	Allowed 2s. by sons
Waiting or cleaning .	,,	None	3	..	?	20/-	No	....
Charing or laundry .	,,	,, ...	3	3	..	18/-	Yes	Living with married son
Cleaning . . .	,,	Drink and bad reputation	4	..	3/6	?	?	6s. allowed by son
Charing	,,	Drink and apoplexy .	3	5	5/-	?	?	Living with married daughter, poor relief, 5s.
,, ...	,,	None	1	..	?	..	?	4s. allowed by children
,, ...	,,	,, ...	1	..	10/-	..	No	Has savings
Charing or farm work .	,,	Ill-health . . .	5	3	..	10/-	Yes	Husband and son-in-law unemployed
Charing. . . .	,,	?	?	?	?	?	,,	Husband of bad character
Laundry or cleaning .	Either	Consumptive tendency	2	4	..	?	?	Only wants work because she is afraid husband will lose his
Washing or cleaning .	Casual	None	1	2	..	?	?	Deserted by husband, poor relief
Domestic service . .	Either	,, ...	3	1	..	25/-	No	Lives with parents, deserted by husband
Washing . . .	Casual	,, ...	2	4	3/6	10/-	Yes	Husband invalid, poor relief, 10s.
Charing. . . .	,,	,, ...	2	6	3/-	19/-	,,	Husband unemployed
Charing or farm work .	,,	,, ...	2	..	1/-	18/-	No	Deserted by husband, maintained by son
Charing or washing .	,,	,, ...	2	..	6/-	7/-	,,	Illegitimate daughter
Charing. . . .	,,	Rheumatism . .	1	1	5/-	?	Yes	Son, aged 15, unemployed, poor relief
,, . . .	,,	Drink and ill-health .	2	1	..	?	,,	Maintained by daughter and charity, 5s.
,, ...	,,	Slowness . .	1	..	10/-	..	No	....
Machinist . . .	Regular	Ill-health . . .	3	6	..	?	?	Living with married daughter, 2 of the children her own
Charing. . . .	Casual	None	1	2	10/-	..	Yes	....

[2] Including regular poor relief, pensions, etc., but not including occasional gifts or savings.   [3] See footnote, p. 61.

WIDOWS, DESERTED WIVES,

Married or Widow.	Age.	Last Regular Employment.				Left Since or Before Marriage.	How long unemployed and dependent on Earnings.	Casual Occupation now followed.
		Nature.	Duration (years).	When Left.	Why Left.			
W	Over 60	?	?	?	?	?	?	?
M	38	Domestic service	2	1893	To keep house	Before	17 years	Charing .
W	58	....	..	..	....	..	2 years	,,
W	?	Information refused .	..	..	....	..	....	....
W	54	Laundress .	3	April 1910	New manageress, change of staff	Since	2 months	....
M	37	Domestic service	5	1894	To marry .	Before	14 weeks	Delivering milk
M	22	Laundress .	3	1907	,,	,,	?	....
M	54	Housekeeping .	4	Nov. 1909	Accident	Since	6 months	Washing, charing .
W	62	Charing .	?	?	?	,,	?	,, ,,
W	42	Housekeeping .	10	?	Employer's removal	,,	?	Charing .
W	72	Laundress .	?	?	?	,,	?	Laundry work
..	30	,, .	2	1907	To keep house for father	..	3 years	Charing (rare)
M	34	Farm service .	3	Nov. 1909	?	Since	?	Washing .

¹ Sixpence per day has been added to earnings of charwomen as estimated value of food received.

especial circumstances before we can say what form
of remedial action is desirable. Such examination
has led us to the following conclusions :—

(1) Six women are almost unemployable. Four of
them drink, and are otherwise of such unsatisfactory
character that they are very unlikely to find more
work than they have at present, and 2 suffer from
physical infirmities. Their ages vary from 48 to 62 ;
5 of them are widows, and none of them have young
children depending on them. Two are living with
their families, who maintain them in part, and could

AND MARRIED WOMEN (45 IN NUMBER)—*continued*

Occupation sought. Nature.	Casual or Regular.	Apparent Personal Handicaps in Search for Work.	Adults.	Children (under 16).	Average Casual Earnings per Week.[1]	Average Weekly Income of Rest of Household.[2]	Is Family under Poverty Line?[3]	Remarks.
Charing . . .	Casual	Age	2	1	..	?	?	Living with deserted daughter and grandchild
Office cleaning . .	,,	None	1	3	6/-	10/-	Yes	Deserted by husband ; poor relief, 10s.
More charing . .	,,	Age, and has to look after delicate child	1	1	2/-	..	,,	Lives on neighbours
....		....	1	2	?	..	?	....
Laundry or field work .	Casual	Age	2	..	..	6/-	Yes	Son too young to maintain her entirely
Charing . . .	,,	None	?	..	..	?	No	Deserted by husband, living with parents
Any day work . .	,,	,, . . .	4	1	..	?	?	Husband in hospital, living with parents
More washing and charing .	,,	,, . . .	4	..	7/-	?	No	Maintained by daughters, left husband
,, ,,	,,	,, . . .	3	..	?	10/-	?	Partly maintained by son, and sister who has 4s. poor relief
Charing . . .	,,	?	?	..	6/6	?	?	....
Laundry work . .	,,	Age	1	..	?	8/-	No	Pension, 3s., old age pension, 5s.
Laundry work and charing	,,	Intemperance and unsatisfactory character	2	2	..	19/-	,,	2 illegitimate children dependent on her, living with father
Charing . . .	,,	Four young children dependent on her	3	4	3/-	?	Yes	Deserted by husband, living with parents in slum home

[2] Including regular poor relief, pensions, etc., but not including occasional gifts or savings.   [3] See footnote, p. 61.

do so entirely, and need not be further considered. One, aged 48, lives with a drunken husband, and it is probably too late to attempt to reform either of them. They somehow manage to make a living, but in future such people will probably be squeezed out by a process of decasualisation, and will be forced to enter some institution. Two others are apparently steady, industrious women, who are prevented from securing more work by their increasing infirmity, but who can still earn a few shillings per week by charing or field work. They seem to be cases for financial support in one form or another, rather than for employment. The sixth is far from strong and somewhat given to drink. A daughter, aged 26, with an illegitimate child, lives with her, and was out of work at the time of inquiry. Another daughter, aged 12, also lives with her. The mother receives help from a private charity, and there would be no difficulty if the daughter were in work. It should not be too late to train her for domestic service, in which case the child might be cared for by its grandmother.

(2) In 7 cases it is entirely undesirable for the women to engage in industrial employment, as they are needed at home. In one case there are 4 children, and a husband ill with Bright's disease. At the time of our inquiry the wife was earning about 3s. a week by charing, and receiving 10s. from the Guardians. Two are cases of deserted women. One of them has 3 young children; she earns 5s. a week and gets 10s. from the Guardians. The other, who earns about 3s. a week by washing, has 4 young children; she lives with her parents in a crowded slum house, and her father is a bricklayer's labourer. There are 4 other women, each with 2 children. Two of them earn a little over 7s. a week by charing, and get 5s. and 6s. respectively from the Guardians. One earns about 10s. a week and receives a little assistance from relatives, and one, who has been deserted by her husband, receives 3s. from the Guardians, to which she adds insignificant earnings by charing. All but one are respectable women with clean homes.

Looking to the future of the children, and the
prospect of turning them into strong, efficient, and
self-supporting workers, surely it would be very bad
policy to help their mothers to secure further industrial
employment which must inevitably lead to neglect of
their home duties. In the first of these cases, no
woman can be expected to do more than look after
4 young children and a sick husband, and she should
be given relief adequate to maintain them without
her work. In the other cases, where the relief from
the Guardians is inadequate, the women should stay
at home ; and we suggest that, by way of supplement-
ing their meagre incomes, children under the care of
the Poor Law should be boarded out with them,
although this would involve an alteration in the
existing law that no children may be boarded out
with women in receipt of Poor Law relief. No doubt
it would also be necessary to increase the relief which
they are now receiving, but the additional sum
required would not be an extravagant payment to
ensure the suitable upbringing of children who are at
present not only suffering from lack of parental care
and training, but also from physical privation due to
the inadequate earnings of their mothers. Moreover,
we think it advisable that in the case of widows and
others receiving relief for the maintenance of children
—their own as well as any who might be boarded
out with them—periodical inspections should be
made, so that the State, having provided an income
adequate for their maintenance in a condition of

physical efficiency, should be able to insist that the money is wisely expended. It is also important that special care should be taken, through the agencies described in Chapter I., to see that the children thus maintained by the State should, when they begin to work, enter employments with prospects of adequate remuneration in the future.

In the case of widows or deserted women having young children dependent on them, with whom other children could not suitably be boarded out, it would probably be wise to arrange for them to go out to work, and for the State or Municipality to make arrangements for their children to be taken care of in their absence. As regards provision of work, they would practically be in the category of women having no children dependent on them. Some suggestions in this connection are made in the subsequent paragraphs of this chapter.

(3) There are 14 women—some having only one child, who could be suitably left with a relative, the others having no children—who are obviously well fitted for domestic work of one kind or another, but cannot earn enough to maintain them. We believe that if they are to become self-supporting, they must first of all, if not sufficiently competent, be properly trained, and in some way protected from the competition of the large number of women who, although not dependent for their livelihood on their own earnings, are glad to add to the family income by doing an occasional day's work. A system of registering

casual domestic workers would here be very helpful, but no one should be registered who was not willing to accept work on at least 5 or possibly 4 days every week. This regulation would practically limit registration to those dependent mainly on their own earnings. Any applicant would have to satisfy a responsible person or authority, both of her good character and of her ability to undertake those branches of domestic work for which she desired to be registered.[1] Thus one woman might only be registered for rough scrubbing and cleaning; another for cleaning and laundry work; a third for laundry work, cleaning, and plain cookery, and so forth. Every registered person would receive a certificate indicating the branches of domestic work for which she was qualified, and a book in which to obtain a brief reference from all her employers.[2] Such a book in the case of a good worker would constitute an increasingly valuable testimonial to her efficiency, and thus augment her chances of regular employment. Registration should be renewed annually, and an examination of the book of reference would enable the registering authority to judge whether the original certificate of efficiency had been well deserved. There is no doubt that the prospect of securing

[1] Such a person or authority should be able to check information regarding the character of applicants for registration, by local knowledge, and should also have the confidence of employers.

[2] The book might be ruled as follows :—

Date employment commenced.	Date employment ceased.	Kind of work.	Was work satisfactorily done?	Signature of employer.	Address of employer.

regular employment would, in the case of many
applicants for registration, be greatly increased by
a little training in one direction or another. For
instance, a woman who had a fair knowledge of
working-class cookery and an evident aptitude for
such work, might soon be enabled to qualify for
better posts. Similarly, some teaching in laundry
work would often materially better a woman's
position. In York, as elsewhere, there is great
difficulty in finding private laundresses who understand their work. Again, working people who cannot
afford to pay fully trained nurses, complain that it
is difficult to secure the help of women who can do
simple sick-nursing, and a little training in this might
open an additional avenue to unemployed women.
It would obviously be an economy for the community
to pay for such training, and to meet any small
expenditure involved by a system of registration, if
a number of women who might otherwise come on
the rates could thus be rendered self-supporting.
But even apart from the possible economy, it is not
unreasonable to ask that some steps should be taken
to help women who, through circumstances over
which they have no control, are suddenly thrown on
the labour market, to earn an adequate income.
Probably if such a scheme were carried out, the
examiner granting certificates of efficiency would be
under the control of the municipal authority, and
the domestic economy schools under the same control
might be used for the suggested training, although it

should be given in classes confined to adults. We also think that instructions should be issued to all Labour Exchanges to give preference to registered workers in filling vacancies for domestic work. Such regulation, while not ruling out the many women who add to the family income by an occasional day's work, would enormously increase the chances of regular employment for women dependent upon it for a livelihood ; and decasualisation of this kind can be strongly recommended.[1]

(4) Next come 12 women who, although they would take more work, are not in distress through lack of it. One of them is keeping house for her father ; the others are living either alone or with children who maintain them, or for whom they keep house. In so far as they were qualified for, and really anxious to secure, regular work, they would be helped by a scheme for the registration of domestic workers, as outlined above. It should, however, be noted that their ages vary from 44 to 61, and since they are already living with their families, it is doubtful whether many of them would accept regular work.

(5) There only remain 6 cases to be considered. Two are women whose husbands are out of work, and another is one whose husband is in temporary work which he may lose any day. All have children

---

[1] The Association of Trained Charwomen and Domestic Workers (7 John Street, Adelphi, Strand, W.C.) has for several years done useful work in training and finding employment for domestic workers, whose characters and qualifications they can certify as satisfactory.

depending on them, and the solution of the difficulty
should be to find work for the husband, rather than
for the wife. Another is a widow of 33, who was
trained as a weaver, and who has one child and a
mother living with her. Here the right solution is
to move her to a district were she can get work at
her own trade, while the mother takes care of the
child. One woman, over 60 years old, lives with a
daughter, who has been deserted by her husband,
and a grandchild. In this case it is desirable that
the daughter, who earns a little by charing, should
obtain more regular work—by the means suggested
above—and thus maintain the woman here returned
as unemployed who is getting infirm. For one case
all information was refused which would enable us to
suggest relief.

We have entered in some detail into the question
of how best to help the women of this class, because,
although the number enumerated in our census was
small, the total number of women in York who at
one time or other are in similar positions must be
considerable, and their distress is often both acute and
prolonged. We have seen that in the case of mothers
with children dependent on them, the remedy called
for is not to provide work which would take them out
of the home, but adequate maintenance, and therefore
the problem they present is not, or rather should not
be, a problem of unemployment. But there are other
women who, through the death of those who have
hitherto maintained them, suddenly find themselves

cast on the labour market, where they struggle for work, often with pitiably unsuccessful results. Almost all of them, through lack of experience, are limited to some branch of domestic work for employment. We believe that the proposals made for their registration would greatly improve their position by increasing their chances of regular work. This registration is really a method of decasualisation, and involves the squeezing out of some workers who obtain occasional employment at present. With women, however, this difficulty is much less serious than with men, because the workers squeezed out would not be those relying entirely upon their own earnings, but wives of working men, and others who merely do an odd day's work to add to the family income." No special steps need be taken to provide employment for them : the attention of reformers should rather be directed to measures which, by increasing the wages of the men, will render work on the part of their wives superfluous.

CHAPTER VII

DETAILED DESCRIPTIONS OF SELECTED FAMILIES

IN order to realise what unemployment actually means when it is so prolonged, or so frequent, as to exhaust any provision made against it in periods of regular work, we have obtained the weekly household budgets of eight unemployed families. In some of these a regular, though inadequate wage was coming in from boy or girl labour, though the principal breadwinner was idle ; in others the family subsisted on casual work of the most precarious character, or on credit; two were helped by the Parish, and another by the Charity Organisation Society, during the four weeks of which we have a record. In one case our investigator was compelled to advance a portion of the sum paid to budget-keepers for their trouble, rather than face the charge of having, for the sake of statistics, conducted the researches in too cold-blooded a manner. Due account has, of course, been taken of all these incomings, as also of gifts in kind received by some of the families during the period under observation.[1]

---

[1] The budgets here given do not represent the lowest level of want ;

The method followed in obtaining the information is the same as that adopted in previous studies by one of the present writers.[1] Each housewife was furnished with a specially ruled notebook of fourteen pages—two for each day—for the entry of all goods purchased on the left page, and that of all food consumed, with the number of persons at each meal, on the right. Each budget was kept for four weeks, and the stock of food in the house was noted at the beginning and end of this period. The investigator paid frequent visits to each house, to ensure absolute accuracy. It may safely be assumed that the food consumed is equivalent to that purchased and given, and that no unnecessary waste has taken place.

The first question which arises is : In how far does the food consumed by each family suffice for the maintenance of physical efficiency ? To answer it, it is necessary to examine its quantity and character, and to reduce it to a common measure. For the method adopted we refer the reader to the Appendix, p. 259, reprinted from *Land and Labour*. He will there find the reasons referred to which have induced us to accept 125 grams (or about $4\frac{1}{2}$ oz.) of protein

rather they represent the level at which underfeeding can continue week after week and month after month. It is practically impossible to obtain records, lasting over four weeks, of the way in which the very poorest families manage to exist. This is partly because, when in the very worst straits, families shrink from letting others know of the shifts to which they are put to exist at all, and partly because no investigator could stand by for a month and watch such a family, without suggesting an appeal to some charitable agency, and thus invalidating the statistics.

[1] See *Poverty : A Study of Town Life*, p. 223 *et seq.*, and *Land and Labour*, p. 341 *et seq.*

and 3500 calories of energy value, as the nutrients required to maintain a man at " moderate muscular work " in physical efficiency.

Next, for the purpose of comparing the diets of the different families, it is necessary to reduce them to a common basis " per man per day," allowance being made for the food requirements of men, women, and children of various ages. The method of doing this is also given in the appendix. The following table, resulting from this analysis and classification, gives us the desired information respecting the adequacy of the diet.

It will be noted that the supply of protein varies from 39 to 74 grams per man per day. In other words, the family best supplied with it has less than two-thirds (60 per cent), and that worst supplied less than one-third (32 per cent), of the amount required for physical efficiency (i.e. 125 grams per man per day).

Or if we turn to the calorific or energy value of the dietaries, this varies from 1086 calories per man per day in the case of the worst fed, to 2374 in that of the best fed family. As the amount necessary for physical efficiency in the case of a man doing moderate work is 3500 calories, it will be noted that the amount of energy value in the dietaries of these families varies, as in the case of the protein, from one-third (31 per cent) to two-thirds (68 per cent) of what is necessary. Broadly speaking, the families suffering most from deficiency of protein in their dietary,

2 Standard requirement 3500 calories.

Number of Budget	Adults	Children	Equivalent to Men	Average Weekly Income of Family (from all Sources) s. d.	Amount s. d.	Percentage of Total Expenditure	Expenditure on Food per Man per Day. d.	Protein per Man per Day. Grams	Deficiency of Protein per Man per Day [1]. Grams	Energy Value per Man per Day. Calories	Deficiency of Energy Value per Man per Day [2]. Calories	Protein. Grams	Calories.	Animal Food.	Vegetable Food.	Animal Food.	Vegetable Food.	Animal Food.	Vegetable Food.	Alcohol.	Other Beverages and Condiments.
1	3	1	3·1	3 6	3 6	67·1	2·13	43	82	1086	2414	242	6119	19·2	80·8	14·2	85·8	31·0	57·3	...	11·7
2	2	2	2·8	15 0½	7 2	44·8	4·65	72	53	2374	1126	186	6120	25·0	75·0	23·3	76·7	47·5	41·9	...	10·6
3	2	3	3·4	9 9½	6 2	76·1	3·01	66	59	2088	1412	249	8058	11·5	88·5	11·2	88·8	22·5	60·1	...	17·4
4	2	2	3·4	11 7	7 7	66·3	3·93	74	51	2236	1264	174	5252	25·8	74·2	14·1	85·9	46·2	44·6	...	9·2
5	3	3	4·0	13 0	7 10	61·5	3·25	63	62	2020	1480	233	7459	18·1	81·9	18·1	81·9	38·8	50·5	...	10·7
6	4	...	3·6	14 7½	9 8½	58·9	4·63	41	84	1321	2179	106	3424	47·6	52·4	37·7	62·3	50·2	40·1	...	9·7
7	2	4	3·4	11 0	5 4	49·0	2·68	39	86	1361	2139	176	6094	23·7	76·3	22·4	77·6	42·0	45·5	...	12·5
8 [3]	2	3	...	4 2	3 7	...	...	54	71	1642	1858	...	...	...	...	...	...	...	...	...	...

1 Standard requirement 125 grams.
3 So much food was given to this family as to render valueless any figures of the family's expenditure on food.

Q

are also suffering most from deficiency in its energy
value.　So we see that some families are actually
having to exist on less than one-third of the food
necessary to keep them physically efficient, and *none*
have more than two-thirds of that amount.　These
facts, especially when it is remembered that unemployment often lasts for months, enable us to gain
some idea of the extent to which the physical
efficiency of such families is being sapped by privation.　The physiological effect of an inadequate
supply of protein, or albuminous food, is thus
described by a well-known writer on dietetics.[1]

The daily consumption (of protein) should never be
allowed to sink below 100 grams, but should preferably be
125. . . . It is well to have an excess of proteid above
that barely required for tissue repair.　To live on a
minimum of proteid is to run the risk of having what one
may call " threadbare tissues," and of having no reserve for
use in emergencies.　And such a condition of things makes
for low resistance and for disease.　There is also reason to
believe that proteid, besides acting as a repairer of
tissue and a source of energy, exerts upon the cells a
stimulating influence which increases vitality and energy.
A deficiency of it, too, seems to impair the condition of the
blood and lower the tone of the muscles and of the heart,
besides enfeebling the digestive powers by restricting the
supply of the material from which the digestive ferments
are elaborated. . . . The difference, in fact, between an
animal fed on highly nitrogenous diet, and one supplied
with little nitrogen, is the difference between a steam engine

---

[1] Dr. Robert Hutchison : *Food and the Principles of Dietetics*, pp. 23, 169.

at half pressure and one which is producing its full horse power. . . . To growing children a deficiency of proteid in the diet is specially disastrous, for the lack of building material which it entails may result in impaired growth and development, the consequence of which may last throughout life. For the same reason persons who habitually live on a minimum of proteid are apt to convalesce but slowly after an acute illness; for once their tissues are broken down they have no ready surplus of building material out of which to repair them.

Those familiar with the extent to which many unemployed persons are underfed, and with the physiological effects of this underfeeding, will recognise that it is often necessary to discount the criticism made of work done by men who have been unemployed, that "the beggars aren't worth helping. They won't work when they have the chance." That the feebleness of their efforts is sometimes due to idleness, we do not dispute, but that it is often due to sheer physical weakness caused by starvation is a fact which the critics are too apt to forget. As a well-known American economist has reminded us : [1]

What an employer will get out of his workman will depend very much on what he first gets into him. Not only are bone and muscle to be built up and kept up by food, but every stroke of the arm involves an expenditure of nervous energy which is to be supplied only through the alimentary canal. What a man can do in twenty-four hours will depend very much on what he can have to eat in those twenty-four hours; or, perhaps, it would be more

---

[1] F. A. Walker : *The Wages Question*, p. 53.

correct to say what he has had to eat the twenty-four hours previous. If his diet be liberal, his work may be mighty. If he be underfed, he must underwork.

But not only should the facts before us make us more discriminating in our criticism of work done by "the unemployed," they should emphasise the urgent need for such measures of reform as will prevent this terrible wastage of human strength, not only that of adults, but of children. The physical deterioration following on unemployment comes home to us with great force when cases are studied individually, and it is well from time to time to be reminded of the personal side of the problems confronting us, which is sometimes overshadowed by masses of figures or by arrays of generalised facts.

Before turning to the detailed descriptions of the 8 families under observation, a few more words may be said regarding the table on p. 225. First let it be noted that with one exception, namely, Budget No. 6, the selection of food stuffs was economical. This economy in selection is especially marked in Budget No. 3. There is no doubt that some of the other families might have got a little more nutriment for the money they expended had their selection of food stuffs been different, but it cannot be expected that they should have a scientific knowledge of the nutriment contained in every article of food, or be able, without notice or education, to change the habits of a lifetime. It may be stated that these families obtained on an average 195 grams of protein, and 6075 calories of energy value for every shilling expended on food, which is considerably higher than the average of 14 poor working-class families whose budgets were examined by one of the present writers some years before, even although food was a good deal dearer in 1910 than when the previous investigation was made.[1]

As regards the expenditure on articles other than food, an examination of the details given on the succeeding pages shows that with the exception of rent—where this is paid—the outgoings are reduced to a minimum. The serious matter is the debt into which the families are obliged to run in order to live at all. The following are the respective amounts of debt incurred during the month in which they were under observation :—

	£	s.	d.			s.	d.
Family No. 1	. . 1	8	3½	Family No. 5	. .	...	
„ 2	. .	3	6½	„ 6	. .	13	4
„ 3	. .	6	2½	„ 7	. .		4½
„ 4	. .	14	1½	„ 8	. .	13	7½

When it is remembered that these figures take no account of debts incurred before or after the particular month for which the budget was kept, it will be recognised how heavy is this burden consequent upon unemployment. It means that the under-feeding and other privations which accompany unemployment itself do not terminate when work is found, but are continued, although in a lesser degree, often for many months, sometimes for years, even when the

---

[1] See *Poverty*, p. 238.

work found is permanent. Of course the time
necessary to repay a debt varies not only with its
amount, but with the wages received when in work,
and the size of the family. When the wages are low
and the family is large, a man who has been out of
work for some time finds it almost impossible ever to
free himself from debt.

BUDGET No. 1

The Nevinsons live in a very small four-roomed house in a very
small street. Fortunately, it is situated in the outskirts of the city,
on pretty high ground, and they are fond of fresh air, so that front
door or back door is generally open, and the rooms, though small, are
not stuffy. Mrs. Nevinson "feels the heat," being tall and very stout,
with a face radiating good nature and even hope. How she achieves
either her expression or her weight, which must be 14 stones, is a
standing mystery, for the wolf which many people contrive to keep
outside the door, crosses the threshold of the Nevinsons pretty continually. Beer, which is popularly supposed to be "feeding," is
tabooed by them, though not because of any conscientious scruples.
As Mrs. Nevinson says, "when he was in regular work he liked his
glass of beer as well as any one, but now we can't get bread, let alone
beer ; and you don't find a man who goes out many a morning at five
o'clock fasting, because he wants to leave what crust there is for the
children and me, dropping into the public with the first shilling he
earns—nor me neither."

Indeed, the general testimony of the neighbourhood is, that the
Nevinsons are a sober, decent, well-living family, always eager for and
willing to do any kind of work, however poorly paid. One of the
children referred to is a delicate girl of twenty, who has worked in
various factories, but always left through ill-health. As she sits by
the fire, inactive, while her mother bustles to and fro, she looks more
like death than life, yet she is to be married in a few weeks to a man
whose employment is quite fitful and precarious.[1]

The other is a lad of twelve, undersized, but fairly healthy.
Another child, the youngest, is at the Blind School, but comes home
for holidays. Moreover, there is a weekly charge of 1s. 6d. for her
keep, though such fees are sometimes remitted in cases of acute poverty,
and though the Nevinsons are in worse arrears with them than with
rent and insurance, the demand is less pressing. If they were not
tenants who kept the property clean and in good repair, and paid up

---

[1] Since this description was written the girl has developed consumption.

whenever it was humanly possible, they would long ago have drifted into the workhouse. As it is, they have been forced to flit time after time, with small sums of rent owing. Yet Nevinson has two first-rate characters, one for twelve years, one for twenty, has never been known to refuse work, and is well liked, both by his mates and his employers. One post he left through the closing of the works, another through illness. His last regular work was for two years, and he left it three years ago, with many other hands, through slackness. Since then he has only had catch jobs, chiefly at the waterside. He is never long with no work at all, in spite of increasing age—he is nearly fifty. It is true that, like his wife, he can neither read nor write, but the deficiency is largely atoned for by a fund of native shrewdness, adaptability, and practical knowledge. He is a silent man, but when he talks he is often original, quaint, and worth hearing, and he always seems to have the serenity and faith in life that are supposed to accompany religious conviction, but are dissociated in his case from any of its organised forms. How far the fact that he has never "darkened the doors" of any place of worship is explained by lack of suitable clothing, and how far by a deep contempt for people who go to church "for what they can get," it is impossible to say, for his faith and doubt alike are dumb.

"Nothing is against Nevinson but bad luck," say the neighbours; and their criticisms may be accepted as true, though once in his record he was dismissed for another man's fault—a thing that happens more frequently than might be imagined. His worst enemy has really been sciatica, which has several times crippled him hopelessly "just as things were beginning to mend," and then the household has had to depend on Mrs. Nevinson's skill as occasional washerwoman or "char."

They have had a very large family, but as Mrs. Nevinson once remarked, "the undertaker has buried them a lot." Only five children are living, two of them married, but unable, owing to their own straitened circumstances, to help their parents.

The house rent is five shillings—a heavy rent for the four small rooms, and miniature scullery, though the yard is a fair size. The smallest room is the parlour, opening out of the narrow passage which leads to the kitchen door (the stairs lead out of the kitchen). It is the conventional artisan parlour, so far as china ornaments, engravings, antimacassars and "gimcracks" are concerned, but there is a suspicious paucity of solid furniture, since all the best of that has gone to the pawnshop, or been sold to individuals, from time to time. The white lace curtains at the window give an impression of comfort and ease within, till Mrs. Nevinson displays the careful draping necessary to conceal the fact that they are really "dropping to pieces," and "won't mend no longer." Moreover, it must be borne in mind, that in the straits the Nevinsons have passed through, even a ball of white mending cotton may be an unattainable luxury.

The budget covers a period of very precarious employment, and further light as to the actual daily life of the family may be gained from a perusal of Nevinson's diary, as taken down by a married son who is a "splendid scholar." Since it was written, after years of casual work that would have hopelessly demoralised most men, but has apparently left Nevinson steady and punctual as ever, a prospect of regular employment has at last dawned on the horizon, and if it comes, the arrears of rent and the heavy bill at the corner shop will be wiped off gradually week by week. Till that is done, the family will continue to live almost entirely on bread and margarine, even if wages are coming in every Friday. That is one form of the insurance practised by the poor against unemployment in the future. They are certainly actuated by honesty in their endeavour to wipe off arrears. But they are also enabled to run up a fresh bill if, after a brief respite, the wolf comes back to the door.

DIARY

Thursday, July 7.—Went to work at Messrs. L.'s, 6 A.M., carrying sacks of wheat. Breakfast 8 to 8.30—one kipper and bread ; dinner 12 to 1—bread and margarine ; left at 6 P.M. ; tea—bread and margarine ; got a bit of twist given. Earned 4s.

Friday, July 8.—Up at 6 A.M. No breakfast. Went round to L.'s and W.'s wharves, stayed out until 12, came home, had dinner—kipper and bread ; walked round and round until tired, came home at 4.30 ; tea—bread and cup of tea.

Saturday, July 9.—Up at 6 A.M., waited at L.'s until 9, no chance ; went round to W.'s wharf, nothing doing ; home at 11, bit of bread and margarine for dinner ; walked round to see if I could pick any work up, home at 7 P.M. ; no supper.

Sunday, July 10.—Up at 4 A.M. and went round the town to see if I could find anything that had been lost, could not see anything, so came home at 7 A.M. ; had breakfast consisting of jam and bread, went to bed until 1 P.M., had dinner—stew, and cup of tea ; to bed at 9 P.M.

Monday, July 11.—Got up at 5.30 ; got a job at L.'s, earning 4s. ; took it for rent. Meals : breakfast—butter and bread ; dinner—nothing ; tea—hot cakes and bacon,—got a pound of bacon given, also some tea and a ¼ stone of flour.

Tuesday, July 12.—Earned a shilling at wharf for working three hours. Breakfast—bacon and bread ; dinner—bacon and bread ; tea—margarine and bread.

Wednesday, July 13.—Went out at 5.30 A.M. ; walked round to several different jobs until 10, cut some old boots up to mend the little boy's boots, went out again until 4, got nothing. Breakfast—margarine and bread ; dinner—dripping and bread ; tea—kipper and bread, and not much of that.

Thursday, July 14.—Went out at 5 A.M., got a job helping a man at L.'s to stow some wheat; worked until 11 A.M., earned 1s. 6d.; bought ¾ stone of flour when I got home. Afternoon earned nothing, wandered round again. Breakfast—a pennyworth of corned beef for five of us and a loaf of bread; dinner—bread and tea; tea—dripping and bread, tea.

Friday, July 15.—Got up 5 A.M., went round the town to several places hoping to find work, but was unsuccessful, back home at 10 A.M.; had some cold tea and bread, went out until 3, carried a bag for a gentleman to the station, got 6d. for the job. On making my way home, a gentleman wished me to show him the way to St. Lawrence's Club, gave me 2d. for my trouble; bought ¼ stone flour, two pennyworth of kippers, two ounces of tea siftings 1½d. Had tea at 7—hot cakes and kippers and cup of tea; went to bed at 9.

Saturday, July 16.—Up at 4 A.M., went into Market Place to see if there was any chance of helping farmers with baskets of " spuds " (potatoes), etc., earned 1s.; went round to L.'s and W.'s wharf, no work there, came home and had some tea and bread. Out again at 11, walked round and round, trusting to luck to see if anything would turn up; came home at 4, fell asleep in chair until 6, had another walk round until 9 P.M., back home to bed.

Sunday, July 17.—Up at 4 expecting that I should get work assisting at L.'s to move a barge, but I was disappointed. Had a walk round the town, but did not find anything; came home again, had a cup of tea and some bread, then went to bed until I had my shirt washed; had dinner, consisting of some stewed pieces and potatoes that the wife had earned by doing some washing. Tea consisted of bread and tea, and then to bed again.

Monday, July 18.—Got up at 5 A.M., went round to several places to see if I could find any work, but did not get any; back at noon, no breakfast, dry bread for dinner; went out again at 2, walked about until 7—nothing; went to bed at 8.30.

Tuesday, July 19.—Up at 5.30 A.M., usual walk round and back at noon, nothing doing; no breakfast, dry bread for dinner, no tea, bed at 8 P.M.

Wednesday, July 20.—Went out at 5.30 A.M., walked round to W.'s and L.'s, came back at 8.30, had breakfast—a cup of tea and bread and margarine; went out again and walked about until 6 o'clock; came back home, had a cup of tea and dry bread, and then went to bed.

(On this day the family had neither breakfast nor dinner. The wife gave her husband the last crust, and he thought there was a loaf left; but at night a neighbour brought 2d. and a bowl of Quaker oats, which the children ate.)

Thursday, July 21.—Went out at 6 A.M., walked to Naburn to meet boats for W.'s wharf, waited there until 12, then walked back home at 2. Dinner—bread and tea; tired out, so went to bed; got up at 7 P.M., had tea and bread, went to bed at 9.30.

Friday, July 22.—Up at 5, walked round and round the town until 12. Nothing doing anywhere, so I was fairly sick of walking about. For dinner I had bread and kipper and a drink of tea; no breakfast, no tea, and no supper; went to bed at 7.30.

(In meantime, chopped wood that he had picked up at waterside.)

Saturday, July 23.—Up at 4, went round Market Place, got a job to carry some baskets for 3d., went round to W.'s wharf, and L.'s, but nothing doing; came home at 11, had some bread and cheese, then went out and got threepence given from a friend; came back home, had a drink of tea and some dry toast, went to bed at 8.

Sunday, July 24.—Got up at 3, had a walk round the town, did not find anything; came home at 7, had a drink of tea, then went to bed until I had my shirt washed; got up at 3 P.M., had some potatoes, then sat in the house the rest of the day; went to bed at 9.

Monday, July 25.—Got up at 5, heard of a job for a few hours emptying a boat, waited for two hours to see the master. When I saw him he had got some one; came home, had some bread and fat for dinner; walked round the town until 6 P.M., came home again and went to bed.

Tuesday, July 26.—Got up at 6, heard tell of a job grave-digging at cemetery, went to see after it at 8, but was disappointed. Walked round town until 12; when I came home—had been sent for to go to the cemetery. Started work at 1 until 5, being told it was for a few weeks. I hope it will be regular. Wages 21s. a week. Two chairs sold for 4s. 6d. to-day to make rent up.

The straits in which this family found itself is shown by the following details regarding their expenditure and dietary. The latter falls short of the standard requirements by 66 per cent as regards protein, and 69 per cent as regards energy value.

STATEMENT OF INCOME AND EXPENDITURE FOR FOUR WEEKS, JUNE 1910

INCOME—				EXPENDITURE—				
Man (unemployed except for three odd days' work).	£0	7	0	Food (including beverages)—				
				Paid for . . £0 8 11				
Wife (occasional charing) .	0	6	9	On trust . . 0 5 0½				
Sale of rags	0	0	1½			£0	13	11½
Gift	0	0	2	Fuel and Light—				
Loan	0	0	6	Paid for . . £0 4 0½				
Obtained by pawning quilts, sheets, and underclothing .	0	1	0	On trust . . 0 1 5½				
Deficit	1	6	9			0	5	6
				Washing and Cleaning Materials—				
	£2	2	3½	Paid for . . £0 0 8				
				On trust . . 0 0 4				
						0	1	0
				Tobacco—				
				Paid for . . £0 0 4				
				On trust . . 0 0 2				
						0	0	6
				Rent not paid		1	0	0
				One week insurance . .		0	1	4
						£2	2	3½

PURCHASES DURING FIRST WEEK

Friday.—Nil.

Saturday.—¾ lb. meat pieces, 3d. ; ¼ lb. tea, 4d. ; ½ lb. margarine, 4d. ; Fish and chips, 1d. ; 1 lb. sugar, 2½d. ; ½ stone potatoes, 1½d. ; gas (1d. in the slot meter), 2d. ; 4 lb. loaf, 6d. ; 10 stone coals, 1s. 5d. ; 4 kippers, 2d. ; 1 lb. soap, 3d. ; 1 washing powder, 1d. ; sticks for fuel, 1d. ; blue for washing, ½d. ; matches, ½d. ; 2 lb. bread, 3d.

Sunday.—Nil.

Monday.—"On trust," ½ oz. twist tobacco, 2d.

Tuesday.—2 oz. yeast, 1d. ; 3 stale buns, 1d. ; "on trust," 1 stone flour, 1s. 8d.

Wednesday.—1 lb. soap, 2½d. ; 3 stale buns, 1d. ; "on trust," ½ lb. jam, 3d.

Thursday.—"On trust," ¼ lb. cheese, 2½d.

MENU OF MEALS PROVIDED DURING FIRST WEEK

	Breakfast.	Dinner.	Tea.	Supper.
Friday .	Tea,[1] kippers, bread.	Tea and dry bread.	Tea and dry bread.	
Saturday	Tea, kippers, bread.	Tea, one penny-worth of fried fish and chips.	Tea, bread and margarine.	
Sunday .	Tea, kippers, bread.	Three penny-worth of meat pieces boiled with potatoes.	Tea, bread and margarine, onions.	Tea.
Monday .	Tea, bread and margarine.	Tea, bread and margarine.	Tea, bread and margarine.	Tea, bread.
Tuesday .	Tea, bread and jam.	Tea, 3 stale buns.	Tea, bread.	Tea, bread.
Wednesday	Tea, bread and jam.	Tea, 3 stale buns.	Tea, bread and margarine.	
Thursday	Tea and bread.	Tea, bread, cheese.	Tea, bread and jam.	

[1] Always without milk, but with sugar when there was any in the house.

BUDGET No. 2

(NOTE.—*This family is suffering from under-employment rather than actual unemployment, but is included here as showing some of the effects of the former evil.*)

The house is in a poor quarter of the town, but it faces a large open square, and is roomier and more solidly built than the majority of workmen's houses. The door opens into a square space, so minute that it would be ironical to call it a passage or a hall, from which the stairs lead up on one side while the living-room is on the other. The latter again opens into a short passage with a combined scullery and wash-house on one side, ending in a yard in which a good-sized sheet may actually be hung out to dry in fine weather, without flapping against the walls if a breeze rises. It is a good house for the money, five shillings a week, paid monthly, but the tenants have lived here many years, and proved themselves so trustworthy in every respect that the landlord would consider it bad policy to raise the rent against them. He is, moreover, a connection of theirs by marriage, but though comparatively well off he never helps them in any way.

Dinner is just over when we enter, and the members of the family are all in the living-room—mother and daughter, and a boy and girl, twelve and ten respectively, the children of the daughter, Mrs. Taylor. Mrs. Taylor's husband drank and gambled, and finally went to America without her when the children were four and two. She has heard nothing of him since ; but he ill-treated and half-starved her, and she is "better without him than with him." She returned to her widowed mother, Mrs. Wade, and the two together tried to extend a small dress-making custom. For the first two years a married sister and her family lived with them, but later on this arrangement had to cease, as the house was overcrowded, and Mrs. Wade and her daughter were left alone with the two children. About that time Mrs. Wade's rheumatism began to interfere with her industry, and it grew steadily worse till the whole of the work fell on her daughter. She is now completely crippled, and lies on a couch in the living-room, as to ascend and descend the narrow stairs is impossible. Her life has been a hard one. She supported an invalid husband for three years before he died, and she brought up a large family, most of whom are now dead—often working till two in the morning and rising again at four—and toil and privation have broken her. She suffers incredible pain, but she is extremely cheery ; and now the Old Age Pension is in sight if she lives to the spring.

Meanwhile, a very heavy burden devolves on the daughter. She is clever, careful, and conscientious, but has no technical training in dressmaking, and her customers are among the poor people of the neighbourhood. But there is a piano in the living-room, a relic of the palmy days long ago, when her father was living and in full work as a "crack" painter, and having some skill she makes an occasional sixpence by giving a music-lesson. Moreover, a day's charing is accepted when dressmaking is slack, or possibly a "bit of washing" is undertaken for a neighbour that brings in a few pence. But these women, no less than the fashionable costumière, have to face deferred payments and bad debts. They have to pay the rent, and even if they are positively starving, the money for this is put aside. They have to bring up the children respectably, and they would as soon dream of begging for them in the streets as for applying for free dinner or breakfast tickets. . . . *Noblesse oblige!*

Again, just when the times are hardest, and coal and gas are most needed, there is least doing. Mrs. Taylor is pallid, pinched, and prematurely old ; but the very spirit of pluck and patience looks out of her eyes, and she and her mother have an invaluable gift of extracting any spice of humour that the situation may hold. They know all the ropes perforce. They know where the biggest "ducks" are to be got for a penny, and where you can sometimes get two for three-halfpence. They know that Bob or Kitty, threadbare perhaps, but clean, neat, and hopeful, is likely to get a bigger "duck" or a larger pennyworth of "fish-chips" than is given to a grown-up person. And they know—what is so rare among the poor—how to extract the utmost value from a pennyworth of bones or a pound of lentils, and how to make the pound of meat purchased for Sunday's dinner, still the *pièce de résistance* on Tuesday, for the same four people.

The real *pièce de résistance*, however, is "bread and scrape." The bread is good and home-made, and always the same ; but there is a variety about the scrape, which sometimes consists of butter, sometimes of a sprinkle of sugar, and sometimes of margarine or dripping—the one invariable quality being the skimpiness. Yet the children are happy children, keen at work and keen at play. Bob is in ex-seventh standard already, a phenomenal thing for a boy of twelve, and Kitty at ten is only held back by her age from the sixth standard. They have, in short, the abnormal precocity of the habitually underfed, for, however they may brave it out, they could always "do with more." And love and care, cleanly and healthy surroundings, and an abundance of fresh air—for, in regard to the latter, both their mother and their grandmother are thoroughly up-to-date—cannot altogether make up for the shortage of nourishing food.

The deficiency of protein in their dietary is 42½ per cent, and that of energy value 32 per cent, measured by standard requirements.

STATEMENT OF INCOME AND EXPENDITURE FOR FOUR WEEKS, NOVEMBER 12 TO DECEMBER 9, 1910

INCOME—

	£	s.	d.
Mrs. Taylor (dressmaking)[1]	3	0	2½
Deficit	0	3	6½
	£3	3	9

EXPENDITURE—

	£	s.	d.
Food (including beverages)	1	8	6½
Rent	0	16	0
Fuel and light	0	7	10
Washing and cleaning materials	0	1	7½
Clothing	0	6	0½
Insurance (four weeks)	0	1	8
Sewing cotton	0	0	10
Pocket money for children [2]	0	0	8
Sundries [3]	0	0	6½
	£3	3	9

PURCHASES DURING WEEK ENDING NOVEMBER 18, 1910

Friday.—½ lb. bacon, 4½d. ; gas, 1d. ; sticks for fuel, 1d. ; cinders, 3d. ; 1 stone flour, 1s. 9d.

Saturday.—2 oz. yeast, 1d. ; ½ lb. tea, 6d. ; 2 tins condensed milk, 3d. ; 3 lb. sugar, 6d. ; gas, 1d. ; 1 lb. scrag-end neck of mutton, 6d. ; 10 stone coals, 1s. 3d. ; insurance, 5d. ; pepper, 1d. ; boy's boots mending, 2s. ; 1 lb. onions, 1d. ; ½ stone potatoes, 2½d. ; ½ lb. butter, 7½d. ; 1 lb. cod, 2d. ; ½ lb. rice, 1d.

Sunday.—½ pint skimmed milk, ½d. ; gas, 1d.

Monday.— 1 lb. soap, 3d. ; 1 washing powder, 1d. ; 1 box starch, 1d. ; blue, ½d. ; gas, 1d. ; 1 pint whole milk, 1½d. ; fried fish and chips, 1d. ; rent, 4s.

Tuesday.—Gas, 2d. ; kippers, 1d. ; "duck" (a kind of black pudding), 1d.

Wednesday.—1½ lb. scrag-end neck of mutton, 8d. ; ½ stone potatoes, 2½d. ; 2 oz. yeast, 1d. ; gas, 2d.

Thursday.—Sewing cotton, 4d. ; matches, ½d. ; sticks for fuel, 1d. ; 2 oz. shrimps, ½d. ; gas, 1d.

[1] The income was larger than usual this month, as extra work was being done for Christmas.
[2] For the Martinmas fair.
[3] Two jars and mustard pot, 3d. ; writing-paper and stamps, 2½d. ; cat's meat, 1d. Total 6½d.

MENU OF MEALS PROVIDED DURING WEEK ENDING
NOVEMBER 18, 1910

	Breakfast.	Dinner.	Tea.	Supper.
Friday . .	Tea (with condensed milk and sugar), bread and butter.	Tea, bacon, bread.	Tea, bread and butter.	Tea, bacon, dripping and bread.
Saturday .	Tea (with condensed milk and sugar), bread and butter.	Tea, fish (cod), potatoes.	Tea, bread and butter.	Bread and dripping.
Sunday . .	Tea (with condensed milk and sugar), bread and butter.	Tea, roast mutton, boiled potatoes, rice pudding.	Tea, bread and butter, sweet cake.	Cold potatoes, a little meat, dripping and bread.
Monday . .	Tea (with condensed milk and sugar), bread and butter.	Tea, cold meat, bread.	Tea, bread and butter.	Fried fish and chips, dripping and bread.
Tuesday . .	Tea (with condensed milk and sugar), bread and butter.	Tea, stewed mutton, potatoes.	Tea, bread, kippers.	"Duck," bread and dripping.
Wednesday .	Tea (with condensed milk and sugar), bread and butter.	Tea, roast mutton, potatoes.	Tea, bread and butter.	Bread and mutton-dripping.
Thursday .	Tea (with condensed milk and sugar), bread and butter.	Tea, potatoes, hash.	Tea, bread, a halfpennyworth of shrimps.	Bread and dripping.

BUDGET No. 3

The Campbells are a Scotch family. Mr. Campbell came to this
city to execute a contract, and in April 1910 was finally dismissed
by the firm for which he had worked for 17 years. It gave him a
good character, but alleged that there was no further work for him.
He thought that his age, 40, might have something to do with it.
At the beginning of the budget it was two months since he finished
his last piece of work as engineer and hot-water fitter, and for some
weeks he had expected daily to be set to work again. Then he grew
doubtful and began his search for work in York, but only after two
months of suspense did the firm give him definitely to understand
that it could employ him no longer, and in that two months the
Campbells had come to the end of their savings, and had begun the
process of pawning and selling. Campbell was not in a trade union,
having left it in a time of slackness to enter the employment of the

firm which had now turned him adrift, at 30s. a week, a wage below the union rate. He had begun his career as a plumber, but not only had his plumber's tools been long parted with, but he had lost his practical skill in the many years in which he had done other work. As for the savings of the Campbells, they were small, the intervals between contracts, and the moving from place to place repeatedly, involved by the character of the man's post, had made that inevitable, even though the family had never or seldom "troubled the doctor." They were careful, economical Scotch people, and by dint of living mainly on bread and oatmeal, they made the utmost both of their slender savings and of the sums obtained for their poor household gods. But the end came. They had been actually starving for days before they appealed to the Parish, and the Parish recommended them to the C.O.S. as superior, self-respecting folk. The latter society gave them a small grant for some weeks, and the record of how they spent it is contained in the budget, which was kept under the supervision of the C.O.S. visitor. At the end of the month Campbell, who had been completely unsuccessful in getting odd days, whether from the Labour Bureau or by his own exertions, got a few weeks' employment during another man's illness. It was hard, rough work, quite unsuitable for a man of very slender build and below the medium height, but he stuck to it like grim death, and gave great satisfaction till the job ended. This enabled them to pull round and pay up the rent, with which they were remarkably little in arrears. And then, as there seemed no hope of anything permanent, they shook the dust of York off their feet, and, with the help of the C.O.S., removed to Mrs. Campbell's native city, Glasgow, where they had relatives who would do their best to put work in their way.

There were five in the family, Mr. and Mrs. Campbell, a boy, and two girls. The boy, who was 12 years old, had begun to earn 1s. 6d. a week as errand boy in the evenings, before the budget was completed. Mr. Campbell was a phenomenally silent man, and his wife, a woman of his own age, was far from talkative. They had always been of the superior skilled artisan class, used to helping others rather than asking for help, and the position in which circumstances had placed them was acutely painful to both. Probably C.O.S. relief had never been more keenly or gratefully appreciated. The greater part of the allowance, as will be seen, was spent on flour, that they might be sure of bread for the week. They were not intimate with the neighbours, who probably never knew the extent to which they were suffering, or else, though poor themselves, they would have offered help. But independence, and possibly their own intense respectability in a more squalid street than they had ever before inhabited, isolated the Campbells pretty completely in spite of a jerry-built house and a crowded neighbourhood.

Mr. Campbell, asked to write an account of himself, proved more expansive through the medium of pen and paper than that of spoken words, and some extracts from his journal are enclosed as a supplement to the budget.

YORK, 20/7/1910.

Having had the misfortune to be paid off my work last Easter, through slackness of trade, I had, like my unfortunate brother out-of-works, to look elsewhere for employment; and York is a very unpromising district, I deeply regret to say, for one to be in, who is by trade an engineer, at a time of unemployment. This I proved, having bitter recollections of the many persistent refusals that met my entreaties for work (including labouring work of any description) while searching York to its very extremities. But with pride I may here mention that, as I had always been a careful and sober man while in employment, I had been able to put away a trifle weekly for a rainy day, which I am pleased to say came in very handy for the first month of my great trial. The first three weeks of my " no work " experience was mostly spent in scanning the different newspapers in the library, hoping against hope to see something to which I could reply, and also making strict inquiries as to any work that was going on in and around York ; also, meanwhile, I was answering advertisements in the *York Press* and *Herald*, all of which came to absolutely nothing in the end. I casually heard of the Labour Bureau, to which office I at once went with great hopes of work, and entered my name and address and duly received my membership card, which I had to hand in at the office every morning for the clerk's consideration of any work which may have reached him by post or otherwise. One morning, in handing in my card as usual, I was completely dumfounded to hear him remark that I was to call only once a month. Now, at this point, I would like any common-sense people to try and put themselves in my position when he closed the small office window and left me to my own keen reflections. I turned away, and the only remaining strength in my body seemed to completely forsake me. I staggered into the street a completely world-forsaken man, with the words continually ringing in my ears— " once a month." However did these people think I was going to manage a month, which seems to the unemployed six months ? But fate being against me, I never did receive any material benefit from this Bureau, although they were very anxious to get me work. Being in such a shattered condition I went home quite unfit to do anything further that day. The next morning, being somewhat refreshed, I started out with just a little boiled oatmeal on my stomach, not very much, one would say, to do any hard work with, and made for the railway shops, and then to the goods station, where I had the pleasure of seeing the manager, with whom I pleaded for some work—which resulted in him summing up with the remark that he was "very sorry indeed that I was not the usual type of man they started for such heavy work." I only was a very light-built chap, which was my greatest failing in many cases where I sought work. . . . But I must remark here that, as my savings were beginning to dwindle away, I became more anxious to get work, being out from early morning until late at night with a stomach as empty as a soap bubble; and of course the necessary walking which I had to do made my feet very sore. This would raise a blister over-night, and next morning, when starting out again, the blister would burst, and would be very painful, which, of course, was a great impediment in my locomotion. But I struggled bravely on; knowing too well those depending upon me at home, I tried to forget the awful soreness which I knew would wear off through time, and returned home again at night with no better success. At last the crisis came when I became absolutely penniless, an awful fix to be in, and I felt my position at this period more than I did when facing complete destruction three times through shipwreck. I was without work, or food for the children, a matter of great importance, when it was proposed that I should try and see if the C.O.S. would grant me a little relief. This they did, I am proud to say, without any unnecessary trouble, and to this society I shall always be greatly indebted for their kindness in coming to my rescue. For five weeks I was entirely depending upon their liberality and kindness; and, while receiving this munificent help, I was still very much in earnest and busy to find work, so that I would not be long a burden to the society's fund. Having been in correspondence with a firm of Engineers, one morning a welcome letter came for me to go and arrange with the foreman to start work at once. Having made the necessary arrangements I was employed as a labourer, and although the pay is small I am pleased to say, through being very careful, I have been able, the short time I have been employed, to put everything straight again at home, and I still live in great hopes that something else will turn up for me when this work is completed.

It is very interesting in many cases to note, if a person be a little industrious at home, how everything can be kept in working order when there is no income coming in. Looking back to the first month I was out of employment, nothing of any importance happened until my little daughter fell sick with measles, but under the care of the parish doctor she got quite well again. He ordered her milk, but, having no money to buy it with, the child got better in the lack of such luxury! Now, during Whit Monday and Tuesday, these days not being suitable for one to look for work, I saw that the children's boots required repairing, so I cut the uppers off some old boots and finally had the satisfaction of making such a good job of them that they will last them for some time to come; and as my boy sold his melodeon for 3d. I was able to buy a card of protectors. During

R

this time the landlord was continually growling, when he called for the rent and I had nothing for him, so in desperation at being annoyed thereby, I took my best suit to the pawnbrokers and pledged it for 4s. and paid 3s. 6d. out of it for rent, much against my will, as I could have made it spin out a good way in food for the children. When I was in receipt of relief from the C.O.S. we were able to get along a little better, but our main support, on the whole, was bread and tea. Now, as I got home at night, tired out and foot-sore with tramping about all day, I always found some little item wanted attention, one in particular being the chimney, which was causing us annoyance with smoking very badly. So, on making a careful inspection, I found a soot-door in the attic which no doubt was for cleaning purposes, and naturally I grasped the idea at once; and after carefully covering the fireplace I took some water and poured it through the soot-door, which I am proud to say had the desired effect. But what a mess everything was in! Now, the next case being the slop-pail which had become worn and would not hold water at any cost, and it being a responsible commodity in the household, I decided to bring my inventive powers to a test once more. So, after a careful consideration I went out and begged a little Portland cement at a new building in Swinegate, which I put into the pail with a little water, until I mixed it into a paste, and next morning it was quite ready for its usual duties, being set and hard and good for some time to come. The next item which was causing some trouble at home, not mentioning the blessings it got from my wife, was the steam pan, which was very much worn and continually putting out our bit of fire. But as this article was made of tin (6½d. bazaar) and completely burned away, I saw at once that it was condemned for any further use, and until I shall be able to buy another one we are cooking potatoes or puddings in the kettle, carefully washing it out when it is required for breakfast and tea.

The details given below show how very economical was the dietary adopted. Yet the deficiency in protein was no less than 47 per cent, and that in energy value 40 per cent.

STATEMENT OF INCOME AND EXPENDITURE FOR FOUR WEEKS, JUNE 1910

INCOME—				EXPENDITURE—				
Received from the C.O.S.—				Food (including beverages) .			£1	4 11
Grocery tickets value . .	£1	2	6	Rent—				
Coal tickets value . .	0	5	8	Two weeks paid . £0 7 0				
Gift from a friend . .	0	1	0	Two weeks in				
,, subscribed by relatives .	0	10	0	arrears . . 0 7 0				
Deficit	0	7	0			—	0 14	0
				Coal			0 5	8
	£2	6	2	Candle			0 0	0½
				Soap			0 0	9
				Balance in hand . .			0 0	9¼
							£2 6	2

PURCHASES DURING FIRST WEEK

Friday.—1 oz. tea, 1d.
Saturday.—1½ stone flour 2s. 6d. ; ¼ lb. tea, 4½d. ; 1 lb. rice, 2d. ; 3 2-lb. loaves, 9d. ; 1 lb. soap, 3d. ; 1 tin condensed milk (12 oz.), 2½d. ; 2 lb. sugar, 5d. ; ½ lb. margarine, 2½d. ; 2 oz. yeast, 1d. ; 1 candle, ½d.
Sunday.—Nil.

Monday.—Nil.
Tuesday.—Nil.
Wednesday.—2½ lb. beef bones, 2d. ; 1 lb. rice, 2d. ; 1 lb. oatmeal, 2d. ; 1 lb. turnips, ½d. ; ¾ lb. carrots, ½d. ; ¼ lb. barley, ½d. ; 1 oz. yeast, ½d.
Thursday.—Nil.

MENU OF MEALS DURING FIRST WEEK FOR WHICH THE BUDGET WAS KEPT, JUNE 1910

	Breakfast.	Dinner.	Tea.	Supper.
Friday	Tea, bread.	Tea, bread.	Tea, bread.	
Saturday.	Tea, bread.	Tea, bread, rice.	Tea, bread and margarine.	Bread.
Sunday .	Tea, bread and margarine.	Tea, bread, rice.	Tea, bread and margarine.	Tea, bread.
Monday .	Tea, bread.	Tea, bread, rice.	Tea, bread.	
Tuesday .	Tea, bread and margarine.	Tea, bread and margarine.	Tea, bread.	
Wednesday	Porridge.	Soup, bread.	Tea, bread.	
Thursday.	Tea, bread, porridge.	Soup, bread.	Tea, bread.	Bread.

BUDGET No. 4

Dunn is a sturdy, honest working-man, who can turn his hands to most things, from cab-driving to hawking or field work, and who has very seldom been idle long together. But his age—57—is against him, and it is eight years since he last had regular employment. Then he certainly had a stretch of it—twenty-five years with one employer, the head of a firm of painters. But at his death Dunn was thrown on the labour market, since the firm who took over the business, though continuing to employ him occasionally, did not put him on their permanent staff. His life has been varied. He left school at 12, in the fourth standard, or what corresponded to it, and became a milk-boy. After five years, wanting to rise in the world, he took a post as carter to a York baker. There he earned 12s. a week, with board and lodging, his money going chiefly to support his mother who, but for him, might have starved, since his father " drank all he earned." He stuck to this post seven years, but the work was " killing." He had known what it was to come in dog-tired at 11.30 P.M., and be compelled to drive right off again as far as Knaresborough (19 miles away) with bread. Sometimes he fell asleep while driving, and had two or three severe falls. Finally, he quitted, and found work at painting and packing, being employed, he told us, for two masters at once. Then came his regular post of twenty-five years, where he averaged 28s. a week, not more, as he could not do " graining." It is hard for a man with so excellent a record to come down to dependence upon catch jobs. He certainly is an adept at picking up work, but the average earned is very slender. "Sometimes 11s. in a week, and then three weeks nothing at all," he says. In winter he has worked at the workhouse for 1s. 6d. a day, but in the spring and summer it is natural to hope for something better. The budget furnished belongs to the spring, and almost every day he expected to be absorbed in the rush of painting or field work. His wife is a pale, delicate woman, who does not look fit for work, but who, nevertheless, earns 2s. or 3s. a week by going out as washerwoman for a day and a half. His son—17—is, according to the general verdict, "a slacker," who "won't have regular work." He has already given notice to quite a number of employers—the last was given just a week before the budget closed—and he is still seeking, in a casual manner, for some ideal post. The daughter, a girl of 15, is of another make. She looks frail, but she is already earning nearly 5s a week, and expects soon to earn more. The house is clean and well kept, but very bare ; and scrutiny in the upstairs rooms would reveal no blankets—the last was pawned some time ago. But Mrs. Dunn does her utmost with the slender resources at her disposal, and they say quite cheerfully that they might be worse off. Certainly Dunn could, and should, dispense with tobacco ; but Mrs. Dunn does not grudge it as he never spends a penny on beer. Besides, he can get it on trust, which must be a great temptation !

He and his wife have shrewd tongues, and an hour spent in hearing their caustic comments on men and things is well worth while. They are people who will break, but not bend ; brusque, active North country folk, and it is an irony of fate that their son should be so weak and characterless—unless his strength of character is displayed by a very distinct talent for being parasitical.

The dietary of this family also falls considerably short of standard requirements, namely by 41 per cent as regards protein, and by 36 per cent as regards energy value.

STATEMENT OF INCOME AND EXPENDITURE FOR FOUR WEEKS, APRIL TO MAY 1910

INCOME—				Fuel and Light—				
Man (unemployed) .	.	.	£0 0 0	Paid for	.	. £0 4 8		
Wife (charing)	.	.	0 7 0	On trust	.	. 0 1 3½		
Son	.	.	0 18 0				£0 5 11¼	
Daughter . .	.	.	0 17 3½	Washing and Cleaning				
Grocery ticket	.	.	0 4 0	materials 1	.	. . .	0 0 11	
Deficit . .	.	.	0 14 1½	Clothing	.	. . .	0 1 2	
				Paid debts	.	. . .	0 8 6¼	
			£3 0 5	Tobacco—				
				Paid	.	. £0 1 6		
EXPENDITURE—				On trust	.	. 0 0 4		
Food (including beverages)—							0 1 10	
Paid for	.	. £1 6 0½		Shaving and hair-cutting		.	0 0 5	
On trust	.	. 0 4 3		Contribution to Hospital				
			£1 10 3½	Fund Collection .		.	0 0 1	
Rent—				Sundries—				
One week paid .	£0 2 9			Thread and tape £0 0 1½				
Three weeks in				Nails . . . 0 0 0½				
arrears .	. 0 8 3			*Evening Press* . 0 0 0½				
			0 11 0				0 0 2½	
							£3 0 5	

1 Soap, starch, blue, soda, and blacking.

Purchases during First Week

Friday.—½ stone flour, 10d.; yeast, ½d.; 2 oz. tea, 2d.; ½ lb. margarine, 4d.; 2 lb.; sugar, 5d.; ½ lb. soap, 1d.; ½ lb. rice, 1d.; ¼ lb. black pudding, 1d.; matches, ½d.; ½ oz. tobacco twist (with matches), 2d. On trust, 4 stone coal, 6d.

Saturday.—2 oz. tea, 2d.; ½ stone potatoes, 1½d.; ½ lb. margarine, 4d.; 4 kippers, 2d.; 3 bundles firewood, 1d.; ½ lb. rice, 1d.; blacking, ½d.; starch, ½d.; soda, ½d.; blue, ½d.; 1 lb. meat pieces, 4d.; 4 stone coals, 6d.; lamp oil, 1d.; ½ pint milk, 1d.; fried fish and potatoes, 2d.; ¼ stone potatoes, 1½d.

Sunday.—½ pint milk, 1d.

Monday.—2 oz. tea, 2d.; 1 lb. sugar, 2½d.; ½ stone potatoes, 1½d.; 1 gill milk, ½d.; 2½ lb. bread, 4d.; 2 kippers, 1d.; ½ oz. tobacco twist (with matches), 2d.

Tuesday.—½ lb. brawn, 4d.; 1 gill milk, ½d.; firewood, 1d.; 4 stone coal, 6d.; ½ lb. margarine, 4d.; 2½ lb. bread, 4d.

Wednesday.—½ stone flour, 10d.; 1 oz. yeast, ½d.; 2 "German ducks," 1 1½d.; tobacco and matches, 2d.; 1 gill milk, ½d.; 1 oz. tea, 1d.

Thursday.—1 lb. sugar, 2½d.; 1 gill milk, ½d.; 3 oz. cheese pieces, 1d.; firewood, 1d.; 1 oz. tea, 1d.; matches, ½d.

Menu of Meals provided during First Week

	Breakfast.	Dinner.	Tea.	Supper.
Friday . .	Tea, bread and margarine.	Tea, black pudding, bread and margarine.	Tea, bread and margarine.	Tea, bread and margarine.
Saturday. .	Tea, bread and margarine.	Tea, fried fish, potatoes, bread and margarine.	Tea, kippers, bread and margarine.	Tea, bread and margarine.
Sunday . .	Tea, bread and margarine.	Tea, meat pieces, potatoes, rice-pudding.	Tea, bread and margarine.	Tea, bread and margarine.
Monday . .	Tea, bread and margarine.	Tea, potato hash.	Tea, bread and margarine.	Tea, bread and fat (rendered down from meat pieces bought on Saturday).
Tuesday . .	Tea, bread and margarine.	Tea, brawn, bread and margarine.	Tea, bread and fat (see Monday).	Tea, bread and fat (see Monday).
Wednesday .	Tea, bread and margarine.	Tea, "German ducks," bread.	Tea, bread and margarine.	Tea, bread and margarine.
Thursday .	Tea, bread and margarine.	Tea, cheese pieces, bread.	Tea, bread and margarine.	Tea, bread and margarine.

1 Kind of black pudding, weighing about 7 oz. each.

BUDGET No. 5

Rafferty lives at the end of a pleasant open yard, named Chestnut Court, after the tree that hangs over from an adjacent garden. He has been a robust, good-looking fellow, but consumption laid its grip on him some years ago, and "the wonder is that he endures so long." Probably the healthy character of the court, and his habit of sitting at the open door of his cottage, has something to do with it. Besides, however badly nourished, he is not so badly nourished as some of the under-employed, though there are six in the family, and his wife's work in the fields is only occasional. His eldest daughter, the one child who is earning anything, is errand girl at a confectioner's shop, and gets 4s. a week and her meals, besides scraps of food to take home from time to time, and even articles of clothing. They also have 9s. a week out-relief. Moreover, in any especial stress, they would sometimes be able to get a milk ticket, or a bag of coal or cinders from the clergyman of the parish, and Mrs. Rafferty, now gaunt and haggard, but still handsome, with coal black hair and an imperious way of wearing an ancient check shawl, is not "backward in coming forward."

The probability is, no doubt, that they never spread their resources evenly through the week, but live in comparative luxury for three or four days, and very meagrely for the other three. But in spite of Mrs. Rafferty's eloquent descriptions of their hardships, they might be considerably worse off. Even so, their subsistence is inadequate, except when she herself is busy in the fields. And at such times there is always the problem of the back rent to face. The landlady is very lenient to them, knowing that Rafferty has been a very diligent workman. But as he himself says, "it ain't in reason that she should let it go for ever." In point of fact, they are about £3 behind. They used to work it off in the summer, when the man "picked up his strength a bit," and went stone-breaking. But for the last two years he has been able to do very little but "mind the children" while his wife goes out.

Yet he was still anxious, when the budget was kept, to recover strength enough at least to do some of the lighter field work; and it is extremely probable that some months of proper treatment, and a plentiful supply of nourishing food, would to a certain extent restore him. But the ordinary convalescent home would not take him, and a consumptive home is so expensive that it is doubtful if any charitable agency would undertake his case, since it could, at best, only "patch him up."

Meanwhile, at home, though the door is wide open in summer, he sleeps in a small, crowded room, and the food is often meagre, and always coarse and unappetising, not calculated to help poor Rafferty towards the new lease of life that he vaguely hopes for still.

The living-room is fairly clean, but very chaotic, with the two youngest children always in evidence. They look grimy, but healthy, and, in spite of the blood-curdling threats addressed to them from time to time by their mother, happy and fearless. Rafferty never scolds them. For the most part he sits silent, eating next to nothing, his wife says, but seeming in a vague way to enjoy the spring and summer when they visit Chestnut Court. The neighbours all like him, calling him "a quiet, peaceable body." His wife, too, is fairly popular, although from time to time "there are words, and one thing leads to another," till the proceeding known as "playing steam" begins in Chestnut Court, and some resident, who is either nervous or

fond of melodrama, " goes for the pleece." One of these periodic rows
has just occurred, and Mrs. Rafferty is endeavouring to persuade the
investigator both of the magistrate's high estimate of her own
unblemished character and the forbearance she displayed in the recent
"difference" between herself and Mrs. Pinnock, and of the pressing
necessity of a subsidy towards the fine imposed upon her for some
mysterious unknown reason by the selfsame magistrate. The feeling
of Chestnut Court, however, is undoubtedly with Mrs. Rafferty, who,
while incidents in Mrs. Pinnock's life, which will not bear investigation, are subjected to "that fierce light which beats upon a cottage"
and hotly condemned, is pronounced unanimously "a decent living
woman." If, in a moment of passion, she did offer to "tear the heart
out of" Mrs. Pinnock, the threat, in the opinion of the neighbours,
was not only provoked, but justified by the nature of Mrs. Pinnock's
allegation against her. . . . The allegation being repeated, the hearer
can only gasp and agree that "it was not a nice thing for one woman
to say of another." As for Rafferty, he accepts all happenings with
but faint melancholy interest. He is probably a spent man, though
only 41. His life has been hard. He left school at 14 and went
straight into the brickyard, where he worked for about six years.
He used to carry bricks for a number of hours a day that seems
incredible—sometimes from 3 A.M. to 9 P.M., and such heavy work in
youth doubtless went far towards undermining his constitution. To
be sure, he had fitted himself for no lighter employment. He was in
the fourth standard at school, and can now read and write very slowly
and imperfectly, but assuredly he knows the meaning of toil. He
told us that he had earned 5s. a day at carrying bricks at 1s. a
thousand. For the past few years, however, his work had been stone-
breaking. He says that the earnings varied greatly, 27s. a week if
a wagon happened to contain small stones that required comparatively
little breaking, but averaging nearer 21s. He stuck to the employment, however, because, when forced to break time through illness,
he could always return to it. He could crawl out a mile and a half to
the heap of stones that stood waiting for him, and work at them
slowly and painfully, to some extent making up for want of strength
by knack and knowledge of the cleavage. . . . But finally he stopped
work with a severe hæmorrhage from the lungs, and though at first he
looked forward to going back in the spring, two years have passed,
and, as his wife said rather wistfully, he is "still going back." But
he lingers on, and the Guardians, in consideration of his years of
faithful toil, do the best they can for him and his.

    If Mrs. Rafferty had regular work—say 12s. a week coming in—
the problem of this family would really be solved, and according to the
parish doctor it is quite possible that Rafferty, with plenty of milk
and eggs and the small luxuries that such an addition to the family
exchequer would procure, might even now pull round, and for a time,

at least, become self-supporting. But there is no prospect of this, though Mrs. Rafferty is strong and willing and never refuses a chance of work. She has no skilled occupation in her hands, and the field work round York, irregular at the best, has become more irregular since the use of fresh machinery by farmers. And, to tell the truth, the Rafferties have almost given up striving after something better, and, in a kind of fatalism, accept the days as they come.

In spite of the fact that this family had nearly every day a "taste" of meat or fish for dinner, the diet, measured by standard requirements, is deficient by 49½ per cent in protein and by 42 per cent in energy value.

STATEMENT OF INCOME AND EX-
PENDITURE FOR FOUR WEEKS,
JULY 1910

INCOME—

Out-door relief (9s. a week) .	£1 16	0
Daughter (4s. a week) . .	0 16	0
Loan	0 0	6
	£2 12	6

EXPENDITURE—

Food (including beverages) .	£1 11	4½
Rent (four weeks) . . .	0 14	0
Fuel and Light . . .	0 4	6
Soap	0 0	4
Balance in hand [1] . . .	0 2	3½
	£2 12	6

[1] Money received on the day the budget period closed.

PURCHASES DURING FIRST WEEK

Friday.—1½ stone flour, 2s. 4½d. ; 2 oz. yeast, 1½d. ; 5 stone coal, 7½d. ; 4 stone coke, 4d. ; 3 lb. sugar, 7½d. ; ¼ lb. tea, 4d. ; ¼ lb. coffee, 3d. ; 1 lb. soap, 2d. ; 3 candles, 1d. ; 1½ stone potatoes, 7d. ; 1 lb. margarine, 8d. ; firewood, 1d. ; 1 tin milk, 2d.
Saturday.—½ lb. bacon pieces, 3d. ; ½ lb. brawn, 1½d. ; 2 lb. rump beef, 1s. ; ½ lb. rice, 1d.
Sunday.—Nil.
Monday.—Nil.
Tuesday.—¼ lb. dripping, 1½d. ; 2 lb. fish-necks, 2d. ; ½ lb. brawn, 1½d.
Wednesday.—½ lb. liver, 2d. ; ½ lb. onions, ½d.
Thursday.—½ lb. treacle, 1d.

MENU OF MEALS PROVIDED DURING FIRST WEEK

	Breakfast.	Dinner.	Tea.	Supper.
Friday . .	Tea (with condensed milk), bread and margarine.	Fish necks, potatoes.	Tea, bread and dripping.	"Drink of tea, and bite of bread."
Saturday .	Tea (with condensed milk), bread and margarine.	Bacon pieces, potatoes.	Brawn, bread, coffee.	
Sunday . .	Tea (with condensed milk), bread and margarine.	Rump beef, rice, potatoes.	Tea, bread and margarine.	Tea, coffee.
Monday . .	Tea (with condensed milk), bread and margarine.	Tea, hashed beef (remainder from Sunday), potatoes.	Tea, bread, 2 bloaters.	Tea, bread.
Tuesday . .	Tea, bread and dripping.	Fish necks, potatoes.	Tea, brawn, bread.	
Wednesday .	Tea, bread and margarine.	Liver, onions, bread.	Tea, bread and margarine.	
Thursday .	Bread and treacle.	Bread and margarine.	Coffee, bread and treacle.	

BUDGET No. 6

The Martins belong to the best type of working people. They live in a suburb of the city, and the house is cheap at the rent—5s. 6d., having three bedrooms, a minute parlour, a roomy kitchen with a tiny scullery, a microscopic square of garden in front, and a good-sized yard behind. Probably the rent would be raised against any new tenants, but the Martins have been there so long, and paid so punctually when Mr. Martin was in work, that hitherto the landlord "has not worried them."

Martin is 49, and a good deal troubled with rheumatism, though he looks hale and strong. He has always been a capable and steady workman, and was with one firm, earning 38s. a week, for thirty-two years, till it failed three years ago. He then, after about six months of unemployment, got work for eight months, but it was merely temporary, and he left at the close of a contract. That was in June 1908, since which time he has only worked about ten months altogether for different employers—if we except occasional days of gardening which he procures through the goodwill of an old friend who is a gardener. It must be remembered that he was 45 when his employers failed, and also that his trade has been extremely slack. Moreover, though industrious, honest, punctual, and reliable, he is without push and self-assertion, and inferior workmen sometimes step in before him. He can neither advertise himself nor his necessity. And while he would accept work if it were offered to him in the heart of a volcanic region, and when flung to the ground by an earthquake shock, merely pick himself up and begin again, he has no very keen *flair*, no natural aptitude for getting hold of something. There are men who, if you send them out in the morning in a desert island, will come back at night and tell you they "begin regular work in the morning." And there are others, as competent and frequently more reliable, who, month after month, wander disconsolately after employment that they cannot find. Mrs. Martin is very thin and careworn. She would be in the doctor's hands, but they cannot afford to call in a private doctor, and have never yet brought themselves even to ask for a dispensary note. She is not strong enough to go out to work, and she has the family to look after, to keep the house exquisitely neat and clean, and to cook and mend, and make the most of the slender resources at her disposal. These are brought in by the girl and boy, aged 18 and 15, who earn respectively 8s. and 5s. They are "good children, none better." But they have the look of care and responsibility too often seen on young faces under the present economic regime, and one of its sorrowful sights, especially when, as in this case, it may mean premature exhaustion. For there can be no doubt that the family is, at present, under-nourished to an appalling degree. Careful washing and mending may preserve an appearance of well-being, but the white faces and black shadows under the eyes of the children, the frequent heart attacks of the mother, the increasing exhaustion of Martin himself when he returns from his vain tramps after work, tell a different story. The family would suffer less if they had not been used to a high standard of comfort. As it is, the chances are that unless Martin secures regular work, even poorly paid, one of them will break down completely— very probably a breadwinner, and no respectable record can save them from the abyss of destitution.

It may be asked, of course, why, under the circumstances, they do not move into a smaller house. To this, the only answer is that the present house is fully occupied, two bedrooms being needed for the boy and girl, while the good air and pleasant neighbourhood outweigh any possible saving that might be effected in rent. As a matter of fact, nowhere in the city would they be likely to get the accommodation, which they with their present standard of living, would consider absolutely necessary, for less rent.

Certainly a more enterprising couple might already have turned the drawing-room into a bed-sitting room and let it to a lodger, unfurnished, for the outlay on furniture would have been quite beyond their means. This would have meant perhaps, provided the lodger were honest, another two shillings a week. It would also have advertised the poverty they have tried to hide, and revolutionised their whole manner of living. Or if, on the other hand, they had boarded the lodger, the ten shillings a week inclusive for board and lodging, which is all they could have hoped for—possibly less if he shared the room of the boy,—would have been so largely swallowed up by his keep that the profit would hardly be greater than if he boarded himself.

No doubt if, at the beginning of Martin's unemployment, they could have known how long it would last, some such scheme would have been determined upon. But every day they have been hoping that he would find something, and the fact that he has worked from time to time, at temporary employment, has kept them from giving up hope. The wonder surely is not that they have failed to adopt other methods of coping with their difficulties, but that after two years of hardship and anxiety, with their savings long since exhausted, they are still, though with failing strength, holding their own.

It is probable that their dietary has for a considerable time been much below standard requirements. For the four weeks covered by our returns it fell below them by 67 per cent in protein and by 62 per cent in energy value.

STATEMENT OF INCOME AND EXPENDITURE FOR FOUR WEEKS,
MARCH 1910

INCOME—				EXPENDITURE—			
Man (unemployed) earned for				Food (including beverages) .		£1 18 10
odd jobs¹	£0	6	0	Rent—		
Daughter (four weeks at 8s.) .	1	12	0	Two weeks paid . £0 11 0		
Son (four weeks at 5s.) . .	1	0	0	Two weeks in arrears 0 11 0		
Gift	0	0	6		————	1 2 0
Deficit	0	13	4	Insurance (one shilling a week)		0 4 0
				Coals and oil		0 6 0
		£3 11 10		Soap		0 1 0
						£3 11 10

PURCHASES DURING FIRST WEEK

Friday.—1 lb. chops (frozen meat), 5d.
Saturday.—1 stone flour, 1s. 10d. ; yeast,
1d. ; 3 lb. sugar, 7½d. ; ½ lb. tea, 10d. ; 1 lb.
butter, 11d. ; 1 lb. soap, 3d. ; 1 lb. rice, 3d. ;
3 lb. beef (frozen), 1s. 6d. ; 1 lb. bacon, 9d. ;
½ lb. Cheshire cheese, 4½d. ; 4 pints milk,
7d. ; 1 stone potatoes, 5d. ; Insurance, 1s.;
coals, 1s. 5d.
Sunday.—Nil.
Monday.—Nil.
Tuesday.—Nil.
Wednesday.—Nil.
Thursday.—Nil.

MENU OF MEALS PROVIDED DURING FIRST WEEK

	Breakfast.	Dinner.	Tea.	Supper.
Friday . .	Tea, bread and butter.	Tea, bread, cheese.	Tea, bread and butter.	Tea, bread and butter.
Saturday. .	Tea, bread and butter.	Chops, potatoes, bread.	Tea, bread and butter.	Tea, bread, cheese.
Sunday . .	Tea, bread and butter.	Beef, potatoes, rice pudding.	Tea, bread and butter.	Remainder of rice pudding.
Monday . .	Tea, bread, bacon.	Tea, beef, potatoes, bread.	Tea, bread and butter.	Tea, bread, cheese.
Tuesday . .	Tea, bread and butter.	Beef, potatoes, bread.	Tea, bread and butter.	Tea, bread and jam.
Wednesday .	Tea, bread, bacon.	Beef, potatoes, bread.	Tea, bread and butter.	Tea, bread, cheese.
Thursday. .	Tea, bread and butter.	Bacon, potatoes, bread.	Tea, bread and butter.	Tea, bread and jam.

BUDGET No. 7

The Lovells live in the last house of Tanner's yard, on the right
hand. It is a fairly spacious yard, which would contain half a dozen
cottages quite comfortably, but which, when crowded with twenty,
looks disconsolate and squalid, in spite of the asphalt pavement that
has just been laid down, in deference to the sanitary inspector's
prejudice against standing puddles. The reform, needless to say, is
most unpopular among the children of the yard, to whom those
puddles, after a heavy rain, represented a seaside holiday. Now the
more enterprising youngsters travel farther afield in quest of adventure,
to be chased or shouted after by their mothers, with the threat of " a
braying " ; while the less enterprising merely contemplate the rain
pensively, as if it were an outworn illusion. Toys are not plentiful in
Tanner's yard, and perhaps, to realise the difference which the absence
of a mere puddle may make to a child, one would have to be a

member of the smart set, whose doctor forbids bridge, or a Stock Exchange merchant who is not allowed to speculate. The asphalt may be healthy, but it is deadly dull!

The Lovell children, on the whole, are livelier than some of their companions, since they possess various old toys, a lame battledore and shuttlecock with one feather, a rag doll, and a railway train that seems to have been in a great many collisions. There are only four children, but, as always happens in a small crowded kitchen, they produce the effect of at least half a dozen, as they creep or wander aimlessly round the room. When the visitor enters Mr. Lovell is minding them, while his wife is out at work, and he picks up one of them from the floor and holds her in his arms to secure quiet. He is a slightly built man of 33, who looks as if even the weight of the two-year child tired him, and as he speaks his voice betrays his weakness. He suffers from a complication of diseases as he says, without the pride of many invalids—he is too depressed for pride. Lead-poisoning, asthma, bronchitis, we forget the rest! Still he does a day's work whenever he can get it, earning 3s. or 4s. a week with his brother-in-law, a coal merchant, whom he helps in the yard, and whose bills he writes out. It is just possible that a light regular employment that took him a good deal into the open air might make a comparatively strong man of him, but at present he is too ill-nourished to have a fair chance.

He has been an excellent workman, and was sixteen years with the firm he left through lead-poisoning. For eight months he got compensation at the rate of 16s. a week, and when that was discontinued he became a caretaker for a few months. But the wage was so small that he made the fatal blunder of returning to his old employment. The lead-poisoning set in once more, and now, not only are his hands so disabled that he can never work rapidly again, but often enough, as his wife says, he "looks like death."

But his wife has gone out to work bravely as often as work could be found, sometimes two days a week, sometimes three, sometimes four. Ten shillings in a week, however, being the utmost she has ever earned. To be sure, she occasionally brings back fragments of food from her employers, and relations only a little better off than themselves help from time to time with a sixpence, but, as the Lovells say wearily, "it's not living, it's existing."

They dread applying to the Board, knowing that they would probably be told to "come inside." And while they can keep a roof over their heads they are determined not to do this, the grim fact being that Lovell has begun to contemplate death as anything but a remote contingency —unless conditions improve—and wants, if he dies, to die at home.

The children look healthy and clean, "too clean," as the neighbours say, "to get meals given at school." These have never been offered, and Mrs. Lovell has never asked for them. The rosy face of the little girl who sits on her father's knee—he has grown tired of standing, and sunk down upon a hard, uncomfortable chair—is a strange contrast to his haggard face.   Probably they ought not to be together, but there is no one else with whom to leave the children while Mrs. Lovell works, without a fee of 6d. that can ill be spared. And the task makes Lovell feel that he is of some use, even when he is not "working."   Meanwhile, day by day, it becomes more difficult for him to go far afield in search of odd jobs.   And, though sober, conscientious, intelligent, and punctual, he has no "push" about him. Moreover, in his best days, he could not have done heavy work.   His father and mother both died when he was a young child, and he comes of a delicate stock.

Altogether the outlook is profoundly melancholy.   Lovell cannot recover his normal health on the diet he gets, and with about 12s. a week coming in from the combined earnings of himself and his wife, and the rent 2s. 9d., no great improvement in the menu is possible. If his wife's work were regular they could " cut their coat according to their cloth "; but from week to week she never knows on how many days she may be employed.   Perhaps, however, Lovell's worst enemy is his own inveterate self-respect.   If he had gone the round of charitable agencies during the last few months, as assiduously as he has gone the round of possible employers, he might have become a moral wreck, but the chances are that he would have been stronger physically.

It is not due to lack of economy that this family is the worst fed of the eight here considered.   Their diet fell short of standard requirements by 69 per cent in protein and 61 per cent in energy value.

STATEMENT OF INCOME AND EXPENDITURE FOR FOUR WEEKS, JULY 1910				PURCHASES DURING FIRST WEEK

STATEMENT OF INCOME AND EXPENDITURE FOR FOUR WEEKS, JULY 1910

INCOME—

	£	s.	d.
Man (casual jobs) . . .	1	6	6
Wife (charing). . . .	0	14	0
Gifts from friends (including 1s.6d. from the investigator)	0	3	6
Deficit	0	0	4½
	£2	4	4½

EXPENDITURE—

	£	s.	d.
Food (including beverages)¹ .	1	1	3
Rent . . . £0 11 0			
„ Payment of arrears at 3d. per week . . 0 1 0			
	0	12	0
Insurance	0	2	0
Repayment of loan . . .	0	1	0
Boot-mending . . .	0	0	3
Fuel and light . . .	0	3	6½
Soap and starch . . .	0	0	4
Baby "mindings" while mother at work, 1s. per week . .	0	4	0
	£2	4	4½

PURCHASES DURING FIRST WEEK

Friday.—Nil.
Saturday.—½ lb. beef pieces, 2d. ; ¼ stone potatoes, 1¼d. ; 1 egg, 1d. ; ½ stone flour, 10d. ; 1 lb. sugar, 2¼d. ; ¼ lb. tea, 5d. ; 2 eggs, 2d. ; milk (for week), 10½d. ; 1½ lb. ox cheek, 7d. ; 2 lb. bread, 3½d. ; ¼ lb. fresh butter, 3d. ; 1 cabbage, 1d. ; yeast, ½d.
Sunday.—Nil.
Monday.—Rent and arrears,3s.; Insurance, 6d.; 5 stone coals, 8d.; baby "minding," 6d.; paid debt, 1s. ; boot-mending, 3d.
Tuesday.—1 lb. soap, 3d. ; 1 pint oil, 1d. ; matches and candle, 1d. ; ¼ lb. jam, 1d. ; 2 short cakes, 1d. ; baby "minding," 6d.
Wednesday.—¼ stone flour, 5d. ; 2 oz. tea, 2½d. ; ¼ lb. butter, 3d. ; 2 lb. potatoes, 1¼d. ; starch, 1d. ; 1 head lettuce, ½d.
Thursday.—Nil.

¹ In addition a little food was given to the family.

MENU OF MEALS PROVIDED DURING FIRST WEEK

	Breakfast.	Dinner.	Tea.	Supper.[1]
Friday . .	Tea (with milk and sugar), bread and dripping.	Tea, bread, ¼ lb. brawn.	Tea, bread and butter.	Bread and butter.
Saturday. .	Tea, bread and dripping for the children, dry bread for man and wife.	½ lb. beef pieces, Yorkshire pudding, potatoes.	Tea, bread and butter.	Tea, bread and butter.
Sunday . .	Tea, bread and butter.	Stewed ox cheek, cabbage, potatoes, Yorkshire pudding.	Tea, bread and butter.	Tea, bread, cold meat.
Monday . .	Tea, bread and dripping.	Cold meat, bread (for children and husband, wife out at work).	Tea, bread and dripping.	Tea, bread and butter.
Tuesday . .	Tea, bread and jam.	Bread, cold meat, jam.	Tea, bread and dripping.	Tea, bread and dripping, short cake.
Wednesday .	Tea, bread and butter.	Hashed remains of Sunday's meat, potatoes, Yorkshire pudding.	Tea, bread and butter, lettuce.	Tea, bread and butter (for two persons).
Thursday .	Tea, bread and dripping.	Tea, bread and butter.	Tea, bread.	Tea, bread.

[1] For the man only.

BUDGET No. 8

Mr. and Mrs. Archer and their three young children live in a rather pleasant court, to which a plane-tree, growing at the end on a small strip of grass, gives an air of distinction, though it makes the last house rather dark. But this does not affect the Archers, who live half-way down. The house is small—three rooms, with a miniature scullery, but it looks clean and fresh, and Mrs. Archer has just washed the red-tiled floor. That operation, by the way, is becoming harder and harder. Not only is her strength failing steadily, but soap is becoming more difficult to procure. It is easy enough to say, and the poor themselves echo it, "you can be clean if you're poor," so long as bread is plentiful, and "a penny lump for the children" does not involve a soapless existence. But it is well to remember that both cleanliness and godliness, so far as the latter is identified with regular attendance at a place of worship, are unattainable luxuries to extreme poverty.

Archer is 31, a good-looking, well-built fellow. He served his apprenticeship as a joiner, but tells us that his training was defective. Whether or no this was the case he drifted from the less skilled branches of his work to mere labouring, and finally, in 1906, was dismissed from the N.E.R. owing to a large reduction of staff. Since then he has only done catch jobs, the longest being four months for the G.P.O. in connection with the Telegraph Department, and the laying down and repairing of wires. For the first twelve months after he left the N.E.R. his wife worked at a laundry, earning about 9s. a week, and paying half a crown for the care of the second child. But she is now too frail for laundry work; moreover, the youngest child is ailing, and has frequently to be nursed night and day. At present the family are "on the rocks." Things have never been so bad before. Archer has relations in the town, who are in fairly comfortable circumstances, but they are tired of helping a man with the luck, as they say, "dead against him." A month ago the Archers applied to the Parish for help, and they have had two grocery orders of four shillings. The Board refuses to help them further, and offers them "the House." "I'd sooner make a hole in the river Ouse and done with it," says Mrs. Archer apathetically; and Archer echoes her from the remotest corner of the room.

Conscious of a patched coat that cannot possibly hold together much longer, and of unspeakable shoes, he keeps well in the background. He has walked eight-and-twenty miles to-day in search of work, with only a crust of bread for breakfast, and more bread for supper on his return; but the walk "nearly did for him." His feet, hidden, or half hidden, by the apologies for shoes, are blistered and swollen, his attitude, and the very set of his shoulders, are those of a man who is giving up all hope.

Mrs. Archer must have been a handsome woman, but her face is colourless, and she is abnormally thin. The baby in her arms, nine months old, wails perpetually, and if she is put down for a moment the low wail rises to a howl of pain and resentment. It is no wonder, she is more than half starved. "Oh do be still, Maudie," says Mrs. Archer, feebly hushing her. "She's never still night or day; she tears the very heart out of me. You see I can't nurse her properly myself, and yet I can't buy milk—and tea and sop isn't the right thing for a baby that age."

Here and there one finds a family that, even out of the circumstances of the Archers, would be capable of extracting some grain of consolation, and would say, "we might be worse off." But the Archers have lost any buoyancy they ever possessed. The chances are that, even if the tide turns—a very unlikely contingency—they will remain permanently embittered and demoralised by the experience they have passed through. "If he'd drunk, or rowed, or horse-raced," says Mrs. Archer, "I'd have said he deserved all he got. And if I'd let the house get lost in dirt while I gossiped, or run up debts with the pedlars, I'd have said serve me right. But we've tried and tried and better tried, and if I'd got my life to live over again I can't say I'd try at all, for it seems to me those that don't, have the best time of it."

"Oh, I don't know! For instance, look at your rent book. No one would have let it run so long if you hadn't been honest people who paid every shilling you could."

"Yes," Mrs. Archer admits, "we're £2 behind. It's more than we could have looked for. But I'm expecting notice to quit every Monday; and when the collector comes I feel I could sink through the floor. Last week, with his having a couple of days helping some people to shift, I did pay the three shillings, but then we had to hunger almost as much as if he'd earned nothing. We should have been without this two days, but for the next-door neighbour. She lent me sixpence, and she said she shouldn't expect to see it back again. And she only gets five shillings a week herself from the Board, and her rent's the same as mine. But she said I was worse off than she, for she'd only herself to keep, and I'd a man and three children."

"It's hard on Archer not to be able to keep you comfortably."

"Aye, he feels it! The day of the King's funeral he started off at six o'clock without a bite. He knew that there was only half a loaf left in the house, and he wouldn't touch it. All the same he went out in good spirits. He seemed to think it was such a grand day he'd pick up something somewhere, if it was only a horse to hold! He didn't come back while dinner-time, and I'd got the cloth set, and part of the bread, and the tea leaves warmed over with a fresh sup of water. He looked through the window, and I called him in, but he just shook his head and away again. The next thing I saw of him was eight at night, and he came in looking more like a ghost than a man and laid down twopence. 'There,' he said, 'that's my day's earnings. I got it for carrying a portmanteau half a mile.' Then the strength seemed to go clean out of him. He just sat down in the arm-chair. 'I do feel done,' he said. Well, I saw he was past bread, and there wasn't but a crust. So I sent Sally for two penn'-orth of fish and chips, and she brought back over a pound and a half, I should think. We had a good meal, and we didn't seem to care where the next meal would come from, or if we died in the night."

"I suppose Archer has registered at the Bureau?"

"Oh yes, and he's had two months from them, taking it altogether. But four years is such a stretch! And he tries everywhere every day (she named places five miles apart), and answers the advertisements if we can borrow a *Press*. I don't see what more he can do. But lately we've both lost heart. I can't keep things clean as I used —I don't seem to care; and I sometimes think if he gets regular work he won't know how to do it."

Certainly the prospect was gloomy.

It may be noted that the menu given for the first week, since it includes 4s. relief from the Board, is hardly typical of the way in which the Archers were living. The investigator was divided between a desire to keep the budgets properly checked, and the impossibility of checking them frequently without being almost compelled to advance some of the payment due at the end of the four weeks. Such budget entries as the following explain the difficulty. They were written by Mrs. Archer.

" *Friday in Third Week.*—Nothing in house till Lily got 2d. given, which bought a penny lump and half a pound of treacle. Father ate nothing through the day, leaving what there was for us. Breakfast—none ; dinner—bread and treacle for mother and children ; tea—a ' mash' given by a neighbour, and the rest of the penny lump ; supper—a neighbour brought a cup of Quaker Oats.

" *Saturday.*—Breakfast—a penny lump given by neighbour, and the scrapings of the treacle ; dinner—none."

In the afternoon, the investigator on coming to check the budget advanced a shilling of the payment, which was expended promptly on two cakes of bread, half a pound of frozen mutton chops, tea, sugar, and margarine.

In spite of the gifts received, the dietary of the Archers is deficient in protein by 57 per cent and in energy value by 53 per cent.

STATEMENT OF INCOME AND EXPENDITURE FOR FOUR WEEKS, JUNE 1910

INCOME—

Man (casual jobs) .	.	.	£0 9 7½
Gifts from friends .	.	.	0 7 0
Borrowed .	.	.	0 2 10½
Sold toasting-fork .	.	.	0 0 3
Sold rags .	.	.	0 0 6½
Deficit .	.	.	0 10 9
			£1 11 0½

EXPENDITURE—

Food (including beverages)—			
Paid .	.	£0 14 1½	
"On trust"	.	0 0 3½	
		£0 14 5	
Fuel and Light	.	.	0 1 2
Rent—			
One week paid	£0 3 0		
Three weeks in arrears .	0 9 0		
		0 12 0	
Washing and cleaning materials	0 0 5½		
Repayment of debts	.	.	0 1 0
Clothing .	.	.	0 2 0
			£1 11 0½

FOOD GIVEN TO THE FAMILY

First Week.—1 box of "Force," 2d. fried fish, 5½ oz. margarine, slice of cold mutton, 2 eggs, cup of tea and bread cake.
Ordered by Doctor called in to attend the woman, who was suffering from the effects of starvation, and paid for by Guardians :—

1 stone flour .	.	.	.	.	£0 1 8
2 oz. yeast .	.	.	.	.	0 0 1
½ lb. butter .	.	.	.	.	0 0 7
½ lb. bacon .	.	.	.	.	0 0 6
1 tin condensed milk .	.	.	.	0 0 3
1 lb. rice .	.	.	.	.	0 0 8
¼ lb. tea .	.	.	.	.	0 0 4
2 lb. sugar .	.	.	.	.	0 0 5
Bread .	.	.	.	.	0 0 2
Soap and candles .	.	.	.	0 0 2
					£0 4 5

Second Week.—1 egg, 1¾ lb. shin beef (for beef tea).
Third Week.—¼ lb. butter, 2 fresh eggs, 1 rhubarb tart (4 oz.), 1 onion, ¼ stone flour, ¼ lb. tea, 1 lb. sugar, 1 oz. yeast, 7 eggs, ¼ lb. butter, 1 packet pea flour, ½ lb. stewing beef, ¼ stone potatoes, ½ lb. onions.
Fourth Week.—3 bread cakes (8 oz. each).

PURCHASES MADE DURING FIRST WEEK

Friday.—1 stone coal, 1½d. ; ¼ lb. margarine, 2d. ; washing powder, ½d. ; ½ lb. soap, 1½d.
Saturday.—2 stone coal, 3d. ; ½ oz. yeast, ½d. ; ½ pint milk, 1d. ; salt, ½d. ; 1 lb. meat for stewing, 5d. ; ¼ stone potatoes, 2½d. ; ½ lb. onions, ½d. ; 2 oz. tea, 2d. ; 1 stone coal (another), bundle of sticks, 2d.

Sunday.—Nil.
Monday.—"On trust," 2 bread cakes, 1d. ; ¼ lb. dripping, 1½d.
Tuesday.—1 stone coal, 1½d. ; 1 cake bread and ½ lb. sugar, 1½d.
Wednesday.—Food ordered by doctor.
Thursday.—½ lb. mutton chops (frozen), 2d. ; ½ lb. onions, ½d. ; 1 gill milk, ½d.

S

MENU OF MEALS PROVIDED DURING FIRST WEEK

	Breakfast.	Dinner.	Tea.	Supper.
Friday . .	Tea, bread and margarine.	Tea, bread and margarine.	Tea, bread and margarine.	
Saturday .	Tea, slice of bread each for children; none for parents.	Tea, bread, plate of Force each for children. Parents— Tea, bread and margarine, 1 egg each.	Tea, bread and margarine.	Tea, two pennyworth of fried fish given by a neighbour.
Sunday . .	Plate of Force each for children. Parents— Tea, bread and margarine.	1 lb. meat (stewed), 4 lb. potatoes (mashed).	Tea, bread and margarine.	Bread and the gravy remaining from dinner.
Monday . .	Plate of Force each for children. Parents— Tea, bread.	"Children had a drop of the gravy left from Sunday's dinner; there was no meat left." Parents— Bread.	Tea, bread.	Slice of cold mutton (given), bread.
Tuesday . .	"Children had 1 cake and dripping. Father and mother nothing but tea."	"Children and father 1 cake and ½ oz. dripping. Mother nothing — was too ill."	"A neighbour brought me a strong cup of tea, and the children a cake."	
Wednesday .	Tea, bread and butter.	Children— Rice pudding (made with water). Parents— ¼ lb. bacon, bread.	Tea, bread and butter.	Children— Bread and butter. Parents— Tea, bacon, bread.
Thursday .	Tea, bread and butter.	Stewed mutton (½ lb.), potatoes, bread, rice pudding.	Tea, bread and butter.	Tea, bread and butter.

APPENDIX

METHOD OF MEASURING ADEQUACY OF DIET

(From *Land and Labour*, pp. 342 *et seq.*)

THE nutrients contained in food fall under three heads :—

Protein—which replaces waste tissues.
Fats—which may be transformed into body-
fat, but not into muscle.
Carbohydrates, *i.e.* sugar and starches—which
may be transformed into fat.

} All serve as fuel, and produce energy.

Since all three nutrients produce energy, it is evident that in one sense the food value of any diet may be expressed in terms of the total energy which it is capable of yielding. This energy is usually measured in calories, a calory being the amount of heat required to raise 1 kilogram of water 1° centigrade (or 1 lb. of water 4° Fahrenheit).[1]

But in estimating the adequacy of a diet for practical purposes, it is not enough to know its total energy value ; another factor has to be considered.

The only nutrient which can repair the constant waste going

---

[1] Taking our common food materials as they are used in ordinary diet, the following general estimate has been made for the energy furnished to the body by 1 gram or 1 lb. of each of the classes of nutrients :—

PROTEIN,   fuel value,   4 calories per gram, or 1820 calories per lb.
Fats,   ,,   8·9   ,,   ,,   4040   ,,   ,,
Carbohydrates,   ,,   4   ,,   ,,   1820   ,,   ,,

These estimates are based on the latest and most reliable research and take into account only the material which is digested and oxidised so that its energy is actually available in the body. Earlier estimates based on less accurate data and not making allowance for the amounts of fats and carbohydrates which escape oxidisation in the body, give 4·1 calories per gram for protein, and for carbohydrates, 9·3 calories per gram for fats.

(Revised edition of Atwater's *Principles of Nutrition and Nutritive Value of Food*, published 1902.)

on in the muscles and various tissues of the body is protein, and consequently a sufficient supply of this must be present in the diet. It is obvious that the greater the muscular work to be done, the greater will be the amount of protein required; but when a sufficient quantity has been secured for the repair of waste, it is a matter of indifference, within limits, whether the additional energy needed is derived from further protein, or from fat or carbohydrates.[1]

Physiologists disagree somewhat as to the number of grams of protein and the number of calories of fuel energy necessary for the maintenance of physical efficiency; and it would obviously be impossible in this volume to give, with any pretence of completeness, the arguments in favour of adopting one or another standard of food requirements.

In a previous volume [2] the writer stated the reasons which led him, after a careful examination of the different standards of food requirements specified by physiologists, to adopt that of Professor Atwater, and he proposes to adopt the same standard in the present volume.[3] Professor Atwater's standards are based upon very extensive observation, and while we recognise that future research may modify his estimates, they appear to be the best substantiated and the most trustworthy at the present time.

The amount of food which a man requires, of course, varies with the severity of the work to be done. The following is Atwater's table showing the food requirements of men doing work of varying severity :—

[1] "It is generally found that when the amount of carbohydrates exceeds about 500 or 600 grams (i.e. 18 or 21 oz.) per man per day the digestive organs begin to be disturbed."
See A Study of the Diet of the Labouring Classes in Edinburgh (Otto Schulze & Co., Edinburgh), p. 9.

[2] Poverty: A Study of Town Life (Macmillan).

[3] The recent work of Professor Chittenden of Yale, if it is fully confirmed by physiologists, will lead to the adoption of a lower standard of protein. His experiments, however, appear to controvert the general experience of mankind. They were carried out on selected groups of men living well-ordered lives under uniform conditions. Most of the experiments were continued for a few months. It would be unwise at present to assume that the lower intake of protein would give equally favourable results over a course of years, or that Professor Chittenden's suggested standard could be applied to people living under average conditions.

	Grams of Protein required daily.	Calories of Energy required daily.
Man without muscular work . .	100	2700
Man with light work . . .	112	3000
Man with moderate work. . .	125	3500
Man with severe work . . .	150	4500

These are, of course, average figures, based upon observations of a large number of persons. The exact food requirements vary from person to person according to body weight and personal idiosyncrasies. Moreover, there is no absolute standard by which to measure the severity of work, but a careful consideration of the work done by the families under observation has convinced the writer that it must at least be classed as "moderate," not only that of the men, but also that of the women, who are occupied for long hours every day in housework which involves much hard manual labour, such as scrubbing floors and washing. As for the children, the active habits and rapid growth make considerable demands upon their muscular tissues.

Accordingly, the diet required for a man at "moderate" muscular work, viz. 125 grams (or about 4½ oz.) of protein and 3500 calories of energy value, has been adopted as the standard by which the adequacy of each of the diets examined has been tested.

The dietary requirements of women and children may be stated as follows :—

Woman, equivalent to 0·8 of a man at moderate work.
Boy, 14 to 16 ,, 0·8 ,, ,,
Girl, 14 to 16 ,, 0·7 ,, ,,
Child, 10 to 13 ,, 0·6 ,, ,,
,, 6 to 9 ,, 0·5 ,, ,,
,, 2 to 5 ,, 0·4 ,, ,,
,, under 2 ,, 0·3 ,, ,,

In order to compare the various diets with the standard, it was necessary to ascertain the proportion of protein, fat, and carbohydrates contained in each. The food value was derived chiefly from tables of American Food Stuffs published by Atwater and Bryant.[1]

[1] Bulletin 28. Revised Edition, U.S. Department of Agriculture, 1899. Bulletin 142. Revised Edition, U.S. Department of Agriculture, 1902.

CHAPTER VIII

A VALUABLE SUGGESTION FROM BELGIUM [1]

THE facts set forth in the preceding chapters, bringing us, as they do, face to face with the actual consequences of unemployment in concrete instances, emphasise the need for effective remedial measures. We have already discussed a number of these, and we believe that though they must ultimately be supplemented by more fundamental changes, they are full of hope and would, if carried out, greatly reduce the volume of unemployment. It would be futile to suggest that they would cure the evil. Even if all of them were put into practice there would still be fluctuations in the demand for labour, both seasonal and cyclical, although much less severe than at present. Men would still grow old and become partially disabled, and frost and rain would still make building impossible at certain periods of the year. While, therefore, the regularity of employment would be enormously increased, periods of

[1] We are indebted to Professor E. Mahaim, of Liége, and M. Louis Varley, of Ghent, for reading the proof of this chapter, and are glad to record the complete agreement of these two authorities on the main facts concerning Belgian conditions here referred to, and the inferences drawn from them.

unemployment would remain in which men must be guarded from destitution and demoralisation. Whatever scheme may be suggested, it must be one which can be put into operation as soon as employment ceases, and which will afford a substantial measure of relief as long as it may be needed, to all who may require it. It must also be one which will develop independence and strength of character rather than impair them. We believe that a scheme enabling men to reside in the country while working in the town would operate with steady and cumulative effect in lessening unemployment and the dire evils which now attend it, and that it would not retard, but tend to further, extensive economic changes making for greater stability of employment. Our proposals in this connection are based upon a careful study of conditions in Belgium, where such a scheme is in operation, and where we have been profoundly convinced of its far-reaching benefits. In this chapter we propose to give an account of these conditions, and inquire how far, and with what modifications, they might be adopted in this country. But we must first point out that while in Great Britain the industrial revolution preceded the development of transit facilities, in Belgium the two movements were practically simultaneous, and the introduction of machinery and of the factory system came later. For this and other reasons, Belgium has never been urbanised to the extent of Great Britain, and the majority of her industrial workers now living in the country have never lived in towns. Here, on the contrary, though many town dwellers or their parents are country-bred, they have, so to speak, become rooted in the towns and it would be necessary to transplant them. Still, as the methods of doing this must be largely identical with those by which country dwellers could be kept from migrating into the towns, a study of Belgian conditions seems to us of importance.

We will begin by stating the striking fact that although only one-quarter (23 per cent) of Belgian workers are engaged in agriculture, more than half of the population (56½ per cent) are living in the country.[1] This means, that probably over a third of the industrial workers are country dwellers, a fact which, while accompanied by certain minor disadvantages, on the whole greatly promotes the national well-being, and mitigates some of the worst evils of industrial employment. It will therefore be amply worth our while to explain in some detail how this has been brought about, and in what way the industrial workers are benefited. The present state of things is due to the interaction of three essential economic conditions, viz. :

(1) The possibility of obtaining without difficulty land in small plots suited to the needs of industrial workers, and in the desired localities.

(2) The provision of cheap and rapid transit between town and country.

---

[1] See *Land and Labour*, p. 217.

(3) The provision, upon easy terms, of capital for the erection of houses.

Before dwelling upon these three factors in further detail, we will give a short description of the results which have been achieved through their agency. First, it may be taken as the general rule, although not without exceptions, that the industrial workers who live in the country have plots of land attached to their houses. These plots vary in size, from a small vegetable garden to one or two acres or even more. Those who live farthest from the towns, where land is cheap, naturally have the largest gardens, but it is amazing to see what a quantity and variety of vegetables are obtained from quite small plots of land. A great many of the men living in the country also add to their income by keeping a goat, or rabbits, or both, not infrequently a pig, and occasionally one or more cows, the last, however, only on the larger holdings situated at some distance from the towns.[1]

It may be said that practically all the gardens are of economic value, though of course to a widely varying degree. The produce from the plots is not, as a rule, sold, but kept for home consumption. Vegetables are grown in great variety, so that some seem to be available at all periods of the year, and potatoes are stored for winter use.

[1] In Belgium there are forty goats for every thousand of the population, and more than three times as many pigs per square mile of territory as in Great Britain; while in 1908, three million rabbits, mostly bred by small-holders, were exported from Belgium for consumption in England.

Now, as regards the effect of this condition of
things upon unemployment, it is found that the
produce from the gardens constitutes a most valuable
buffer between the family and destitution. A family
with a substantial garden, a quarter of an acre, for
instance, may have to live hardly when no wages are
coming in, but if there is a supply of potatoes and
green vegetables, with possibly bacon, and milk from
a goat, they do not starve. These things just furnish
that little reserve of wealth which tides over the
difficulties. A man securing such a reserve is
provided with an insurance against unemployment,
the amount of which depends upon his own industry.
It comes to him regardless of the reasons why he
left his work, and the period during which it is paid
is not limited. The benefits, moreover, are received
whether he is unemployed or not.

Men in regular work generally cultivate their plots
of land on Sundays and public holidays, getting their
wives and children to help with the lighter work, including the care of live-stock. It must be remembered
that men work longer hours in Belgium than in Britain
and have no recognised half-holiday, so there is little
time to do anything in the gardens during the
week.[1] If a man's work is very regular he is usually
contented to take a house with a smaller garden

[1] It should, however, be remarked that many Belgian workmen *font le
lundi*, *i.e.* refuse to work on Mondays, and some of them spend the day
gardening. In some districts, also, what are known colloquially as "potato
strikes" take place. This means that the men take a day or two off work
to plant their potatoes.

than one who, because his work is seasonal or casual, can devote a considerable amount of free time during each year to the cultivation of his land. Plasterers, bricklayers, and other similar workers, often do not trouble to look for work in the towns when it is scarce. We were informed, for instance, that some of the Antwerp dockers, if they learn on arrival at the docks that very few ships are coming in, return home instead of swelling the army, already far too large, of men scrambling for the few vacancies which occur. They find it pays them better to cultivate their land, doing the heavier work which their wives and children cannot do, such as digging and manuring, and often getting outside work from farmers and others in the country districts at busy seasons. Many an unemployed man can pick up odd jobs from farmers, who would have stood a poor chance of finding any in the towns. This extension of the field in which chance jobs can be met with is a great advantage to the unemployed.

But not only is he better off economically than if he resided in the town, his industrial unemployment is not accompanied by the disastrous deterioration which so rapidly affects the town dweller when out of work, for, instead of walking aimlessly up and down the streets, he can spend his enforced leisure in the cultivation of his plot. Unfortunately, the *full* benefit of this is not experienced in Belgium, because there is no effective system of Labour Exchanges, and therefore men must spend a portion of their time in looking for work in the towns. The extent to which this is required differs, of course, according to individual circumstances. Sometimes the search for work may be necessarily limited to two or three factories, and if a promise is obtained of the first vacancy in one of these, constant attendance in the towns is superfluous. If the use of Labour Exchanges in England became general, it would be possible for an industrial worker living in the country, as soon as he became unemployed, to register his name at the Labour Exchange. He could deposit sixpence if he wished, with the understanding that directly an offer of employment came to hand a telegram should be sent to him, so that he might apply with the least possible delay. Meanwhile, he could remain at home and utilise the period of unemployment to cultivate his garden.

In Belgium there is no such absolute severance between town and country as in England. If an agricultural worker determines to take up an industrial career he does not leave the village of his birth, but travels to his work in the morning and returns at night. Thus his children grow up with a knowledge of country life and an aptitude for agricultural pursuits. They have helped their parents in the cultivation of the plot and the feeding of the live-stock, and do not necessarily enter the industrial world because their father has done so. Moreover, the man himself, still being resident in the country, not infrequently, after having spent some years working in the town, returns to agricultural work, adding to his holding and settling down as an independent small-holder. An industrial workman, with a plot of land in the country, in the cultivation of which he is fairly expert, always has in his hands a possible alternative to industrial employment, and there is no doubt that in Belgium the fact that many such men gradually increase their holdings, and by the time they have reached middle life relinquish town industries altogether, tends not a little to lessen the amount of unemployment. It is well known, and the inquiry we have made in York is eloquent testimony to the fact, that when a man past middle life falls out of regular employment, it is intensely difficult for him, unless he is a skilled workman of known ability, again to secure a permanent post. We have seen how man after man, by no fault of his own, but solely through the pressure of circumstances, has thus degenerated into a casual labourer. But in Belgium it is easy for a country dweller, as he sees the chances of regular work in town diminish, to supplement his income by increasing the amount of land he cultivates, until eventually he comes to rely entirely upon the land for a living.[1]

To a man who is growing old the ability to do this is of inestimable value, for he competes at a great disadvantage with young and vigorous men in

[1] The capital necessary to cultivate more land could be obtained from an Agricultural Credit Bank.

the industrial market, and if he does not get the job for which he is competing, he remains entirely unemployed. But when he is working on the land he can get out of it just what he can put into it, and there is never any question of working for less than a standard wage.

In England at present a man must, generally speaking, be either a country workman and a country dweller, or a town worker and a town dweller; there is no compromise.

Country life in England is dull, and the prospects of an agricultural labourer are poor. Hours are long and wages are comparatively low. What wonder that the towns with their higher wages, their numerous openings for strong country-bred men, and their liberal provision of excitement and amusement, present attractions which it is difficult to resist? And so the villagers move thither by thousands, and their children grow up with no knowledge of country life and no aptitude for agricultural occupations. On the other hand, it is a serious step for a town dweller, even one who has tasted the bitterness of city life, completely to change his whole method of living, to leave an industrial career behind him and to plunge suddenly into conditions in which he and his family depend entirely upon his winning a living from the soil. He cannot readily draw back if his hope of doing so fails, but must risk everything, and suffer the full consequences if he has misjudged his prospects of success.

But the system which we are describing alters this, since under it a man becomes equally at home in town and country.   And we have not yet spoken of the enormous gain to health, especially to that of the children, from living in a comparatively roomy house in the country, with plenty of fresh air and the opportunity for healthy exercise and light occupations, such as simple gardening or the tending of goats, rabbits, or poultry.   Contrast it with their probable life in the town, too often in overcrowded and squalid neighbourhoods, with all the consequent deterioration, physical and moral ; and its advantages are readily seen.

In the case of unemployed youths, we saw how many were handicapped from the very outset of their industrial career by the deteriorating influence of their home environment.   It goes without saying that even poverty and squalor are less pernicious if the homes in which they occur are dispersed over the country-side, than if they are crowded together in slum quarters.

It has been suggested to us that if working men in employment were obtaining a certain amount from their land, this would enable them to take smaller wages without lowering their standard of comfort. There is absolutely no evidence of this result in Belgium, and we are convinced that such a contention is entirely false, and that the position of the workers would be strengthened, and not weakened, by providing them with an alternative to industrial employment.

In the first place, a man with a supply of food in the house, sufficient to last him for some weeks, is less at the mercy of an employer when making a bargain as to wages, than one who must earn money immediately or starve. And secondly, a man who had done well on his land and proved his ability as a cultivator, could always increase his holding, and depend entirely upon the land for a living rather than submit to a wage which he considered too low.

Now let us revert to the three economic factors stated on pp. 264-5, which are necessary to enable town workmen to live in the country. The first is the opportunity of securing land in the desired localities, and in quantities suited to their requirements. This need is very fully met in Belgium, for there is no country in Europe where land is so much subdivided, and where, in consequence, small plots are so frequently in the market, either to let or sell. There are practically no great landlords in Belgium. Every tenth inhabitant, and every fifth adult, is a landowner, and the accumulation of land in a few hands is rendered impossible by the laws of succession, in consequence of which the whole of a man's property, whether real or personal, is divided equally at his death among his children or other heirs, whether male or female.

We will discuss later how far land in suitable quantities and localities is available in England, and now consider the facilities given in Belgium for cheap and rapid transit. Let it be said at once, that transit facilities in Belgium are better than in any other country in the world. Area for area, she has 30 miles of main railways, as compared with 22 miles in Great Britain, and, area for area, for every mile of light railways in this country, she has 70.

Not only has she a wonderful system of railways, but the fares charged for workmen's tickets are the cheapest in the world. A ticket, enabling a workman to travel 3 miles to and fro for six consecutive days, costs 9d., or $\frac{1}{4}$d. a mile. If the distance to be travelled daily, each way, is $6\frac{1}{4}$ miles, the ticket costs 1s. or $\frac{1}{6}$d. per mile. For $12\frac{1}{2}$ miles each way it costs 1s. $2\frac{1}{2}$d. a week, or $\frac{1}{10}$d. per mile. For 25 miles each way it costs 1s. 7d., or $\frac{1}{15}$d. per mile. And to travel 62 miles each way daily, which is the maximum distance for which workmen's tickets are issued, costs 2s. 6d. a week, or $\frac{1}{25}$d. per mile. These fares are for special workmen's trains on the main railways, which are national property. The fares on the light railways are somewhat higher, and the traffic is considerably less.

Unfortunately, the published accounts of the railway enterprises do not show whether this branch of the service pays. According to published statistics, the main railways have, during the 70 odd years since the State began to acquire them, made a small profit, but the methods of book-keeping are open to criticism, and it is probable that if the books had been kept like those of an ordinary business enterprise they would really have shown a small loss.

T

Even if this be so, Belgium has paid very cheaply for the marvellous railway facilities which have done so much to develop her industry and agriculture, and to increase the mobility of her population, and thus contribute to the solution of the problem of unemployment.

As regards her light railways, the methods by which these are financed are extraordinarily ingenious and interesting, but as they are somewhat complicated, we will not here give a description of them, but will relegate it to an appendix at the end of this chapter (see p. 290). It may, however, be noted that upon the average the light railways have paid about $3\frac{1}{4}$ per cent. Not a high rate of interest, it may be said. No, but the Belgians have learnt the vital lesson that it is more important to develop their country districts than to earn high dividends on their railway enterprises, and that it is worth while for the State to give guarantees enabling the capital to be borrowed at a low rate of interest, since no wide development of transit facilities is likely to take place if the matter is left entirely to private initiative. Light railways, and other transit facilities in country districts, are seldom likely to earn dividends sufficiently high to make them attractive to the ordinary investor.

While we have spoken of railways alone as a means of transit, it must be remembered that a very large number of working-men go to and from their homes in the near vicinity of towns, either on foot or on bicycles. The extensive use of the latter has been an important factor in distributing town populations over country districts.

We now pass to the third factor essential to the development of a scheme enabling town workers to dwell in the country, viz. the provision, at reasonable rates, of the capital necessary for the erection of houses. In Belgium this provision has been made through the agency of a Housing Act passed in 1889, which has been so successful that, since it was passed, over 100,000 workmen have built houses. Without, at this point, going into details,[1] it may be said that the Act enables a working-man to obtain $\frac{9}{10}$ths of the capital necessary for the erection of his house at about 7 per cent, which covers interest at 4 per cent, and sinking fund in 25 years ($2\frac{1}{2}$ per cent). It also covers an insurance policy under which, should he die before he has paid for his house, it immediately becomes the property of his widow or other legal representative without further payment.

In the majority of cases the man buys land sufficient for his house and a small garden, and pays for them in the manner referred to above. If he wants more land he very often rents it. It may be urged that by acquiring his own house a workman lessens his mobility. This is certainly true, but the drawback is minimised by the excellent facilities for cheap and rapid transit which enable him to reside in one part of Belgium and work in another. In our

[1] These will be found in an appendix, p. 295.

opinion, however, little is gained by the actual purchase of a house, and a scheme giving security of tenure would often be preferable. This matter is referred to later in the chapter.

We have described briefly some of the principal advantages which Belgium derives from the residence of so many of her town workers in the country, and the means by which they have been secured. To us, who have studied Belgian conditions on the spot for four years, they seem well worth securing, and there is no doubt that it can be done. We do not, of course, forget that the conditions in any two countries differ in many respects, and that difficulties must be overcome in Great Britain which do not exist in Belgium, or not to the same extent. They may briefly be stated as follows :—

(1) It may be urged by some that the British people are essentially urban in their tastes ; that an industrial workman would never be happy unless his house were wedged in between a cinematograph and a public-house, and that life in the country, even if combined with work in the town, would appeal to very few. We very much doubt the truth of this objection. The fact is that hitherto town workmen have had hardly any chance of living in the country. The wealthier classes, however, are moving farther and farther out every year, and coming into the town every day to attend to their various duties, and we believe that large numbers of the working-classes would promptly avail themselves of reasonable

facilities for doing the same thing. They would probably go to the districts in the immediate vicinity of the towns, but as the advantages came to be recognised, others, and especially their own children, having become accustomed to a country life, would take up land farther out. If, besides adding to their family incomes during times of employment, men could lay by a reserve for periods of unemployment, by growing potatoes and other crops, or feeding a pig—the prospect would attract large numbers who, after days possibly spent in close factories, might find work on the land a positive recreation, going far to counterbalance the allurements of the publican or bookmaker. They would feel that they were working for themselves, and that every spadeful of soil turned over represented additional wealth.[1] Any who have watched the enthusiasm with which town workers take up allotments, even a long distance from their homes, and at very high rentals (in York they pay as much as £12 an acre), will be apt to reject the argument that the scheme here outlined would fail from lack of support.

(2) It may be urged that the class of men who would be sufficiently enterprising to move out into the country would not be those who suffer seriously from unemployment, but almost exclusively steady and good workmen in regular work. No doubt, at first it would be the best and most enterprising men

---

[1] As stated later, it is essential that the cultivator of the soil should have adequate security of tenure.

who would move out. But it must be remembered that a large proportion of the casuals have once been in regular employment, and that many of them, especially those who have lost their jobs after reaching middle life, have been forced into the casual class through no fault of their own, but through sheer inability to secure permanent posts. But if, when in regular work, they had lived in the country, their position would be infinitely better, as their work became more casual, than if they had remained in the town, for they would find themselves with two alternative occupations—such jobs as they could secure, and work on their land—to be dove-tailed one into the other, as the need arose.

It is practically certain that the advantages of decentralisation would be so great that although at first, as in every new movement, only the most enterprising men would move out, once they had shown the way their example would be followed by less enterprising workers. Moreover, in a few years there would rise up a generation of those who had been brought up in the country, and who would naturally, as they married, tend to remain there. Thus the movement would spread until a continually growing proportion of casual workers were living in country districts.

(3) If it be urged that the cost of houses is much less in Belgium, and therefore the problem of providing them is much easier, on the other hand, the wages of Belgian industrial workmen are as much

lower, in proportion, as the houses are cheaper. And, further, it must not be forgotten that agricultural land costs twice as much in Belgium as in Britain.[1]

(4) Others may urge that the yield from any plot of land which a workman could possibly cultivate in his leisure time would be insignificant in amount. Fortunately, we have in our possession figures obtained by one of the writers a few years ago, but not hitherto published, which show the actual yields, over a period of three years, of small allotments held by a number of York men.

These figures show that 24 industrial workmen, cultivating allotments of rather less than the fourteenth part of an acre, situated at a considerable distance from their homes, obtained on the average, taking the lowest market rates, produce to the net value of £30 : 17 : 2 per year, per acre.[2] Judged by value, one-third of their crop consisted of potatoes, the rest of other ordinary vegetables such as cauliflowers, cabbages, peas, beans, lettuce, etc., which enter into the dietary of a working-class family. The soil was not especially good, and only two of the men had greenhouses (7' × 8' 6" each), and so the conditions were in no way abnormally favourable. It is not,

[1] There are many reasons why wages in Belgium are so much lower than in Britain, which have been explained at length by one of the writers in a previous volume. They are rising rapidly now. (*Land and Labour*, p. 82 *et seq.*)

[2] The gross value was £53 : 5 : 10 per acre ; the figure given above is arrived at by subtracting from this all out-of-pocket expenses for seeds, manure, etc., but *not* subtracting the sum paid for rent (in this case £7 an acre).

however, suggested that equally high yields could be obtained if the size of the allotments were greatly increased, for with the increase of area cultivation would no doubt become less intensive ; but the figures prove that in England, as in Belgium, a very substantial addition to the family income, and consequently a very substantial insurance against unemployment, might be obtained by an industrial workman cultivating half an acre or an acre of land. No doubt, to secure the best results, the British Board of Agriculture should appoint a number of local agricultural experts to give advice to all small-holders and other agriculturists on any matters in which they required help. Such a service has been established very thoroughly in Belgium, where there are 27 officials known as *Agronomes de l'État*. Each of these men has a certain district allotted to him, and is at the call of any agriculturist within it who desires his advice. The *agronomes* attend the local markets, and many agriculturists interview them there. Others seek advice by correspondence, while some are visited on their farms or small holdings. In this way the best expert advice is obtainable easily, and without payment, and it is given, not in the form of literature which simple agriculturists cannot understand, but chiefly through conversations, where questions can be asked and answered. We have gone round farms in Belgium with these *agronomes*, and been greatly impressed by the practical value of the aid they render. Valuable educational work is already done

in England among allotment holders, and with the
help of the Agricultural Development Fund, it should
be possible to enlarge it in accordance with the
growing need. It would also be advisable to establish
Agricultural Credit Banks similar to the Raiffeisen
Banks, which are so numerous in various European
countries. These would assist cultivators to secure
the capital necessary for the development of their
holdings.[1]

(5) There is one further argument, which may be
raised against the very principle of the suggestion for
the rural settlement of industrial workers, viz. that
trade unionism may suffer if individual workers are
living in isolation. But our proposal implies nothing
of the kind. In the first place, every increase in
the distance between home and workshop would be
accompanied by a corresponding increase of transit
facilities. In the second, it would have to be proved
that workmen residing at the heart of some industrial
centre were more faithful to their unions than those
living in the suburbs, before it was argued that a
man's removal beyond the city boundaries was likely
to diminish his loyalty. On the contrary, the progress of trade unionism, like every other movement
towards the solidarity of labour, is closely bound up
with the growing prosperity and economic independence of the workers, and if these were increased by

---

[1] For suggestions as to the organisation of co-operative banks, see
People's Co-operative Banks, by H. C. Devine (Cassell & Co.), and for an
account of co-operative banks on the Continent see *People's Banks*, by
H. W. Wolff (P. S. King & Son).

our scheme, the chances are that all federations for mutual aid would benefit.

We must now consider how such a system as the Belgian one could be established here. And first we must ask whether suitable land is available near enough to towns, and low enough in price, to serve our purpose.

If cheap transit facilities were given on such a scale as in Belgium, men might easily travel 20 or 30 miles to and from their work every day; but, generally speaking, nothing of the kind would be necessary. Within 3 or 4 miles of towns like York (population about 82,000), and within 8 or 10 miles of most of the larger towns, there is plenty of suitable land which there should be no difficulty in obtaining for the purpose outlined above at from £70 to £80 an acre downwards. The price would, of course, depend not only upon the distance from a centre of population, but on the road and water facilities which the site possessed. Land fronting a road would be worth more than back land, and perhaps for our purpose it would be better to take into consideration the cost of land with the necessary roads. For this our own experience, supplemented by inquiry among experts, suggests £100 an acre as a safe figure. It must, of course, be borne in mind that people living in the country cannot expect, and must not demand, the various advantages and facilities of towns, and the figure of £100 an acre is based on this assumption.

It does not, for instance, allow anything for elaborate sewerage; a system of dry closets is quite suitable for people having an ample extent of land around their houses. The cost of roads can be kept down to a minimum if the land is carefully plotted out. The houses should be grouped near the roads, with the land attached to each stretching out behind; and further back there should be an allotment ground, reached, not by a costly highway, but by a small country road, cheap both to construct and maintain. In this way a small mileage of roads could be made to serve a large extent of country.

It would probably be advantageous in many cases to limit the land actually attached to each house to what is required for live-stock and such crops as need constant care. Those who wanted more could take plots of back land in the near vicinity, on which they could grow crops like potatoes, rhubarb, and fruit-trees, which demand comparatively little attention. Such an arrangement would make it possible for a man who, because his industrial employment was becoming more irregular, or for some other reason, wished to add to his holding, to do so without removing. No doubt men whose work was irregular in its nature could manage more land than those in steady employment.

As regards fences, these might be largely dispensed with, as is done abroad.

Turning now to transit facilities, the methods by which these could be provided are so many that we cannot here describe them in detail. We would, however, put before the reader, once again, the view frankly adopted by the Belgians, that all transit facilities should be regarded as an essential condition of the development of the country's resources, and not solely as a means of earning dividends, and that fresh enterprises should be viewed from the standpoint of whether they are desirable in the national interests. Belgium has shown that great development of light railways is possible without incurring loss, and what is possible in Belgium should be equally possible here. If it is advisable to encourage town workers to dwell in the country, the provision of adequate transit facilities is essential, and although the task is a large one, it will have to be faced.

Hitherto, we have spoken of railways alone as a means of cheap and rapid transit. But there are other possibilities, and perhaps trackless trams running on the country roads, and adapted to carry light goods as well as passengers, might, for some years to come, supply the needs of many districts, while the capital involved would, of course, be much less.

Cheap transit is a *sine qua non* of any scheme for enabling town workers to live in the country, as it is indeed for the whole development of rural England. Nor must it be forgotten that cheap transit will enormously lessen the evil of high rents and overcrowding in towns. If a worker is enabled to get quickly and cheaply into the country, he will not submit to the housing conditions from which he suffers so often in British towns to-day.

The Provision of the Necessary Capital

The success of any scheme of decentralisation will largely depend upon the terms on which the capital necessary for the purchase of land and erection of buildings can be secured.[1] There are various ways in which such a scheme may be financed. For instance, under the existing powers given by the Small Holdings and Allotments Act, 1908, the necessary land could be bought and developed, and all the buildings erected thereon by the local authorities or the County Councils, the money being borrowed from the central Government at $3\frac{1}{2}$ per cent. Under this Act, money borrowed for land must be repaid in 80 years, and for houses in 50 years. The sinking fund would therefore amount to about $\frac{1}{4}$ per cent in the case of the land and $\frac{3}{4}$ per cent in the case of the houses, bringing the combined interest and sinking funds to $3\frac{3}{4}$ and $4\frac{1}{4}$ per cent respectively. At present, in fixing the rents which they charge for land and buildings acquired on these terms, the County Councils add a considerable amount, frequently as much as 20 per cent on the total rental, for management charges. Part of these charges, at any rate, might reasonably be borne by the Council, since the

---

[1] As will be seen later, we do not suggest that working-men should necessarily *buy* their houses in the country, but that these might be owned by County Councils, or other public bodies.

tenants are paying the whole of the sinking fund although eventually both land and buildings will become the absolute possession of the Council.

The items which must be taken into account in fixing rents, in addition to interest, sinking fund, and management, are repairs, insurance, and a reserve for empties.

With regard to the first, there is no doubt that since the houses will be situated in scattered groups or hamlets in the country, repairs should be done by the tenants themselves, the landlord only providing the necessary material. Experienced house-owners inform us that if that plan were adopted $\frac{1}{4}$ per cent on the capital cost of house and land should suffice for this item, while $\frac{1}{2}$ per cent should amply cover insurance and empties. Assuming then that $4\frac{1}{4}$ per cent were charged for interest and sinking fund (which, it will be noticed, would leave a small margin towards the cost of management), and $\frac{3}{4}$ per cent for all other outgoings, we arrive at 5 per cent on the capital cost of land and buildings as the amount which must be covered by the rent. There is no doubt that houses with adequate accommodation could be erected at from £200 to £250 each, exclusive of land. If we take the higher figure and allow half an acre of land, at £100 an acre, to each house, we get a total capital cost of £300, which at 5 per cent gives a rental of £15 a year, or 5s. 9d. per week. But if, to make our figures perfectly safe, we fix a rental to pay $5\frac{1}{2}$ per cent on this capital cost, it would amount to £16 : 10s., or 6s. 4d. a week for a good house with half an acre of land.   If further land were required in the immediate neighbourhood it should, on the assumption that it could be bought for £100 an acre, be available at a rental of £4 an acre, which would more than cover interest and sinking fund ; and as we saw, the produce from half an acre of land, after paying all out-of-pocket expenses for seed, manure, etc., should be worth not less than £10 a year.

It has been suggested to us that little progress is likely to be made with the erection of houses if the matter be left with the County Councils.   In that case private associations working on the lines of the Co-Partnership Tenants Association could, we are assured, afford to erect such houses in the country if the rentals were fixed at $5\frac{1}{2}$ per cent on the total capital.   In view, however, of the fact that a wide extension of this scheme would largely increase the value of agricultural land in the vicinity of towns, it would be much more satisfactory for the work to be done by public bodies than by private societies, so that the community as a whole should profit from the increased land values.   Possibly, however, local experiments might first be made by private societies, in the hope that their success would lead to action on a national scale.   It may be held that the scheme could best be developed if men were encouraged to buy their own houses, as in Belgium.   But a sinking fund enabling them to do this in a period which would hold out any attraction, say not more than 25 years, would, of course, add largely to the annual payment, and although this does not discourage the Belgians, we believe that it would prevent many working-men in England from moving from the towns. But, while there would be nothing to prevent those who could afford it from purchasing their houses, it would be a mistake to assume that the success of the scheme depended on the extent to which this was done. All that it is necessary to provide for is *security of tenure at a reasonable rental*, which can be had without a scheme of purchase. Again, even when transit facilities are good, mobility of labour, in the case of men who have bought their houses, is to a certain extent hampered, and anything which hampers it tends to increase unemployment.

To sum up, we have seen how many and how important would be the advantages of a scheme of decentralisation enabling town workers to live in the country, and how by this means they would have access to an alternative employment, which would materially increase the security of their lives. Such a scheme would, moreover, greatly diminish the demoralisation which, under present conditions, so rapidly follows in the train of unemployment. In addition, it would bridge the gulf—at present almost impassable—between country and town, and it would lessen the flow of the population townwards, and encourage it in the other direction. It is, further, a reform which would render the people more healthy, and so far from costing money, it would increase the national wealth. It would do this in the broad sense, by combining land, labour, and capital where at present they are uncombined; and also in the narrow sense, since, if the scheme were financed by the County Councils, valuable land and buildings would, through the operation of the sinking fund paid by the tenants, become public property in a comparatively few years. If, therefore, on the one hand, the scheme is a large one and the capital involved is great, on the other, the risk is comparatively small and the advantages to the nation are incalculable.

U

APPENDIX A

THE FINANCING OF LIGHT RAILWAYS IN BELGIUM

(From *Land and Labour*, p. 295 *et seq.*)

PRIOR to 1881 the creation of light railways, although desired and encouraged by the Government, was left to private initiative, with the result that nothing was done. But in that year a Commission was appointed to "study the best means of creating a system of secondary or local railways," and the creation of the light railway system of Belgium dates from the appointment of this Commission. At its second sitting, two of its members, MM. Bischoffsheim and Wollens, submitted a document which set forth in detail proposals for the institution of a National Society of Local Railways. These proposals, slightly amended by the Commission, formed the basis of the legislation of 1884 and 1885, and were the starting-point of the extraordinary development of the light railway system.

Acting upon the suggestions of the Commission, the State has granted the sole right to construct and control light railways to a society known as the National Society for Local Railways, whose administration is entrusted to a Council of four members, two appointed by the King, and two elected by the general body of shareholders in the different lines.[1] The King also appoints the chairman of the Council and the general manager. The interests of the shareholders are further safeguarded by a supervising committee of nine members, one from each province, elected by the shareholders.

No light railway in Belgium may be constructed except through the instrumentality of the National Society.[2] If the inhabitants in a rural district desire to have one, their communal

---

[1] As will be explained later, each line belongs to a separate limited company. The shareholders of all the different lines unite to appoint two persons to represent them on the National Council.

[2] Unless the National Society fails to take action within a year after receiving a request for the construction of a light railway.

council communicates this desire to the National Society, and undertakes to meet the expenses of a preliminary inquiry.[1] The Society then ascertains the density of the population and the probable amount of traffic, and sends down engineers, who roughly survey the ground. The report of this inquiry, which is not at all costly, is submitted to the Government. The Minister of War examines the proposal from the point of view of national defence, and the Minister for Railways with reference to any possible competition with the State main railway system. If the Government expresses its provisional approval of the rough proposals which have been submitted, the next step is for the National Society to raise the necessary capital. In England this provision of capital has hitherto been one of the chief stumbling-blocks in the way of any considerable development of the light railway system.

It will be interesting, therefore, to see how Belgium finances her light railways. First, the National Society ascertains how much capital will be necessary in connection with any proposed line; then a limited liability company is formed for its construction and equipment. The State promises—subject to its approval of the detailed plans to be submitted at a later stage—to take half the shares. Some of the provinces subscribe one-quarter, and some one-third, of the capital required for the construction of lines within their boundaries.[2] Thus we see that from three-quarters to five-sixths of the total capital is furnished by the State and Provincial Governments. The remainder of the shares are taken up by the Communes through which the light railway passes, or by private individuals; but, as a matter of fact, the latter have only subscribed $1\frac{1}{2}$ per cent of the total share capital invested in light railways in Belgium. As the development of the system is proceeding very rapidly, the immediate provision of the large amount of capital required might sometimes prove burdensome to the public authorities,

---

[1] It is interesting to note that up to the end of 1908, applications for the building of 3859 miles of lines had been acceded to, and only 240 miles refused.

[2] The State and Provinces now subscribe a larger portion of the total cost than they did in the early days of the National Society.

especially to the smaller Communes whose financial resources are not great. Therefore, the custom invariably followed has been for the State, the Provinces, and the Communes to pay for their shares by annual instalments, instead of in a lump sum. They spread the payment over a period of ninety years, paying each year to the National Society, which issues the shares, $3\frac{1}{2}$ per cent upon their value. This sum covers interest and sinking fund, so that at the end of ninety years the shares become the absolute property of the State, Provinces, and Communes respectively. But of what service to the National Society, it may be asked, is an arrangement such as this, which does not appear to give that immediate command of capital which is the object of issuing shares ? The answer is that the State guarantees not only a dividend of $3\frac{1}{2}$ per cent upon all the share capital subscribed by the three public authorities, but the security of the principal. Furnished with this guarantee, the National Society has no difficulty in issuing 3 per cent debentures, which are redeemed as the sinking fund accumulates ; and it is in this way that the whole of the capital for the light railway system of Belgium has been raised.[1] The company, under this arrangement, obtains the needed capital on terms as low as those on which the State can borrow, while the latter is not burdened by any addition to its debt, or by the heavy responsibilities which would result from complete nationalisation. It will be remarked at once how very lightly the burden of such an arrangement rests upon public bodies. All they have to do in any year is to pay or to receive the difference between the percentage earned upon the capital, and the $3\frac{1}{2}$ per cent which they have to pay annually for ninety

---

[1] The price at which these debentures can be issued varies according to the state of the money market ; but in order to maintain stability, the National Society has built up a reserve fund from profits realised on the issues of debentures above par, out of which losses due to the issue of any debentures below par are met. As a consequence of this policy, the shareholders have not in any instance been called on to guarantee more than 3·5 per cent to cover interest and sinking fund on account of the purchase of their shares. At the time of writing (1909), a guarantee of 3·65 per cent is provisionally demanded for new lines, but with the understanding that if the condition of the money market becomes more favourable before the capital is actually required, the annual charge on the shares to cover interest and sinking fund will be reduced to 3·5 per cent.

years to the National Society.   If the capital invested in any
railway steadily earns more than $3\frac{1}{2}$ per cent, the public bodies
actually receive cash each year, although at the same time they
are buying their shares.[1]   It should be noted in passing that the
National Society is exempted from all state and provincial
royalties upon the concessions granted, and from all national,
provincial, and communal taxes and rates on property directly
utilised for the railways ; and enjoys the privilege of free postage
for official correspondence.[2]   In return for these privileges and
for the financial guarantees referred to above, the National Society
undertakes to perform certain services for the State, such as the
free carriage of mails, and the carriage of soldiers and voters at
half-fares.   As soon as the arrangements for the provision of
capital have been made, it prepares detailed plans for the construction of the line and draws up the necessary specifications,
and after these have received the approval of the Government,
the work of construction begins.   This is always let on contract,
but is supervised by the National Society's own officers.

The methods employed for the working of the line are
interesting and suggestive.   The National Society never works
its own railways, but as soon as one is ready, with all necessary

---

[1] Any profits earned in excess of $3\frac{1}{2}$ per cent, after the payment of certain
bonuses to the members of the administrative council and the general
manager, are distributed as follows :—One-quarter towards the constitution
of a reserve fund for the particular line earning the dividend ; three-eighths
in additional dividends to the shareholders ; three-eighths for the constitution of a national reserve fund, to assist lines which are not prospering.   It
is only through this national fund that the different lines are in any way
financially connected with one another : in everything else the accounts are
kept rigidly separate.   (These reserve funds are, of course, quite distinct
from that mentioned in the previous footnote.)

[2] The only exemption, other than special facilities for obtaining an
advance from the treasury, granted to the constructors of light railways in
Great Britain by the Light Railways Act of 1896, consists in the provision
that : "Where the Treasury agree to make any such special advance as a
free grant, the order authorising the railway may make provision as regards
any parish that, during a period not exceeding ten years to be fixed by the
order, so much of the railway as is in that parish shall not be assessed to
any local rate at a higher value than that at which the land occupied by the
railway would have been assessed if it had remained in the condition in
which it was immediately before it was acquired for the purpose of the
railway. . . ."

stations and rolling stock, tenders are obtained from industrial companies for its working. The usual arrangement made is for the company to which the working of the lines is farmed out, to undertake to hand over to the National Society an agreed percentage of its gross receipts, usually from 30 to 40 per cent. The National Society provides the whole of the rolling stock, the contracting company being responsible for all repairs and replacements. Usually the agreements are entered into for thirty years, with the right of cancellation at the end of fifteen.[1] It frequently happens that one company contracts with the National Society to work several separate railways. At the end of 1906, 138 different light railways in Belgium were worked by thirty-seven companies, some of which were working as many as eleven separate lines. The accounts of each line are kept entirely distinct by the National Society.

The wisdom of farming out the working of the lines is much debated by railway experts in many countries, but whatever may have been the experience elsewhere, there is no doubt that this policy has worked well in Belgium. The greatest care must, of course, be taken only to farm out the working of lines to companies of financial stability and of thoroughly good reputation. An interesting development, much favoured by the National Society at the present time, is the farming out of the working of lines to industrial companies, in which the Communes through which the lines run are the principal, if not the only shareholders. This experiment is giving satisfactory results in the thirteen cases where it has been tried.

---

[1] Among the items stipulated in the agreements, the following may be noted. The contractors have to deposit an approximate sum to guarantee their ability to effect renewals and repairs of lines and stock, when they become necessary. Additions to the rolling stock are usually supplied by the National Society (of course at the expense of the shareholders in the line concerned). The contractors are obliged to insure all buildings and material against the risk of fire. The minimum number of trains to be run per day is fixed, and also the maximum fares and rates which may be charged. The fares and rates are subject to the approval of the Government, with a view to prevent the undercutting of those on the national railways. The stations and stopping places, and the junctions of private lines and sidings are also fixed by the National Society. At the end of 1908, the number of private junctions was 372.

APPENDIX B

THE BELGIAN HOUSING ACT OF 1889

(From *Land and Labour*, p. 453 *et seq.*)

THE provisions of the law fall under three heads :—

1. The creation of a number of local committees to endeavour to improve housing conditions.

2. The reduction by one-half, in the case of working men, of the heavy Government duties imposed on the sale or mortgage of property.

3. Arrangement for the provision at a low rate of the capital necessary for the purchase of land and the cost of erection of workmen's houses.[1]

The first and last of these conditions must be further explained.

The local committees appointed under the Act are called *Comités de Patronage des Maisons ouvrières et des Institutions de Prévoyance.* Their duties are to encourage the building of work men's houses, either to be let or sold to the occupants, to study health conditions in working-class localities, and to stimulate thrift. They number fifty-six at the present time (1909), and are nominated partly by the central and partly by the provincial Governments. The members are unpaid, but their management expenses are met from public funds, and they must report annually to the central Government. The usefulness and activity of these committees really depends upon their personnel. In some cases they are doing a great deal to improve matters in their district, in others they exist in little more than name.

Coming now to the question of the provision of capital, the law empowers the National Savings Bank, whose deposits have largely been made by working people, to loan up to $7\frac{1}{2}$ per cent of its reserve fund for the purpose of cottage construction.[2]

---

[1] It is possible for a workman to borrow nine-tenths of the money required to build his house, including the cost of the land.

[2] About £3,200,000 at the present time (1909).

But as it would be difficult for the central Savings Bank to enter into direct relationship with every workman who wishes to build a house, a number of local Credit Associations have sprung into existence, financed largely by philanthropists and public-spirited men, which act as intermediaries between the central Savings Bank and the individual workman. The great majority of these have taken the form of Limited Companies, whose function it is to lend money to working men desirous of building houses. The great bulk of the money they lend comes, as we shall see directly, from the central Savings Bank ; but in order to give some security to the bank for the money lent, the shareholders, in those Credit Societies which have taken the form of Limited Companies, themselves subscribe a certain amount of capital. No Limited Company can be registered in Belgium unless the whole of the capital is subscribed and one-tenth paid up. The liability of the shareholders to pay up a larger amount, if necessary, acts as a very good security to the National Savings Bank for any sums which it may lend.

After the payment, then, of this legal minimum, the whole of the capital required is obtained from the National Savings Bank, which will lend to these Limited Companies capital equal to 50 per cent of their unsubscribed capital, plus about two-thirds of the value of any mortgages held by them. To take an example— suppose a Credit Society has taken the form of a Limited Company with a capital of £4000, of which one-tenth—namely, £400 —has been paid up by the shareholders, leaving £3600 unpaid, the National Savings Bank will lend half the unpaid capital— £1800. Thus the Company can immediately begin operations with an available capital of £2200, in addition to which the National Savings Bank will grant capital equal to two-thirds of all the loans made by the Limited Company for which it holds mortgages. The National Savings Bank charges 3 or 3¼ per cent interest to the Limited Companies, which in their turn charge 4 per cent to the workmen, that being the maximum interest allowed by law. The difference covers the cost of management and payment of interest on shares (limited to 3 per cent). The remainder, if any, goes to a Reserve Fund.

Thus, any *bona fide* workman in Belgium can borrow nine-tenths of the money required to build a house, at a rate of interest which cannot exceed 4 per cent. To this, of course, must be added the annual sums necessary to repay the loan. The period of repayment may be fixed by the workman, but must not exceed twenty-five years, and all loans must be repaid by the time he is sixty-five years old.

By an excellent arrangement the workman is usually induced to insure his life through the Credit Associations for a sum equal to the amount of his loan. As this life insurance is only valid until the loan is repaid, the additional cost is comparatively small. Should he die before repaying it, not only does the house become the absolute property of his heirs without further payment, but they receive in cash a sum equal to that portion of the loan which has already been paid off.[1] About five-sixths of the loans granted by the National Savings Bank have had life policies of this kind associated with them. Of course workmen desiring to insure their lives must first be examined by a doctor, and the rate of insurance varies with their age. Assuming that a man is thirty years of age, and that he obtains a first-class policy, he can, under the provisions of the 1889 law, become the absolute possessor of his house at the end of twenty-five years by payment of $7\frac{1}{2}$ per cent on the capital borrowed—viz. interest 4 per cent per annum, repayment $2\frac{1}{2}$ per cent, and life policy 1 per cent. As we have seen, he can borrow nine-tenths of the capital required for the purchase of land and the construction of his house. There are a number of associations in Belgium willing to provide suitable applicants with the whole or part of the remaining one-tenth ; and in some cases local authorities put aside a fund, from which grants are made to enable persons who are temporarily out of work or handicapped by illness, to pay their periodical instalments. Practically, any working-man who chooses can become the owner of his house.

---

[1] In 1904 a plan was introduced whereby the life insurance policy was altered to cover only that portion of the loan which remained unpaid at the time of death, and this materially reduced the cost of the life policy. This method of insurance is now generally adopted.

APPENDIX C

THE YIELD FROM ALLOTMENT GARDENS IN YORK

DURING the three years 1902-1904, one of the present writers obtained detailed particulars of the actual yields procured by a number of working-men from allotments in the immediate neighbourhood of York. Each man who volunteered to supply information was provided with a diary, in which he entered particulars of everything obtained from his allotment during the period under observation, and of all out-of-pocket expenses. Certain crops, such as cabbages, lettuce, etc., were to be entered by count; others, such as peas, potatoes, strawberries, etc., by weight. A shed was erected on the allotment grounds, where the books were kept, and where scales were provided for weighing produce. Altogether 24 men kept these records for three years. All the entries were periodically checked. The size of each allotment was 345 square yards, but part of this was devoted to flowers or poultry. The average area per allotment devoted to vegetables was 319 square yards. Eleven of the allotments were on a light loam, and thirteen on a heavy loam over clay. All the men were engaged in industrial occupations, principally on the railway or at the Cocoa Works, and they were all amateurs. The method adopted in valuing the produce from each allotment was as follows :—A number of working-class women, who were known to be particularly clever housekeepers and good buyers, set down daily the prices which they paid for fruit and vegetables during the three years. At the same time, a greengrocer who sold his goods at reasonable rates gave a statement week by week of the prices which he was charging. These were compared with those paid by the women, and if there was any difference the lower prices were adopted for the purpose of these statistics. Thus we satisfied ourselves that our figures really represented what people buying

as economically as possible would have been obliged to pay.
As no useful purpose would be served by giving particulars of
each individual allotment, we have added them together, and
show in Table 1, following p. 300, the money value of the fruit
and vegetables raised each year on the 24 allotments, viz.—

1902	.	.	.	£86	1	9
1903	.	.	.	£94	1	11
1904	.	.	.	£72	17	0

It will be seen that these sums vary greatly. Apart from the
fact that potatoes were dear in 1903, which added about £6 to
the value of that year's produce, there were no changes in the
market price of fruit and vegetables which would account for
such a variation, which must therefore be put down to difference
in the seasons.[1]

Making allowance for the area of land devoted to flower-
growing and to poultry, the gross yield per acre has been £54,
£59, and £46 in each year respectively, an average of £53,
but if we subtract the out-of-pocket expenditure for seeds,
manure, and rent (at £7 per acre), we arrive at £29, £39, and
£25 as the net yield per acre—an average of £31.

If we examine the kind of produce grown, we find that
potatoes, cauliflowers, celery, peas, and cabbages together account
for about two-thirds of the total value in each year.

Although we do not give particulars of the crops grown on
each separate allotment, it will be of interest if we show what
was grown on the three allotments which gave the best results.
These figures are given in Tables 2-4, following p. 300. It will
be noted that the gross yield from these allotments was very
high, averaging £77 per acre in 1902, and £76 and £68

---

[1] The average values attributed to the principal crops were as follows :—

	Potatoes, per 100 lb.	Cauliflowers, per 100 heads.	Celery, per 100 heads.	Brussels Sprouts, per 100 lb.	Cabbage, per 100 heads.	Peas, per 100 lb.
	s. d.	s. d.	s. d.	s. d.	s. d.	s. d.
1902	4 5	17 0½	11 9½	14 11	6 2	11 11
1903	5 6	14 3	12 3	16 7	8 4	12 7½
1904	4 5½	17 0	11 1	13 4	8 2	10 0

respectively in the following two years, the net yields in the three years averaging £52, £54, and £44 respectively.

Although these best allotments represent various modes of cropping, taking them *together*, the cropping does not differ greatly from that of the other allotments, which shows that the greater yield they gave was due to care and skill in their cultivation, rather than to the selection of crops.

In 1902

Crop	Lb.	Bunches	Heads or Single Vegetables	Value (£ s. d.)	Per cent of Total Value
Potatoes	13,960		898		35·5
Cauliflowers			1073		8·7
Celery		291	1535		7·3
Peas		285	1137		6·4
Cabbage			109		5·5
Brussels sprouts					4·5
Lettuce		144	251		3·7
Tomatoes			402		2·5
Onions		362	378		1·9
Broad beans			348		1·8
Beetroot		218	208		1·8
Carrots			60		1·8
Shalots					1·7
Herbs			73		1·7
Red cabbage			303		1·6
Savoys					
Rhubarb					
Black currants	84				
Mustard and cress	16		45		
Red currants					
Radish	108	337			
Kidney beans					
Turnips	21	62	38		
Parsnips	70	71	57		
Dwarf beans			40		
Vegetable marrow					
Broccoli					
Cucumber			47		
Leek	78				
Spinach	1				
Runner beans	44		40		8·4
Beans for seed	12		26		
Marrow plants	20		18		
French beans					
Mushrooms					
Artichokes	5				
Cabbage plants	35				
Greens	19				
Kale	19				
Strawberries					
Raspberries					
Gooseberries					
Total				**£86 1 9**	**100·0**

Gross receipts . £86 1 9 from 7663 sq. yds. = £24 7 5 per acre
Expenditure . 40 12 3
Net receipts . £45 9 6 from 7663 sq. yds. = £28 14 5 per acre

In 1903

Crop	Lb.	Bunches	Heads or Single Vegetables	Value (£ s. d.)	Per cent of Total Value
Potatoes	11,054		979		32·2
Cauliflowers			149		7·4
Celery	1,050		1610		6·8
Peas	512		1314		7·1
Cabbage					4·5
Brussels sprouts	29½	230	585		3·9
Lettuce	394		245		0·5
Tomatoes	590	217			3·6
Onions	215	234			3·1
Broad beans	144				2·1
Beetroot	88	279	245		1·4
Carrots	7				1·4
Shalots		192	348		3·3
Herbs		498	268		2·9
Red cabbage	42		20		1·7
Savoys	74				0·7
Rhubarb	120				1·1
Turnips	130		630		1·2
Dwarf beans					
Kidney beans					
French beans	1		652		
Cabbage plants			12		
Radish	125	244			
Vegetable marrow					
Cucumber	124	81			
Parsnips	31	112			
Leeks	62				
Spinach	42				
Broccoli		12			
Runner beans			26		
Kale					
Mustard and cress					
Greens	26				
Strawberries	35				
Raspberries	23				
Gooseberries	33				
Red currants	26				
Total				**£94 1 11**	**100·0**

Gross receipts . £94 1 11 from 7663 sq. yds. = £29 9 9 per acre
Expenditure . 32 9 9
Net receipts . £61 12 2 from 7663 sq. yds. = £28 18 ? per acre

In 1904

Crop	Lb.	Bunches	Heads or Single Vegetables	Value (£ s. d.)	Per cent of Total Value
Potatoes	10,600		857		32·5
Cauliflowers			829		10·9
Celery	896		1300		6·3
Peas	537	95	1022		7·1
Cabbage	18½	170			4·5
Brussels sprouts	804				2·4
Lettuce	90				2·7
Tomatoes	610	102			2·5
Onions	95		157		2·7
Broad beans	294	449	281		2·5
Beetroot		60	57		2·3
Carrots		488			2·2
Shalots		218			2·1
Herbs	276		540		3·4
Red cabbage	54		270		1·6
Savoys	120		9		0·6
Rhubarb	92		50		1·4
Turnips	112	276	20		1·0
Dwarf beans					
Runner beans	150	22			
Kidney beans					
French beans					
Cabbage plants					
Cauliflower plants					
Radish					
Cucumber					
Vegetable marrow					
Parsnips					
Savoy plants					
Spinach					
Broccoli	19				
Mustard and cress	5½				
Artichokes	21				
Kale	4½				
Raspberries	31				
Black currants	40				
Gooseberries					
Red currants					
Strawberries					
Total				**£72 17 0**	**100·0**

Gross receipts . £72 17 0 from 7663 sq. yds. = £46 0 3 per acre
Expenditure . 33 7 2
Net receipts . £39 9 10 from 7663 sq. yds. = £24 18 10 per acre

To follow page 340.—1.

QUANTITY AND VALUE OF CROPS PRODUCED ON THREE ALLOTMENTS IN 1902

A (329 Square Yards)[1]

Crop	Lb.	Bunches.	Heads or Single Vegetables.	Value.	Per cent of Total Value.
Potatoes	641				25·1
Cauliflowers			68		10·5
Celery			53		6·7
Peas	3½				4·4
Cabbages			124		7·8
Brussels sprouts	55				1·8
Lettuce			196		10·1
Onions	21		90		2·7
Beetroot			28		1·8
Carrots	28				0·7
Shalots	5				1·2
Herbs		2			1·4
Red cabbage			16		1·3
Savoys			46		4·5
Turnips					
Dwarf beans					
Radishes	37½	15			1·1
Vegetable marrow			1		
Broccoli					
Total				£4 17 11	100·0

Gross receipts £4 17 11 = £72 0 6 per acre.
Expenditure £1 9 ...
Net receipts £3 8 2 = £50 0 3 per acre.

[1] Grown on light loam.

B (345 Square Yards)[1]

Crop	Lb.	Bunches.	Heads or Single Vegetables.	Value.	Per cent of Total Value.
Potatoes	1002				50·8
Cauliflowers			15		1·9
Celery			52		6·9
Peas	8				0·4
Cabbages			76		4·3
Brussels sprouts	24½		167		3·3
Lettuce			168		8·6
Beetroot		2			6·7
Herbs		30			2·3
Red cabbage			3		
Turnips	2½	9	3		1·4
Dwarf beans					
Radishes	1–2½	14			3·0
Mustard and cress		5			
Runner beans					
Kidney beans					
Total				£5 10 8	100·0

Gross receipts £5 10 8 = £77 12 6 per acre.
Expenditure 1 11 ...
Net receipts £3 19 0 = £55 8 3 per acre.

[1] Grown on light loam.

C (279 Square Yards)[2]

Crop	Lb.	Bunches.	Heads or Single Vegetables.	Value.	Per cent of Total Value.
Potatoes	734				36·4
Cauliflowers			35		9·4
Celery					0·7
Peas	80				9·1
Cabbages			35		2·3
Brussels sprouts	33		18		4·7
Lettuce		21			3·4
Onions		30			2·8
Beetroot					0·5
Carrots	7	3			3·7
Shalots	31				1·0
Herbs		11			2·1
Red cabbage			12½		1·5
Savoys		2	11½		
Turnips					2·0
Radishes		10			
Mustard and cress	1	5			6·7
Broad beans	12½				0·6
Tomatoes	9½	6			2·0
Greens	3				1·6
Gooseberries	17½				1·7
Strawberries	2				
Raspberries	1				
Red currants	6½				1·1
Black currants					
Rhubarb					
Total				£4 13 5	100·0

Gross receipts £4 13 5 = £81 0 7 per acre.
Expenditure 1 16 3
Net receipts £2 17 2 = £40 11 9 per acre.

[2] Grown on heavy loam over clay.

QUANTITY AND VALUE OF CROPS PRODUCED ON THREE ALLOTMENTS IN 1903

D (329 Square Yards) [1] [2]

Crop	Lb.	Bunches	Heads or Single Vegetables	Value	Per cent of Total Value
Potatoes	445				22.9
Cauliflowers			71		9.8
Celery			55		6.6
Peas					3.3
Cabbages	26		52		7.3
Brussels sprouts					3.6
Lettuce	21		315		14.3
Onions					3.3
Beet-root	51	17			2.8
Carrots	42	48			3.8
Shalots	6				0.7
Herbs		26			2.3
Red cabbage			18		4.3
Savoys			14		1.1
Turnips	20		184		6.8
Dwarf beans					3.2
Radishes		21	8		1.9
Vegetable marrow					1.9
Broad beans	25				2.3
Total				£5 4 7	100.0

Gross receipts £5 4 7 = £76 18 6 per acre.
Expenditure 0 17 0
Net receipts £4 7 7 = £64 8 5 per acre.

[1] Grown on light loam.

E (345 Square Yards) [1]

Crop	Lb.	Bunches	Heads or Single Vegetables	Value	Per cent of Total Value
Potatoes	610		37		31.0
Cauliflowers			74		5.1
Celery					9.1
Peas	27				3.6
Cabbages	32		52		8.0
Brussels sprouts			57		5.2
Lettuce			44		3.0
Onions			12		1.1
Beet-root					1.8
Carrots					1.0
Shalots	12				1.5
Herbs		7	21		2.2
Red cabbage			59		5.2
Savoys					4.8
Turnips		24			1.8
Broad beans	34				4.3
Kidney beans	35				5.7
Cabbage plants					1.6
Other plants		8			0.3
Cucumber			40		3.0
Rhubarb			12		0.7
Total				£5 1 4	100.0

Gross receipts £5 1 4 = £71 1 7 per acre.
Expenditure 1 15 11
Net receipts £3 5 5 = £45 17 9 per acre.

[1] Identical with allotment A (1902).

F (328 Square Yards) [1]

Crop	Lb.	Bunches	Heads or Single Vegetables	Value	Per cent of Total Value
Potatoes	740		25		35.1
Cauliflowers			53		3.5
Celery	24				6.2
Peas			103		2.9
Cabbages					8.0
Lettuce		67			2.9
Onions		54			4.7
Beet-root	105	25			4.4
Carrots					1.9
Mint		10	12		0.8
Red cabbage			8		2.8
Savoys					0.6
Turnips		36			2.8
Radishes		29	1		1.0
Vegetable marrow	73				5.7
Broad beans	87				7.2
Kidney beans					0.6
Rhubarb	19				8.9
Strawberries		1			
Total				£5 7 2	100.0

Gross receipts £5 7 2 = £79 1 4 per acre.
Expenditure 1 15 10
Net receipts £3 11 4 = £58 12 4 per acre.

[1] Identical with allotment A (1902).

QUANTITY AND VALUE OF CROPS PRODUCED ON THREE ALLOTMENTS IN 1904

G (345 SQUARE YARDS)[1]

Crop	Lb.	Bunches	Heads or Single Vegetables	Value	Per Cent of Total Value
Potatoes	452		38	£ s. d. 0 19 6	21·5
Cauliflowers			67	0 6 8	7·2
Celery			53	0 7 4	8·1
Peas	98			0 9 9	10·7
Cabbages	28			0 4 3	5·0
Brussels sprouts				0 3 7	4·1
Lettuce				0 0 10	0·9
Onions				0 3 2	3·4
Beetroot	25			0 2 4	2·6
Shalots				0 3 0	3·4
Parsley		7		0 0 2	0·2
Red Cabbage			20	0 1 6	1·7
Savoys		7		0 2 1	2·6
Turnips	1		7	0 1 11	2·1
Dwarf beans				0 1 9	
Radishes				0 0 8	0·8
Vegetable marrow				0 1 6	1·6
Mustard and cress				0 0 3	0·3
Scarlet runners	10			0 1 8	1·8
Kidney beans	51			0 8 6	9·4
Rhubarb		10		0 6 6	7·2
Gooseberries				0 0 4	0·4
Strawberries				0 1 0	1·1
Raspberries				0 0 6	0·6
Broad beans	3			0 1 1	1·2
Spinach	6			0 1 10	2·0
Cauliflower plants			220	0 1 0	1·0
Total				**£4 10 6**	**100·0**

Gross receipts . . . £4 10 6 = £63 9 7 per acre.
Expenditure . . . 1 13 1
Net receipts . . . £2 17 5 = £40 5 6 per acre.

[1] Grown on light loam.

H (328 SQUARE YARDS)[1][3]

Crop	Lb.	Bunches	Heads or Single Vegetables	Value	Per Cent of Total Value
Potatoes	698		46	£ s. d. 3 1 9	36·7
Cauliflowers			19	0 9 1	9·1
Celery			104	0 7 2	7·1
Peas	24			0 2 4	2·3
Cabbages	7		106	0 9 8	11·0
Brussels sprouts	21			0 1 3	1·3
Lettuce	24	105		0 3 2	3·9
Onions				0 5 9	6·9
Beetroot	12	26		0 1 8	1·9
Carrots				0 2 7	2·5
Shalots		66		0 1 9	1·9
Herbs				0 5 9	6·9
Turnips	13	5		0 0 3	0·6
Dwarf beans		35		0 2 0	2·7
Radishes				0 0 11	1·1
Scarlet runners	10			0 1 8	2·1
Rhubarb		9		0 1 1	1·4
Strawberries	6			0 2 1	3·2
Total				**£3 19 6**	**100·0**

Gross receipts . . . £3 19 6 = £58 13 2 per acre.
Expenditure . . . 1 12 0
Net receipts . . . £2 7 6 = £33 0 11 per acre.

[2] Grown on heavy loam over clay.

I (243 SQUARE YARDS)[2]

Crop	Lb.	Bunches	Heads or Single Vegetables	Value	Per Cent of Total Value
Potatoes	258			£ s. d. 0 12 9	15·6
Cauliflowers			68	0 12 11	15·8
Peas	24		61	0 2 6	3·1
Cabbages	51		80	0 5 6	6·8
Brussels sprouts				0 6 2	8·5
Lettuce	58			0 4 4	3·9
Beetroot				0 4 4	5·3
Herbs		9	9	0 6 1	7·8
Red cabbage			14	0 1 6	1·8
Savoys				0 1 1	1·4
Turnips					
Dwarf beans				0 0 11	1·1
Radishes		32		0 0 11	
Rhubarb		153		0 14 11	18·3
Broad beans	14			0 0 11	1·1
Cabbage plants			120	0 2 0	2·4
French beans	1			0 1 4	1·5
Tomatoes	10			0 0 5	6·5
Total				**£4 1 8**	**100·0**

Gross receipts . . . £4 1 8 = £81 6 7 per acre.
Expenditure . . . 1 4 4
Net receipts . . . £2 17 4 = £57 1 11 per acre.

[3] Identical with Allotment F (1903).

PRICES OF VEGETABLES AND FRUIT IN 1902 (IN PENCE)

Week ending		January				February				March					April				May					June				July				August					September				October				November					December			
		4	11	18	25	1	8	15	22	1	8	15	22	29	5	12	19	26	3	10	17	24	31	7	14	21	28	5	12	19	26	2	9	16	23	30	6	13	20	27	4	11	18	25	1	8	15	22	29	6	13	20	27
Beet																																						1	1	1	1	1	1		1							
Beans (broad)	per lb.																													1	1	1	1	1	1																		
" (French)	"																															8	8	8	8		8	8		8	8			8	8	8	8	8			8	8	8
Brussels sprouts	"																																															
Cabbages	each										2					2																					each																

Week ending		January	February	March	April	May	June	July	August	September	October	November	December
Artichokes	per stone												
Beet	each												
Broccoli	each												
Beans (broad)	per lb.												
" (French)													
" (runner)													
Brussels sprouts													
Cabbages (red)	each												
"													
Carrots													
Cauliflowers	each												
Celery													
Cucumbers													
Greens	per lb.												
Leeks													
Lettuce													
Marrows													
Onions	per stone												
Parsnips													
Peas	per stone												
Potatoes													
Radishes	per bunch												
Rhubarb	per lb.												
Shalots													
Spinach	per bunch												
Tomatoes	each												
Turnips													
Currants (black)	per lb.												
" (red)													
Gooseberries													
Raspberries													
Strawberries													

To follow page 300.—6.

PRICES OF VEGETABLES AND FRUIT IN 1904 (IN PENCE)

Week ending		Jan. 9	Jan. 16	Jan. 23	Jan. 30	Feb. 6	Feb. 13	Feb. 20	Feb. 27	Mar. 5	Mar. 12	Mar. 19	Mar. 26	Apr. 2	Apr. 9	Apr. 16	Apr. 23	Apr. 30	May 7	May 14	May 21	May 28	June 4	June 11	June 18	June 25
Beet		..	..	..	..	..	..	..	..	..	..	..	..	..	..	..	..	..	..	..	..	..	..	..	..	..
Broccoli	each	..	..	..	..	..	..	..	..	3	..	..	..	..	..	..	..	..	2	..	..	2	2	..	..	..
Beans (broad)	per lb.	..	..	..	..	..	..	..	..	..	..	..	..	..	..	..	..	..	..	..	..	..	..	..	..	..
,, (French)	,,	..	..	..	..	..	..	..	..	..	..	..	..	..	..	..	..	..	..	..	..	..	..	..	..	..
,, (runner)	,,	..	..	..	..	..	..	..	..	..	..	..	..	..	..	..	..	..	..	..	..	..	..	..	..	..
Brussels sprouts	,,	1½	..	..	1½	1½	..	..	1½	2	..	..	2	2	..	..	..	2	1½	..	..	..	..	..	..	..
Cabbages	each	1	..	..	1	1	..	..	1	1	..	..	1	1	..	..	..	1	spring 1½	..	..	spring 1½	1	..	..	..
Carrots		..	..	..	..	..	..	..	..	..	..	..	..	..	..	..	..	..	..	..	..	..	..	..	..	bch. 1
Cauliflowers	each	..	..	..	..	..	..	..	..	3	..	..	3	3	..	..	..	3	2	..	..	2	2	..	..	..
Celery	,,	1½	..	..	..	..	..	..	..	..	..	..	..	..	..	..	..	..	..	..	..	..	..	..	..	..
Cucumbers	,,	..	..	..	..	..	..	..	..	..	..	..	..	..	..	..	..	..	..	..	..	..	..	..	..	..
Curly kale	,,	1	..	..	..	..	..	..	..	..	..	..	..	..	..	..	..	..	..	..	..	..	..	..	..	..
Greens	per lb.	1	..	..	..	..	..	..	..	..	..	..	..	..	..	..	..	..	1½	..	..	1½	..	..	..	..
Lettuce		..	..	..	..	..	..	..	..	..	..	..	..	..	..	..	..	..	bch. ½	..	..	bch. ½	3 for 1	..	..	..
Marrows		..	..	..	..	..	..	..	..	..	..	..	..	..	..	..	..	..	..	..	..	..	..	..	..	..
Mint					1d. bunch right through, also other herbs (green)																					
Onions		..	..	..	..	..	..	..	..	..	..	..	..	..	..	..	..	..	bch. ½	..		1 per lb. 3 for 1	..	..	..	..
Parsnips	per bunch	1	..	..	..	..	..	..	..	..	..	..	..	..	..	..	..	..	..	..	..	..	..	..	..	..
Peas	per lb.	..	..	..	..	..	..	..	..	..	..	..	..	..	..	..	..	..	..	..	..	..	..	..	..	..
Potatoes	,,	..	..	..	..	..	..	..	..	..	..	..	..	..	..	..	..	..	new 3	..	..	..	1½	1½	1½	1½
Radishes		..	..	..	..	..	..	..	..	..	..	..	..	..	..	..	..	..	bch. ½	..	..	3 for 1	..	..	..	..
Rhubarb	per bunch	..	..	..	..	..	..	..	..	1½	..	..	..	..	..	..	..	..	..	..	..	1	1	1	1	1
Shalots	per lb.	..	..	..	..	..	..	..	..	..	..	..	..	..	..	..	..	..	..	..	..	..	..	..	..	..
Spinach		..	..	..	..	..	..	..	..	..	..	..	..	..	..	..	..	..	..	..	..	..	..	..	..	..
Tomatoes	per lb.	..	..	..	..	..	..	..	..	..	..	..	..	..	..	..	..	..	..	..	..	..	..	..	..	..
Turnips		..	..	..	..	..	..	..	..	..	..	..	..	..	..	..	..	..	..	..	..	..	..	..	..	..
Currants (black)	per lb.	..	..	..	..	..	..	..	..	..	..	..	..	..	..	..	..	..	..	..	..	..	..	..	..	..
,, (red)	,,	..	..	..	..	..	..	..	..	..	..	..	..	..	..	..	..	..	..	..	..	..	..	..	..	3
Gooseberries	,,	..	..	..	..	..	..	..	..	..	..	..	..	..	..	..	..	..	..	..	..	2	2	..	..	..
Raspberries	,,	..	..	..	..	..	..	..	..	..	..	..	..	..	..	..	..	..	..	..	..	..	..	..	..	..
Strawberries	,,	..	..	..	..	..	..	..	..	..	..	..	..	..	..	..	..	..	..	..	..	..	10	..	..	6

Week ending		July 2	July 9	July 16	July 23	July 30	Aug. 6	Aug. 13	Aug. 20	Aug. 27	Sept. 3	Sept. 10	Sept. 17	Sept. 24	Oct. 1	Oct. 15	Oct. 29	Nov. 5	Nov. 12	Nov. 19	Nov. 26	Dec. 3	Dec. 10	Dec. 17	Dec. 24	Dec. 31
Beet		..	..	..	..	..	..	..	..	..	1 for 3 roots	..	..	..	1 ea.	..	..	st. 8	..	..	..	..	..	..	..	..
Broccoli	each	..	..	..	..	..	..	..	..	..	..	..	..	..	..	..	..	..	..	..	..	..	..	..	..	..
Beans (broad)	per lb.	..	..	..	1½	1	¾	¾	..	..	..	..	..	..	..	..	..	..	..	..	..	..	..	..	..	..
,, (French)	,,	..	..	2½	2	1½	..	..	..	..	2	2	..	..	..	..	..	..	..	..	..	..	..	..	..	..
,, (runner)	,,	..	..	3	2½	2	..	..	..	..	..	..	..	..	..	..	..	..	..	..	..	..	..	..	..	..
Brussels sprouts	,,	..	..	..	..	..	..	..	..	..	..	..	..	..	2	2	2	1½	..	..	1½	..	..	..	..	..
Cabbages	each	..	..	..	..	..	..	..	Red cabbage ¾ ea.	..	2d. each right through	..	..	..	1 ea.	..	..	..	..	..	..	..	..	..	..	..
Carrots		..	..	..	..	..	..	..	..	..	..	..	..	..	6 st.	..	..	..	..	..	..	..	..	..	..	..
Cauliflowers	each	..	..	..	..	..	..	..	..	..	..	..	..	..	..	..	..	..	..	..	..	..	..	..	..	..
Celery	,,	..	..	..	..	..	..	..	..	..	..	..	..	..	1½	1½	..	..	..	..	1	1	..	..	..	1½
Cucumbers	,,	..	4	..	..	5	..	4	..	..	..	..	..	..	..	..	..	..	..	..	..	..	..	..	..	..
Curly kale	,,	..	..	..	..	..	..	..	..	..	..	..	..	..	..	..	..	..	..	..	..	..	..	..	..	..
Greens	per lb.	..	..	..	..	..	..	..	..	..	..	..	..	..	..	..	..	..	..	..	..	..	..	..	..	..
Lettuce		..	..	..	..	..	..	..	..	..	..	..	..	..	..	..	..	..	..	..	..	..	..	..	..	..
Marrows		..	..	..	..	each 8	..	2	..	..	..	..	..	..	..	..	..	..	..	..	..	..	..	..	..	..
Mint																										
Onions		..	..	..	bch. 1	..	lb. 1	1 lb. 1/- st.	..	..	..	..	..	..	1½ lb. 1/6 st.	..	..	..	..	..	..	st. 1/9	..	..	..	..
Parsnips	per bunch	..	..	..	..	..	..	..	..	..	..	..	..	..	..	..	..	..	..	..	..	..	..	..	..	..
Peas	per lb.	..	2	1½	1	1	1	..	..	..	..	..	..	..	..	..	..	..	..	..	..	..	..	..	..	..
Potatoes	,,	1½	1	stone 10	10	9	8	8	8	8	7	7	6	6	6	6	6	6	..	..	5	5	..	..	..	6
Radishes		..	..	..	..	..	..	..	..	..	..	..	..	..	..	..	..	..	..	..	..	..	..	..	..	..
Rhubarb	per bunch	..	..	..	..	..	..	..	..	..	..	..	..	..	..	..	..	..	..	..	..	..	..	..	..	..
Shalots	per lb.	..	..	..	..	1½	..	..	..	..	..	..	..	..	..	..	..	..	..	..	..	..	..	..	..	..
Spinach		..	..	..	..	..	..	..	..	..	..	..	..	..	..	..	..	..	..	..	..	..	..	..	..	..
Tomatoes	per lb.	..	8	..	7	..	..	..	..	..	6	..	..	..	..	..	..	..	..	..	..	..	..	..	..	..
Turnips		..	bch. 1	..	..	..	..	..	..	..	..	..	..	..	..	..	Swedes ½d. each or 4d. stone	..	..	..	..	..	..	..	..	..
Currants (black)	per lb.	..	5	4	..	..	..	..	..	3	..	..	..	..	..	..	..	..	..	..	..	..	..	..	..	..
,, (red)	,,	..	..	..	2½	..	..	..	..	2	..	..	..	..	..	..	..	..	..	..	..	..	..	..	..	..
Gooseberries	,,	..	1½	1½	..	..	..	..	..	..	..	..	..	..	..	..	..	..	..	..	..	..	..	..	..	..
Raspberries	,,	..	4	4	..	..	..	..	..	per qt. 4	..	..	..	..	..	..	..	..	..	..	..	..	..	..	..	..
Strawberries	,,	..	..	3½	..	..	..	..	..	..	..	..	..	..	..	..	..	..	..	..	..	..	..	..	..	..

To follow page 300.—7.

CHAPTER IX

IN the preceding pages we have reviewed the problem of unemployment in York, a city, it will be remembered, of about 82,000 inhabitants. All that remains is so to summarise our main facts as to grasp the problem as a whole more clearly, and to state the conclusions to which we have been led.

THE STATEMENT OF THE PROBLEM

The different classes of persons we have described in this book as unemployed in York on June 7, 1910, total up to 1278. This does not include many who returned themselves as unemployed in our original census, but who, as further inquiry showed, did not come within the scope of our definition of an "unemployed person," namely, *a person is unemployed who is seeking work for wages, but unable to find any suited to his capacities and under conditions which are reasonable, judged by local standards.*

These 1278 persons were divided into the following classes :—

301

	Number.	Per cent of Total.	Per cent of Total occupied persons above 10 years of age.
Youths under 19 years of age . .	129	10·1	
Men who have been in regular employment within the last two years, and are still seeking it. . .	291	22·8	Male. 4·4 [1]
Casual workers	441	34·5	
Workers in the Building Trades .	173	13·5	
Work-shy	105	8·2	Female.
Women and girls	139	10·9	1·5 [1]

Although we give a figure representing the sum of all these classes, we wish at once to warn the reader that such a figure may prove very misleading unless we recognise that it is made up of elements which vary greatly in character. Over one-half of the total number (viz. the casuals, the work-shy, and the majority of the women) are persons most of whom have for years habitually depended on casual work for a livelihood. The majority of them seldom expect to have a full week's work—a few of them would not take it if they could get it. Although they were unemployed on the date of our census, it is probable that many were in work the day before, and would be in work again a day or two after. Such people suffer from under - employment and irregularity of

[1] These figures represent the percentage of *all* occupied workers, as enumerated in the 1901 Census (and corrected for 1910). There are no accurate figures available showing what proportion of these belonged to the classes of workers dealt with in this inquiry, but we shall probably not be far wrong in estimating it at about 80 per cent, in which case the proportion of "occupied persons" in these classes who were found unemployed would be Male 5·5, Female 1·9.

work rather than from unemployment proper, and the social and industrial problems which they present are entirely different from those connected with the unemployment of men seeking regular work, and of youths. The men in the building trades come halfway between the regular and casual workers.

But while this total figure need not lead us to take an exaggerated view of the extent of unemployment in York, we must remember that *it only represents 'those who happened to be out of work on the day of the census.* The number of persons who, for a shorter or longer period, have been unemployed or under-employed *in the course of the whole year* certainly far exceeds those enumerated, although we have no means of determining exactly to what extent.

The Immediate Causes of Unemployment

We have only discussed in this volume the immediate causes of unemployment, but we do not forget those underlying economic conditions which affect the whole social structure — the extent to which land, labour, and capital are brought into fruitful contact, and the distribution of wealth. We remember too that social conditions in the long run reflect the soul of a people, and that reforms are likely to be short-lived which are unaccompanied by a growing sense of brotherhood and mutual interdependence among all classes in the community. Bearing these facts in mind, we have sought to

advocate measures for reducing the evil of unemployment, that would facilitate rather than retard wise
legislative changes of a more comprehensive character.

Turning, then, to the immediate causes of unemployment, let us summarise what has been stated in
more detail in the preceding pages.

CHARACTER AND EFFICIENCY OF THE UNEMPLOYED

We have seen that in the two principal classes of
unemployed workers, namely, those seeking regular
work and the casual workers, numbering altogether
732, or 57·3 per cent of the whole, about half were
men of good character and physique, while the others
were more or less handicapped by some physical,
mental, or moral defect. Of the unemployed lads,
four-fifths had a bad start in life, and the majority of
them were certainly below the average in ability and
character. In the building trade, on the other hand,
the ability of the unemployed men was not markedly
inferior, but we found that moral defects which did
not actually lessen their value as workers were here
less of a handicap than in any other trade.

The majority of the women were of good character
and physically capable. Leaving aside the 105
work-shy, it may be roughly stated that about one-
half of the unemployed in York were not in any way
disqualified for work. This does not imply that they
were on the same level with the best section of
employed workers, for when the demand for labour

shrinks, the less efficient men are generally the first to be dismissed, although, as we have seen, there may be striking exceptions to this rule. But our figures show very clearly that it is quite a mistake to regard the unemployed problem as primarily one of the character and efficiency of the workers. On the contrary, improved morale and increased technical ability, important as they are, can never solve that problem unless they are associated with wide industrial and economic reforms. Moreover, the defects by which some of the unemployed are handicapped are very frequently the direct outcome of unemployment in the past.

Casual Work

The large number of men in York who depend upon casual work for a livelihood is surprising in a town where there is no great industry conducted principally by casual workers, such as that of the London docks. We have shown that, apart from the building trades, probably about 1000 persons are only casually employed, and we have seen the injurious effect upon them of this irregularity.

Such, in brief outline, is the character of our problem; let us now briefly summarise our suggestions for its solution.

Suggestions for Reform

1. *Training for Youths.*—The facts disclosed by our inquiry point quite unmistakably to the need for

a larger measure of oversight for all lads up to the age of, say, 19, and for their compulsory training during periods of unemployment. Having dealt fully with this matter in Chapters I. and V., we will now only express our strong conviction that public opinion would support such a reform, and that its beneficial effects on the morale and technical ability of the workers would be far-reaching. The scheme we have outlined might be introduced immediately, being comparatively inexpensive, and not arousing strong popular opposition by postponing the period when lads would begin to contribute to the family income. It would not impede, but rather facilitate, the adoption of the proposal made in the Minority Report on the Poor Laws and elsewhere, that all youths should stay at school until they were 15, and that for some years after they should be obliged to spend a large part of their time in training—a system which would decrease the supply of juvenile labour, and thus very probably lead to a partial absorption of unemployed adult labour. If, however, the nation is not yet ready to accept such proposals, it might support the scheme we have outlined above, as an intermediate measure.

2. *Regulation of Work of Public Bodies.*—Many writers and speakers on the problem of unemployment have suggested that the work given out by public bodies might be so regulated as largely to neutralise the effects of cyclical and seasonal fluctuations in the demand for labour. We have no data enabling us to

measure the extent to which this might be done, but that such a policy would be of great value in preventing periods of exceptional trade depression there can be little doubt. There is no valid argument against it, and it is a course of action to be strongly commended.

3. *Afforestation, etc.*—While accepting the view that the mere multiplication of ordinary industries will not, in the long run, decrease the volume of unemployment, because each one will develop its own margin of unemployed labour, we have shown that the work of afforestation stands on a different footing. It can, in large measure, be used as a regulator of the labour market—being pushed forward when the general demand for labour slackens, and kept back when it is active. We have shown that it could be carried out on profitable lines, and that if the $8\frac{1}{2}$ million acres of land in Great Britain which the Royal Commission on Forestry and Coast Erosion reported as suitable for the purpose were planted, work would be found immediately for over 50,000, and eventually for nearly 200,000 men for four months each winter, in addition to a permanent staff of over 20,000. On a population basis, York's quota of these men at the commencement would be about 100, which number would gradually increase as the forests became established, ultimately reaching nearly 400. These numbers could be modified according to the state of trade. It would be best for York to participate in a national scheme of afforestation, but, failing that, there appears to be no valid reason why

a financially profitable municipal scheme could not be at once undertaken, if the necessary borrowing powers were obtained. It is obvious that the absorption for four months each winter of so large a body of unemployed men would substantially help to solve the problem of unemployment.

4. *Decasualisation of Labour.* — Our inquiry points to the conclusion that though in a town like York, where masters and men are fairly well known to each other, the Labour Exchange may do little directly to reduce unemployment among regular workers, save by informing men of vacancies in other towns, the supremely important work of decasualising the labour market can only be effected through its agency, and if only for that reason it should be warmly supported both by masters and men. It will be remembered that by "decasualisation" is meant the concentration of all casual work available upon selected men, who thus receive practically constant work, although for different employers, instead of its distribution over an indiscriminate body of workers, all of whom remain under-employed. Obviously the policy involves the squeezing out of a number of individuals who are at present getting a certain amount of the casual work, and some method must be devised for dealing with them. We have on p. 140 *et seq.* suggested certain schemes whereby surplus labour might be absorbed, and, in so far as it is efficient and adaptable, it must be possible to absorb it, unless there is a shortage of either capital

or land, which in this country is not the case. The
demoralising effects of casual work upon this and the
next generation are so widespread and so serious, that
they must needs be dealt with, and decasualisation
through the instrumentality of a central agency, like
the Labour Exchange, is the most effective remedy
for the evil.

5. *Insurance.*—We have considered the part which
insurance can play in mitigating the evil consequences
of unemployment. We saw that any scheme must
necessarily have many drawbacks, such as the limitation of the period for which benefits are paid, the
refusal of their payment altogether in certain cases,
and the fact that insurance can do very little to
lessen the deleterious effect of unemployment on a
man's character, although it may retard his physical
deterioration. In considering any scheme it is
important to bear such limitations in mind, and to
regard it, as the Government Bill is regarded by
those who framed it, as only one of several measures
necessary to lessen the hardships resulting from want
of work.

6. *Decentralisation of Town Populations.*—In
Chapter VIII. we have shown that much might be
done to increase the security of industrial workers,
and to mitigate the consequences of unemployment,
if facilities were given for town workers to reside in
the country and to cultivate a plot of land. This
would provide them with an alternative to industry,
which might be developed as the latter failed them.

No doubt in the first instance only the most enterprising workmen would adopt this mode of living, but when the advantages which they derived from it were recognised, others would follow their example, and the children, being brought up in the country, would often settle there. Thus in time, increasing numbers of industrial workers of all grades would be resident outside the towns and cultivating their plots of land when they had no other work.

CONCLUSIONS

This is a brief summary of the main conclusions to which we have come in the preceding pages, and of the reforms which have been suggested. As we have proceeded with our investigations, the urgency of the need for a determined attempt to deal effectively with the problem of unemployment has been impressed upon us with growing force.

It is a terrible blot on the face of the richest country in the world, that in a town of 82,000 people, the unemployed army on a day in the middle of summer should number over 1200 persons. We do not forget that York lagged behind in recovering from the wave of industrial depression which had swept over the whole country, and we know that no one town can ever be perfectly typical, but if the conditions here described approximate even roughly to those in other towns, they point to a social evil appalling in its magnitude. But though at first

we may be filled with a sense of despair, analysis of
the evil leads us to believe that it is one which will
yield to wise treatment, and that if the cumulative
experience and careful thought of social reformers
cannot yet point to a complete remedy, they can, at
any rate, go a very long way in this direction. For
while, at first, the unemployed present themselves
as an undifferentiated crowd of suffering humanity,
closer investigation gradually resolves them into distinct groups, each afflicted with some definite social ill,
and allows the social physician to diagnose the causes
of the disease and to prescribe its treatment. While,
therefore, our inquiry has convinced us, and we hope
will convince others, of the magnitude of the evil, it
has contributed not a little to clear our minds as to
its exact character, and to indicate some, at least, of
the directions in which its cure is to be sought.

If we have succeeded in helping the reader to
analyse the problem of unemployment into its con-
stituent parts, he will, we believe, feel not less, but
more hopeful of its solution than he did when it
presented itself to his mind as one vast, confused,
and entangled whole.

INDEX

Printed by R. & R. CLARK, LIMITED, *Edinburgh.*

The List of Titles
in the Garland Series

11. Edward G. Howarth and Mona Wilson. **West Ham. A Study in Social and Industrial Problems.** London, 1907.

12. B.L. Hutchins. **Women in Modern Industry.** London, 1915.

13. M. Loane. **From Their Point of View.** London, 1908.

14. J. Ramsay Macdonald. **Women in the Printing Trades. A Sociological Study.** London, 1904.

15. C.F.G. Masterman. **From the Abyss. Of Its Inhabitants by One of Them.** London, 1902.

16. L.C. Chiozza Money. **Riches and Poverty.** London, 1906.

17. Richard Mudie-Smith, Ed. **Handbook of the "Daily News" Sweated Industries' Exhibition.** London, 1906.

18. Edward Abbott Parry. **The Law and the Poor.** London, 1914.

19. Alexander Paterson. **Across the Bridges. Or Life by the South London River-side.** London, 1911.

20. M.S. Pember-Reeves. **Round About a Pound a Week.** London, 1913.

21. B. Seebohm Rowntree. **Poverty. A Study of Town Life.** London, 1910 (2nd ed.).

22. B. Seebohm Rowntree and Bruno Lasker. **Unemployment. A Social Study.** London, 1911.

23. B. Seebohm Rowntree and A.C. Pigou. **Lectures on Housing.** Manchester, 1914.

24. C.E.B. Russell. **Social Problems of the North.** London and Oxford, 1913.

25. Henry Solly. **Working Men's Social Clubs and Educational Institutes.** London, 1904.

26. E.J. Urwick, Ed. **Studies of Boy Life in Our Cities.** London, 1904.

27. Alfred Williams. **Life in a Railway Factory**. London, 1915.

28. [Women's Co-operative Guild]. **Maternity. Letters from Working-Women, Collected by the Women's Co-operative Guild with a preface by the Right Hon. Herbert Samuel, M.P.** London, 1915.

29. Women's Co-operative Guild. **Working Women and Divorce. An Account of Evidence Given on Behalf of the Women's Co-operative Guild before the Royal Commission on Divorce.** London, 1911.

   bound with Anna Martin. **The Married Working Woman. A Study.** London, 1911.

57

61

40

15% 8.55

13% 9.15

20% 8